GRAPHIC NOVEL

endants of Darkness™

Yami no Matsuei

5

Story & Art by Yoko Matsushita

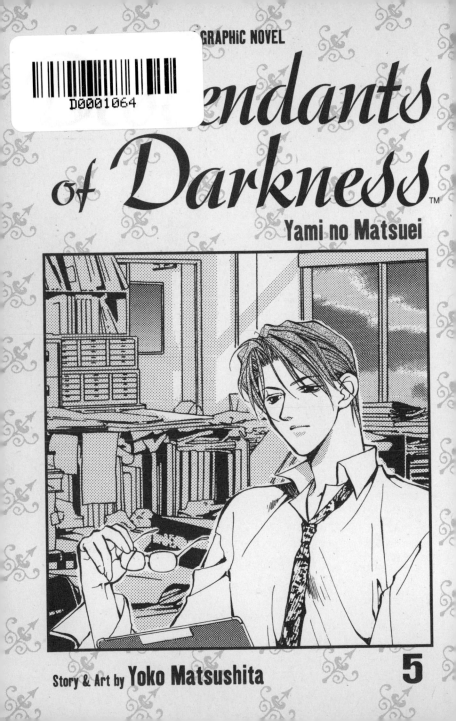

Descendants of Darkness
Yami no Matsuei

Vol. 5
Shôjo Edition

Story & Art by
Yoko Matsushita

English Adaptation/Lance Caselman
Translation/David Ury
Touch-Up & Lettering/Gia Cam Luc
Graphics & Cover Design/Courtney Utt
Editor/Pancha Diaz

Managing Editor/Annette Roman
Production Manager/Noboru Watanabe
Editorial Director/Alvin Lu
Sr. Director of Acquisitions/Rika Inouye
VP of Sales & Marketing/Liza Coppola
Executive Vice President/Hyoe Narita
Publisher/Seiji Horibuchi

Printed in the U.S.A.

Published by VIZ, LLC
P.O. Box 77064
San Francisco, CA 94107

Shôjo Edition
10 9 8 7 6 5 4 3 2 1
First printing, April 2005

For advertising rates or media kit, e-mail advertising@viz.com

www.viz.com store.viz.com

Table of Contents

I HOPE THAT YOU...

MAY COME TO BE...

THE HAPPIEST ONE OF ALL.

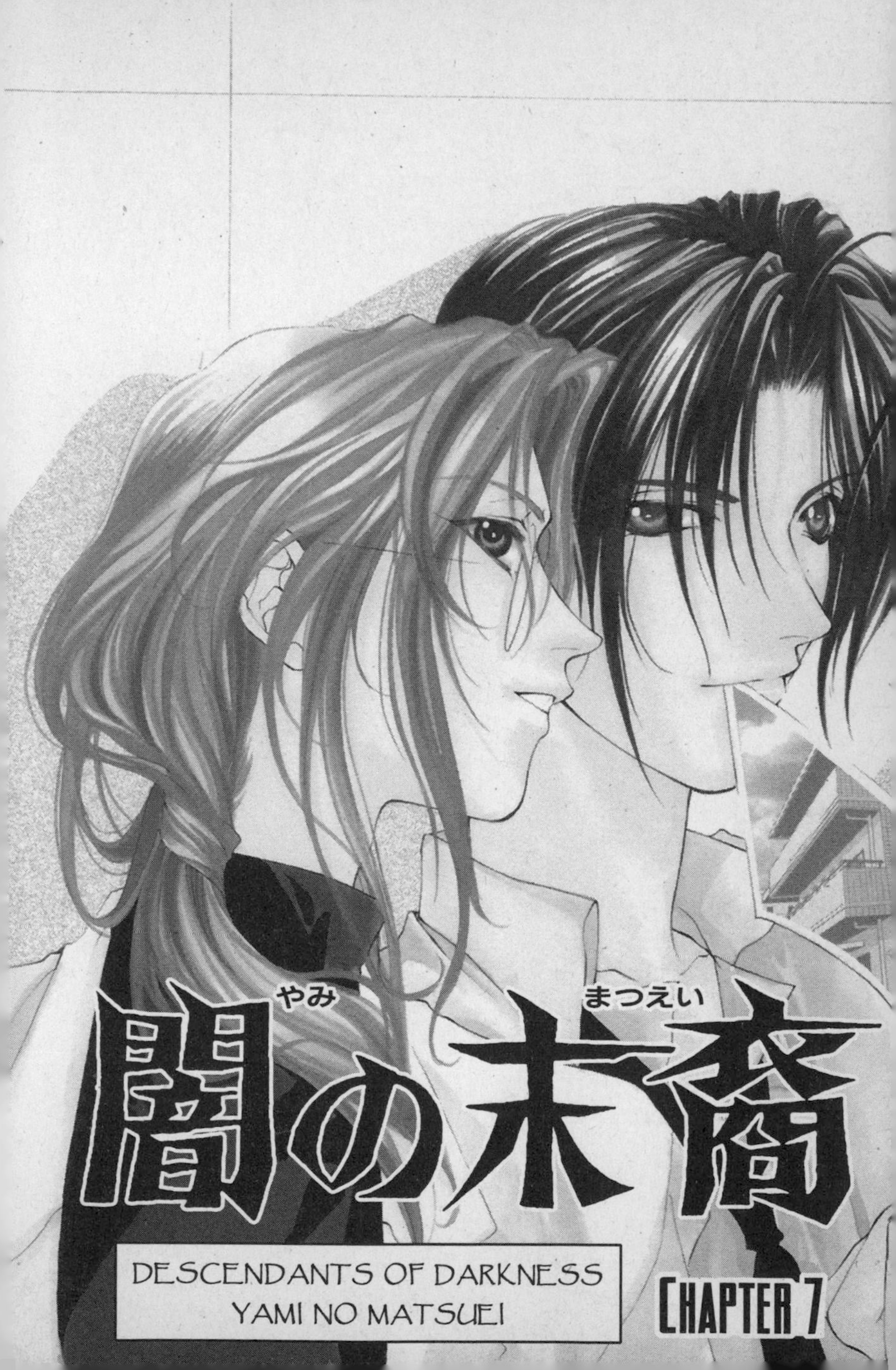
やみ まつえい
闇の末裔
DESCENDANTS OF DARKNESS
YAMI NO MATSUEI
CHAPTER 7

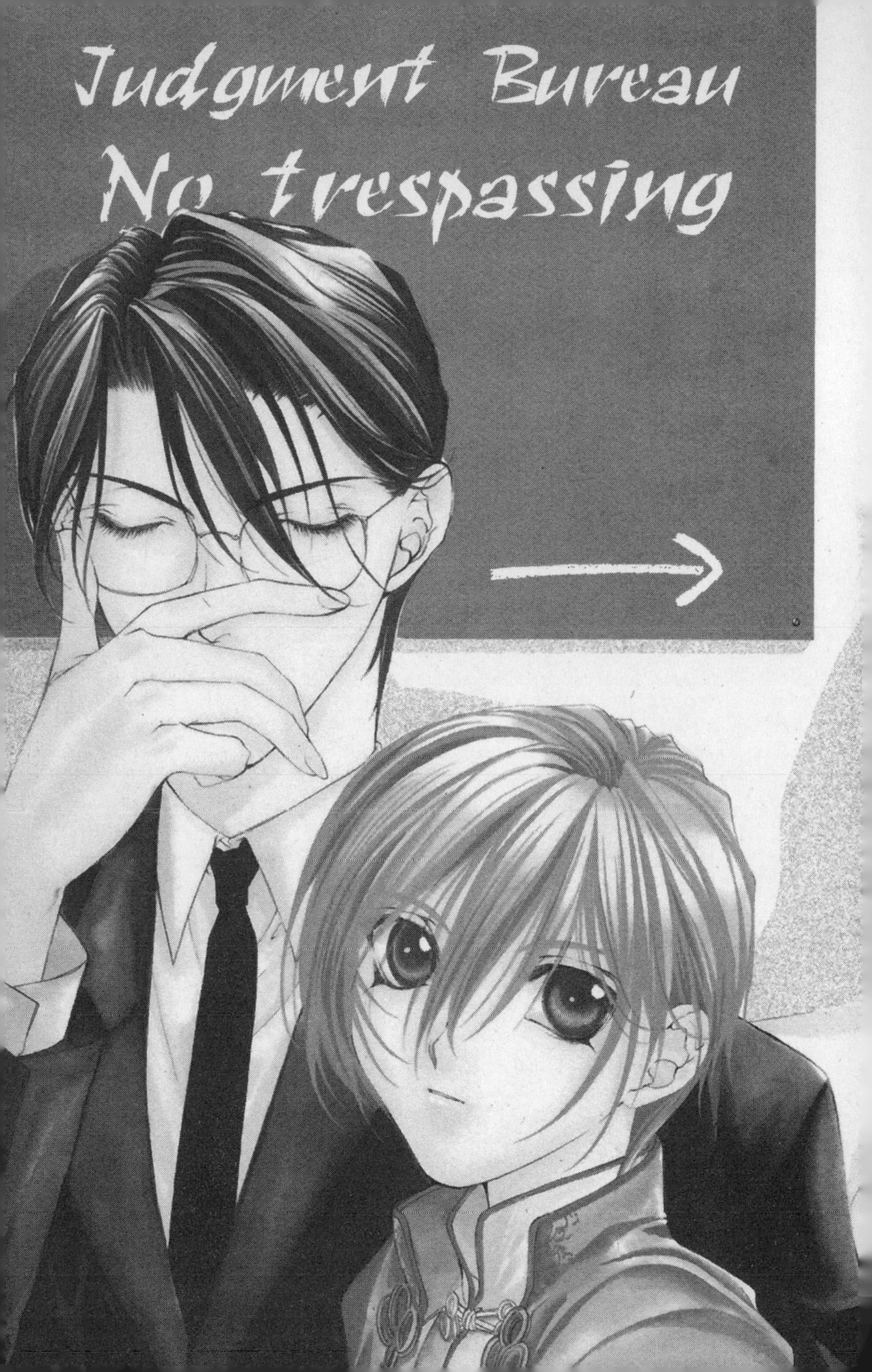
Judgment Bureau
No trespassing

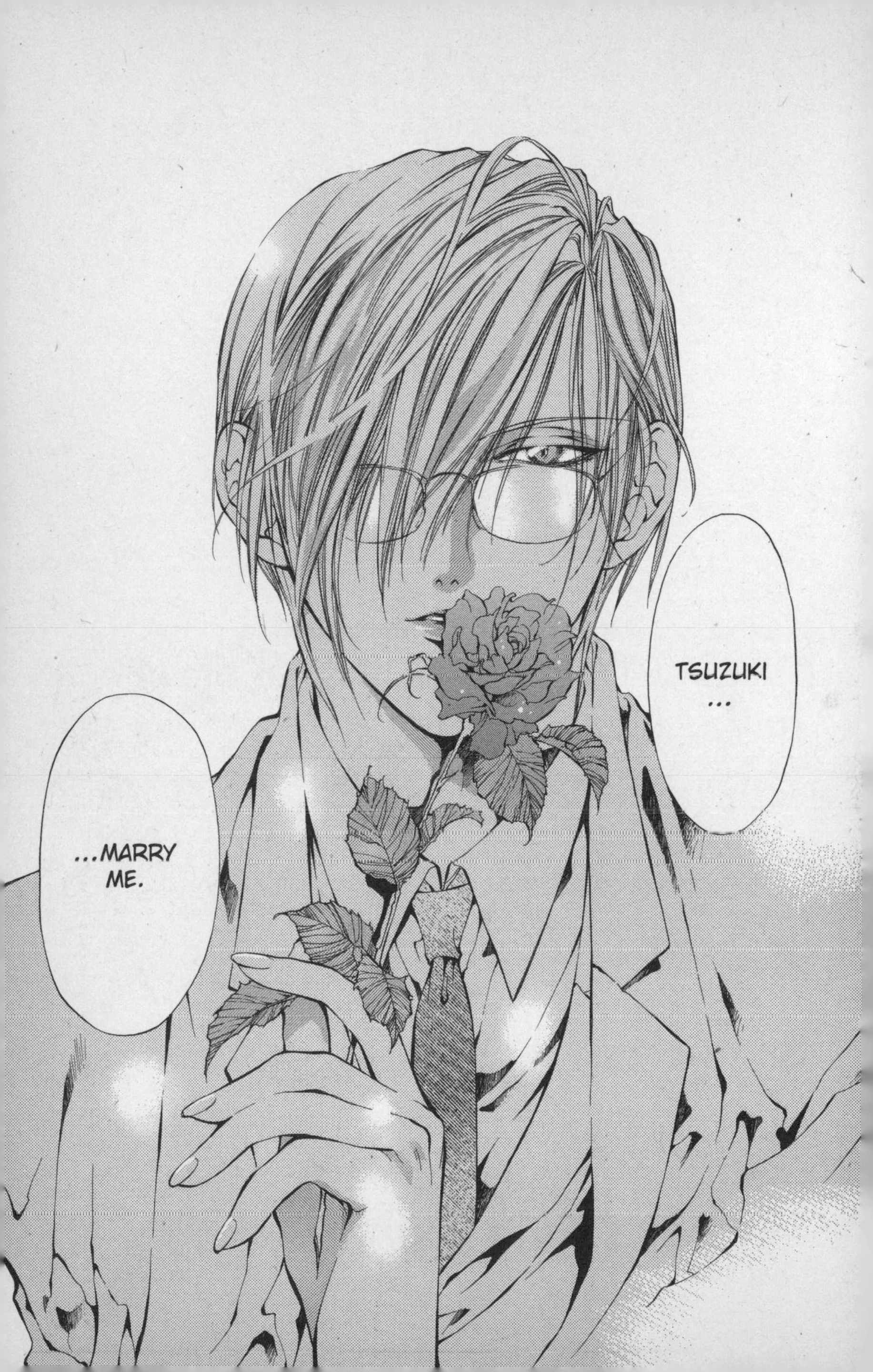
TSUZUKI ...
...MARRY ME.

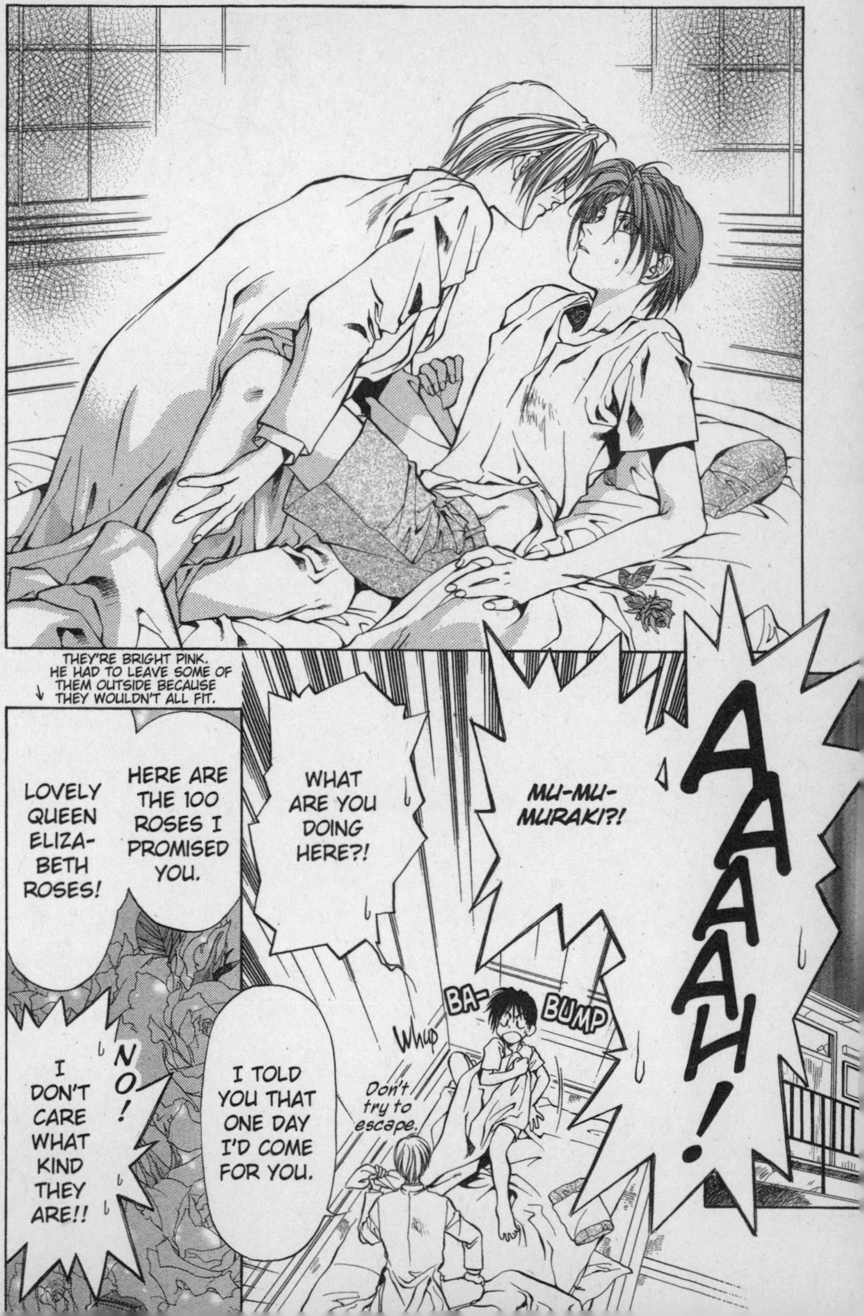
AAAAH!
MU-MU-MURAKI?!
WHAT ARE YOU DOING HERE?!
BA-BUMP
Whup
Don't try to escape.
I TOLD YOU THAT ONE DAY I'D COME FOR YOU.
HERE ARE THE 100 ROSES I PROMISED YOU.
LOVELY QUEEN ELIZABETH ROSES!
THEY'RE BRIGHT PINK. HE HAD TO LEAVE SOME OF THEM OUTSIDE BECAUSE THEY WOULDN'T ALL FIT.
NO!
I DON'T CARE WHAT KIND THEY ARE!!

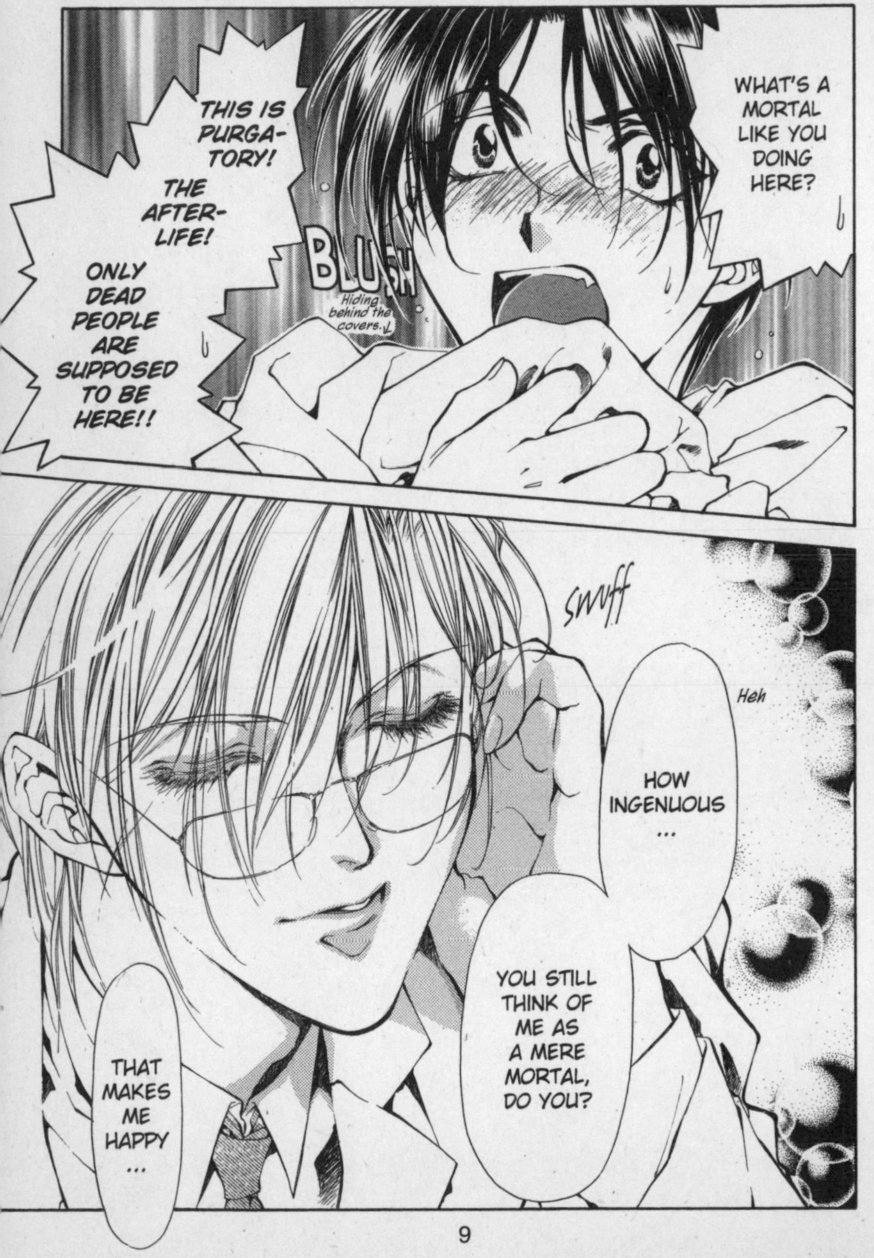
WHAT'S A MORTAL LIKE YOU DOING HERE?
THIS IS PURGATORY!
THE AFTER-LIFE!
ONLY DEAD PEOPLE ARE SUPPOSED TO BE HERE!!
BLUSH
Hiding behind the covers.
Heh
SNUFF
HOW INGENUOUS ...
YOU STILL THINK OF ME AS A MERE MORTAL, DO YOU?
THAT MAKES ME HAPPY ...

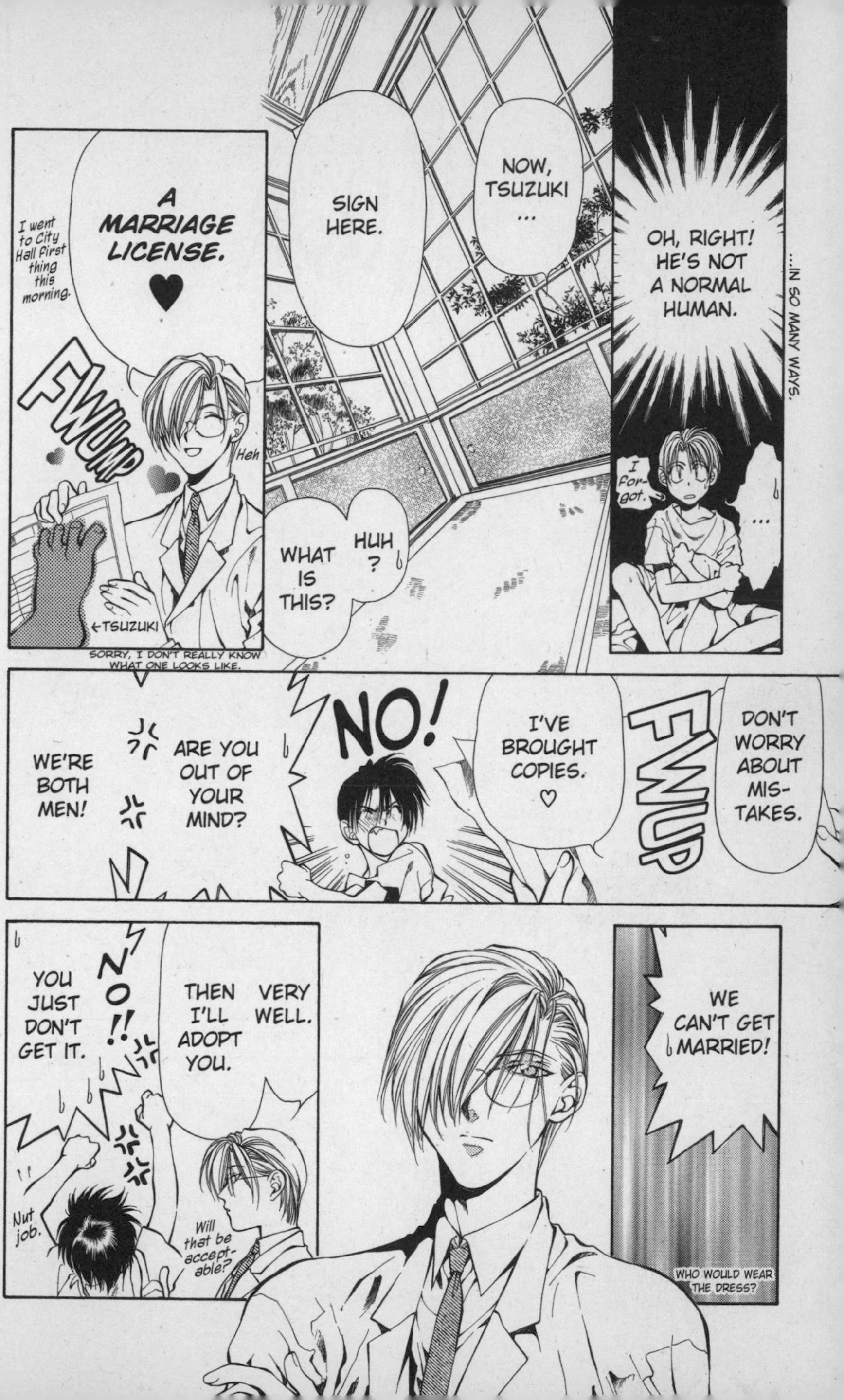
OH, RIGHT! HE'S NOT A NORMAL HUMAN.
...IN SO MANY WAYS.
I for-got.
...
NOW, TSUZUKI ...
SIGN HERE.
HUH?
WHAT IS THIS?
A MARRIAGE LICENSE. ♥
I went to City Hall first thing this morning.
FWUMP
Heh
←TSUZUKI
SORRY, I DON'T REALLY KNOW WHAT ONE LOOKS LIKE.
DON'T WORRY ABOUT MIS-TAKES.
FWUP
I'VE BROUGHT COPIES. ♡
NO!
ARE YOU OUT OF YOUR MIND?
WE'RE BOTH MEN!
WE CAN'T GET MARRIED!
WHO WOULD WEAR THE DRESS?
VERY WELL.
THEN I'LL ADOPT YOU.
Will that be accept-able?
NO!!
YOU JUST DON'T GET IT.
Nut job.

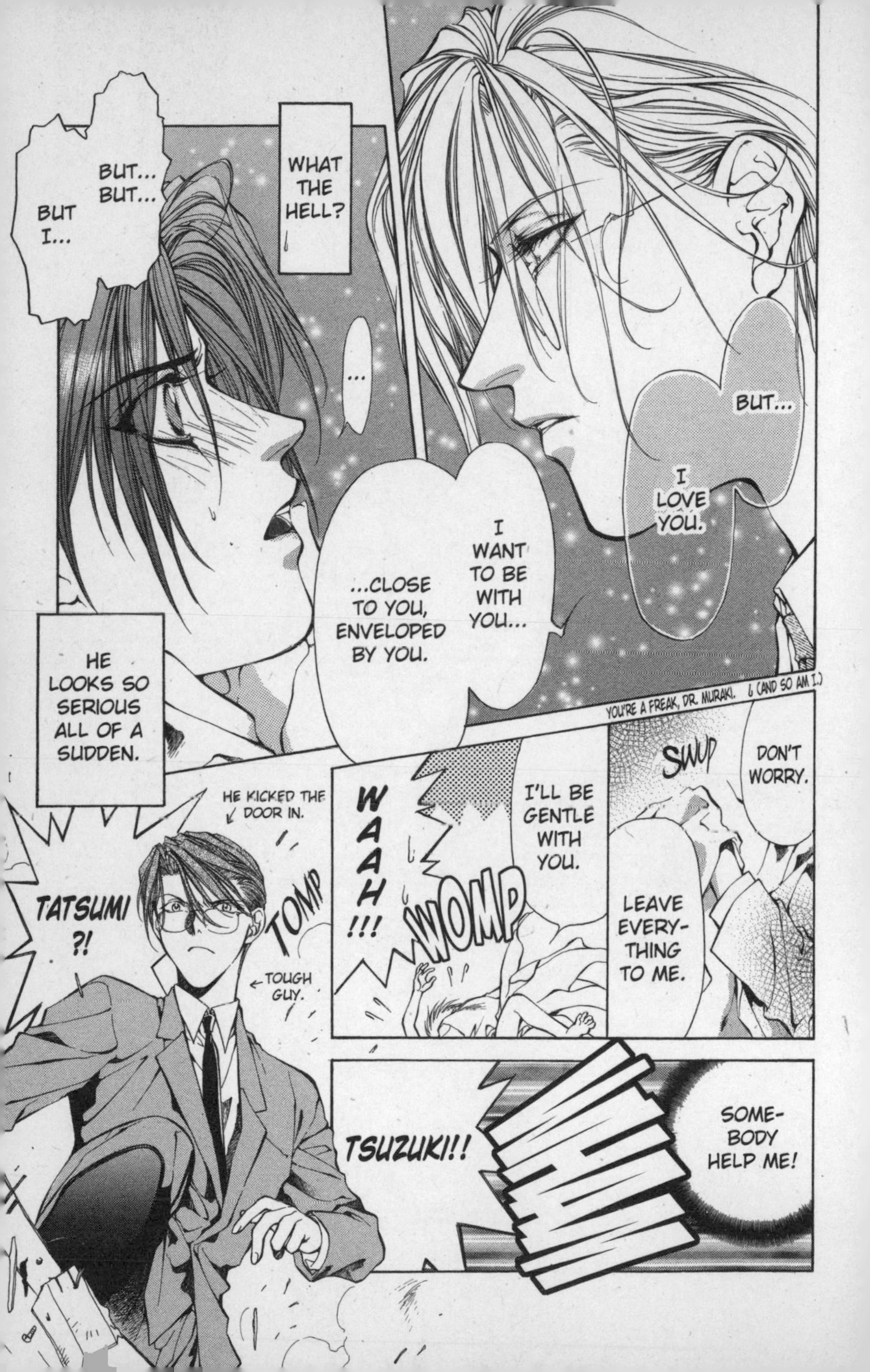
BUT...
I LOVE YOU.
I WANT TO BE WITH YOU...
...CLOSE TO YOU, ENVELOPED BY YOU.
...
WHAT THE HELL?
BUT... BUT...
BUT I...
HE LOOKS SO SERIOUS ALL OF A SUDDEN.
YOU'RE A FREAK, DR. MURAKI. (AND SO AM I.)
SWUP
DON'T WORRY.
LEAVE EVERY-THING TO ME.
I'LL BE GENTLE WITH YOU.
WAAAH!!!
WOMP
SOME-BODY HELP ME!
TSUZUKI!!
HE KICKED THE DOOR IN.
TOMP
TATSUMI?!
TOUGH GUY.

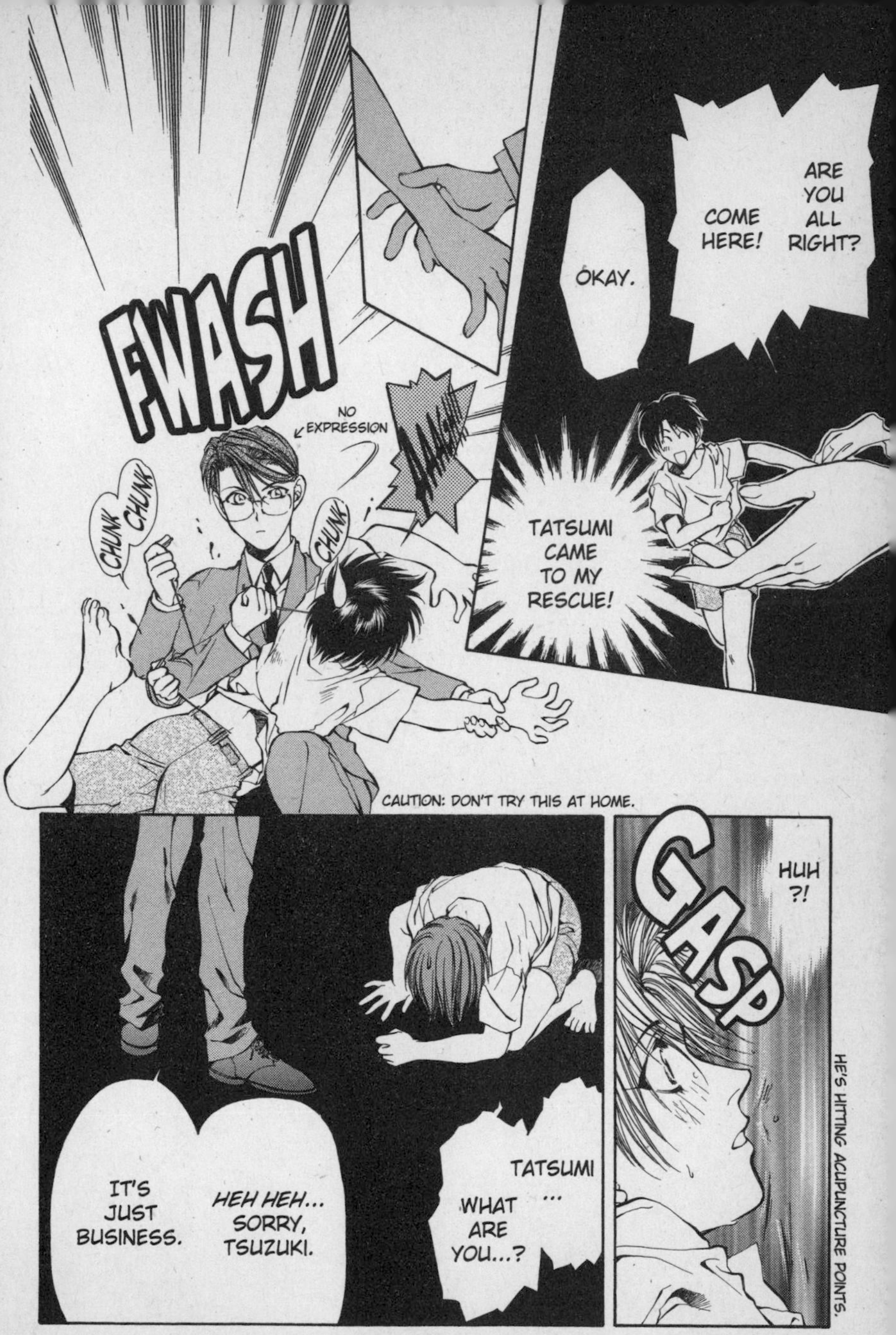
ARE YOU ALL RIGHT?
COME HERE!
OKAY.
TATSUMI CAME TO MY RESCUE!
FWASH
NO EXPRESSION
CHUNK CHUNK
CHUNK
CAUTION: DON'T TRY THIS AT HOME.
GASP
HUH?!
HE'S HITTING ACUPUNCTURE POINTS.
TATSUMI...
WHAT ARE YOU...?
HEH HEH... SORRY, TSUZUKI.
IT'S JUST BUSINESS.

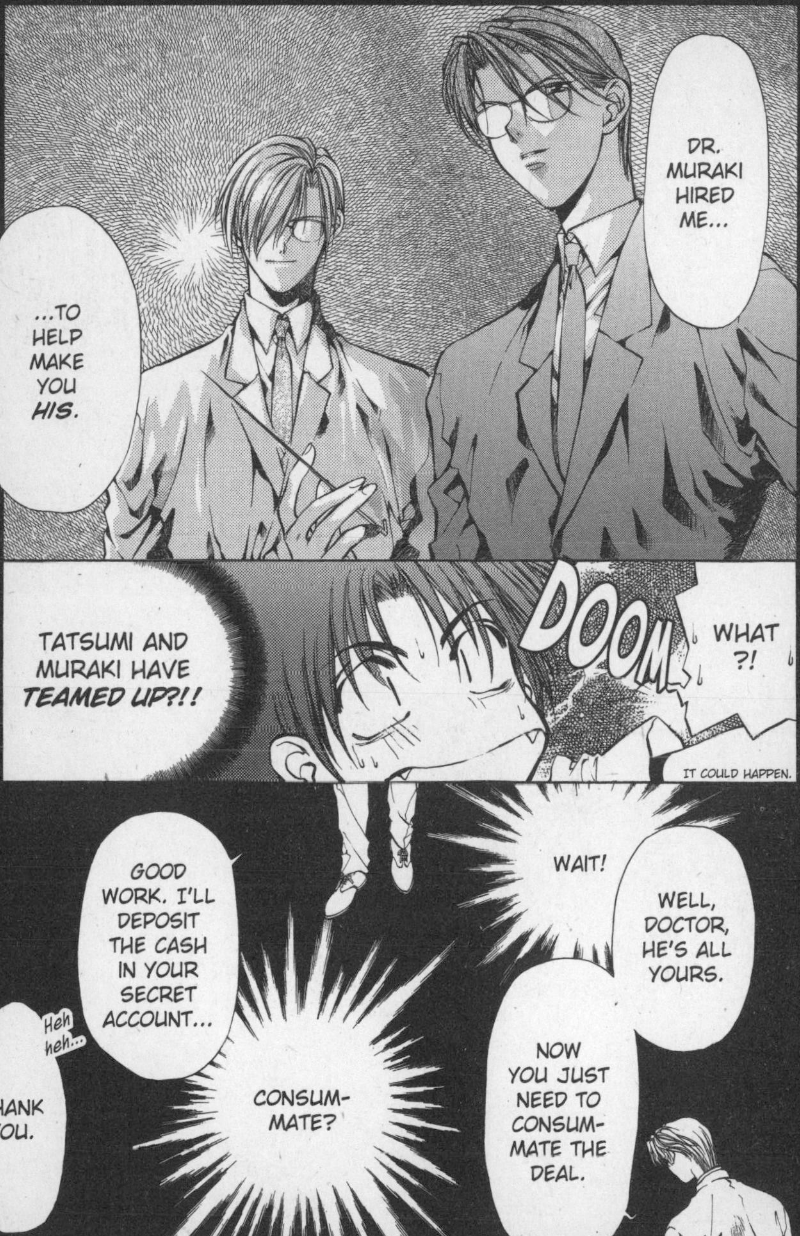
DR. MURAKI HIRED ME...
...TO HELP MAKE YOU *HIS.*
WHAT ?!
DOOM
TATSUMI AND MURAKI HAVE *TEAMED UP?!!*
IT COULD HAPPEN.
WELL, DOCTOR, HE'S ALL YOURS.
NOW YOU JUST NEED TO CONSUM-MATE THE DEAL.
WAIT!
CONSUM-MATE?
GOOD WORK. I'LL DEPOSIT THE CASH IN YOUR SECRET ACCOUNT...
Heh heh...
THANK YOU.

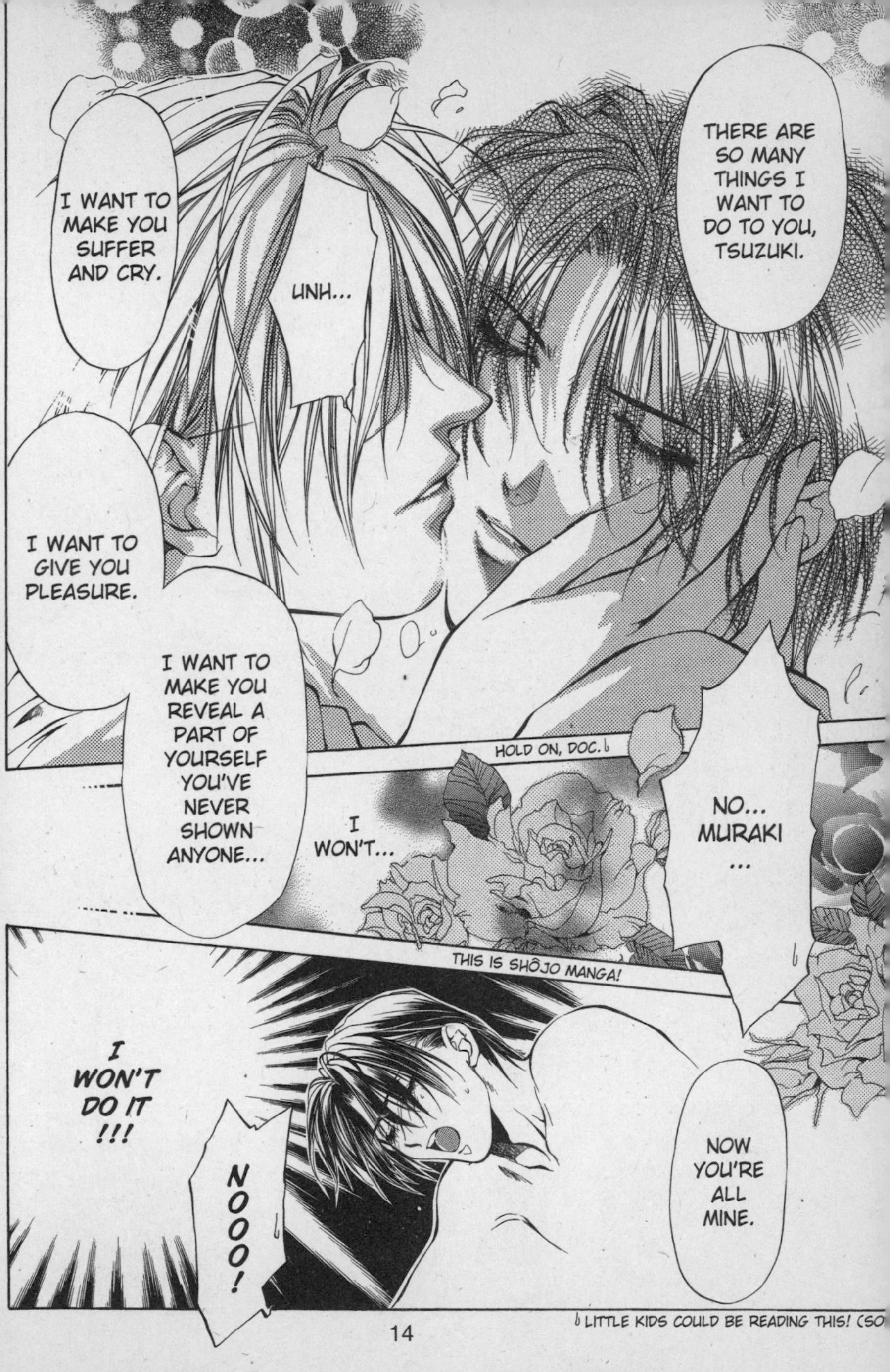
THERE ARE SO MANY THINGS I WANT TO DO TO YOU, TSUZUKI.
UNH...
I WANT TO MAKE YOU SUFFER AND CRY.
I WANT TO GIVE YOU PLEASURE.
I WANT TO MAKE YOU REVEAL A PART OF YOURSELF YOU'VE NEVER SHOWN ANYONE...
NO... MURAKI ...
HOLD ON, DOC.
I WON'T...
THIS IS SHÔJO MANGA!
NOW YOU'RE ALL MINE.
NOOO!
I WON'T DO IT !!!

LITTLE KIDS COULD BE READING THIS! (SO

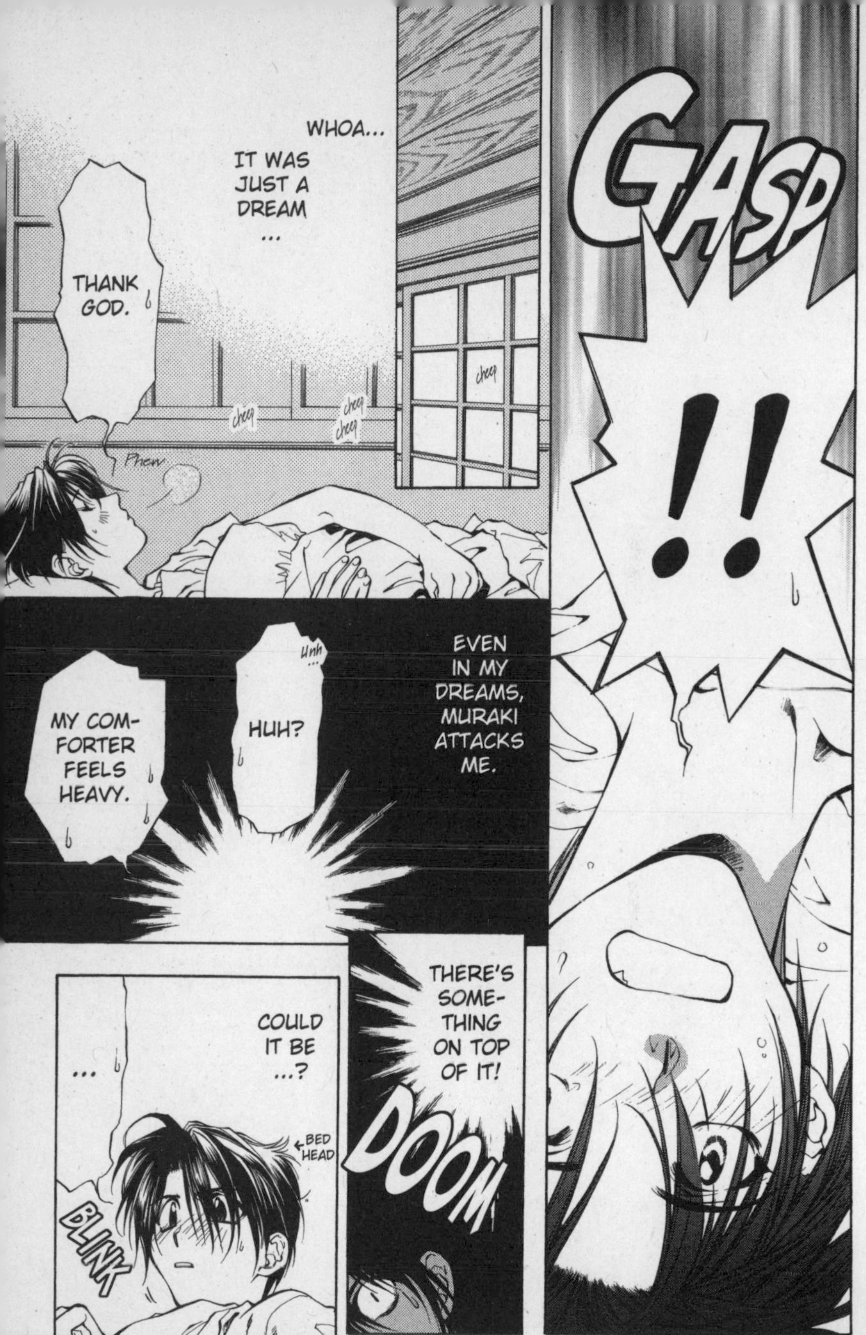
GASP
!!
WHOA...
IT WAS JUST A DREAM ...
cheep
cheep cheep
cheep
THANK GOD.
Phew
EVEN IN MY DREAMS, MURAKI ATTACKS ME.
Unh ...
HUH?
MY COM-FORTER FEELS HEAVY.
THERE'S SOME-THING ON TOP OF IT!
DOOM
COULD IT BE ...?
...
BED HEAD
BLINK
LOOKS PATHETIC, HUH?

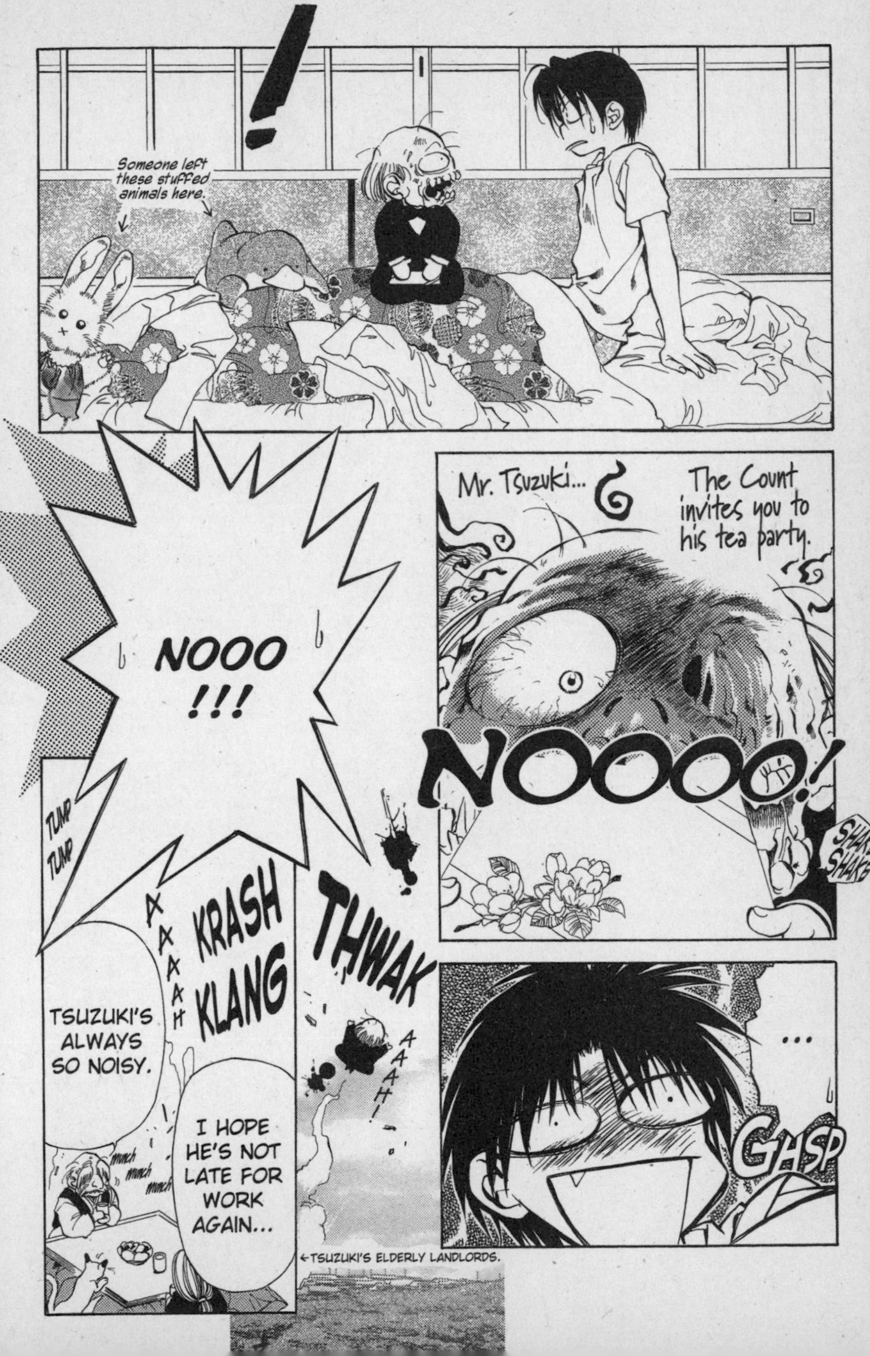
!
Someone left these stuffed animals here.
Mr. Tsuzuki...
The Count invites you to his tea party.
NOOOO!
SHAKE SHAKE
NOOO !!!
...
GHSP
THWAK
AAAAH!
KRASH KLANG
AAAAAH
TUMP TUMP
I HOPE HE'S NOT LATE FOR WORK AGAIN...
TSUZUKI'S ALWAYS SO NOISY.
munch munch munch
←TSUZUKI'S ELDERLY LANDLORDS.

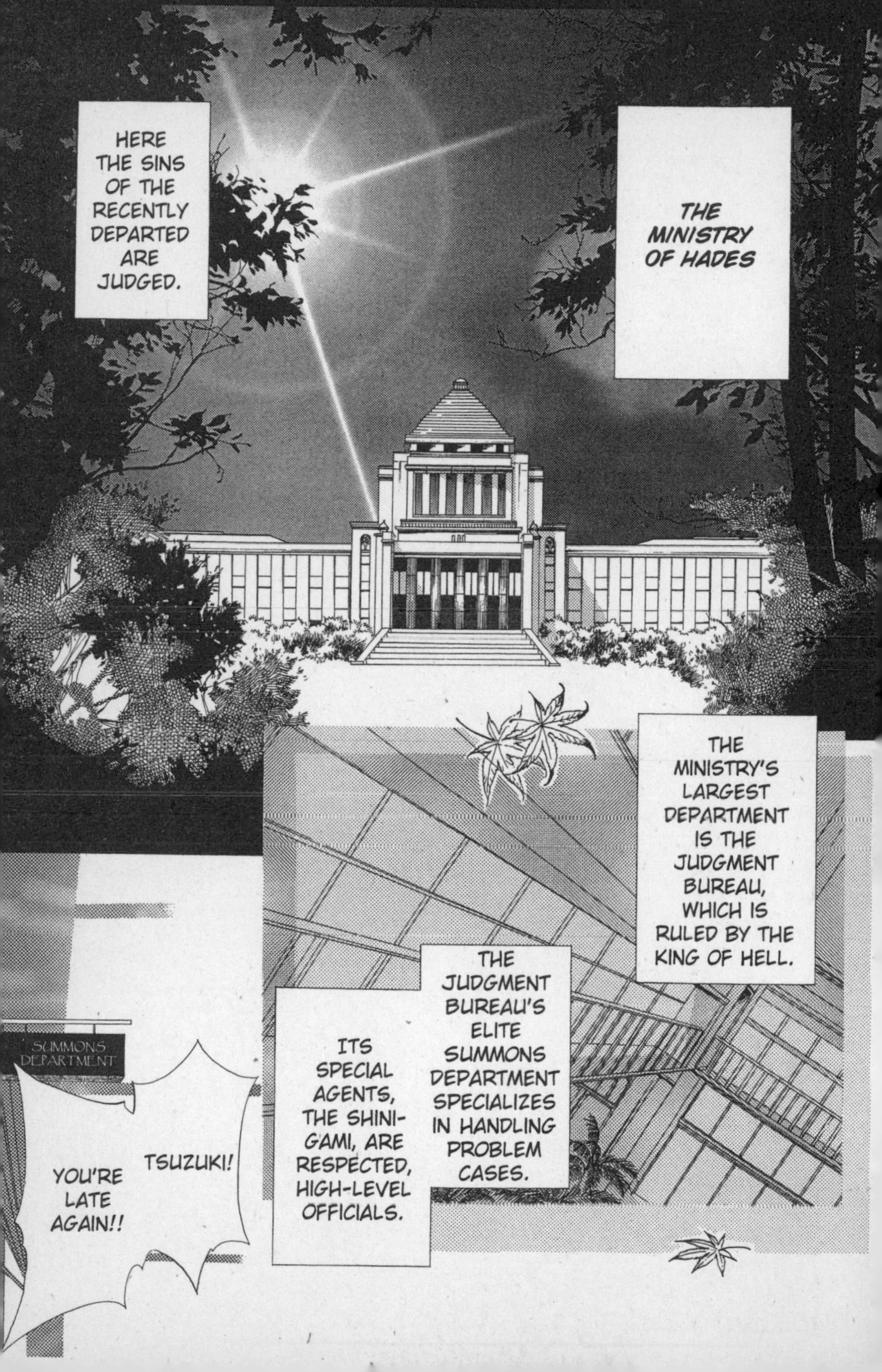
THE MINISTRY OF HADES
HERE THE SINS OF THE RECENTLY DEPARTED ARE JUDGED.
THE MINISTRY'S LARGEST DEPARTMENT IS THE JUDGMENT BUREAU, WHICH IS RULED BY THE KING OF HELL.
THE JUDGMENT BUREAU'S ELITE SUMMONS DEPARTMENT SPECIALIZES IN HANDLING PROBLEM CASES.
ITS SPECIAL AGENTS, THE SHINIGAMI, ARE RESPECTED, HIGH-LEVEL OFFICIALS.
SUMMONS DEPARTMENT
TSUZUKI!
YOU'RE LATE AGAIN!!

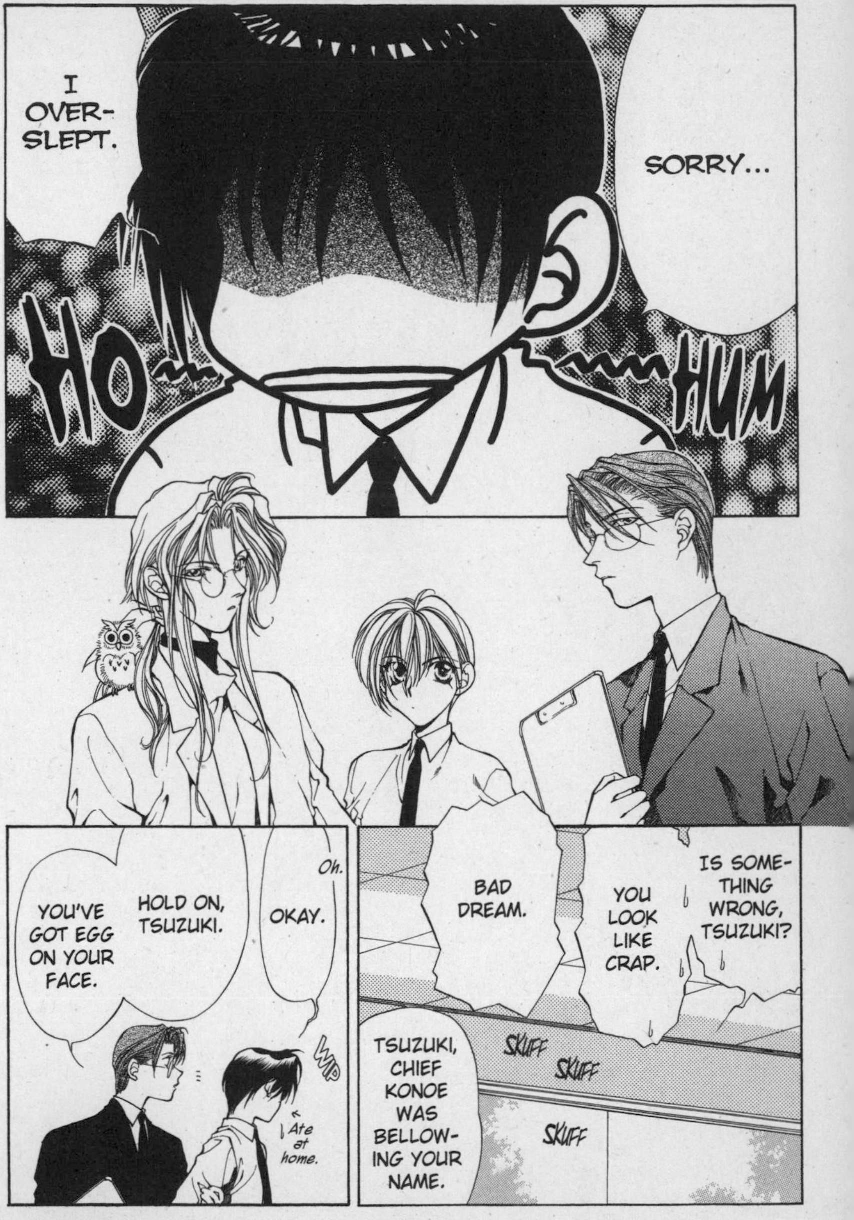
SORRY...
I OVER-SLEPT.
HO
HUM
IS SOME-THING WRONG, TSUZUKI?
YOU LOOK LIKE CRAP.
BAD DREAM.
TSUZUKI, CHIEF KONOE WAS BELLOW-ING YOUR NAME.
SKUFF
SKUFF
SKUFF
Oh.
OKAY.
HOLD ON, TSUZUKI.
YOU'VE GOT EGG ON YOUR FACE.
WIP
Ate at home.

HE'S 98 YEARS OLD.

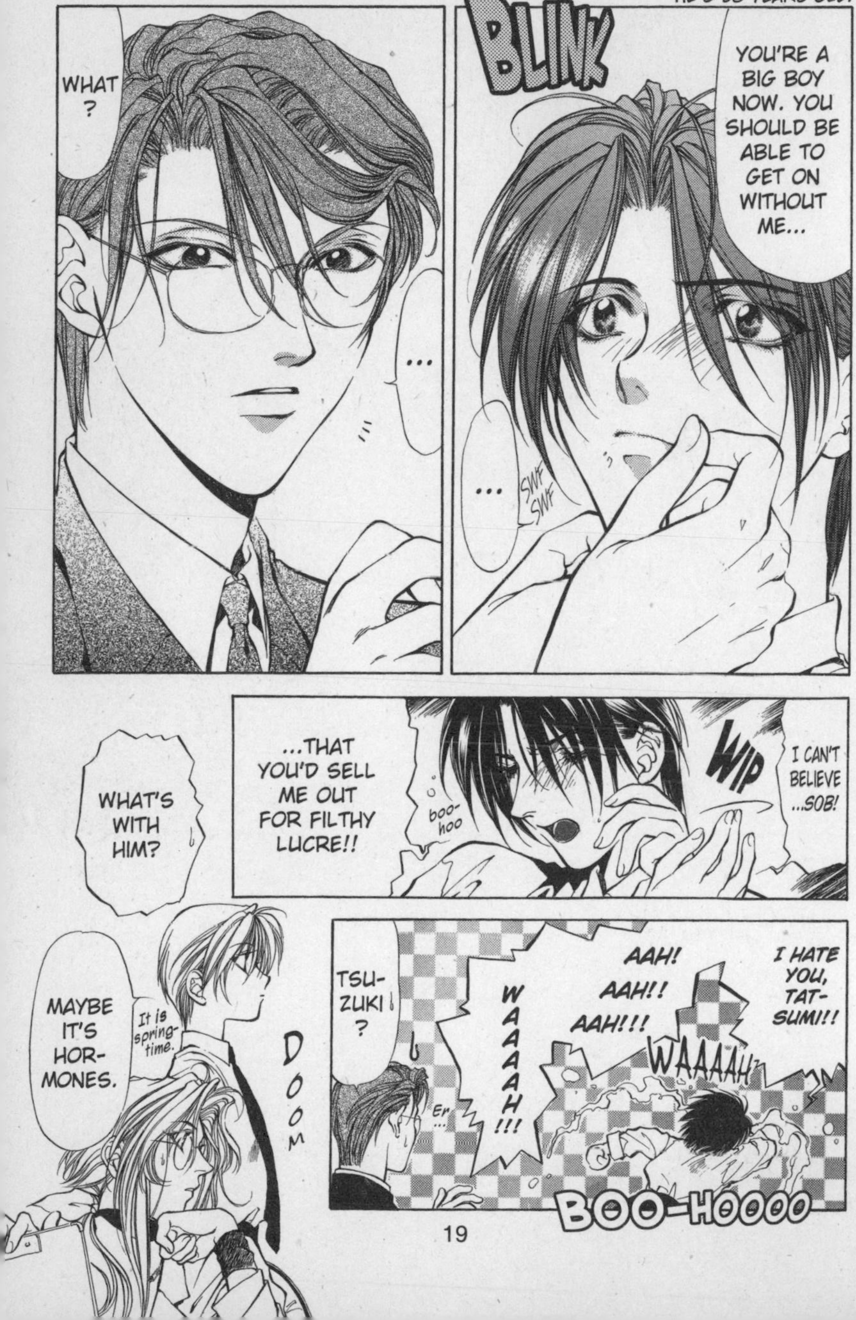
BLINK
YOU'RE A BIG BOY NOW. YOU SHOULD BE ABLE TO GET ON WITHOUT ME...
...
SWF SWF
WHAT?
...
I CAN'T BELIEVE ...SOB!
WIP
boo-hoo
...THAT YOU'D SELL ME OUT FOR FILTHY LUCRE!!
WHAT'S WITH HIM?
I HATE YOU, TAT-SUMI!!
AAH! AAH!! AAH!!!
WAAAAH
WAAAAAH!!!
TSU-ZUKI?
Er...
BOO-HOOOO
MAYBE IT'S HOR-MONES.
It is spring-time.
DOOM

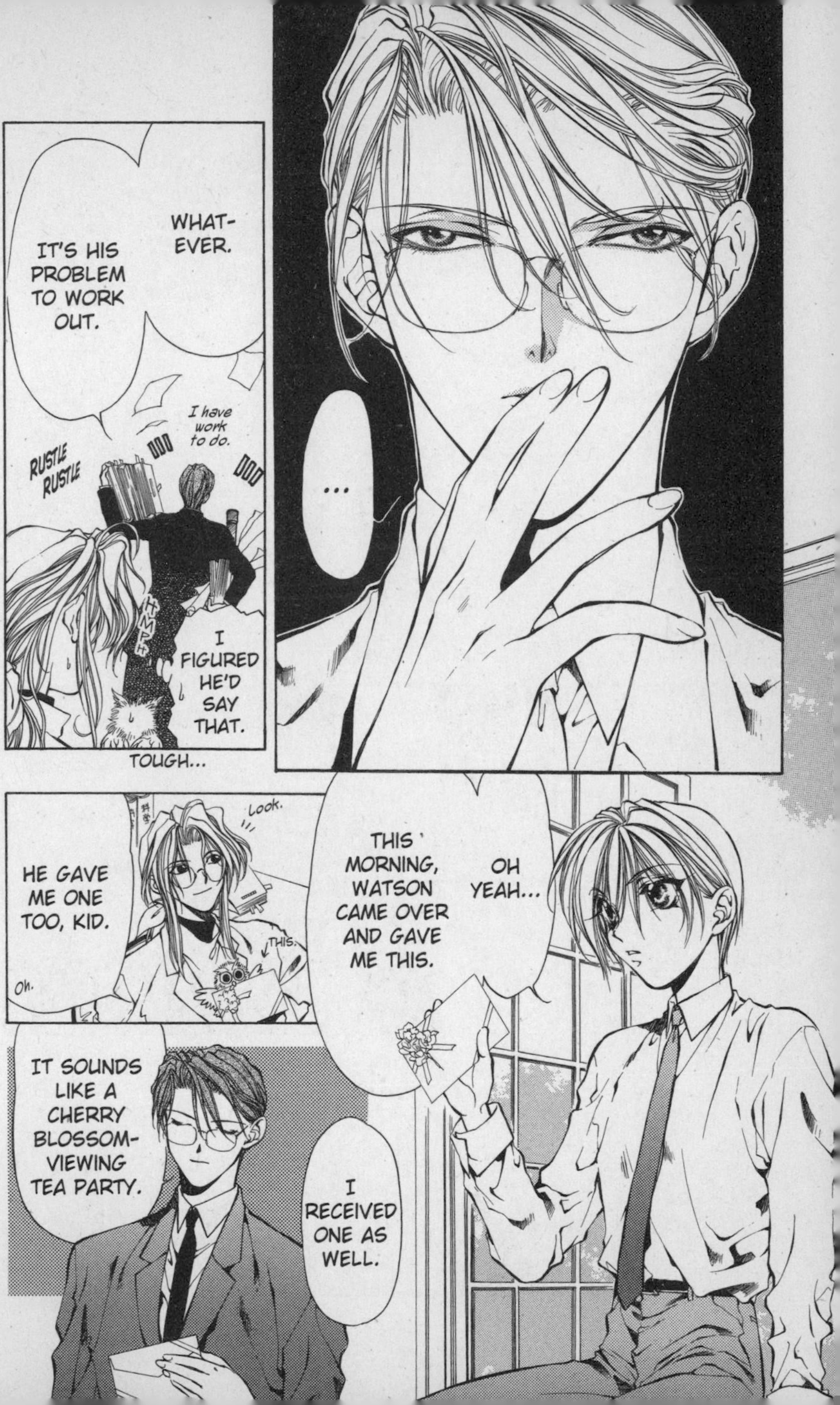
...
WHAT-EVER.
IT'S HIS PROBLEM TO WORK OUT.
I have work to do.
RUSTLE RUSTLE
HMPH
I FIGURED HE'D SAY THAT.
TOUGH...
OH YEAH...
THIS MORNING, WATSON CAME OVER AND GAVE ME THIS.
Look.
HE GAVE ME ONE TOO, KID.
THIS.
Oh.
I RECEIVED ONE AS WELL.
IT SOUNDS LIKE A CHERRY BLOSSOM-VIEWING TEA PARTY.

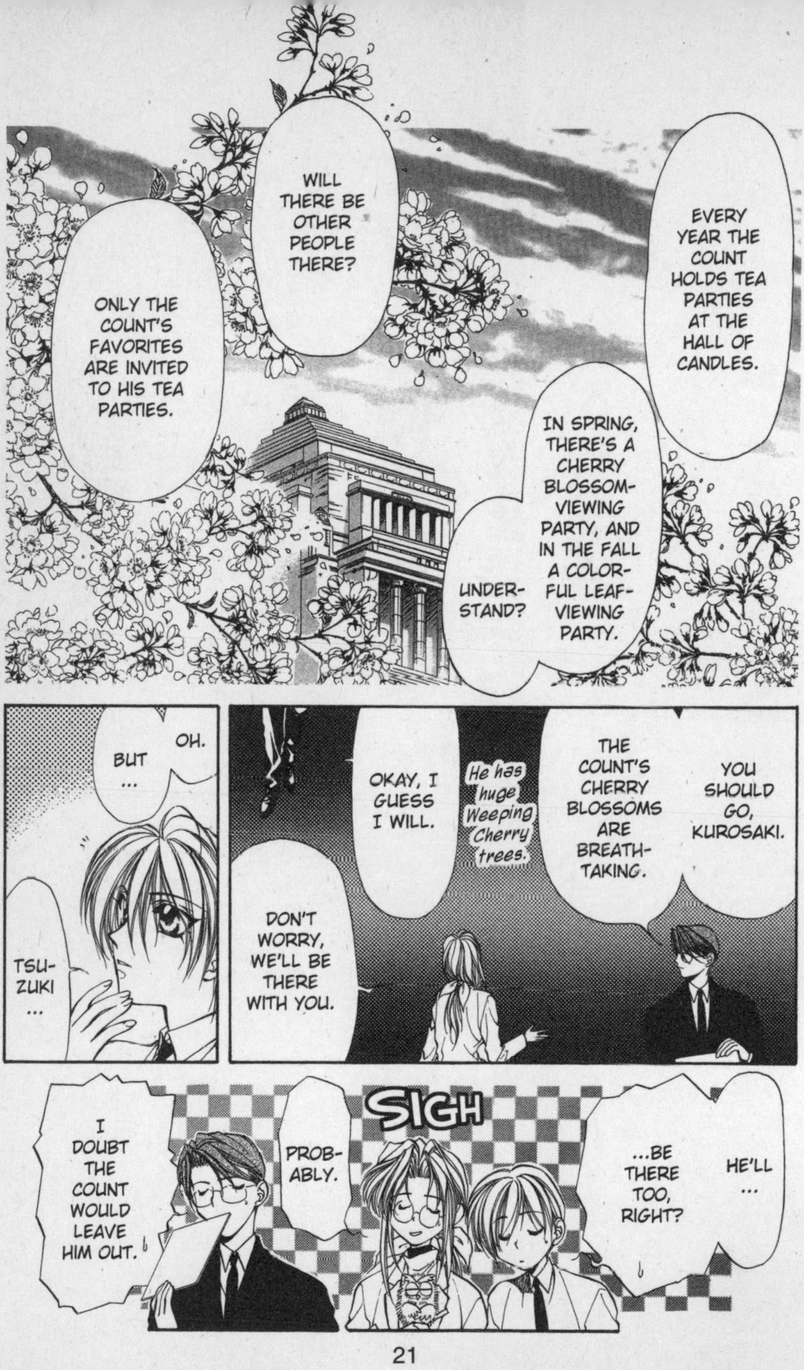
EVERY YEAR THE COUNT HOLDS TEA PARTIES AT THE HALL OF CANDLES.
IN SPRING, THERE'S A CHERRY BLOSSOM-VIEWING PARTY, AND IN THE FALL A COLORFUL LEAF-VIEWING PARTY.
UNDERSTAND?
WILL THERE BE OTHER PEOPLE THERE?
ONLY THE COUNT'S FAVORITES ARE INVITED TO HIS TEA PARTIES.
YOU SHOULD GO, KUROSAKI.
THE COUNT'S CHERRY BLOSSOMS ARE BREATHTAKING.
He has huge Weeping Cherry trees.
OKAY, I GUESS I WILL.
DON'T WORRY, WE'LL BE THERE WITH YOU.
OH.
BUT ...
TSUZUKI ...
HE'LL ...
...BE THERE TOO, RIGHT?
SIGH
PROBABLY.
I DOUBT THE COUNT WOULD LEAVE HIM OUT.

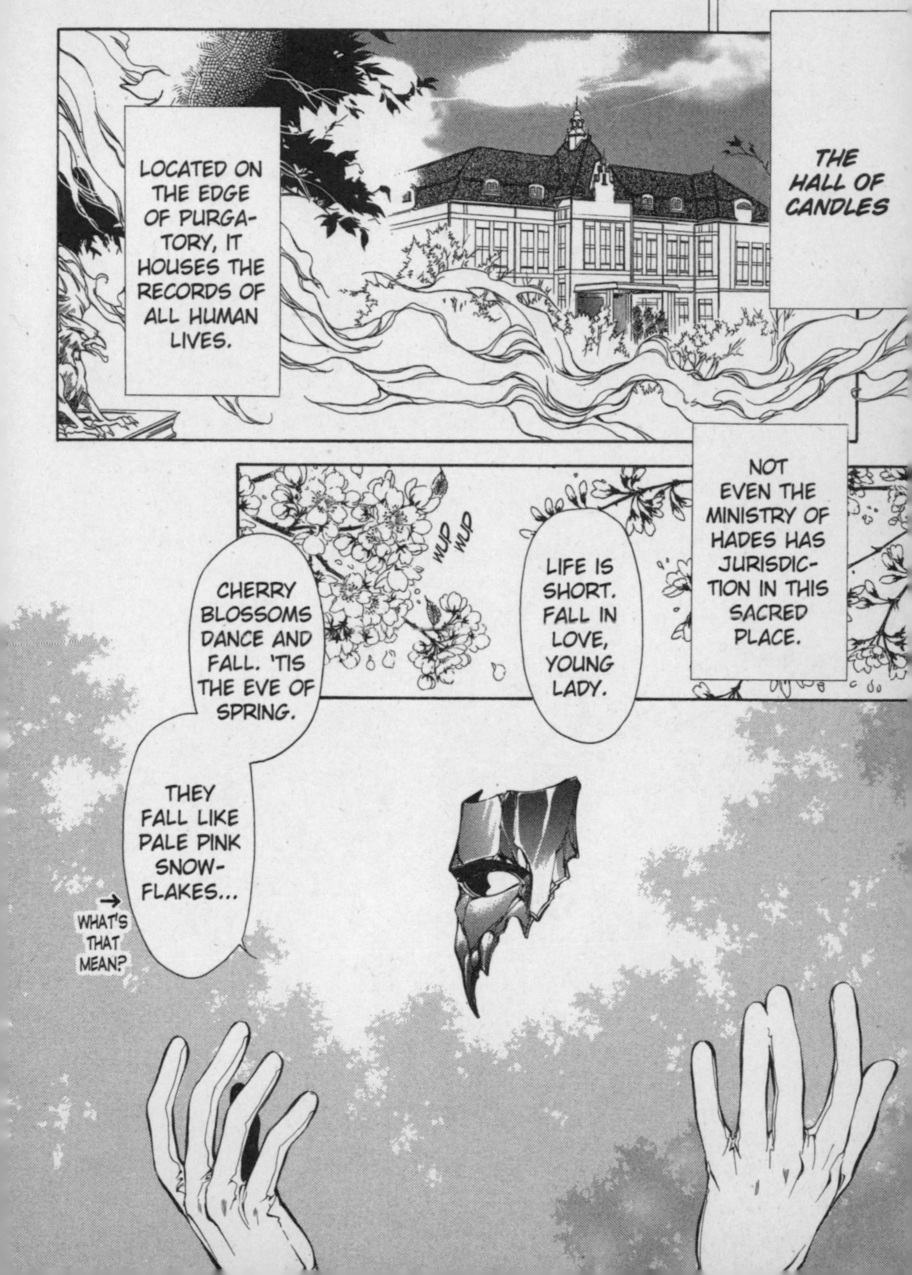
THE HALL OF CANDLES
LOCATED ON THE EDGE OF PURGA-TORY, IT HOUSES THE RECORDS OF ALL HUMAN LIVES.
NOT EVEN THE MINISTRY OF HADES HAS JURISDIC-TION IN THIS SACRED PLACE.
LIFE IS SHORT. FALL IN LOVE, YOUNG LADY.
WUP WUP
CHERRY BLOSSOMS DANCE AND FALL. 'TIS THE EVE OF SPRING.
THEY FALL LIKE PALE PINK SNOW-FLAKES...
WHAT'S THAT MEAN?

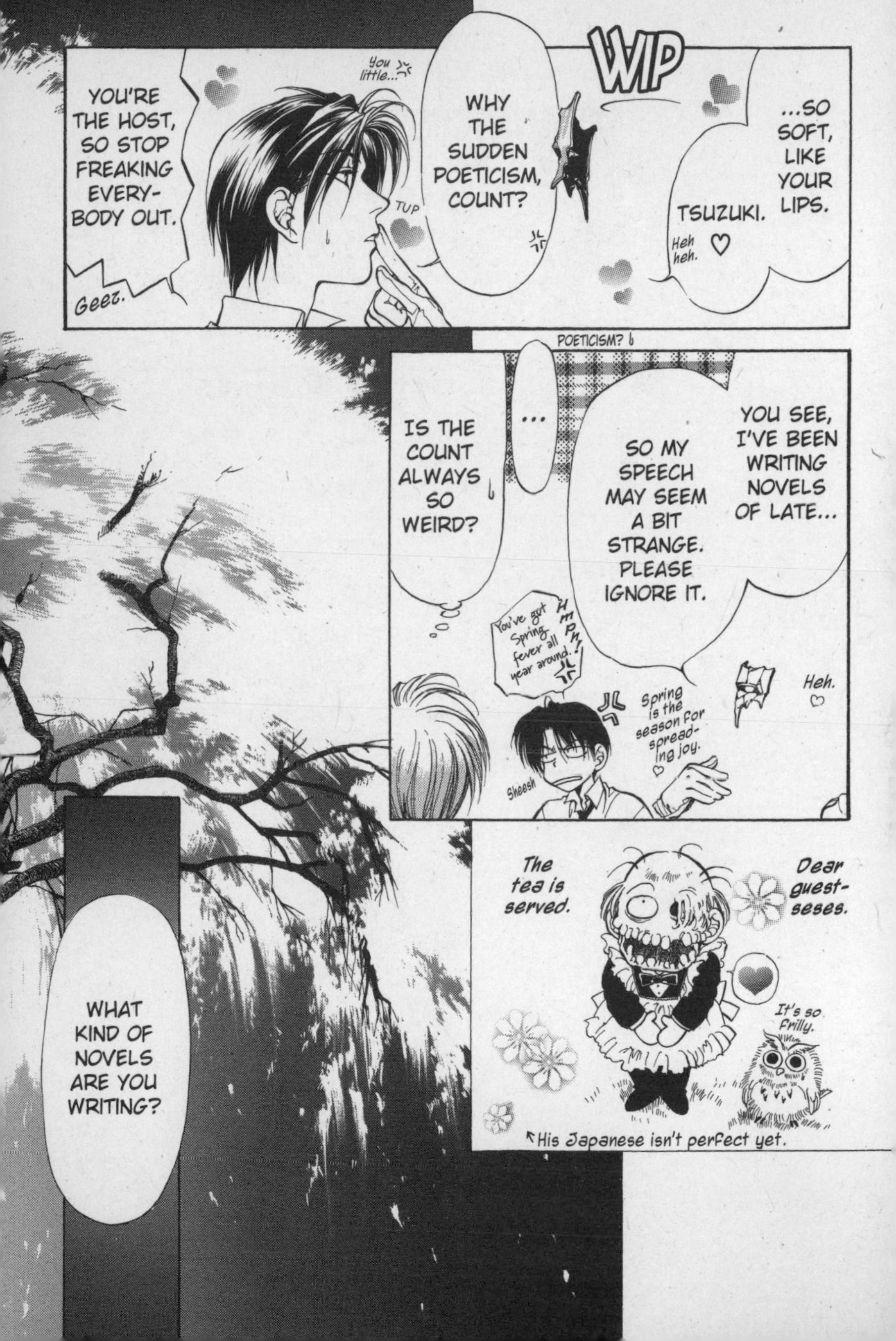
...SO SOFT, LIKE YOUR LIPS.
TSUZUKI.
Heh heh. ♡
WIP
WHY THE SUDDEN POETICISM, COUNT?
You little...
TUP
YOU'RE THE HOST, SO STOP FREAKING EVERY-BODY OUT.
Geez.
POETICISM?
YOU SEE, I'VE BEEN WRITING NOVELS OF LATE...
SO MY SPEECH MAY SEEM A BIT STRANGE. PLEASE IGNORE IT.
...
IS THE COUNT ALWAYS SO WEIRD?
Heh. ♡
Spring is the season for spread-ing joy. ♡
HMPH!
You've got Spring fever all year around!
Sheesh
Dear guest-seses.
The tea is served.
It's so frilly.
His Japanese isn't perfect yet.
WHAT KIND OF NOVELS ARE YOU WRITING?

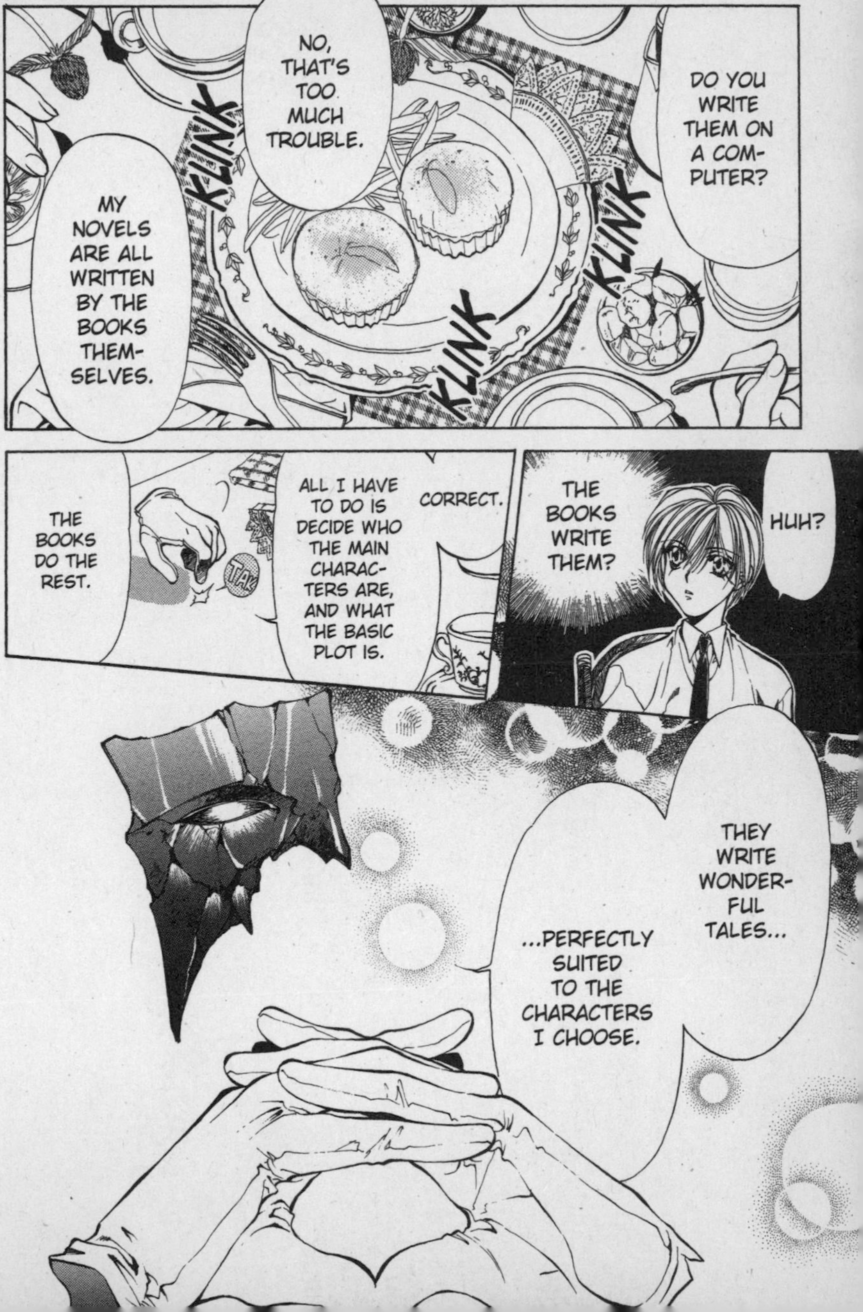
DO YOU WRITE THEM ON A COMPUTER?
KLINK
KLINK
KLINK
KLINK
NO, THAT'S TOO MUCH TROUBLE.
MY NOVELS ARE ALL WRITTEN BY THE BOOKS THEMSELVES.
HUH?
THE BOOKS WRITE THEM?
CORRECT.
ALL I HAVE TO DO IS DECIDE WHO THE MAIN CHARACTERS ARE, AND WHAT THE BASIC PLOT IS.
TAK
THE BOOKS DO THE REST.
THEY WRITE WONDERFUL TALES...
...PERFECTLY SUITED TO THE CHARACTERS I CHOOSE.

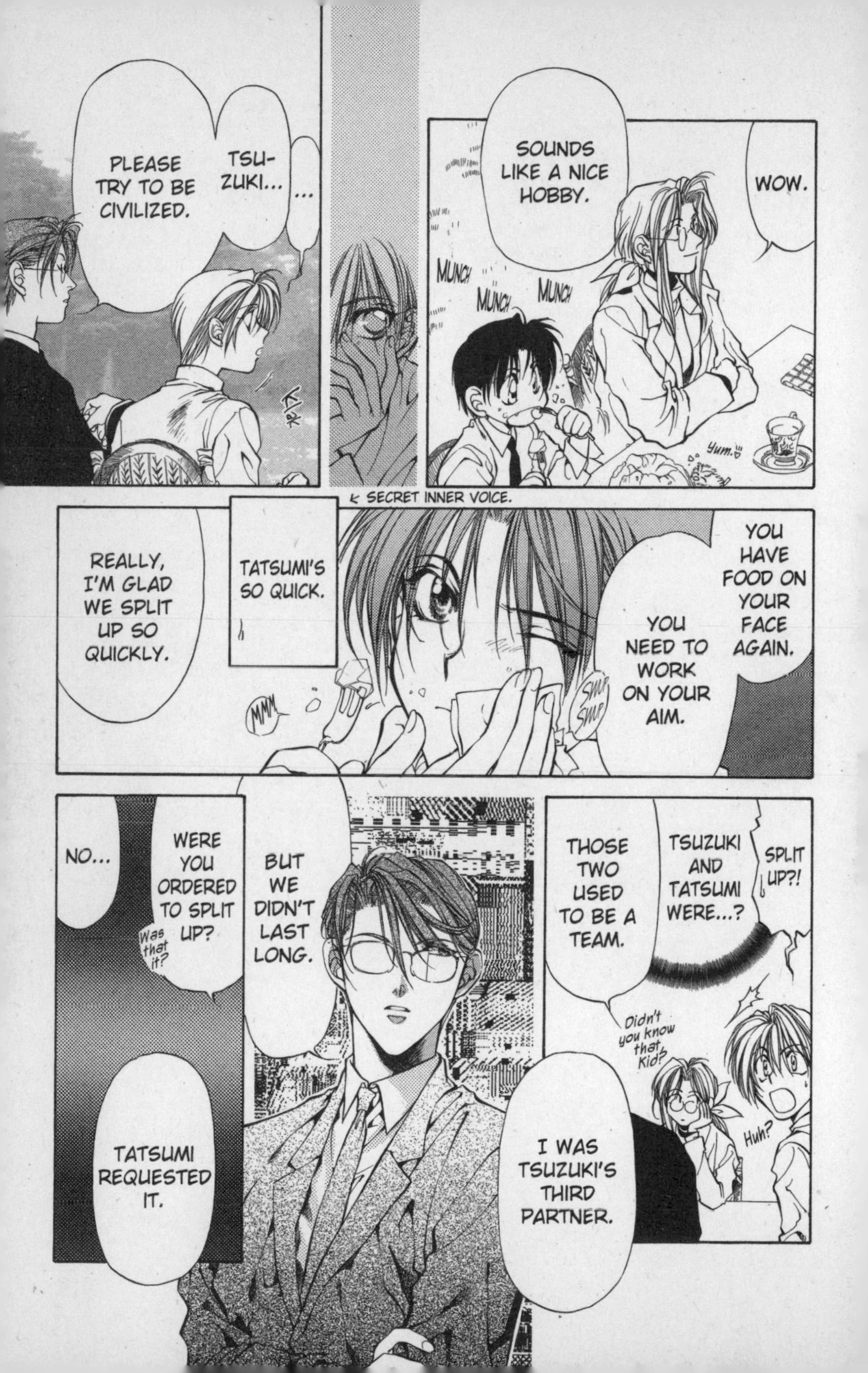
WOW.
SOUNDS LIKE A NICE HOBBY.
MUNCH
MUNCH
MUNCH
Yum.
...
TSU-ZUKI...
PLEASE TRY TO BE CIVILIZED.
Klak
← SECRET INNER VOICE.
YOU HAVE FOOD ON YOUR FACE AGAIN.
YOU NEED TO WORK ON YOUR AIM.
SMP SMP
TATSUMI'S SO QUICK.
MMM
REALLY, I'M GLAD WE SPLIT UP SO QUICKLY.
SPLIT UP?!
TSUZUKI AND TATSUMI WERE...?
THOSE TWO USED TO BE A TEAM.
Didn't you know that Kid?
Huh?
BUT WE DIDN'T LAST LONG.
WERE YOU ORDERED TO SPLIT UP?
Was that it?
NO...
I WAS TSUZUKI'S THIRD PARTNER.
TATSUMI REQUESTED IT.

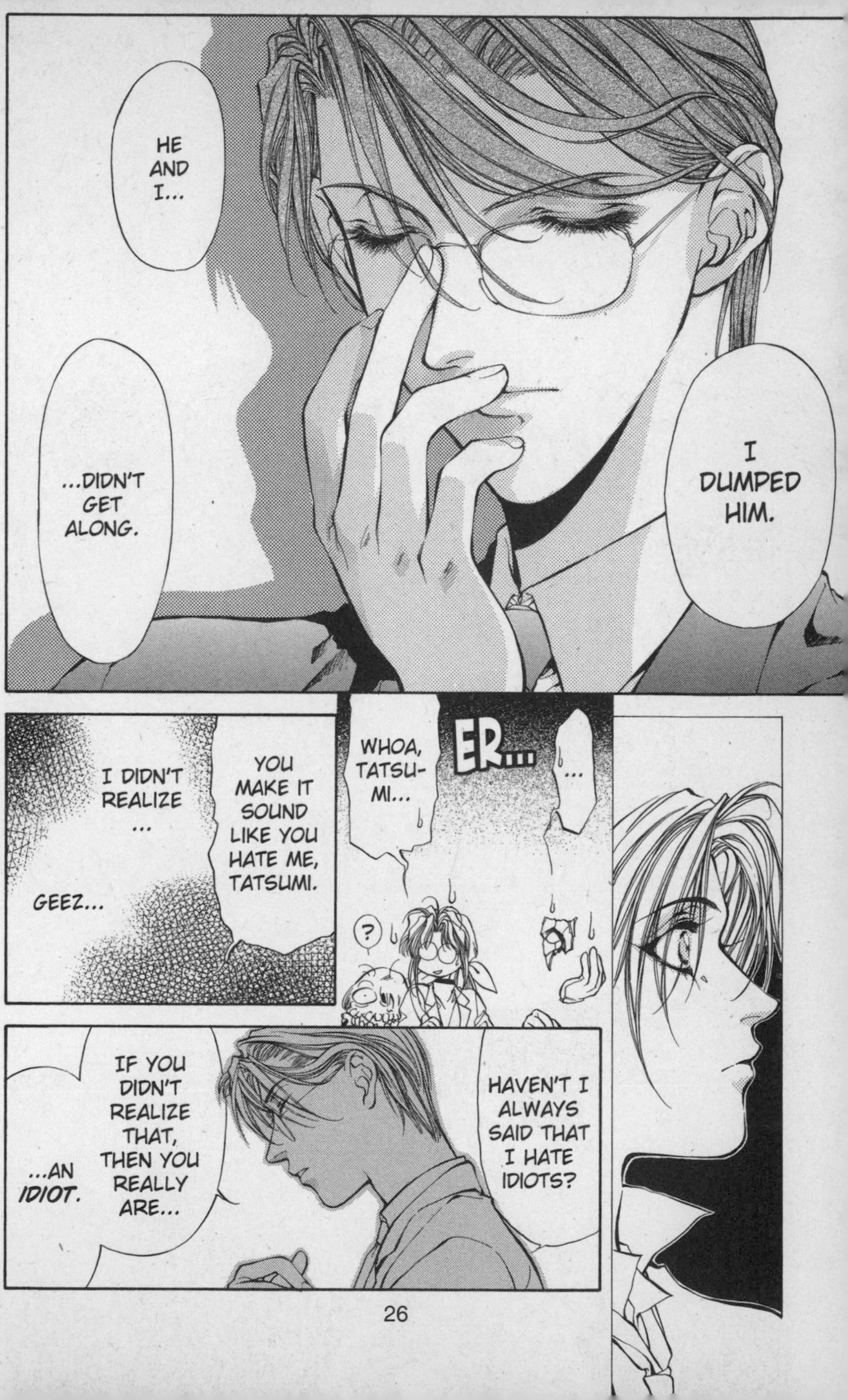
HE AND I...
...DIDN'T GET ALONG.
I DUMPED HIM.
...
ER...
WHOA, TATSU-MI...
YOU MAKE IT SOUND LIKE YOU HATE ME, TATSUMI.
I DIDN'T REALIZE ...
GEEZ...
?
HAVEN'T I ALWAYS SAID THAT I HATE IDIOTS?
IF YOU DIDN'T REALIZE THAT, THEN YOU REALLY ARE...
...AN *IDIOT*.

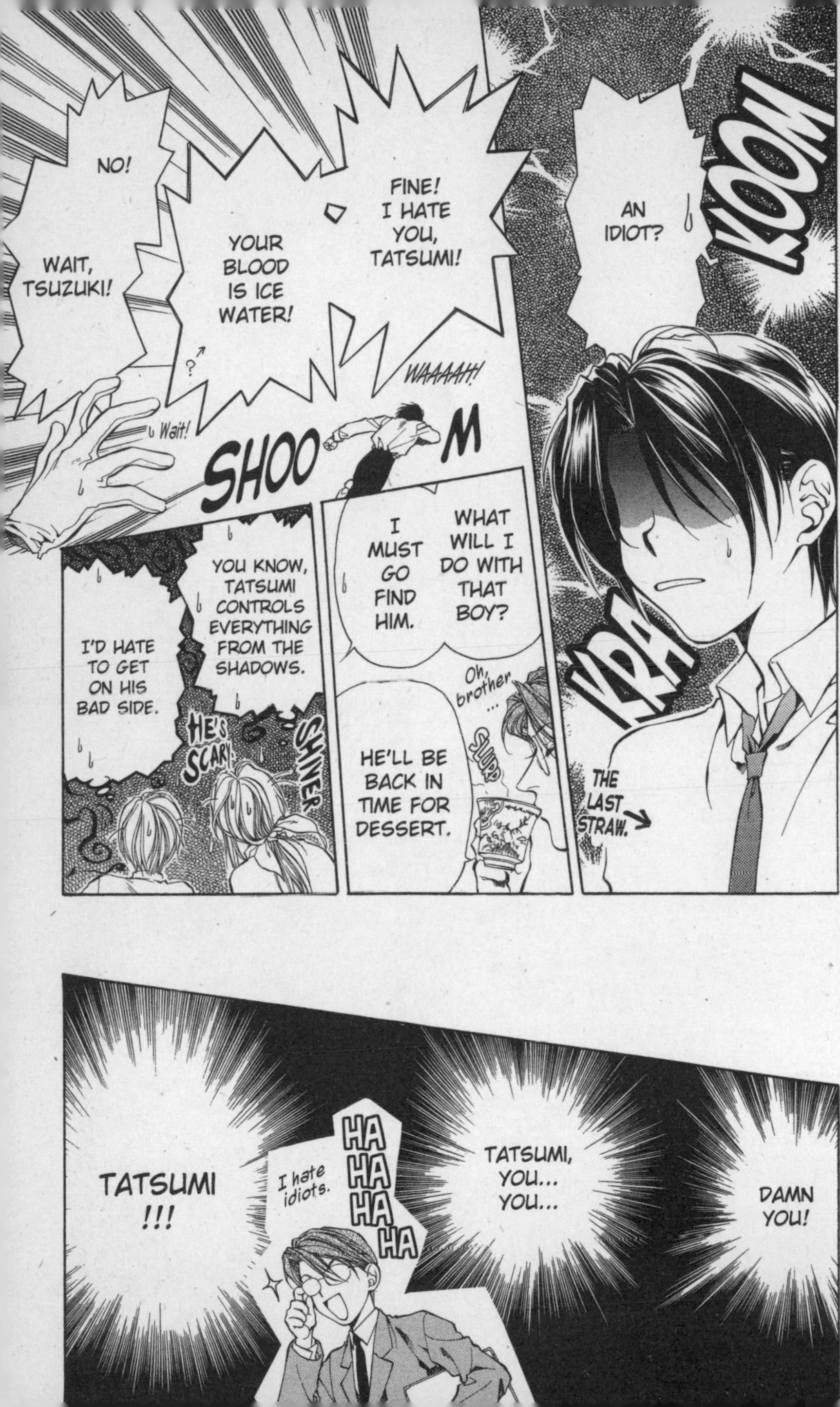
KOOM
AN IDIOT?
KRA
THE LAST STRAW.
FINE! I HATE YOU, TATSUMI!
YOUR BLOOD IS ICE WATER!
?
WAAAAH!
SHOOM
NO!
WAIT, TSUZUKI!
Wait!
WHAT WILL I DO WITH THAT BOY?
I MUST GO FIND HIM.
Oh, brother ...
SLURP
HE'LL BE BACK IN TIME FOR DESSERT.
YOU KNOW, TATSUMI CONTROLS EVERYTHING FROM THE SHADOWS.
SHIVER
I'D HATE TO GET ON HIS BAD SIDE.
HE'S SCARY.
DAMN YOU!
TATSUMI, YOU... YOU...
HA HA HA HA HA
I hate idiots.
TATSUMI !!!

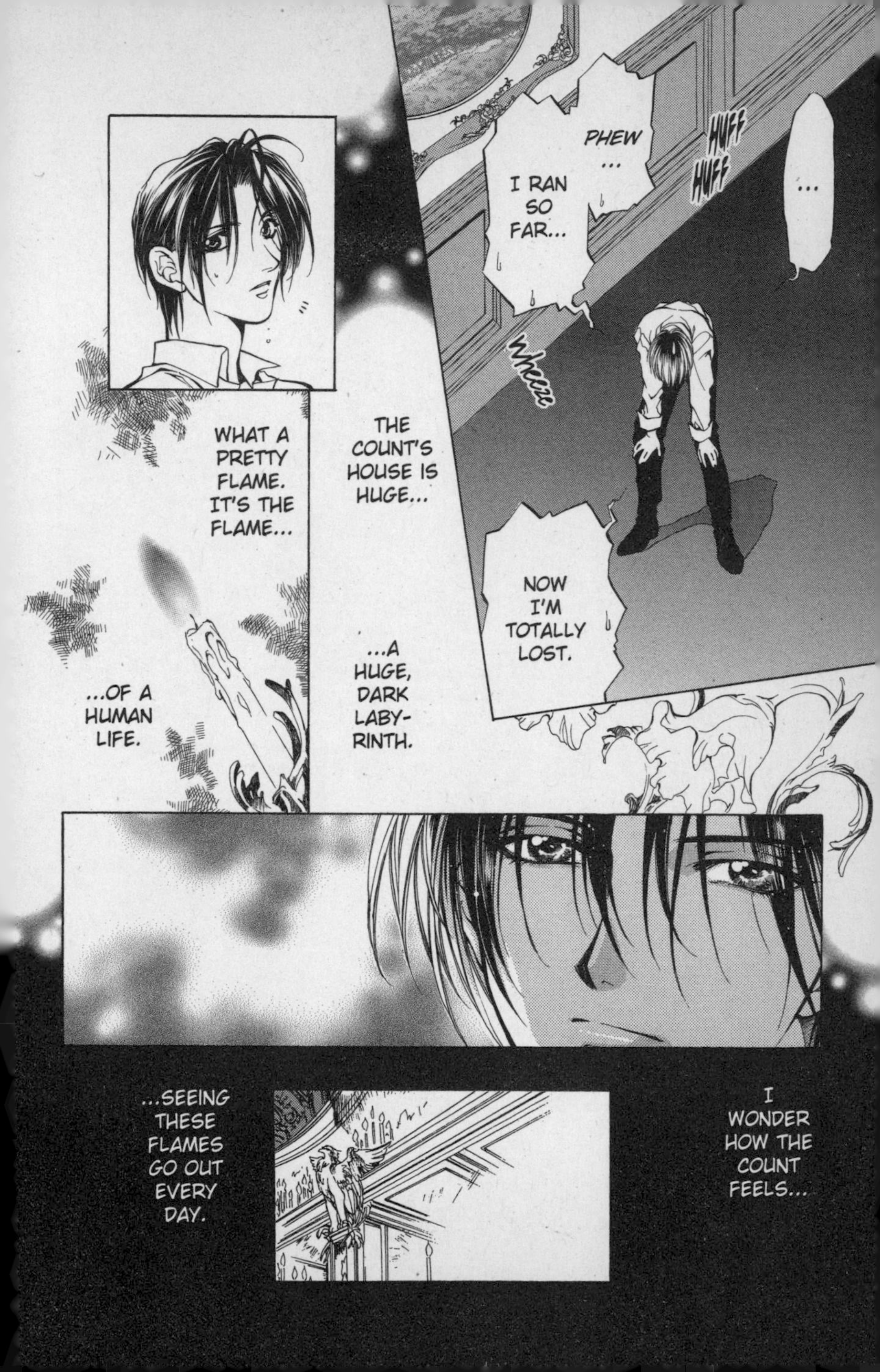
...
HUFF HUFF
PHEW...
I RAN SO FAR...
WHEEZE
NOW I'M TOTALLY LOST.
THE COUNT'S HOUSE IS HUGE...
...A HUGE, DARK LABYRINTH.
WHAT A PRETTY FLAME. IT'S THE FLAME...
...OF A HUMAN LIFE.
I WONDER HOW THE COUNT FEELS...
...SEEING THESE FLAMES GO OUT EVERY DAY.

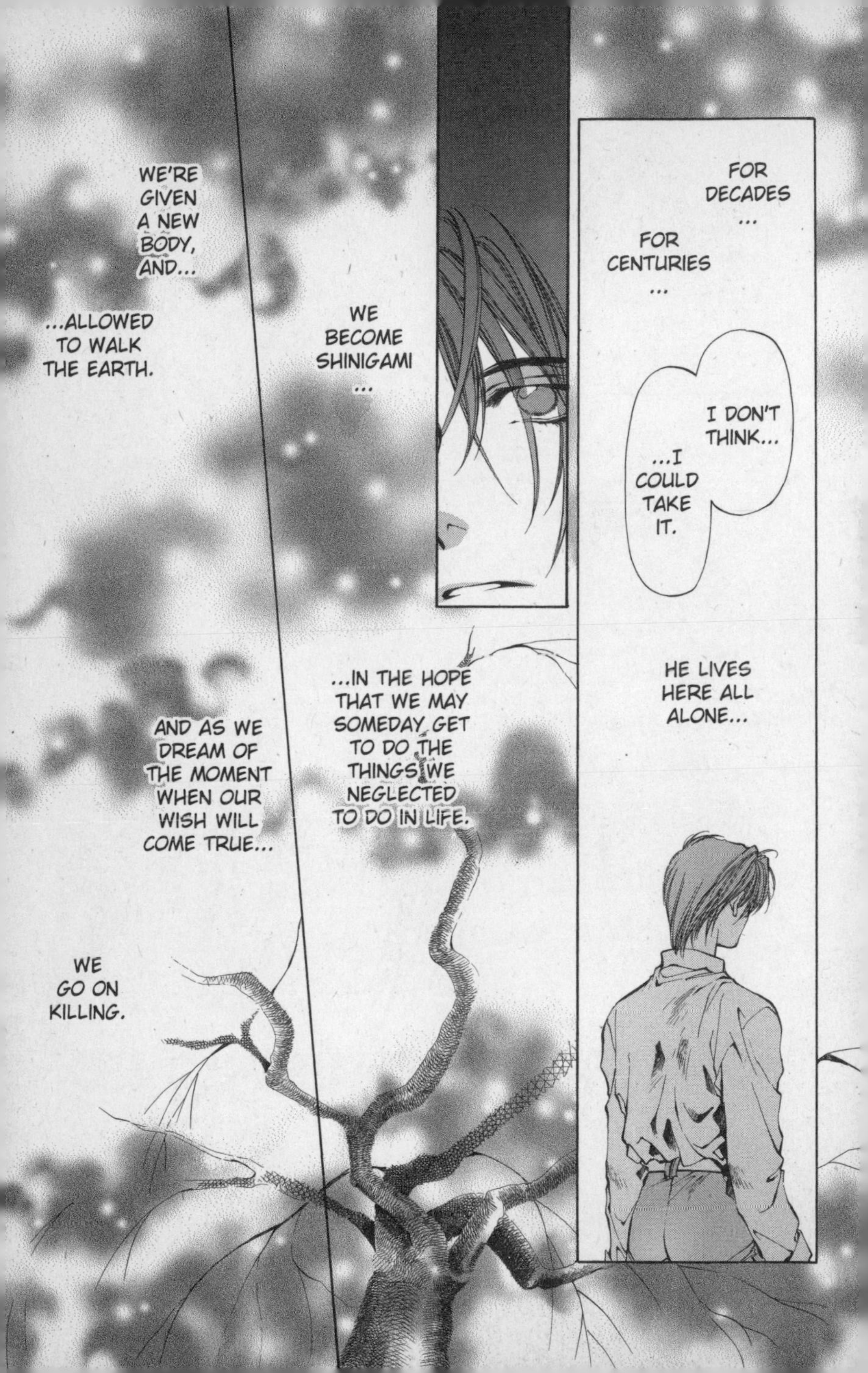
FOR DECADES...
FOR CENTURIES...
I DON'T THINK...
...I COULD TAKE IT.
HE LIVES HERE ALL ALONE...
WE BECOME SHINIGAMI...
...IN THE HOPE THAT WE MAY SOMEDAY GET TO DO THE THINGS WE NEGLECTED TO DO IN LIFE.
WE'RE GIVEN A NEW BODY, AND...
...ALLOWED TO WALK THE EARTH.
AND AS WE DREAM OF THE MOMENT WHEN OUR WISH WILL COME TRUE...
WE GO ON KILLING.

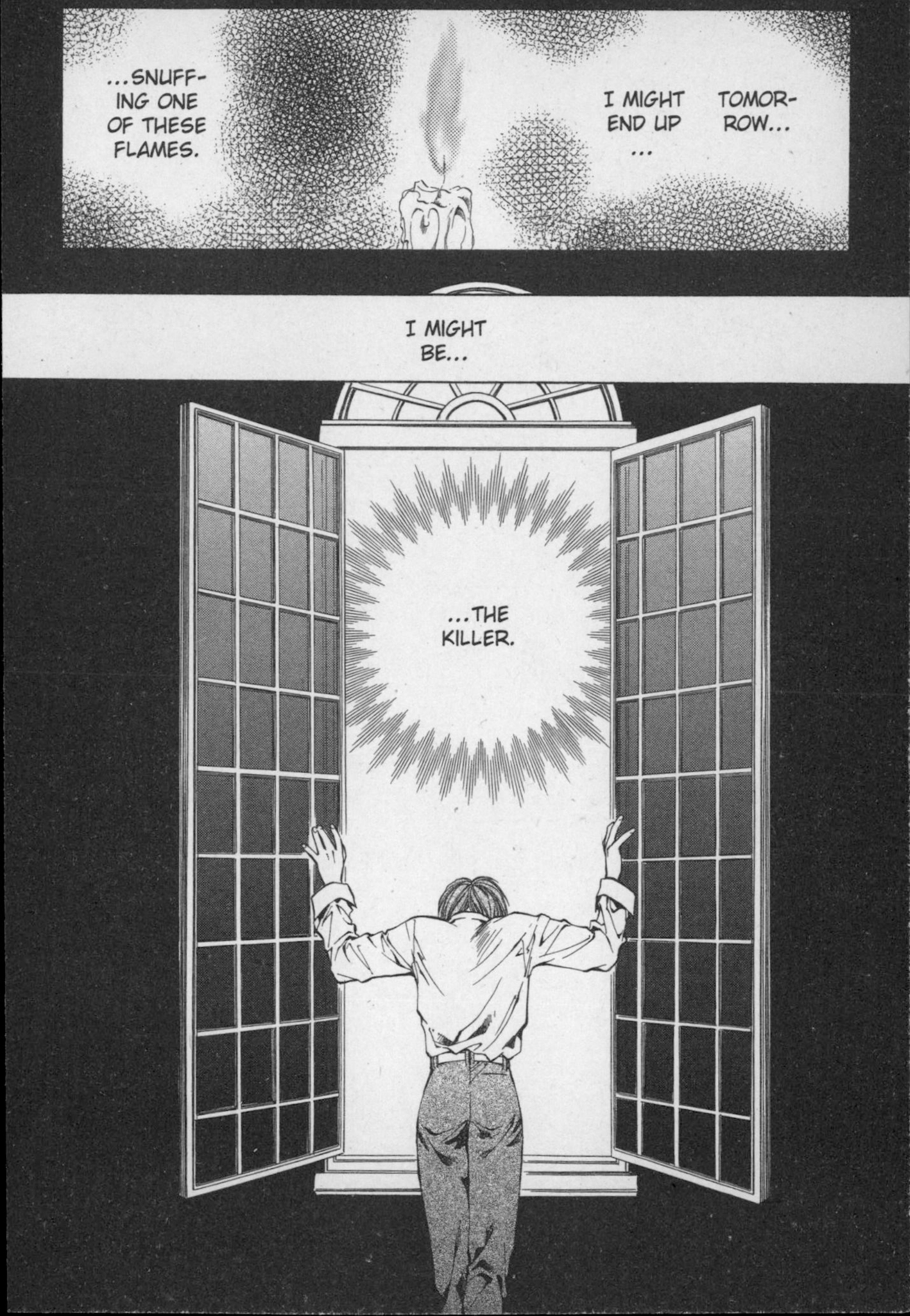
TOMOR-ROW...
I MIGHT END UP ...
...SNUFF-ING ONE OF THESE FLAMES.
I MIGHT BE...
...THE KILLER.

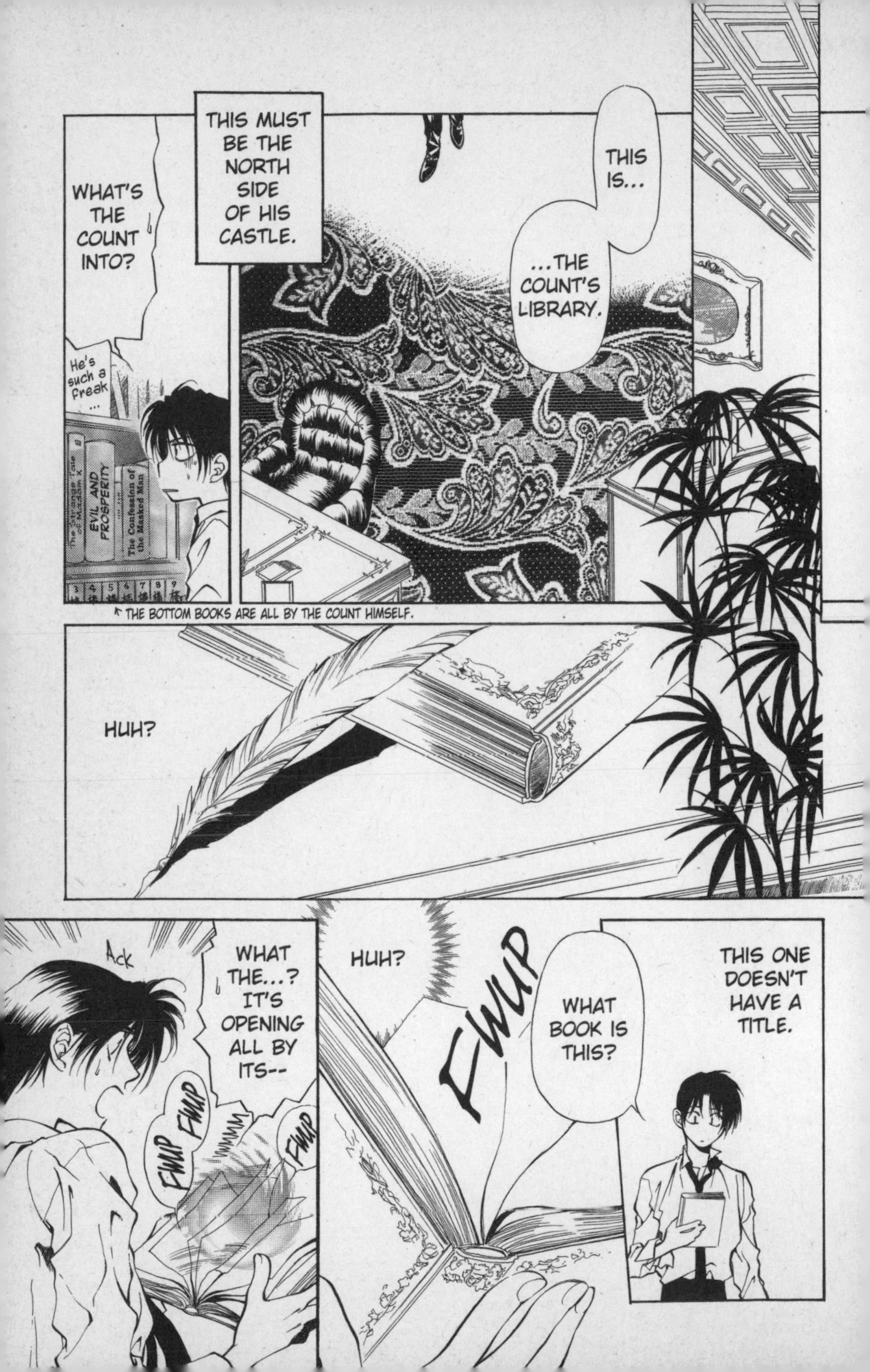
THIS IS...
...THE COUNT'S LIBRARY.
THIS MUST BE THE NORTH SIDE OF HIS CASTLE.
WHAT'S THE COUNT INTO?
He's such a freak...
EVIL AND PROSPERITY
The Confession of the Masked Man
↖ THE BOTTOM BOOKS ARE ALL BY THE COUNT HIMSELF.
HUH?
THIS ONE DOESN'T HAVE A TITLE.
WHAT BOOK IS THIS?
FWUP
HUH?
WHAT THE...? IT'S OPENING ALL BY ITS--
Ack
FWUP
FWUP
FWUP

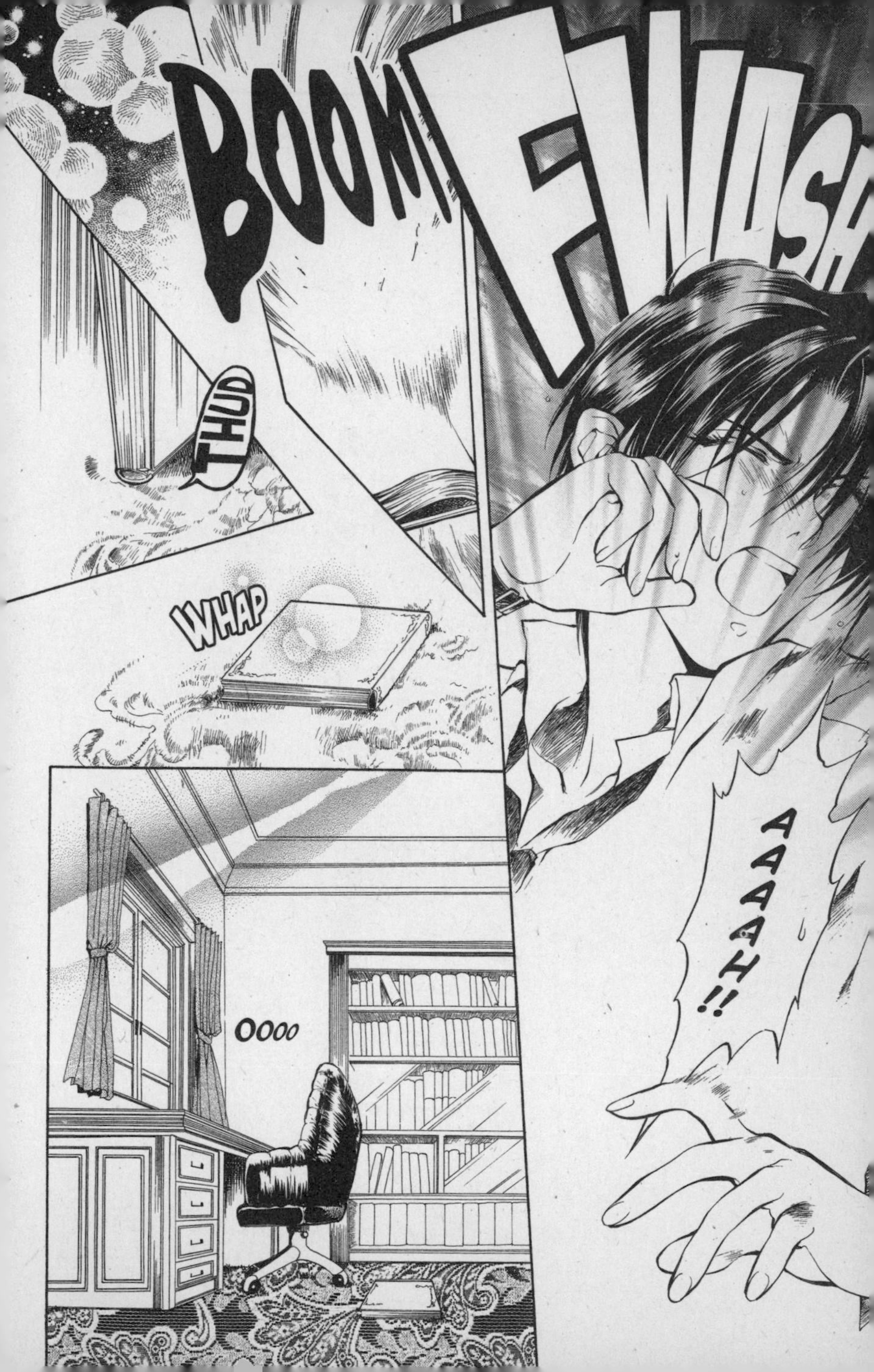
FWISH
AAAAAH!!
BOOM
THUD
WHAP
OOOO

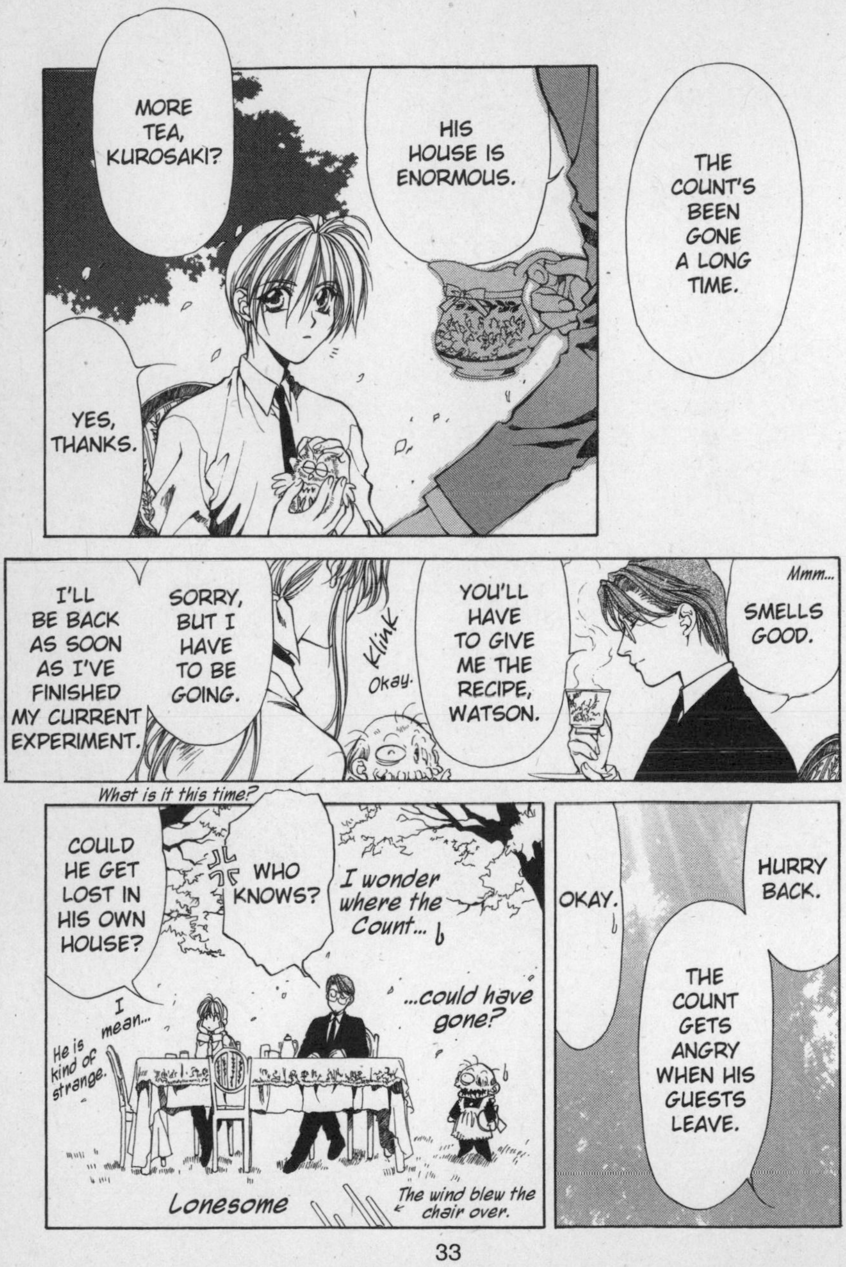
THE COUNT'S BEEN GONE A LONG TIME.
HIS HOUSE IS ENORMOUS.
MORE TEA, KUROSAKI?
YES, THANKS.
Mmm...
SMELLS GOOD.
YOU'LL HAVE TO GIVE ME THE RECIPE, WATSON.
Okay.
Klink
SORRY, BUT I HAVE TO BE GOING.
I'LL BE BACK AS SOON AS I'VE FINISHED MY CURRENT EXPERIMENT.
HURRY BACK.
THE COUNT GETS ANGRY WHEN HIS GUESTS LEAVE.
OKAY.
I wonder where the Count...
...could have gone?
What is it this time?
WHO KNOWS?
COULD HE GET LOST IN HIS OWN HOUSE?
I mean...
He is kind of strange.
The wind blew the chair over.
Lonesome

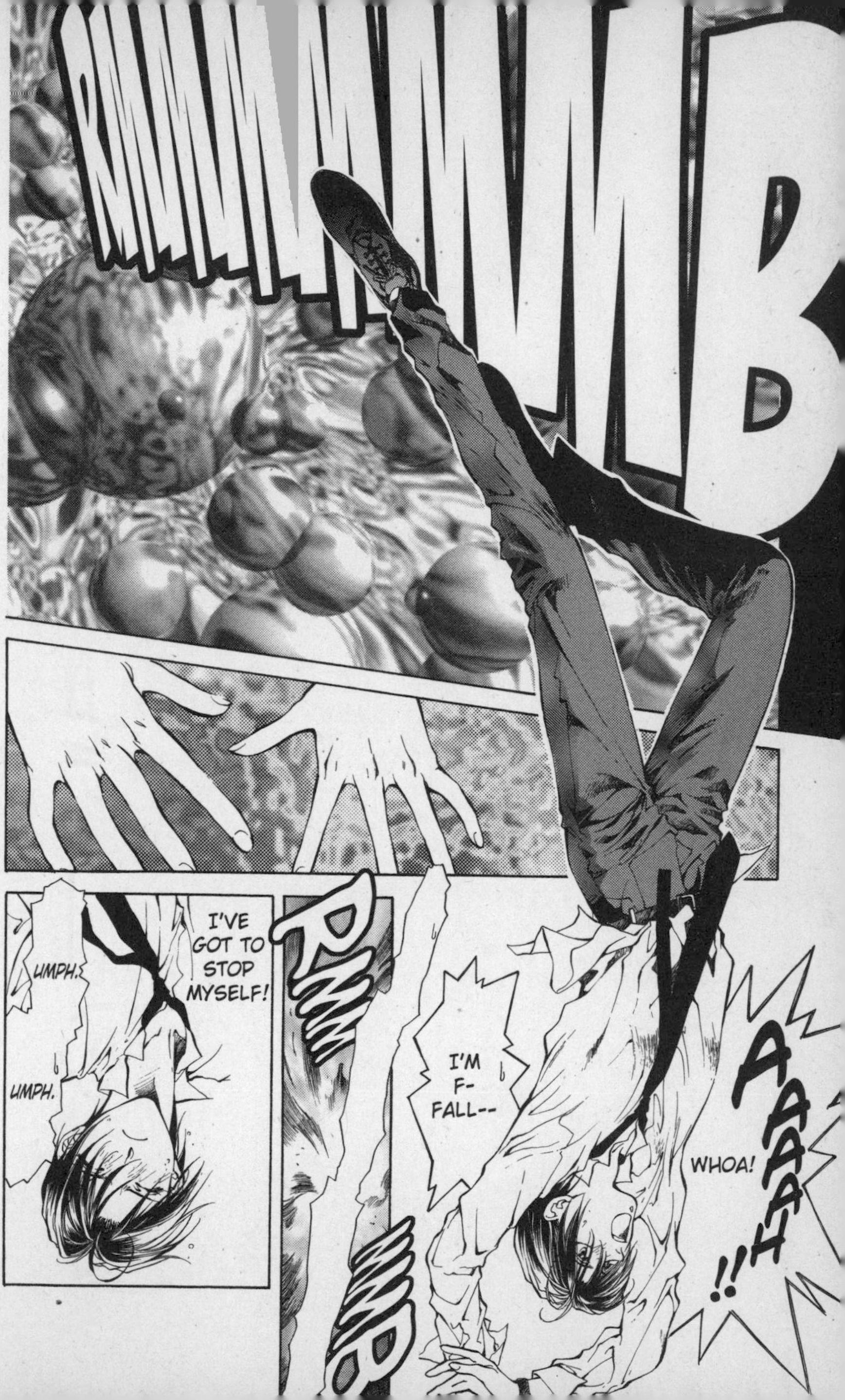
RMMMMMMMMB
AAAAH!!
WHOA!
I'M F-FALL--
RMMMMMB
I'VE GOT TO STOP MYSELF!
UMPH.
UMPH.

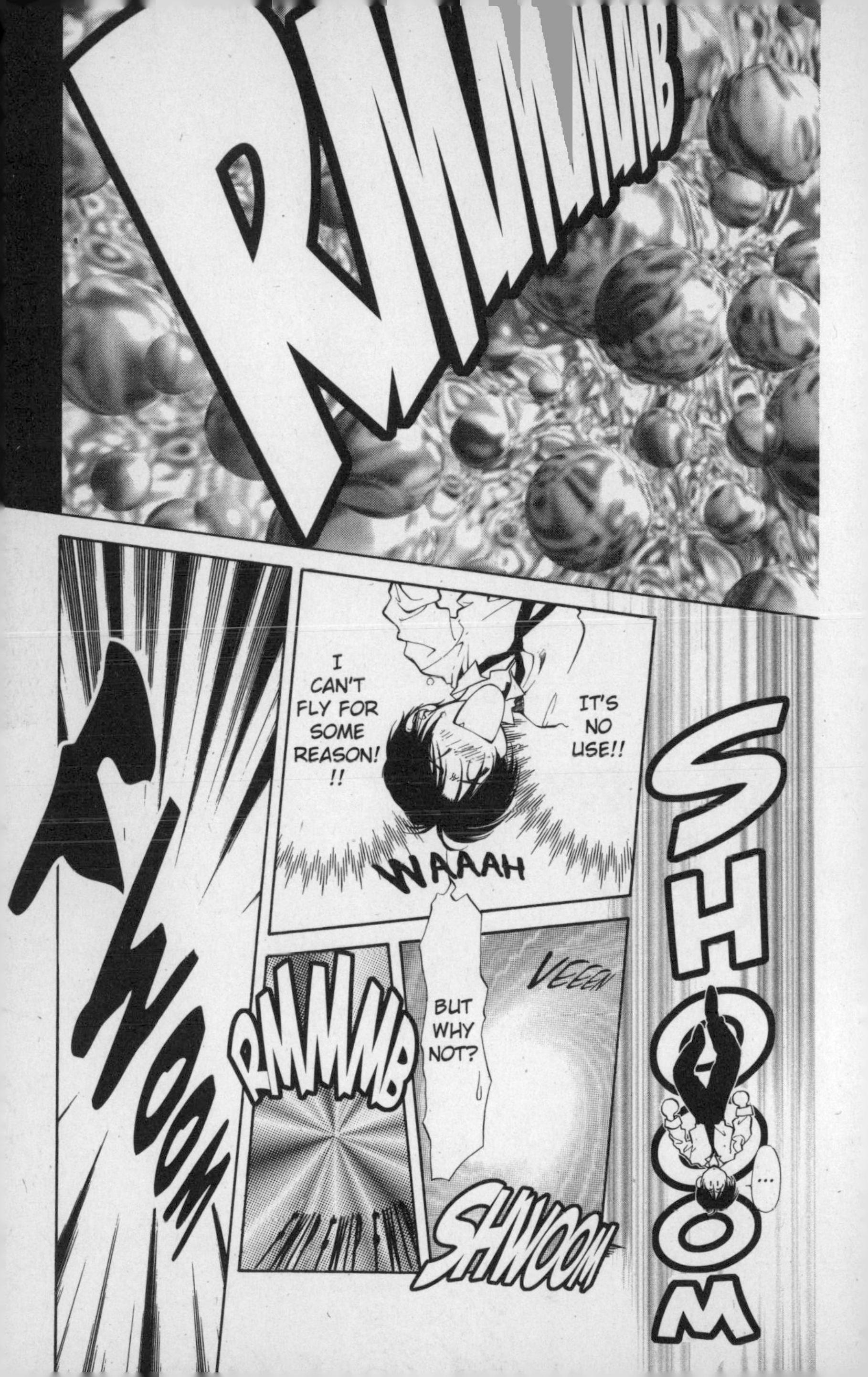
RMMMMMB
SHOOOOM
...
IT'S NO USE!!
I CAN'T FLY FOR SOME REASON!!!
WAAAH
VEEEN
BUT WHY NOT?
SHWOOM
RMMMMB
THWOOM

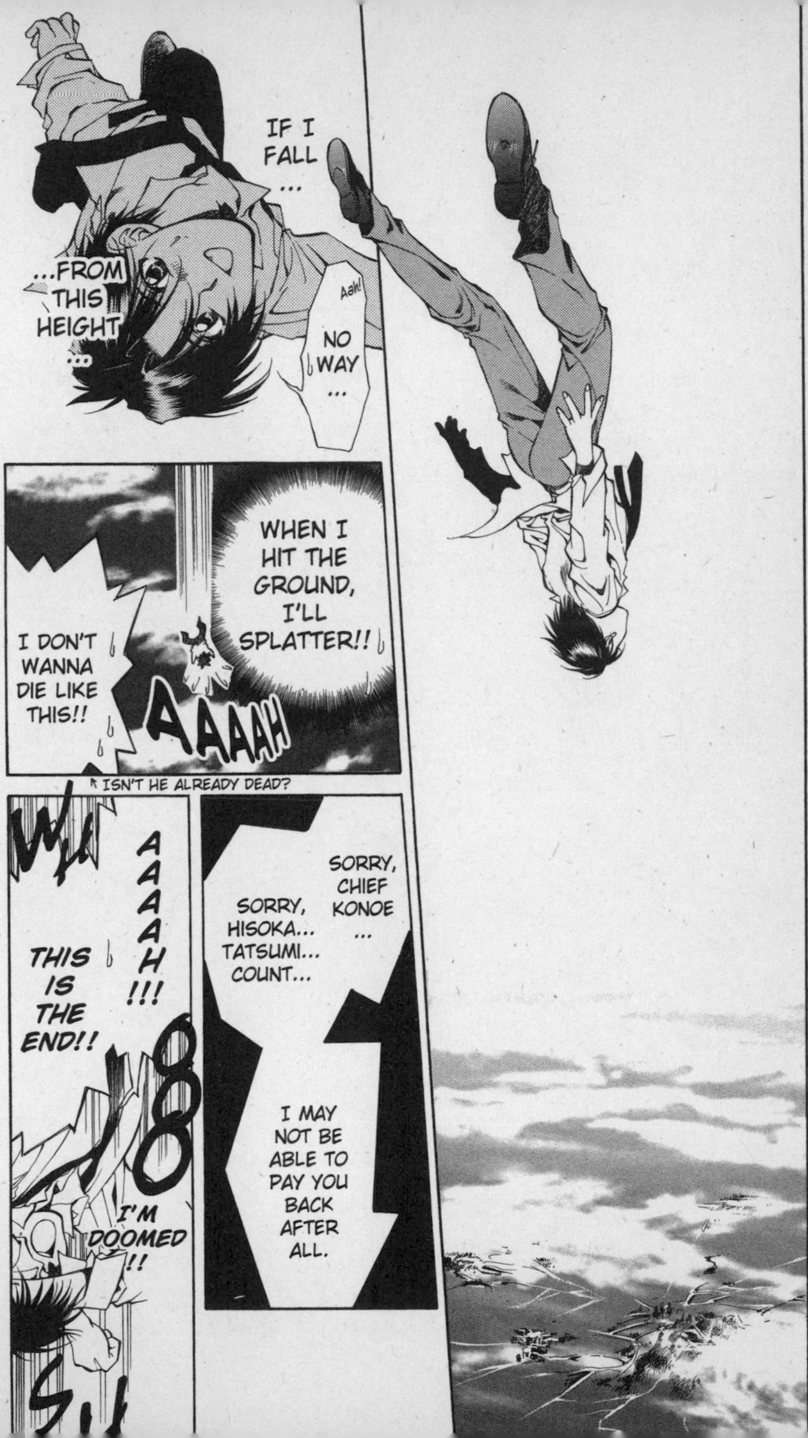
IF I FALL ...
...FROM THIS HEIGHT ...
Aah!
NO WAY ...
WHEN I HIT THE GROUND, I'LL SPLATTER!!
I DON'T WANNA DIE LIKE THIS!!
AAAAH
ISN'T HE ALREADY DEAD?
SORRY, CHIEF KONOE ...
SORRY, HISOKA... TATSUMI... COUNT...
I MAY NOT BE ABLE TO PAY YOU BACK AFTER ALL.
AAAAAH!!!
THIS IS THE END!!
I'M DOOMED!!

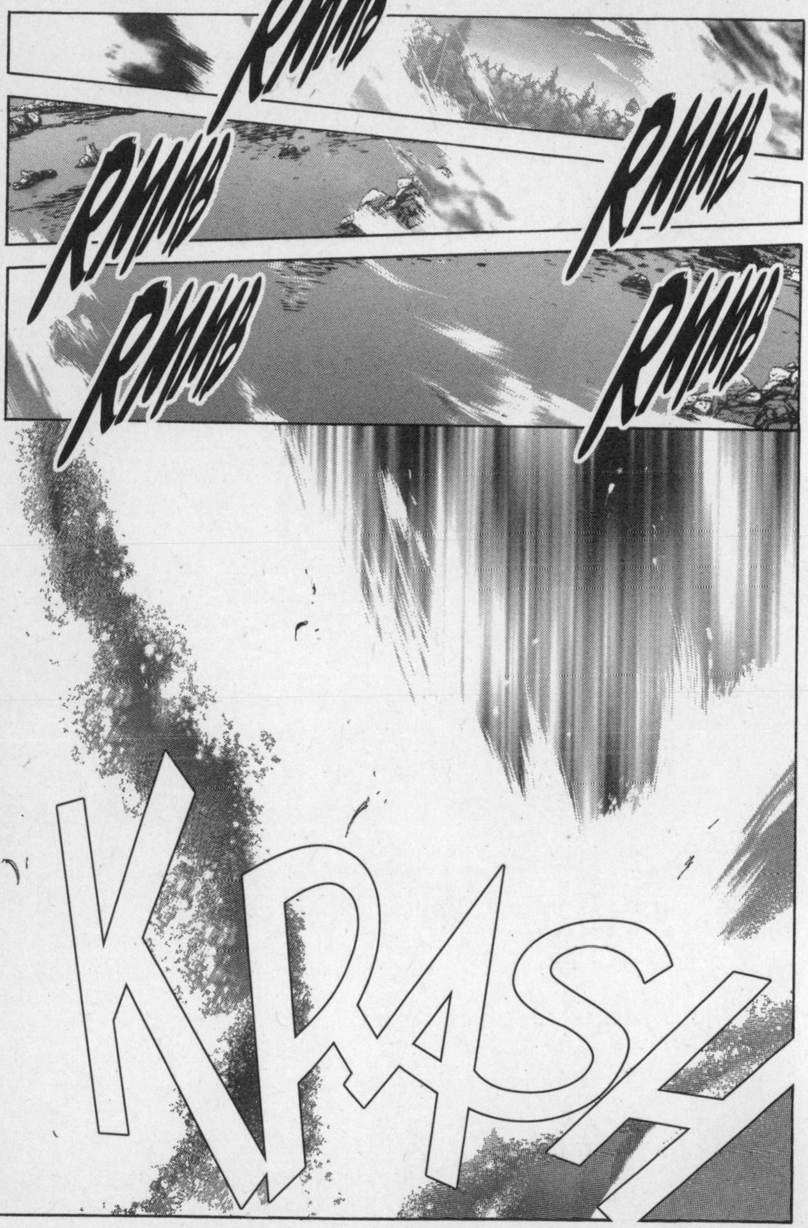
KRASH

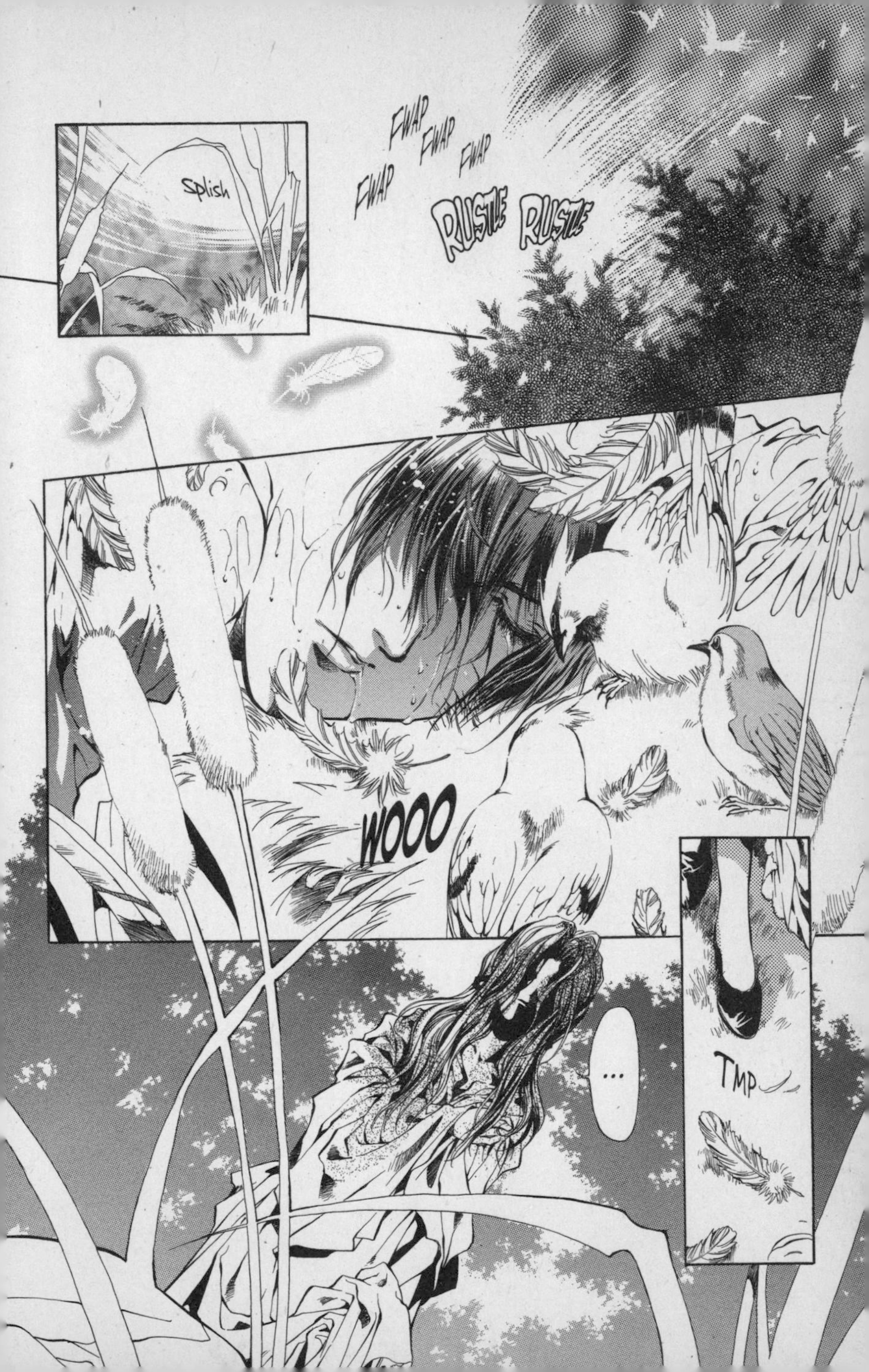
FWAP
FWAP
FWAP
FWAP
RUSTLE
RUSTLE
Splish
WOOO
TMP
...

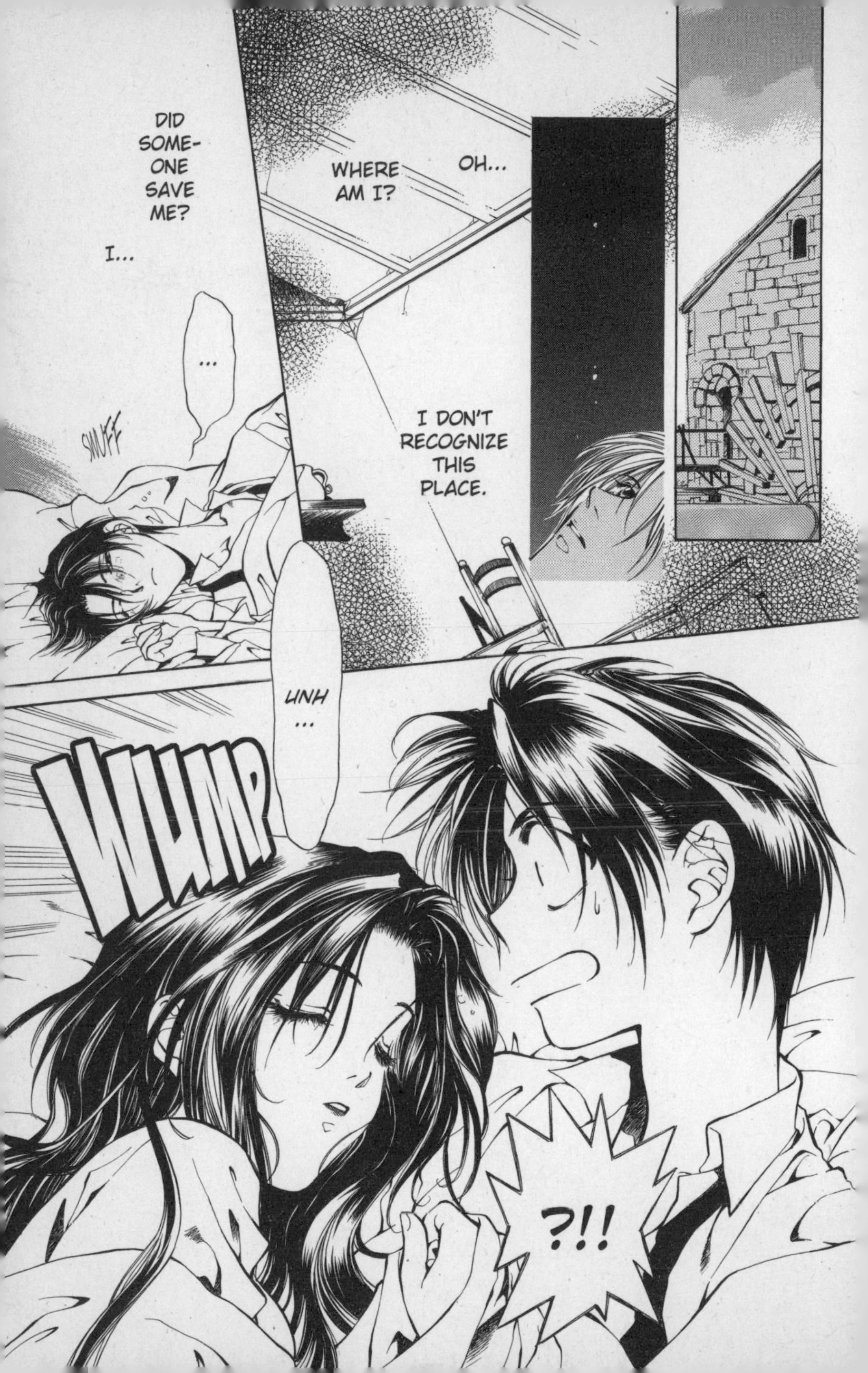
OH...
WHERE AM I?
I DON'T RECOGNIZE THIS PLACE.
DID SOME-ONE SAVE ME?
I...
...
SNUFF
UNH ...
WHUMP
?!!

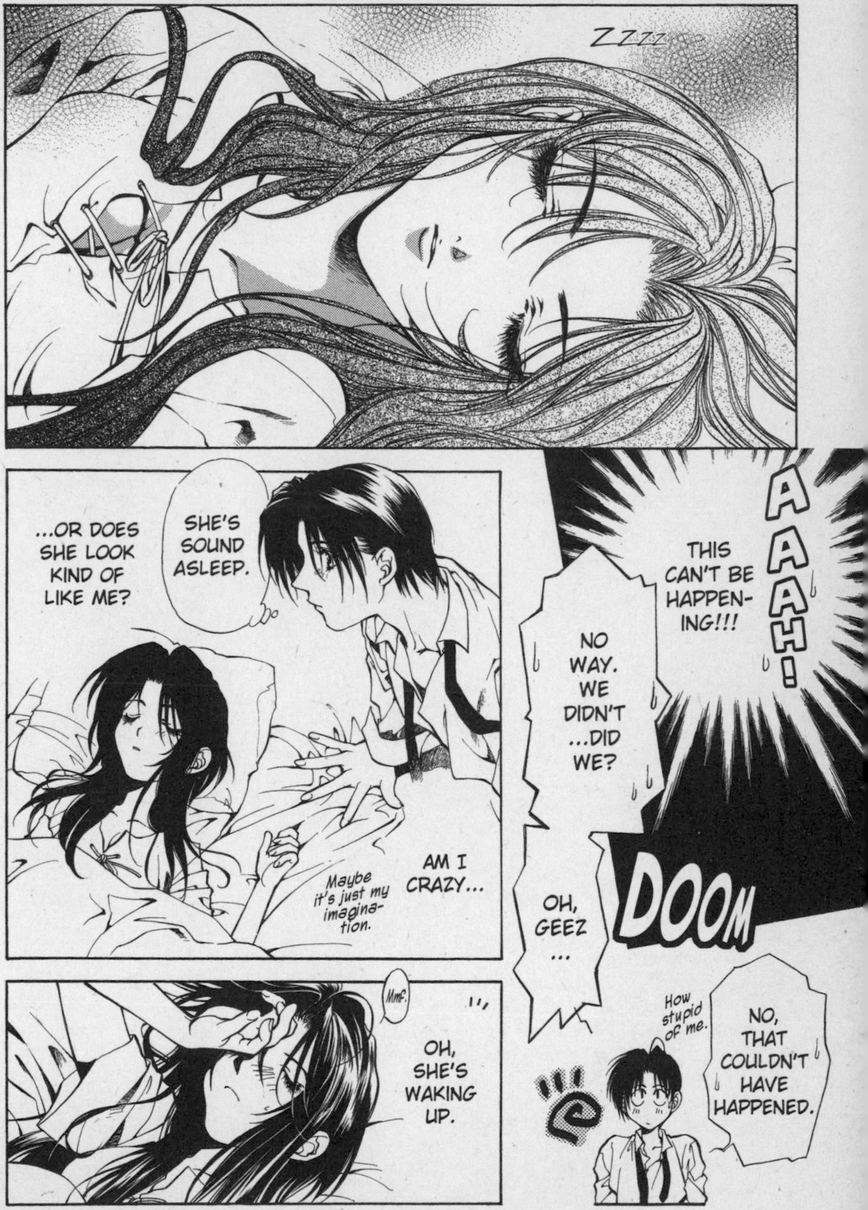
ZZZZ
AAAAH!
THIS CAN'T BE HAPPEN-ING!!!
NO WAY. WE DIDN'T ...DID WE?
DOOM
OH, GEEZ ...
NO, THAT COULDN'T HAVE HAPPENED.
How stupid of me.
SHE'S SOUND ASLEEP.
...OR DOES SHE LOOK KIND OF LIKE ME?
AM I CRAZY...
Maybe it's just my imagina-tion.
Mmf.
OH, SHE'S WAKING UP.

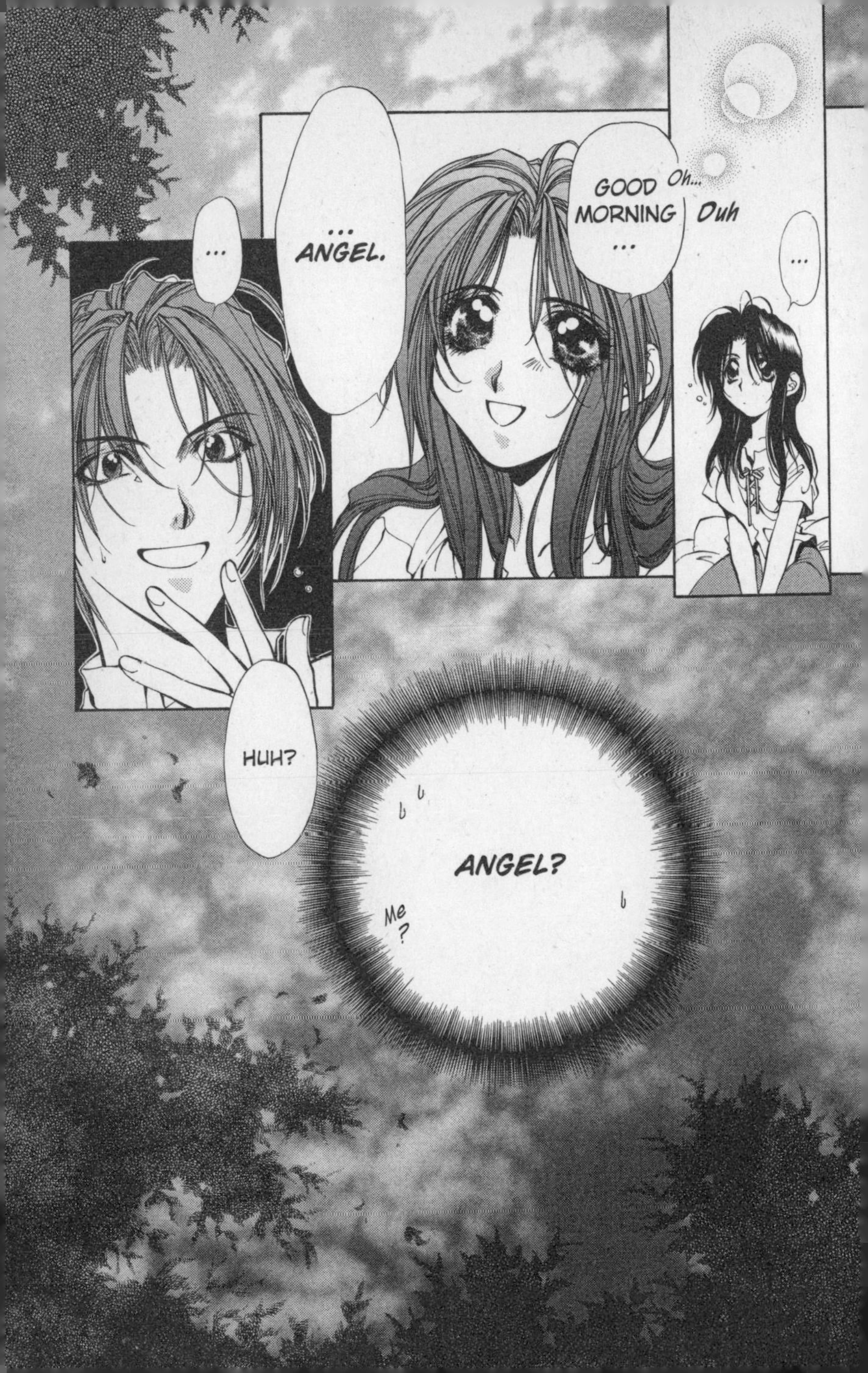
...
Oh... Ouh
GOOD MORNING ...
... ANGEL.
...
HUH?
ANGEL?
Me?

No.JPN-682-C

Patented Brit.906,034 : : 2.589 803 : 3.131.106. Japan
414,218 Other Patent & Patent Pending
Countries of the World. all Principal
: • •3581 1.967 PRINTED IN ENGLAND

Aji

CHAPTER 8

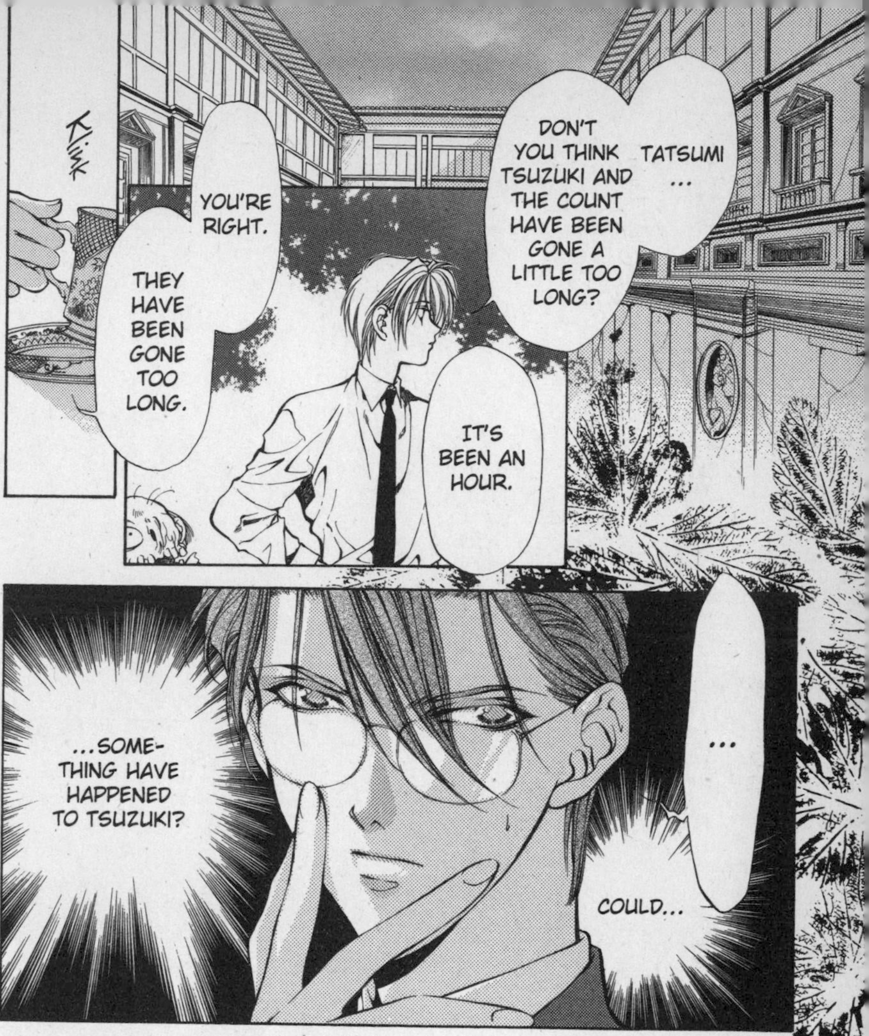
TATSUMI ...
DON'T YOU THINK TSUZUKI AND THE COUNT HAVE BEEN GONE A LITTLE TOO LONG?
IT'S BEEN AN HOUR.
YOU'RE RIGHT.
THEY HAVE BEEN GONE TOO LONG.
Klink
...
COULD...
...SOME-THING HAVE HAPPENED TO TSUZUKI?

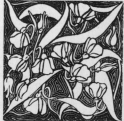

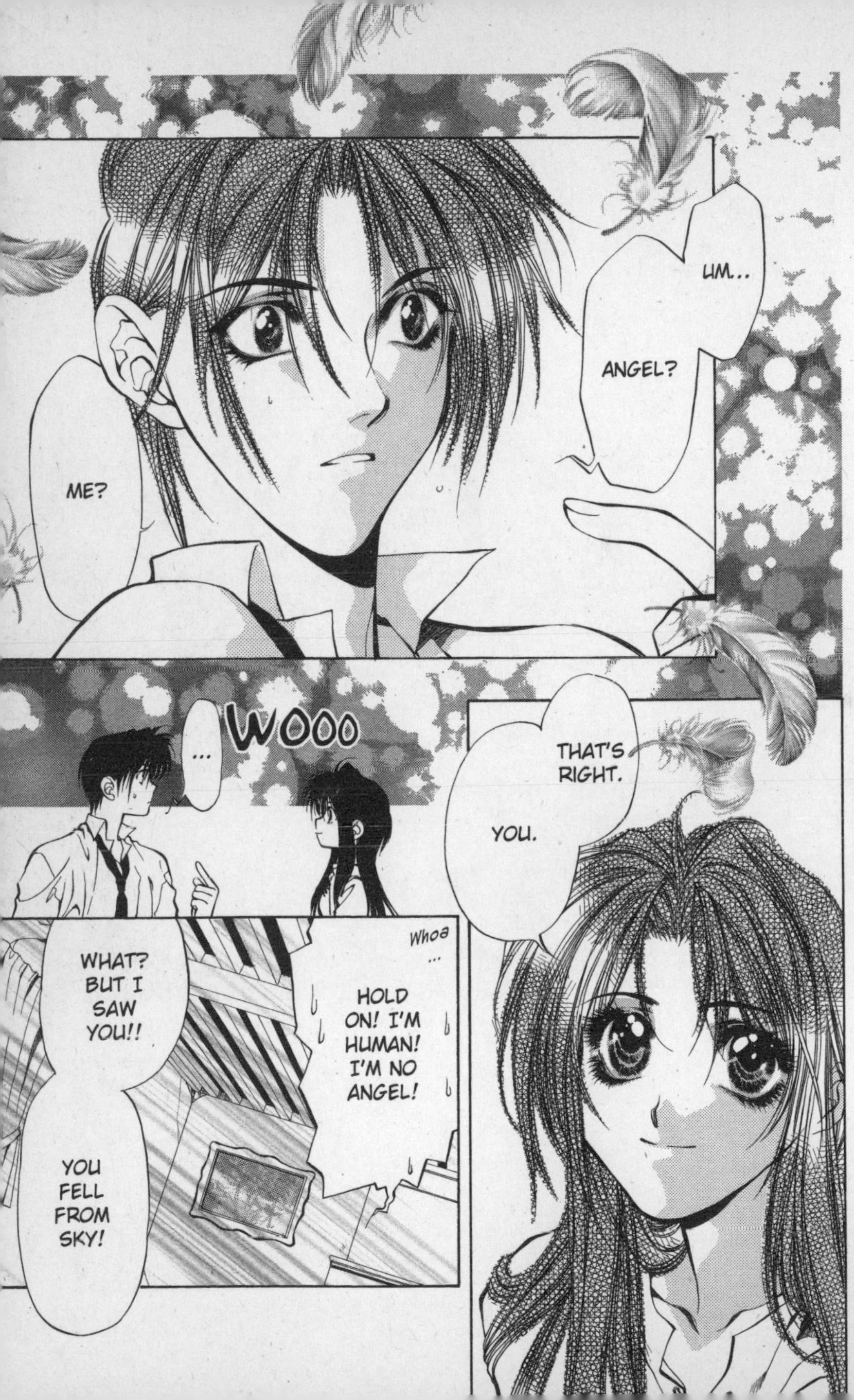
UM...
ANGEL?
ME?
THAT'S RIGHT.
YOU.
WOOO
...
Whoa ...
HOLD ON! I'M HUMAN! I'M NO ANGEL!
WHAT? BUT I SAW YOU!!
YOU FELL FROM SKY!

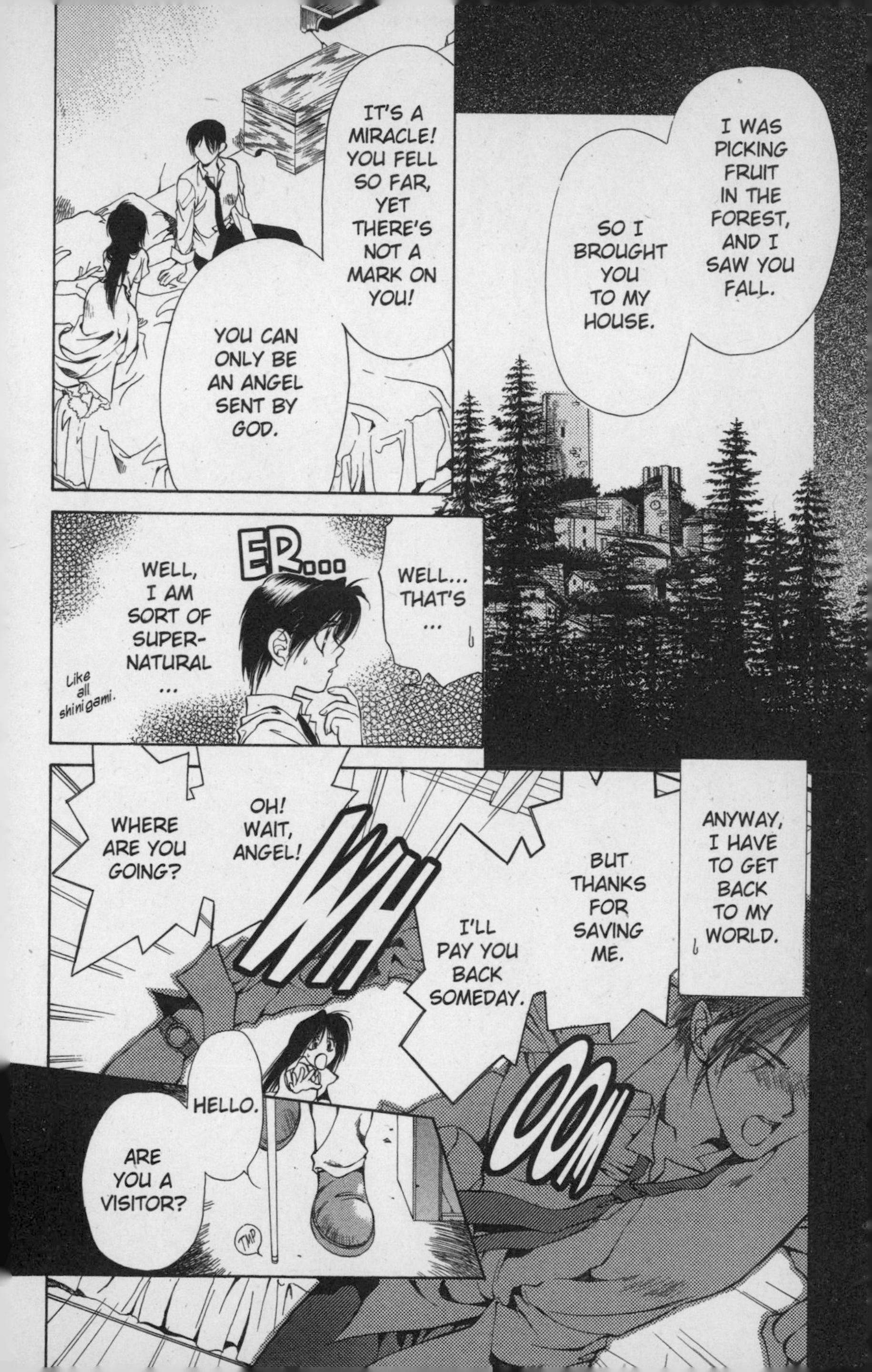
I WAS PICKING FRUIT IN THE FOREST, AND I SAW YOU FALL.
SO I BROUGHT YOU TO MY HOUSE.
IT'S A MIRACLE! YOU FELL SO FAR, YET THERE'S NOT A MARK ON YOU!
YOU CAN ONLY BE AN ANGEL SENT BY GOD.
WELL... THAT'S ...
ERooo
WELL, I AM SORT OF SUPER-NATURAL ...
Like all shinigami.
ANYWAY, I HAVE TO GET BACK TO MY WORLD.
BUT THANKS FOR SAVING ME.
I'LL PAY YOU BACK SOMEDAY.
WH
OOM
OH! WAIT, ANGEL!
WHERE ARE YOU GOING?
HELLO.
ARE YOU A VISITOR?
TMP

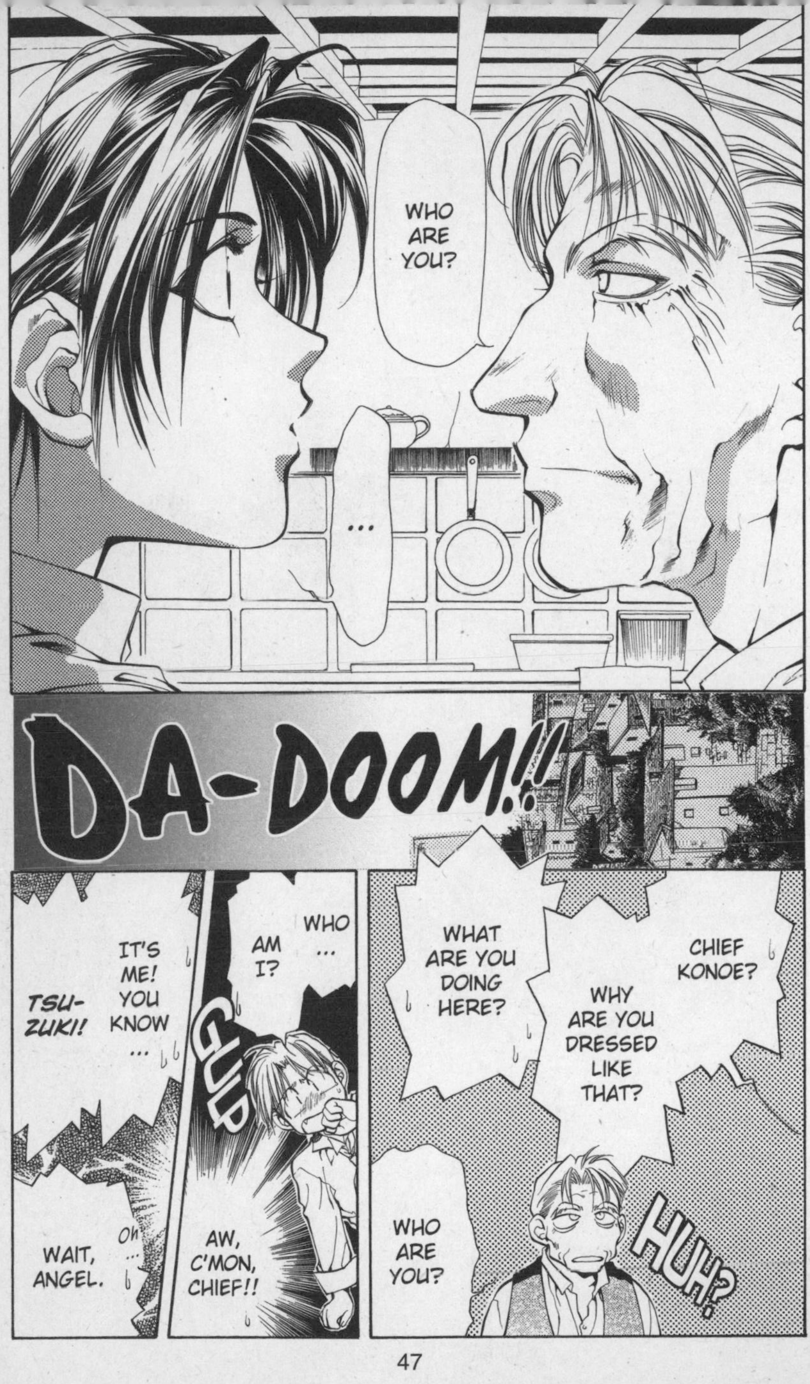
WHO ARE YOU?
...
DA-DOOM!!
CHIEF KONOE?
WHY ARE YOU DRESSED LIKE THAT?
WHAT ARE YOU DOING HERE?
HUH?
WHO ARE YOU?
WHO ... AM I?
GULP
AW, C'MON, CHIEF!!
IT'S ME! YOU KNOW ...
TSU-ZUKI!
Oh ...
WAIT, ANGEL.

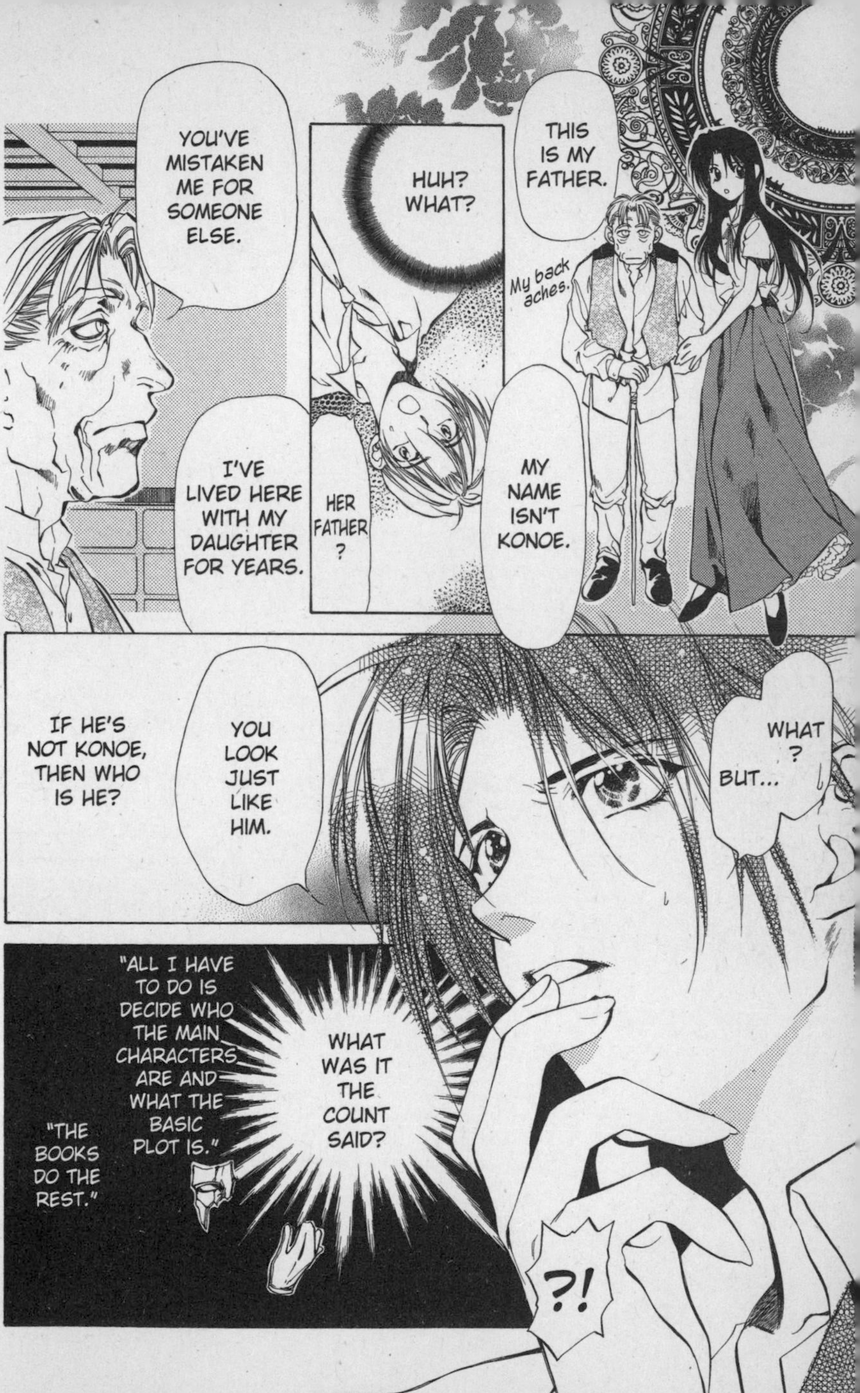
THIS IS MY FATHER.
My back aches.
MY NAME ISN'T KONOE.
HUH? WHAT?
HER FATHER?
YOU'VE MISTAKEN ME FOR SOMEONE ELSE.
I'VE LIVED HERE WITH MY DAUGHTER FOR YEARS.
WHAT? BUT...
YOU LOOK JUST LIKE HIM.
IF HE'S NOT KONOE, THEN WHO IS HE?
?!
WHAT WAS IT THE COUNT SAID?
"ALL I HAVE TO DO IS DECIDE WHO THE MAIN CHARACTERS ARE AND WHAT THE BASIC PLOT IS."
"THE BOOKS DO THE REST."

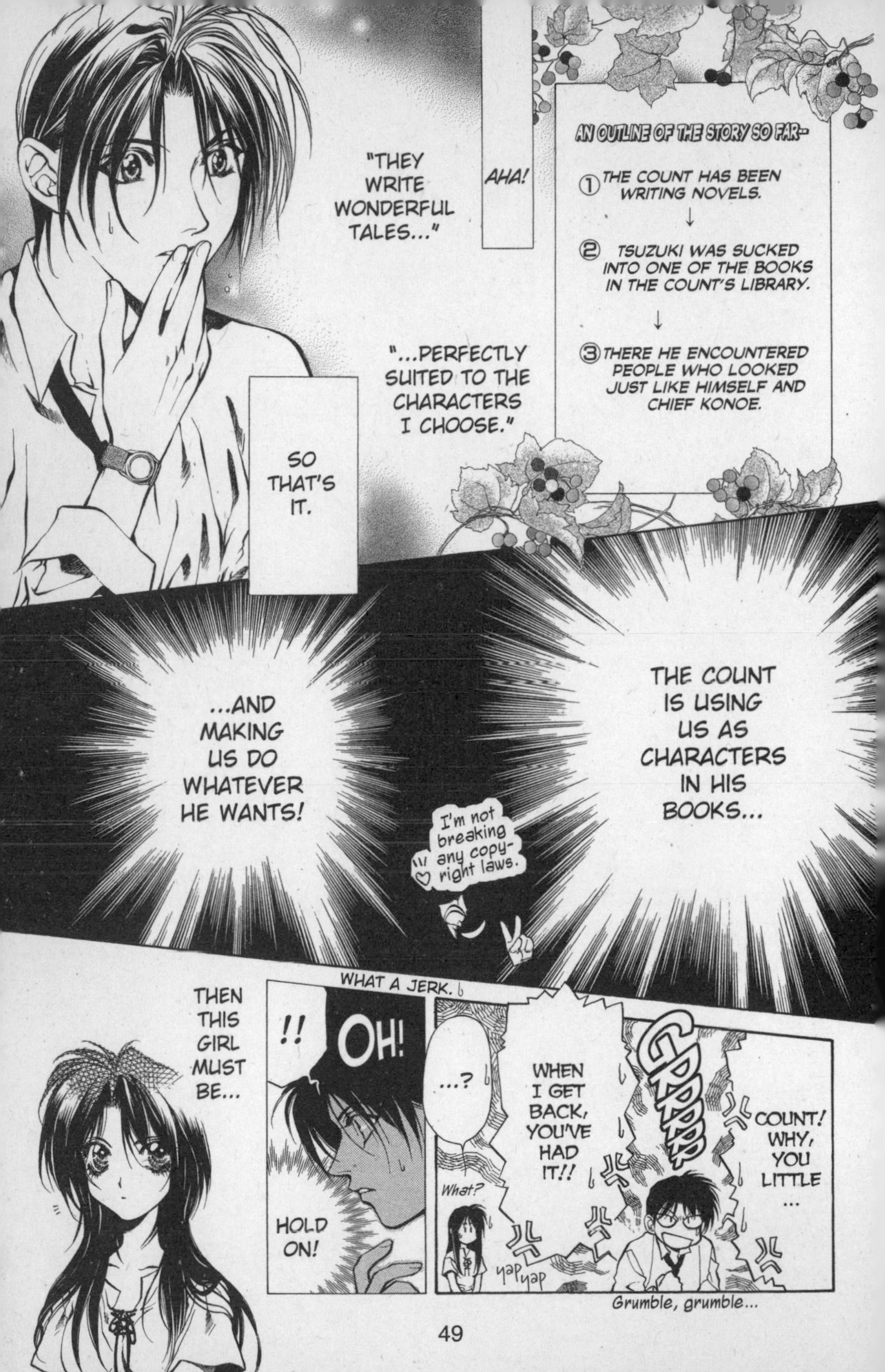
AN OUTLINE OF THE STORY SO FAR–
① THE COUNT HAS BEEN WRITING NOVELS.
↓
② TSUZUKI WAS SUCKED INTO ONE OF THE BOOKS IN THE COUNT'S LIBRARY.
↓
③ THERE HE ENCOUNTERED PEOPLE WHO LOOKED JUST LIKE HIMSELF AND CHIEF KONOE.
AHA!
"THEY WRITE WONDERFUL TALES..."
"...PERFECTLY SUITED TO THE CHARACTERS I CHOOSE."
SO THAT'S IT.
THE COUNT IS USING US AS CHARACTERS IN HIS BOOKS...
...AND MAKING US DO WHATEVER HE WANTS!
I'm not breaking any copyright laws.
WHAT A JERK.
COUNT! WHY, YOU LITTLE ...
GRRRR
WHEN I GET BACK, YOU'VE HAD IT!!
...?
What?
yap yap
Grumble, grumble...
OH!
!!
HOLD ON!
THEN THIS GIRL MUST BE...

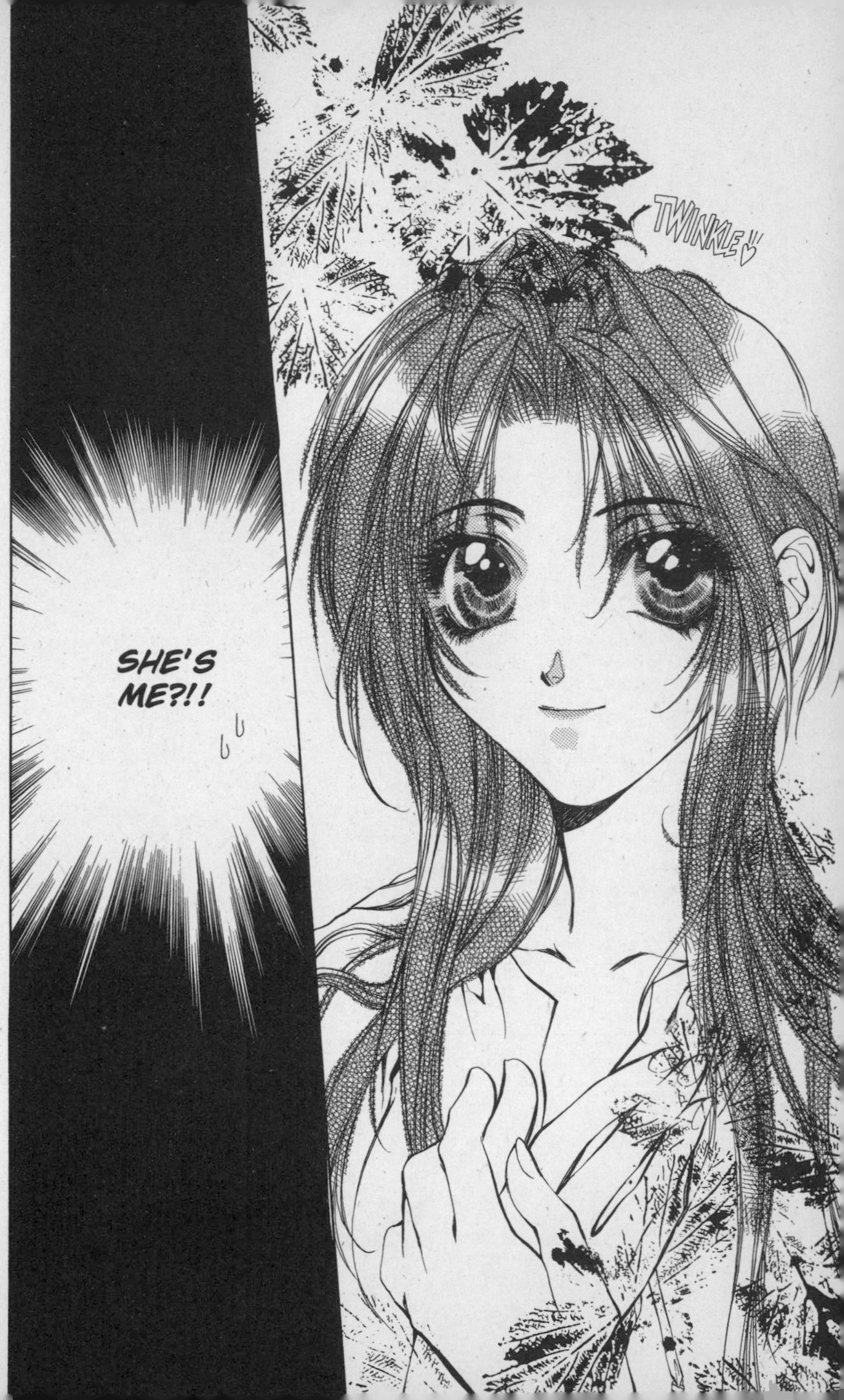
TWINKLE
SHE'S ME?!!

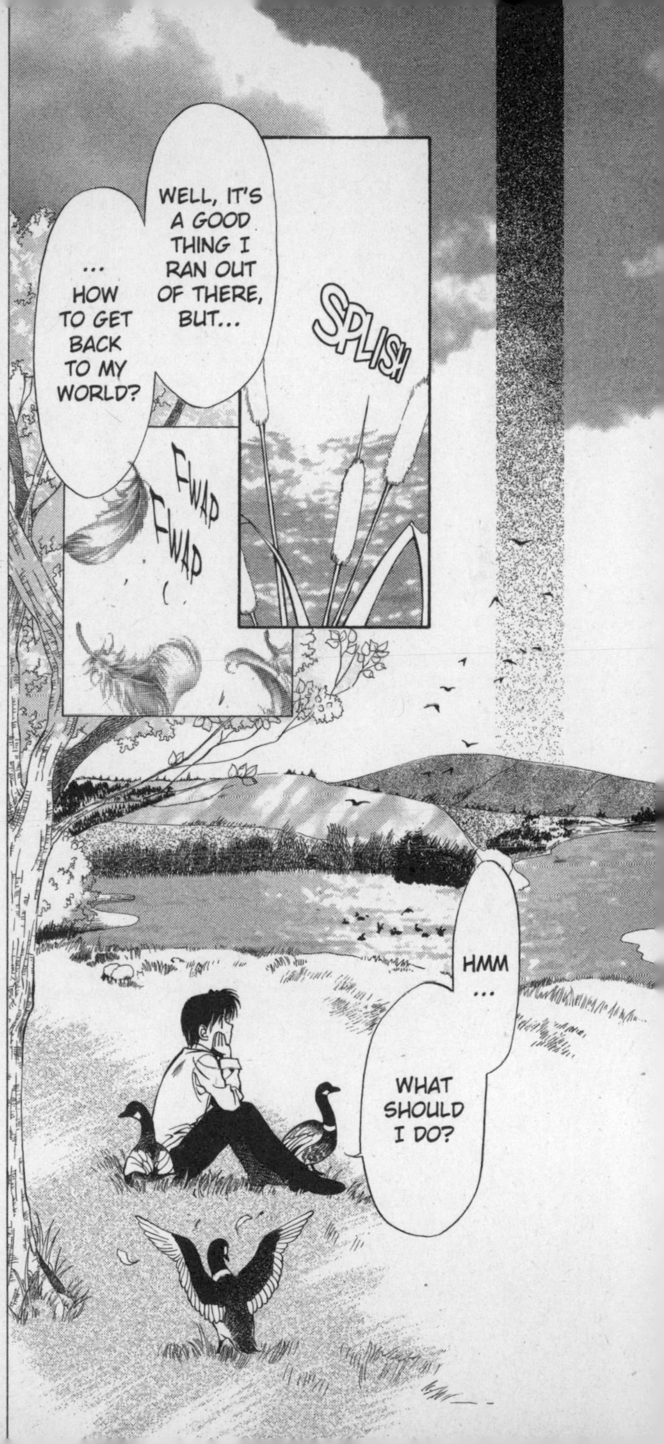
SPLISH
WELL, IT'S A GOOD THING I RAN OUT OF THERE, BUT...
... HOW TO GET BACK TO MY WORLD?
FWAP FWAP
HMM...
WHAT SHOULD I DO?

IT'S VOLUME FIVE!! HOORAY!!!

It happens so fast. This is already book five. Tatsumi is all over this book. Originally, I was going to make this story only three or four chapters long, but the St. Michel story in the last volume was so bad, I thought I'd better write a proper story. So I included a little about Tatsumi and Tsuzuki's past. I made it twice as long. Tatsumi's true nature really comes out in this story. He's turned into such a powerful man. (Ha!) He's exactly my type--I guess I like intelligent guys with glasses who are hard to get along with. (HA!!) Really, I'd love to have a super-handsome secretary who looks great in a suit.

TATSUMI! HE'S THE MAN!!

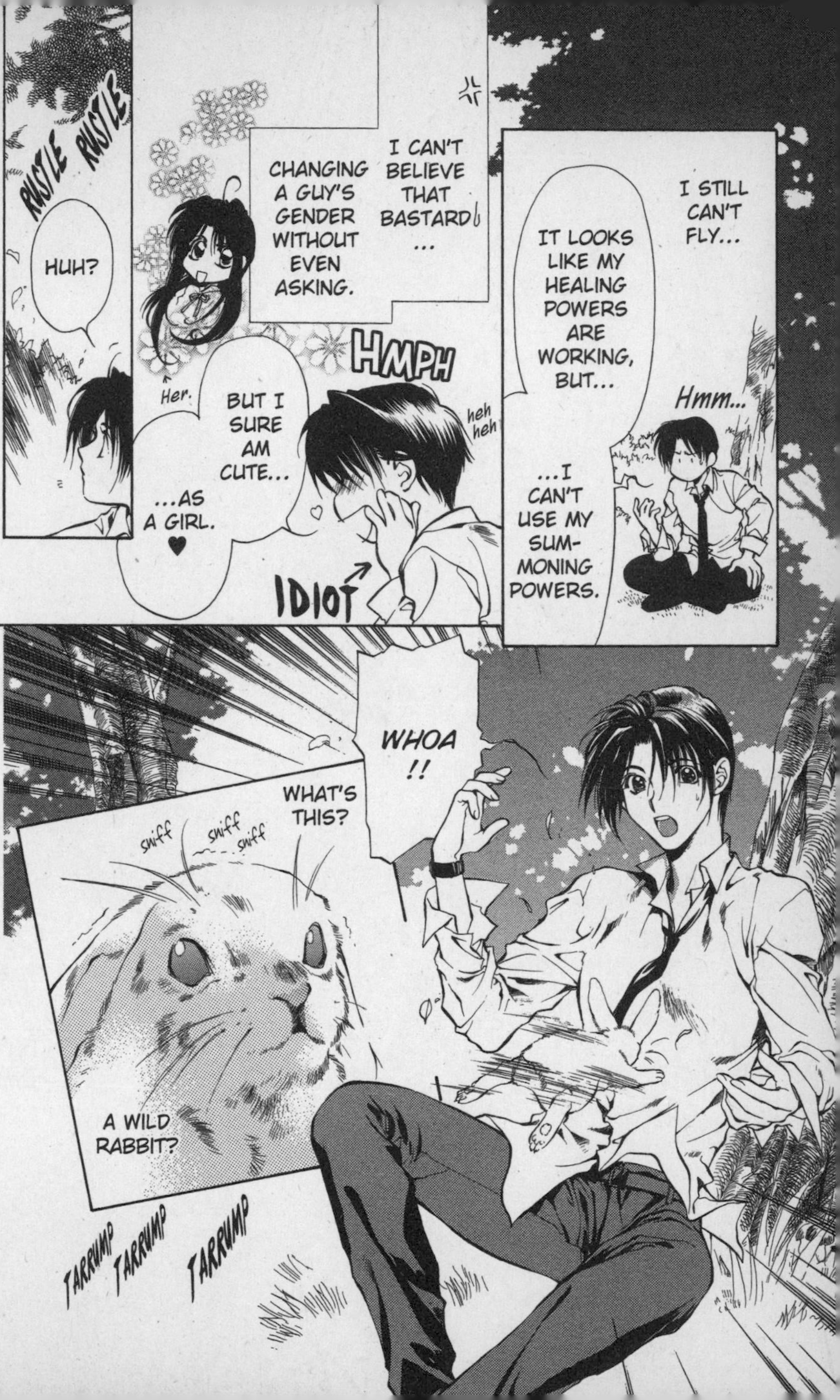
I STILL CAN'T FLY...
Hmm...
IT LOOKS LIKE MY HEALING POWERS ARE WORKING, BUT...
...I CAN'T USE MY SUM-MONING POWERS.
I CAN'T BELIEVE THAT BASTARD...
CHANGING A GUY'S GENDER WITHOUT EVEN ASKING.
HMPH
heh heh
BUT I SURE AM CUTE...
...AS A GIRL. ♥
Her.
IDIOT
RUSTLE RUSTLE
HUH?
WHOA!!
WHAT'S THIS?
sniff sniff sniff
A WILD RABBIT?
TARRUMP TARRUMP TARRUMP

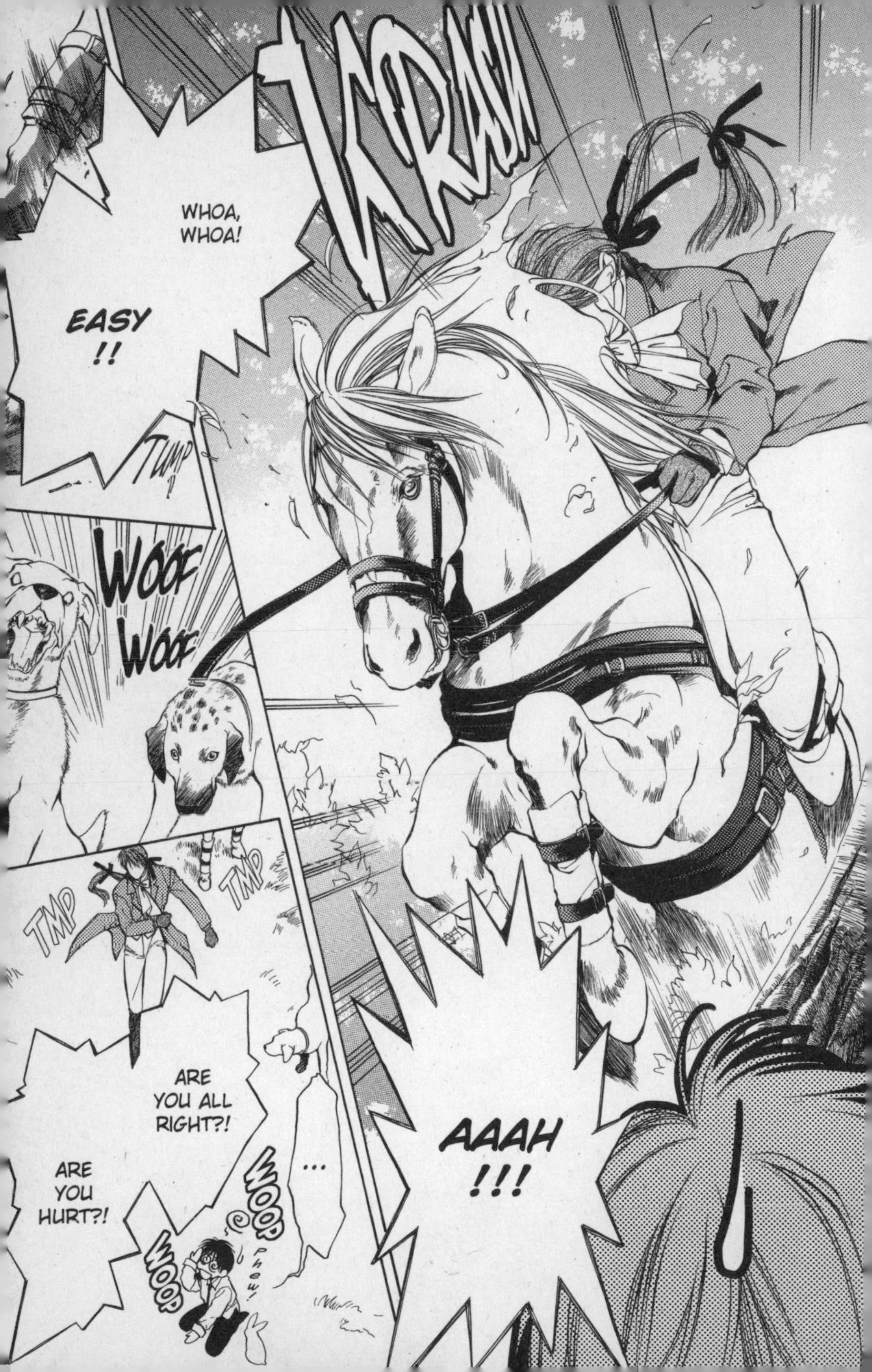
CRASH
AAAH !!!
WHOA, WHOA!
EASY !!
TUMP
WOOF WOOF
TMP
TMP
ARE YOU ALL RIGHT?!
...
ARE YOU HURT?!
WOOP
WOOP
Phew!

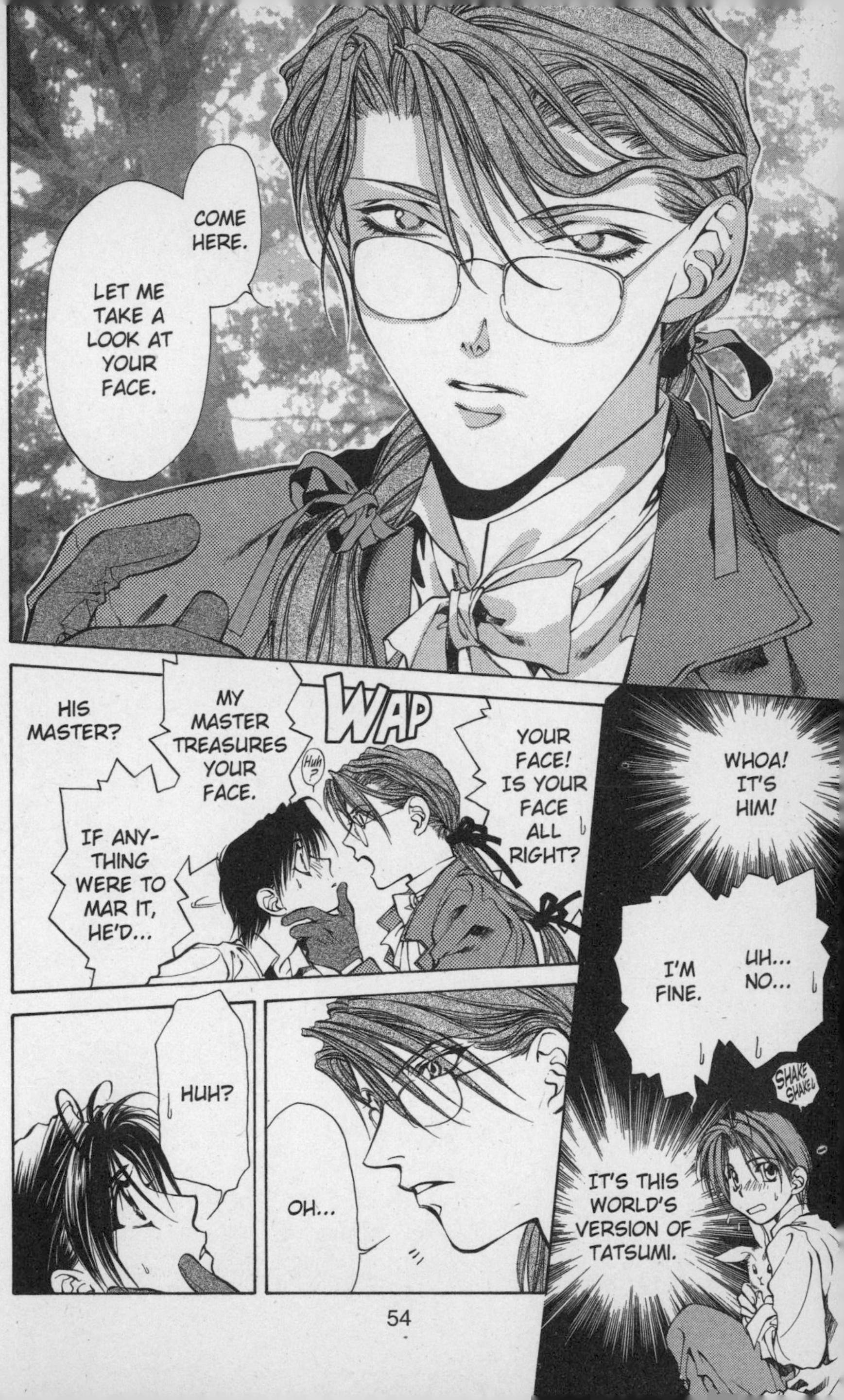
COME HERE.
LET ME TAKE A LOOK AT YOUR FACE.
WHOA! IT'S HIM!
UH... NO...
I'M FINE.
SHAKE SHAKE
IT'S THIS WORLD'S VERSION OF TATSUMI.
WAP
YOUR FACE! IS YOUR FACE ALL RIGHT?
Huh?
MY MASTER TREASURES YOUR FACE.
HIS MASTER?
IF ANY-THING WERE TO MAR IT, HE'D...
OH...
HUH?

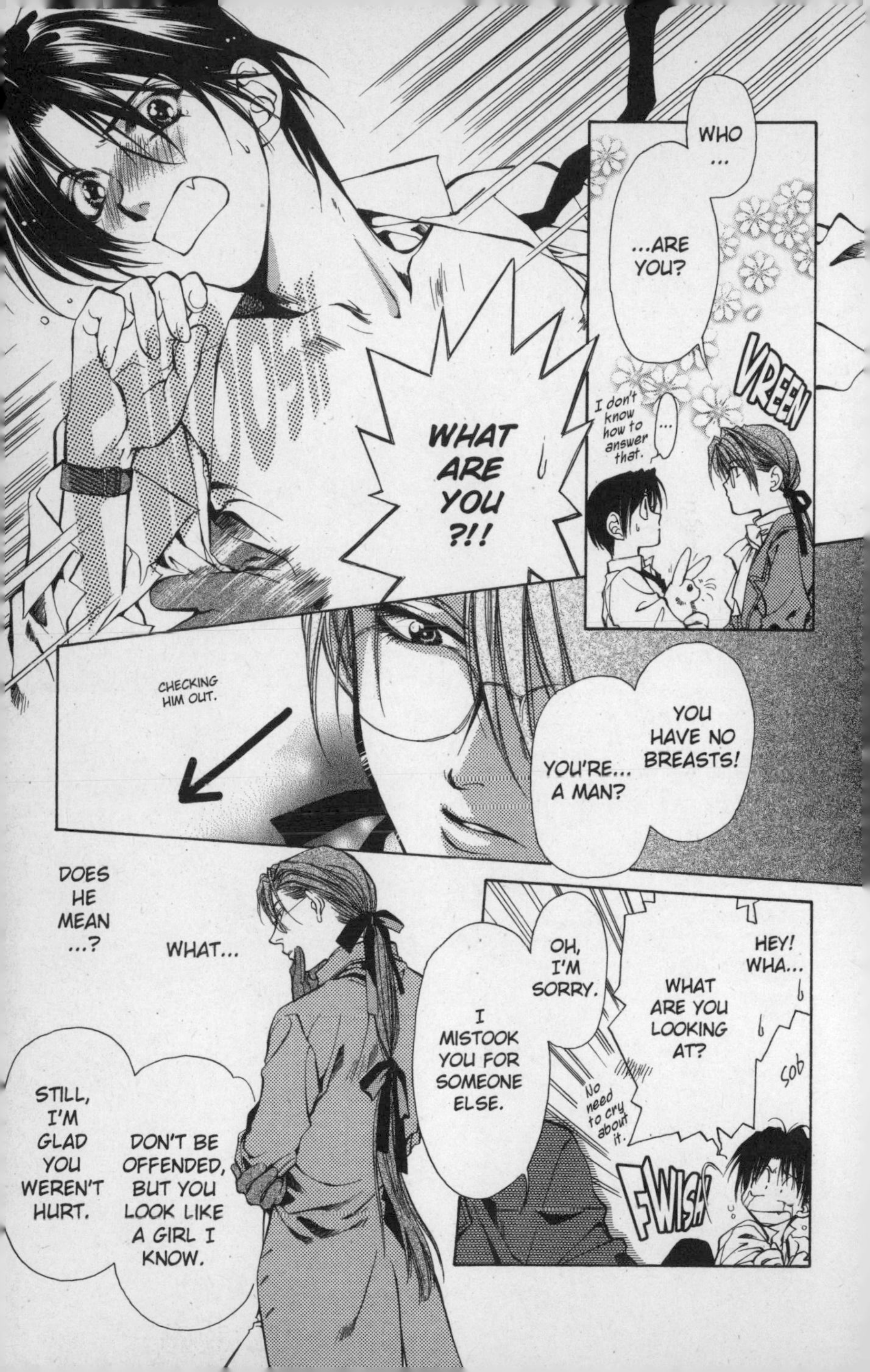
WHO ...
...ARE YOU?
VREEN
...
I don't know how to answer that.
WHAT ARE YOU ?!!
YOU HAVE NO BREASTS!
YOU'RE... A MAN?
CHECKING HIM OUT.
HEY! WHA...
WHAT ARE YOU LOOKING AT?
sob
OH, I'M SORRY.
I MISTOOK YOU FOR SOMEONE ELSE.
No need to cry about it.
FWISH
WHAT...
DOES HE MEAN ...?
DON'T BE OFFENDED, BUT YOU LOOK LIKE A GIRL I KNOW.
STILL, I'M GLAD YOU WEREN'T HURT.

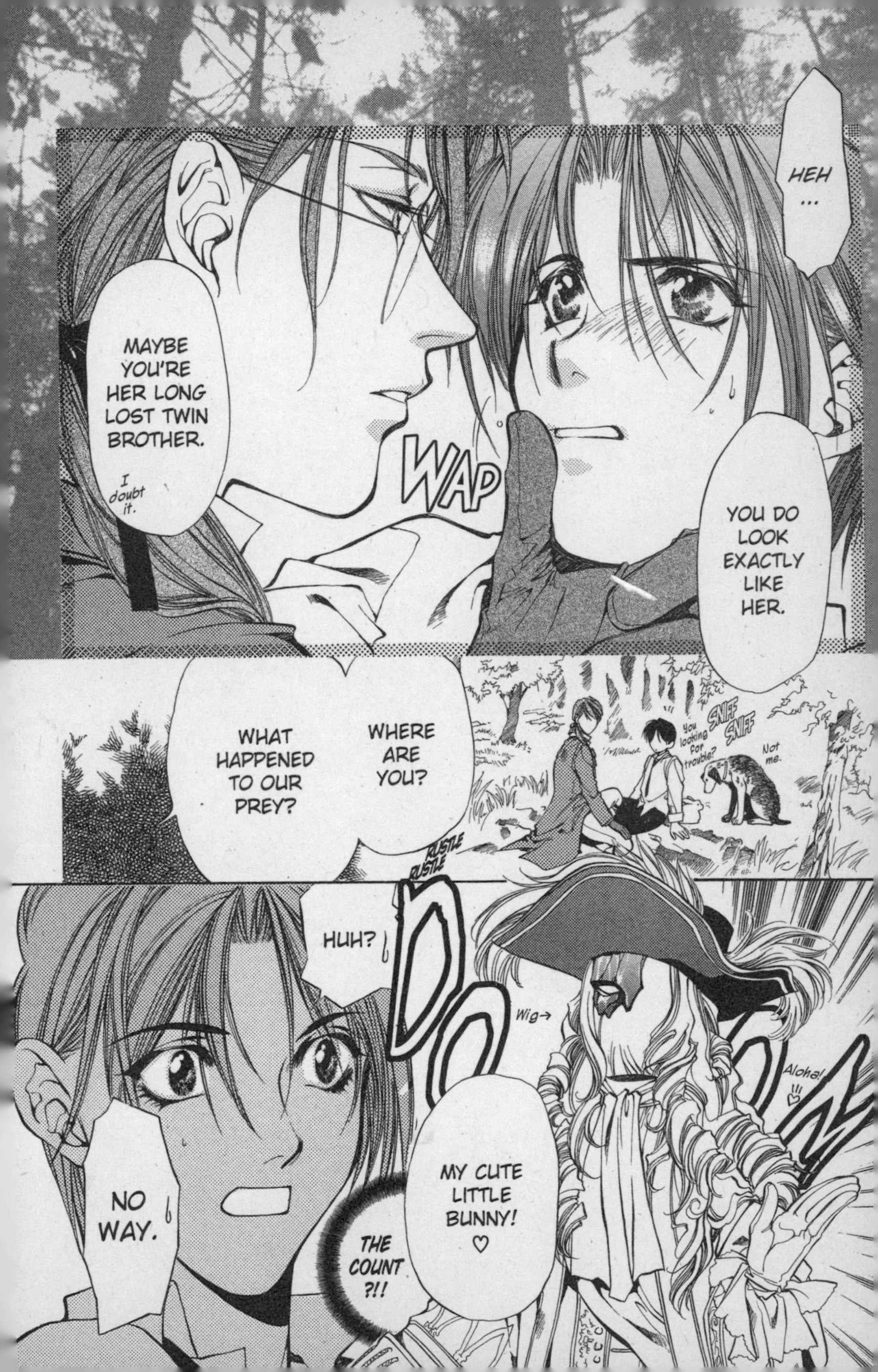
HEH ...
YOU DO LOOK EXACTLY LIKE HER.
WAP
MAYBE YOU'RE HER LONG LOST TWIN BROTHER.
I doubt it.
SNIFF SNIFF
you looking for trouble?
Not me.
WHERE ARE YOU?
WHAT HAPPENED TO OUR PREY?
RUSTLE RUSTLE
Aloha! ♡
Wig→
MY CUTE LITTLE BUNNY! ♡
THE COUNT ?!!
HUH?
NO WAY.

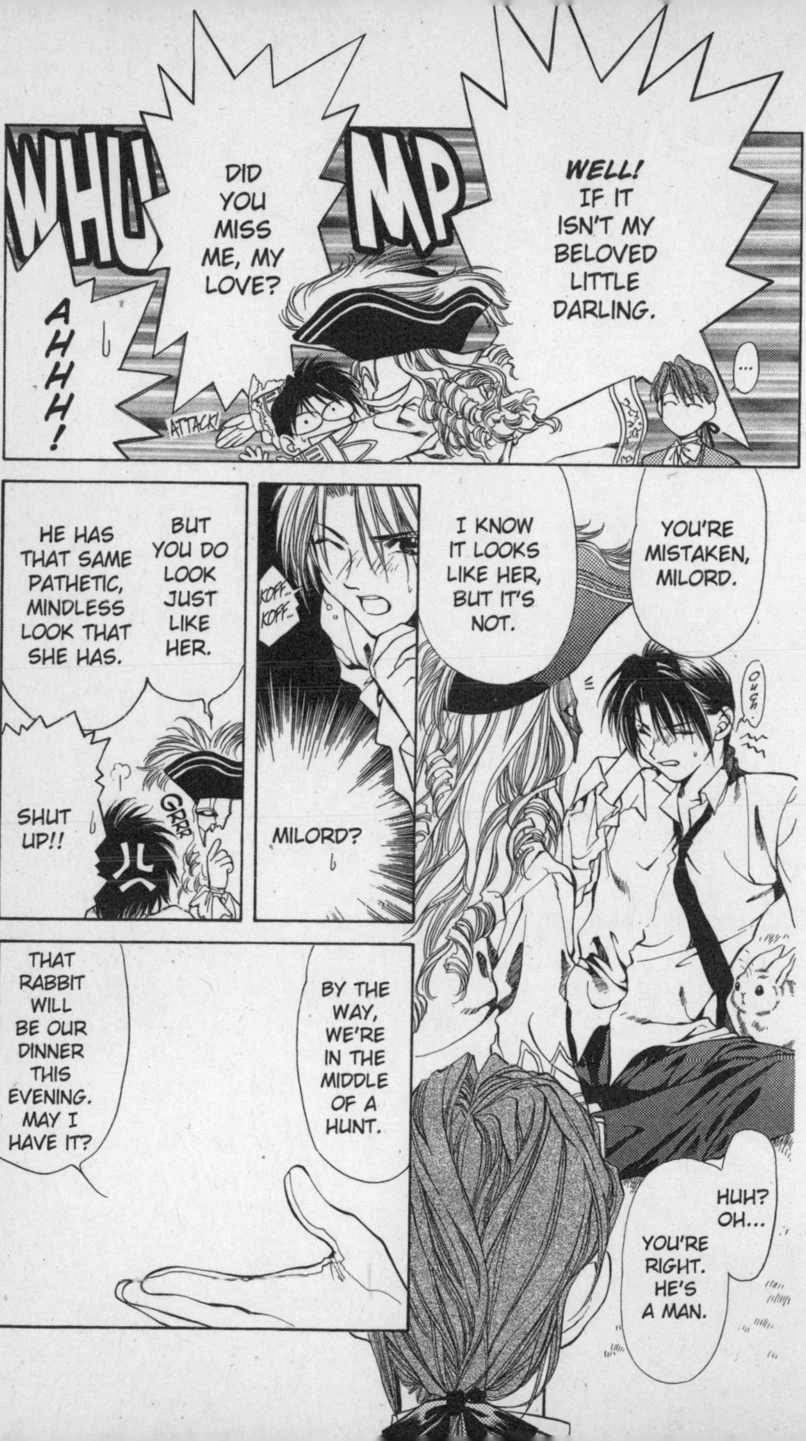
WELL! IF IT ISN'T MY BELOVED LITTLE DARLING.
...
DID YOU MISS ME, MY LOVE?
WHUMP
AHHHH!
ATTACK!
YOU'RE MISTAKEN, MILORD.
I KNOW IT LOOKS LIKE HER, BUT IT'S NOT.
OUCH.
HUH? OH... YOU'RE RIGHT. HE'S A MAN.
KOFF... KOFF...
MILORD?
BUT YOU DO LOOK JUST LIKE HER.
HE HAS THAT SAME PATHETIC, MINDLESS LOOK THAT SHE HAS.
GRRR
SHUT UP!!
BY THE WAY, WE'RE IN THE MIDDLE OF A HUNT.
THAT RABBIT WILL BE OUR DINNER THIS EVENING. MAY I HAVE IT?

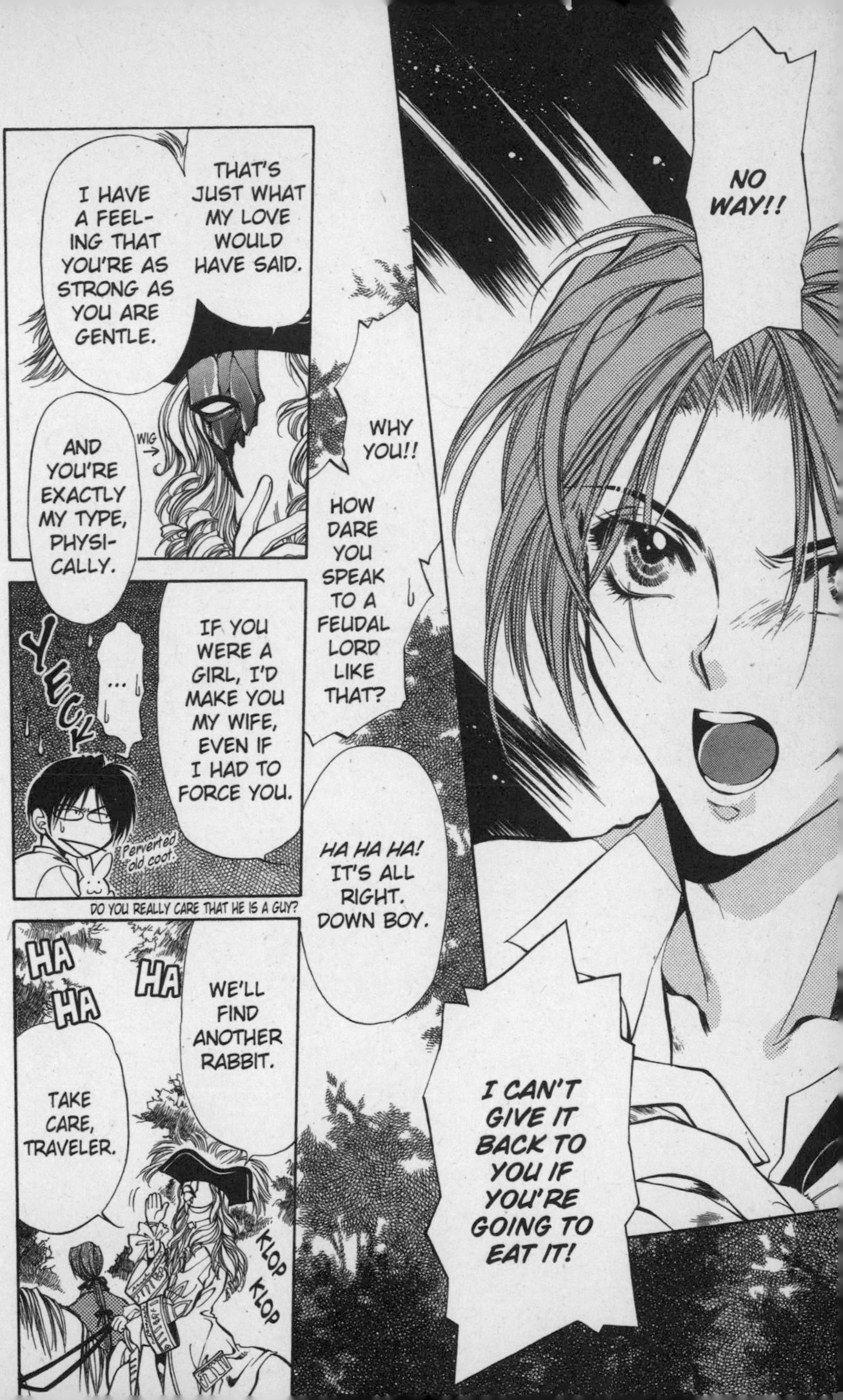

NO WAY!!
I CAN'T GIVE IT BACK TO YOU IF YOU'RE GOING TO EAT IT!
WHY YOU!!
HOW DARE YOU SPEAK TO A FEUDAL LORD LIKE THAT?
HA HA HA! IT'S ALL RIGHT. DOWN BOY.
THAT'S JUST WHAT MY LOVE WOULD HAVE SAID.
I HAVE A FEELING THAT YOU'RE AS STRONG AS YOU ARE GENTLE.
WIG
AND YOU'RE EXACTLY MY TYPE, PHYSICALLY.
IF YOU WERE A GIRL, I'D MAKE YOU MY WIFE, EVEN IF I HAD TO FORCE YOU.
YECK
...
Perverted old coot.
DO YOU REALLY CARE THAT HE IS A GUY?
WE'LL FIND ANOTHER RABBIT.
HA HA HA
TAKE CARE, TRAVELER.
KLOP KLOP

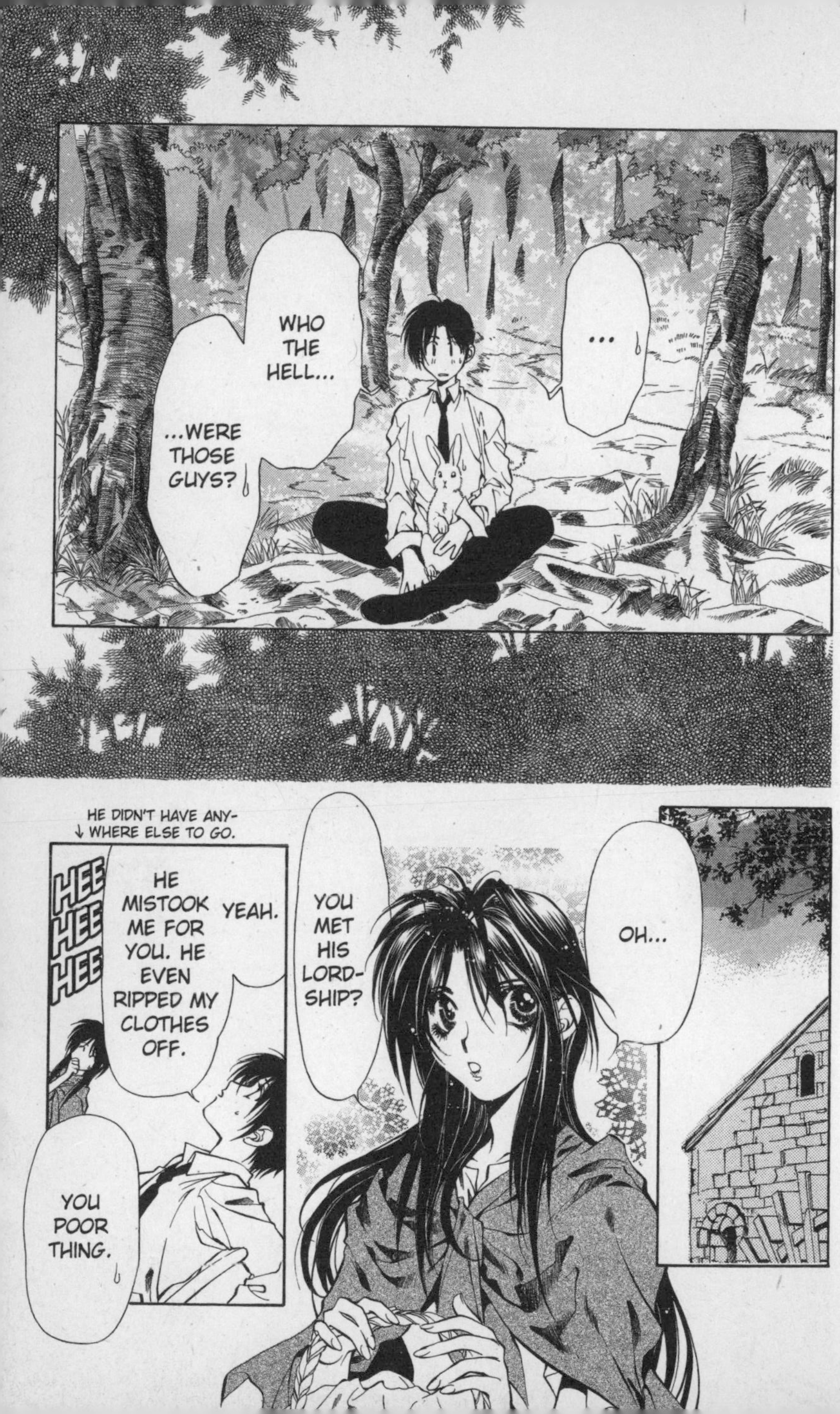
...
WHO THE HELL...
...WERE THOSE GUYS?
OH...
YOU MET HIS LORDSHIP?
YEAH.
HE DIDN'T HAVE ANYWHERE ELSE TO GO.
HE MISTOOK ME FOR YOU. HE EVEN RIPPED MY CLOTHES OFF.
HEE HEE HEE
YOU POOR THING.

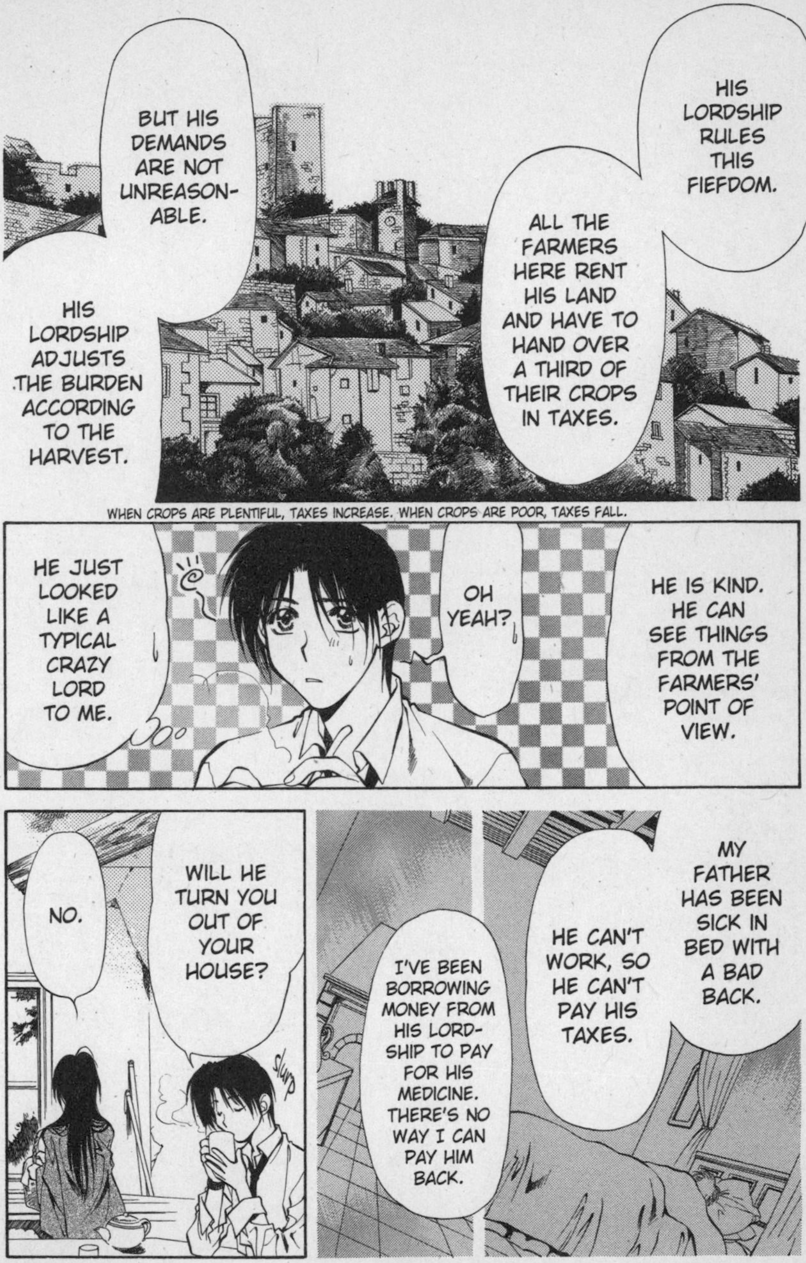
HIS LORDSHIP RULES THIS FIEFDOM.
ALL THE FARMERS HERE RENT HIS LAND AND HAVE TO HAND OVER A THIRD OF THEIR CROPS IN TAXES.
BUT HIS DEMANDS ARE NOT UNREASON-ABLE.
HIS LORDSHIP ADJUSTS THE BURDEN ACCORDING TO THE HARVEST.
WHEN CROPS ARE PLENTIFUL, TAXES INCREASE. WHEN CROPS ARE POOR, TAXES FALL.
HE IS KIND. HE CAN SEE THINGS FROM THE FARMERS' POINT OF VIEW.
OH YEAH?
HE JUST LOOKED LIKE A TYPICAL CRAZY LORD TO ME.
MY FATHER HAS BEEN SICK IN BED WITH A BAD BACK.
HE CAN'T WORK, SO HE CAN'T PAY HIS TAXES.
I'VE BEEN BORROWING MONEY FROM HIS LORD-SHIP TO PAY FOR HIS MEDICINE. THERE'S NO WAY I CAN PAY HIM BACK.
WILL HE TURN YOU OUT OF YOUR HOUSE?
slurp
NO.

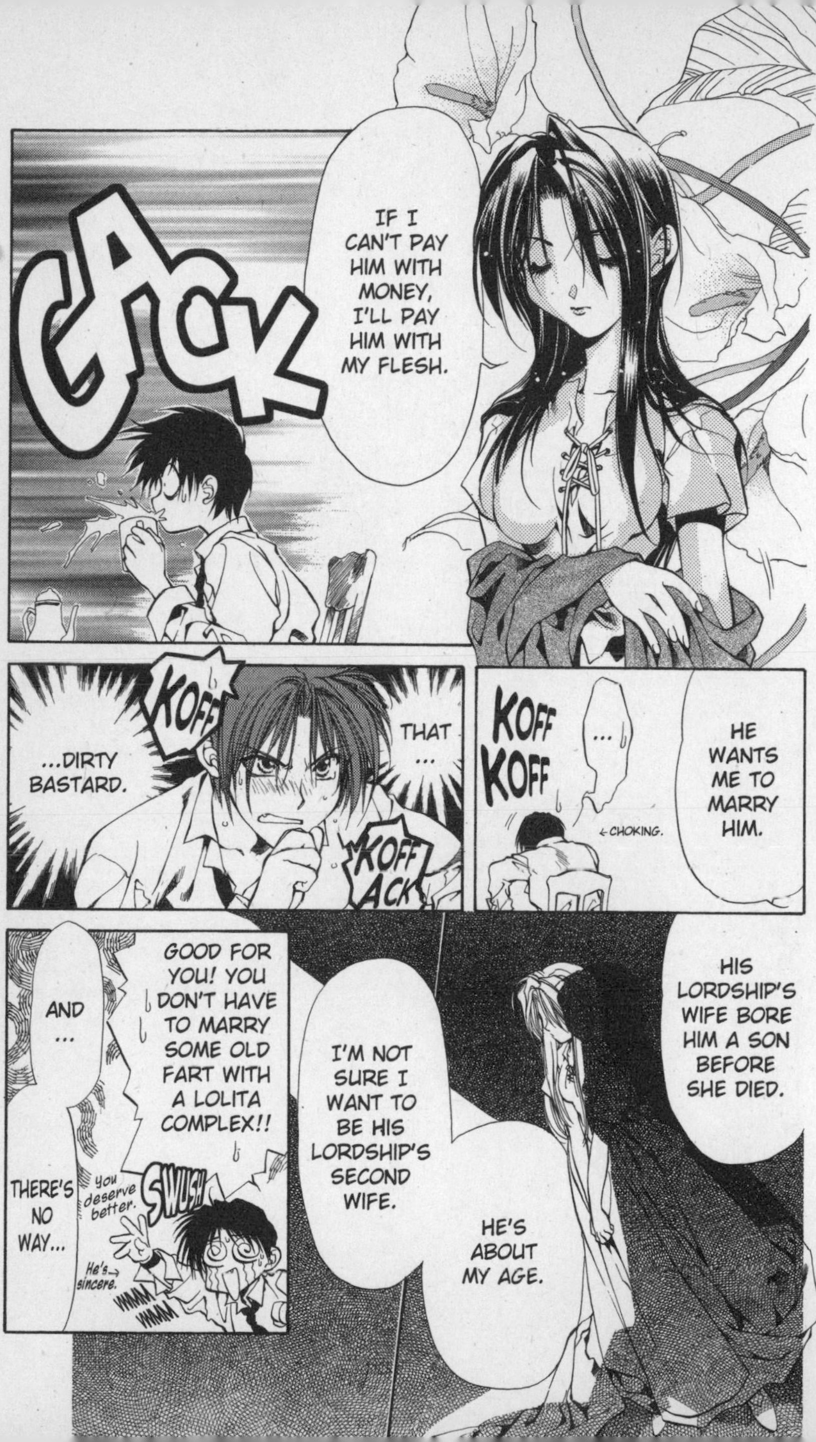
IF I CAN'T PAY HIM WITH MONEY, I'LL PAY HIM WITH MY FLESH.
CACK
HE WANTS ME TO MARRY HIM.
...
KOFF KOFF
← CHOKING.
THAT ...
KOFF
...DIRTY BASTARD.
KOFF ACK
HIS LORDSHIP'S WIFE BORE HIM A SON BEFORE SHE DIED.
I'M NOT SURE I WANT TO BE HIS LORDSHIP'S SECOND WIFE.
HE'S ABOUT MY AGE.
GOOD FOR YOU! YOU DON'T HAVE TO MARRY SOME OLD FART WITH A LOLITA COMPLEX!!
AND ...
SWUSH
You deserve better.
He's sincere.
THERE'S NO WAY...
WMM WMM

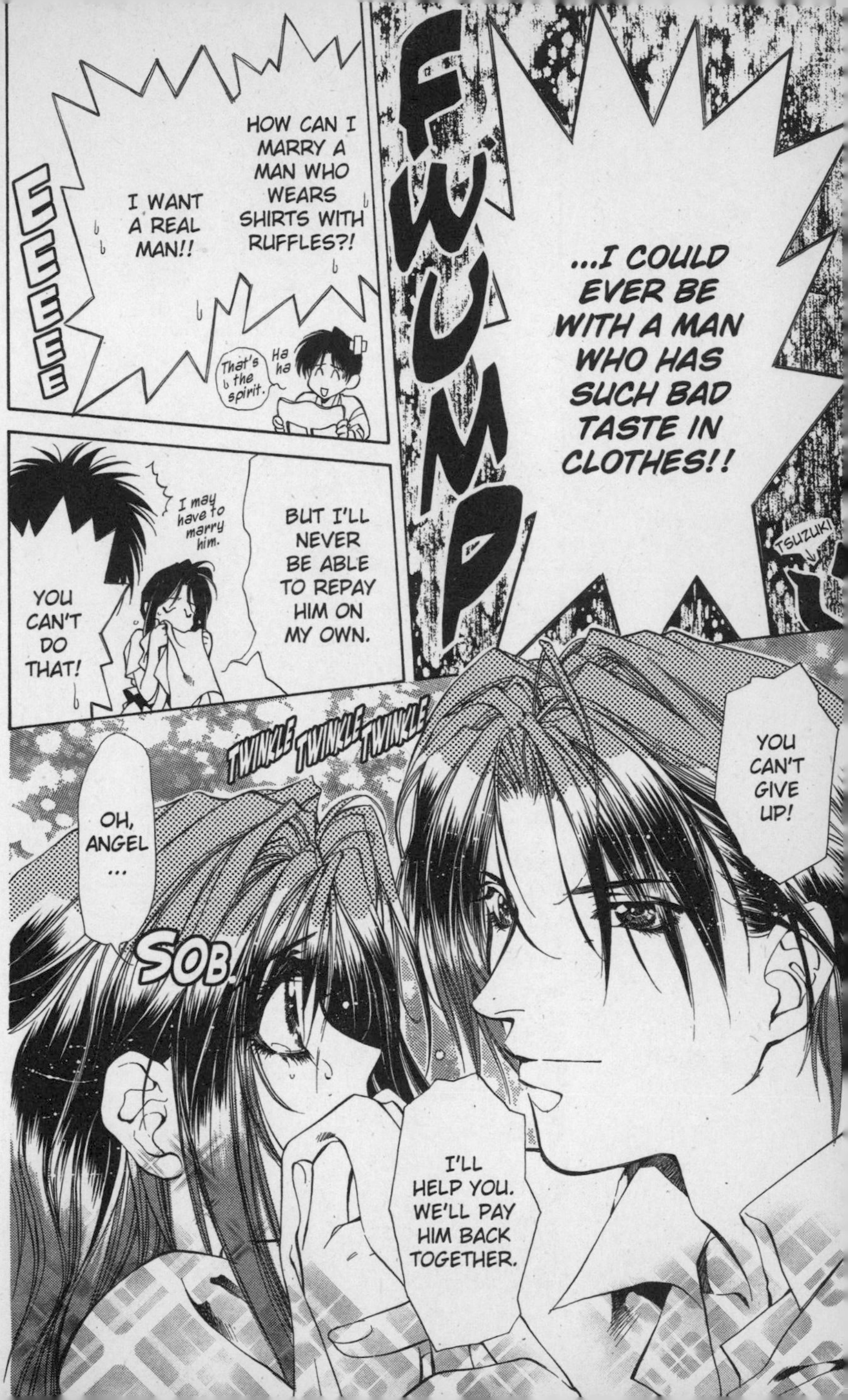
FWUMP
...I COULD EVER BE WITH A MAN WHO HAS SUCH BAD TASTE IN CLOTHES!!
TSUZUKI
HOW CAN I MARRY A MAN WHO WEARS SHIRTS WITH RUFFLES?!
I WANT A REAL MAN!!
EEEEEE
Ha ha
That's the spirit.
BUT I'LL NEVER BE ABLE TO REPAY HIM ON MY OWN.
I may have to marry him.
YOU CAN'T DO THAT!
YOU CAN'T GIVE UP!
TWINKLE TWINKLE TWINKLE
OH, ANGEL ...
SOB
I'LL HELP YOU. WE'LL PAY HIM BACK TOGETHER.

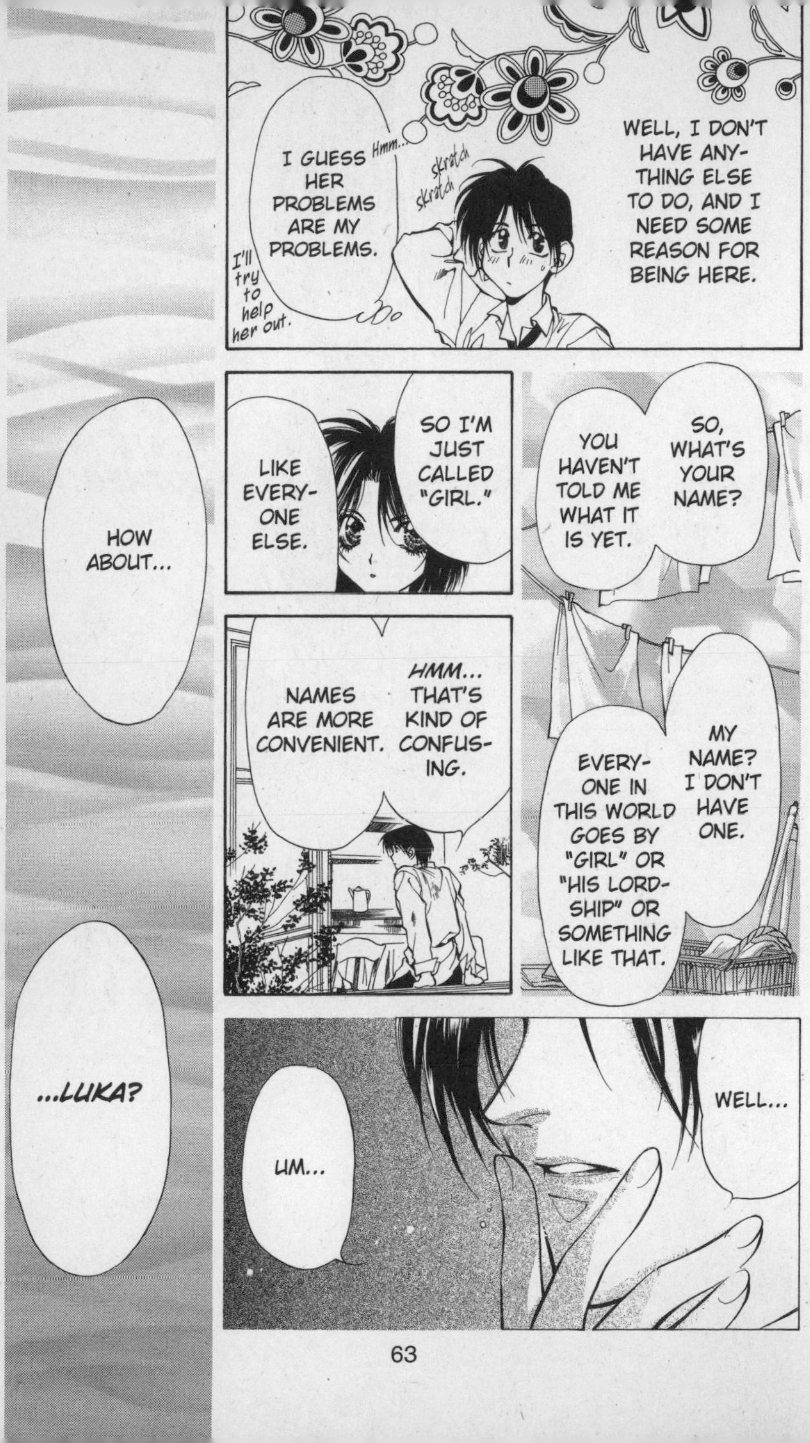
WELL, I DON'T HAVE ANYTHING ELSE TO DO, AND I NEED SOME REASON FOR BEING HERE.
skratch skratch
Hmm...
I GUESS HER PROBLEMS ARE MY PROBLEMS.
I'll try to help her out.
SO, WHAT'S YOUR NAME?
YOU HAVEN'T TOLD ME WHAT IT IS YET.
MY NAME? I DON'T HAVE ONE.
EVERYONE IN THIS WORLD GOES BY "GIRL" OR "HIS LORDSHIP" OR SOMETHING LIKE THAT.
SO I'M JUST CALLED "GIRL."
LIKE EVERYONE ELSE.
HMM... THAT'S KIND OF CONFUSING.
NAMES ARE MORE CONVENIENT.
WELL...
UM...
HOW ABOUT...
...LUKA?

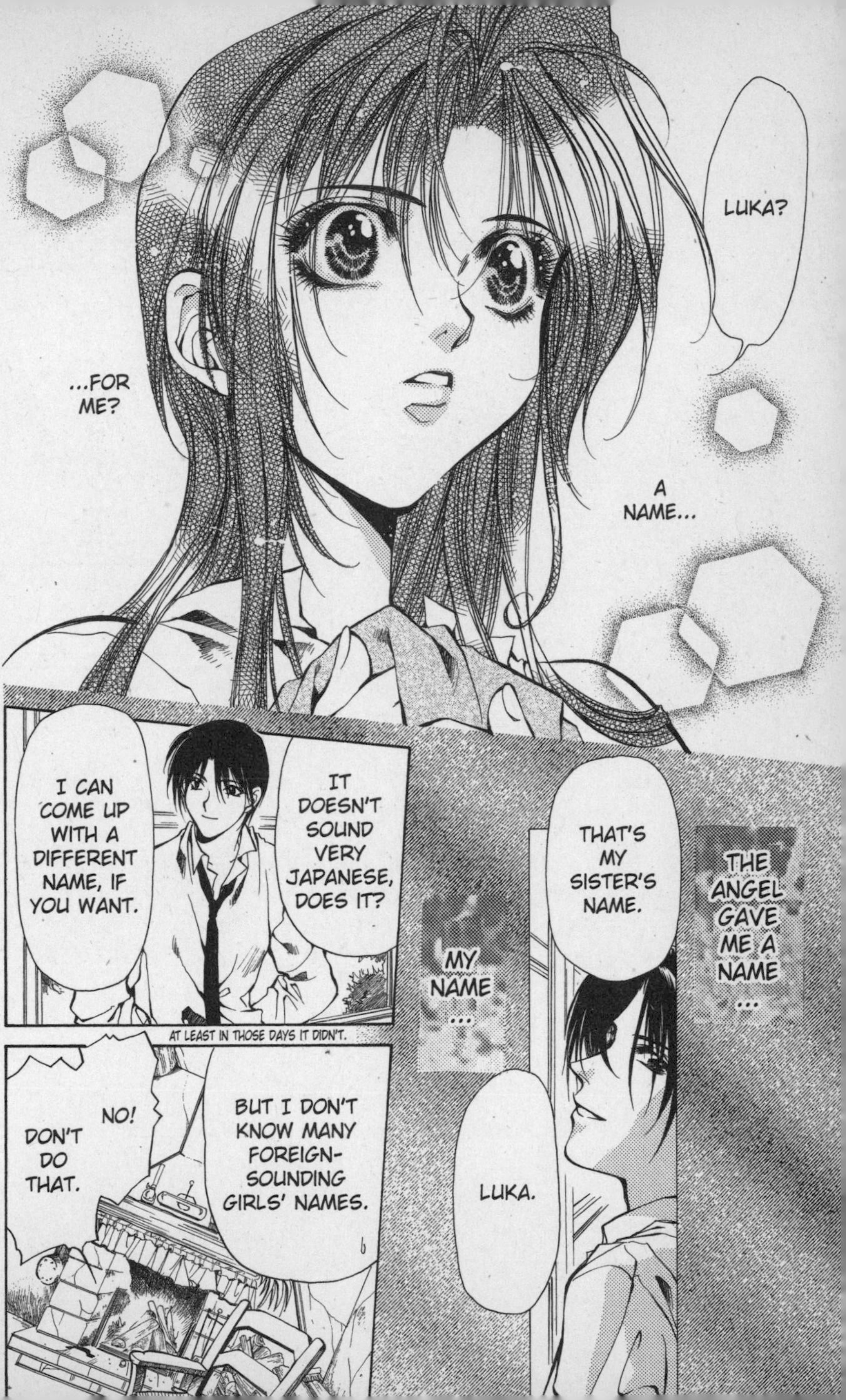
LUKA?
A NAME...
...FOR ME?
THE ANGEL GAVE ME A NAME...
THAT'S MY SISTER'S NAME.
MY NAME...
LUKA.
IT DOESN'T SOUND VERY JAPANESE, DOES IT?
I CAN COME UP WITH A DIFFERENT NAME, IF YOU WANT.
AT LEAST IN THOSE DAYS IT DIDN'T.
BUT I DON'T KNOW MANY FOREIGN-SOUNDING GIRLS' NAMES.
NO!
DON'T DO THAT.

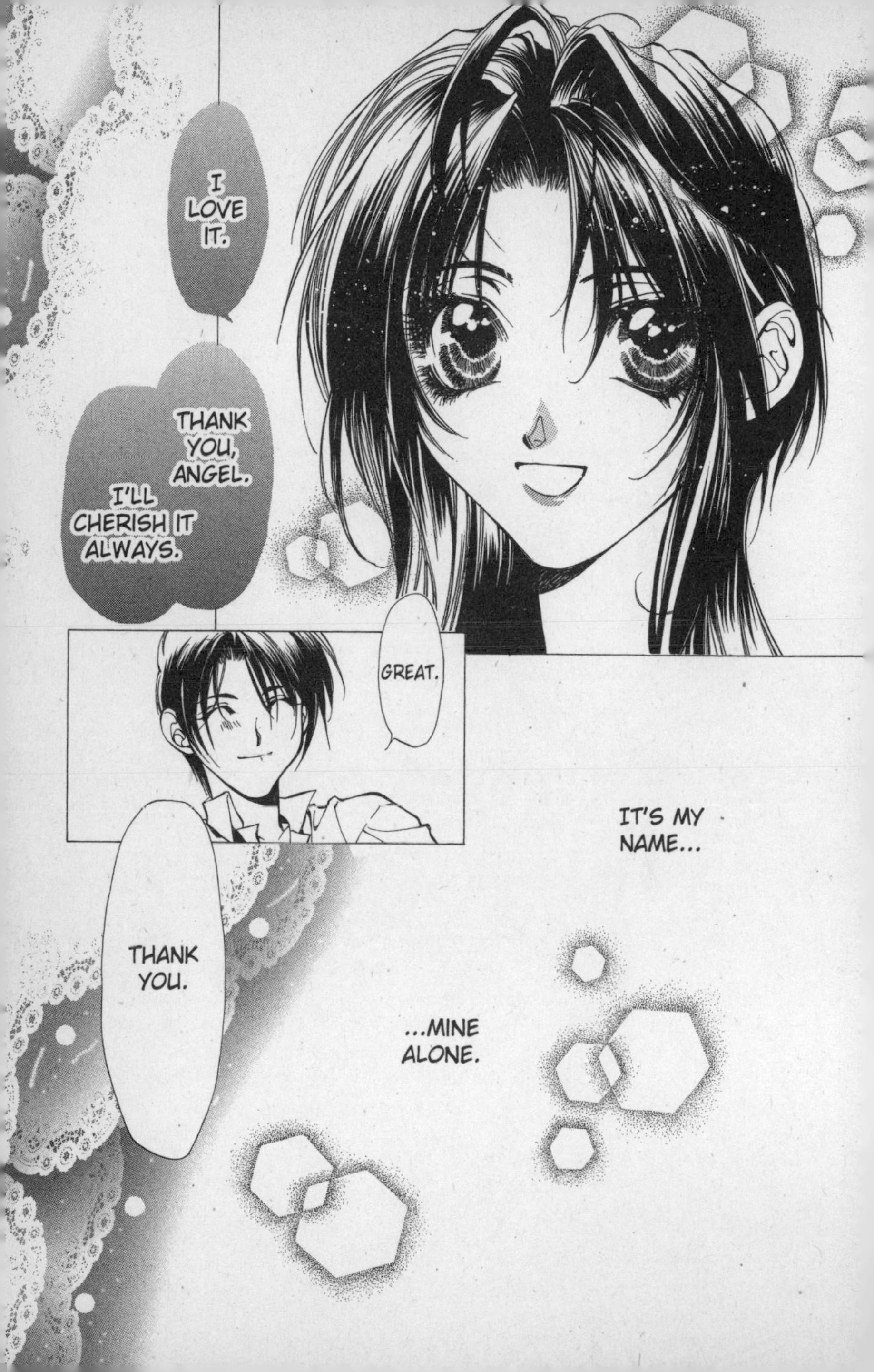
I LOVE IT.
THANK YOU, ANGEL.
I'LL CHERISH IT ALWAYS.
GREAT.
IT'S MY NAME...
THANK YOU.
...MINE ALONE.

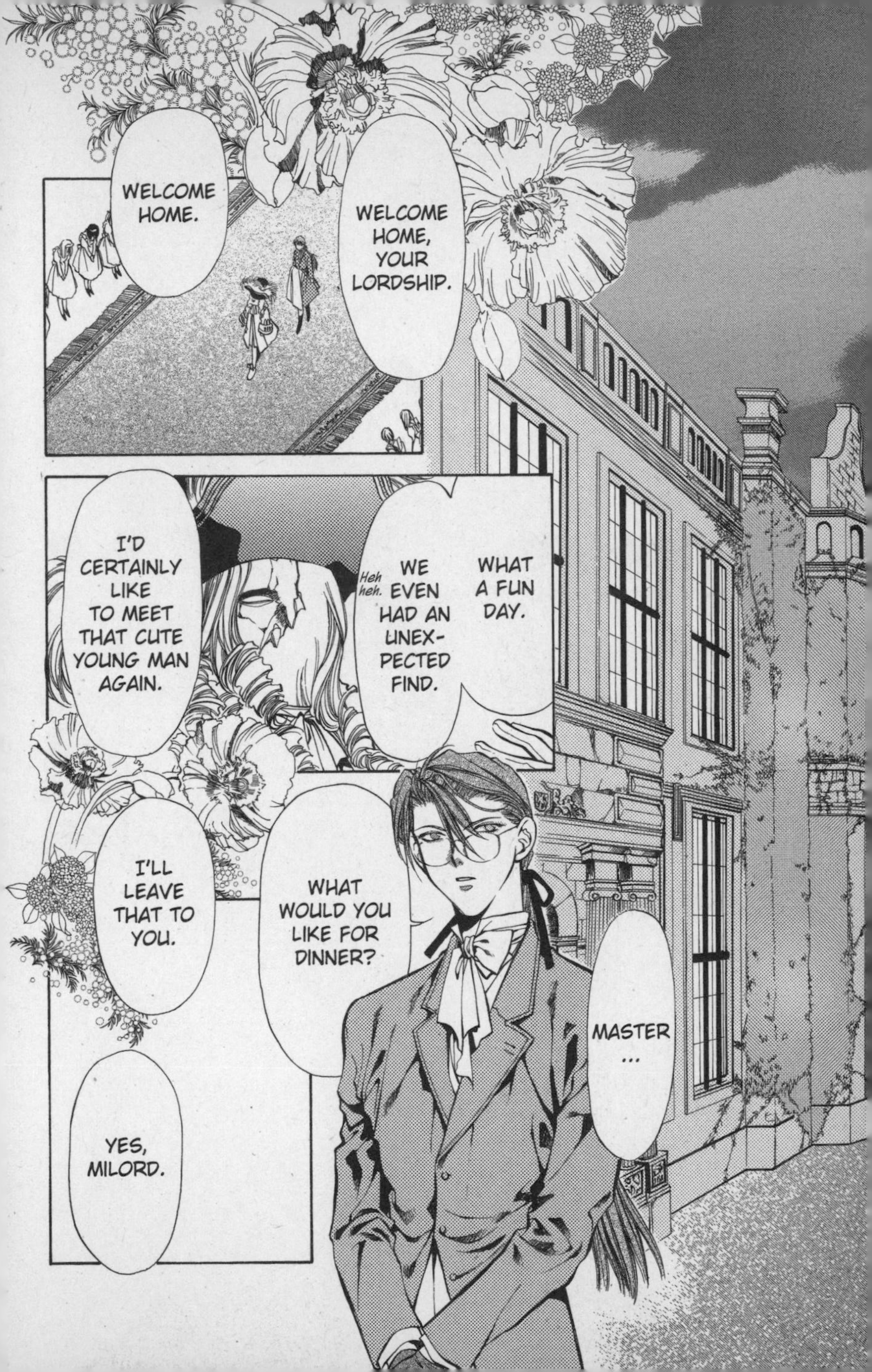
WELCOME HOME, YOUR LORDSHIP.
WELCOME HOME.
WHAT A FUN DAY.
Heh heh.
WE EVEN HAD AN UNEXPECTED FIND.
I'D CERTAINLY LIKE TO MEET THAT CUTE YOUNG MAN AGAIN.
MASTER...
WHAT WOULD YOU LIKE FOR DINNER?
I'LL LEAVE THAT TO YOU.
YES, MILORD.

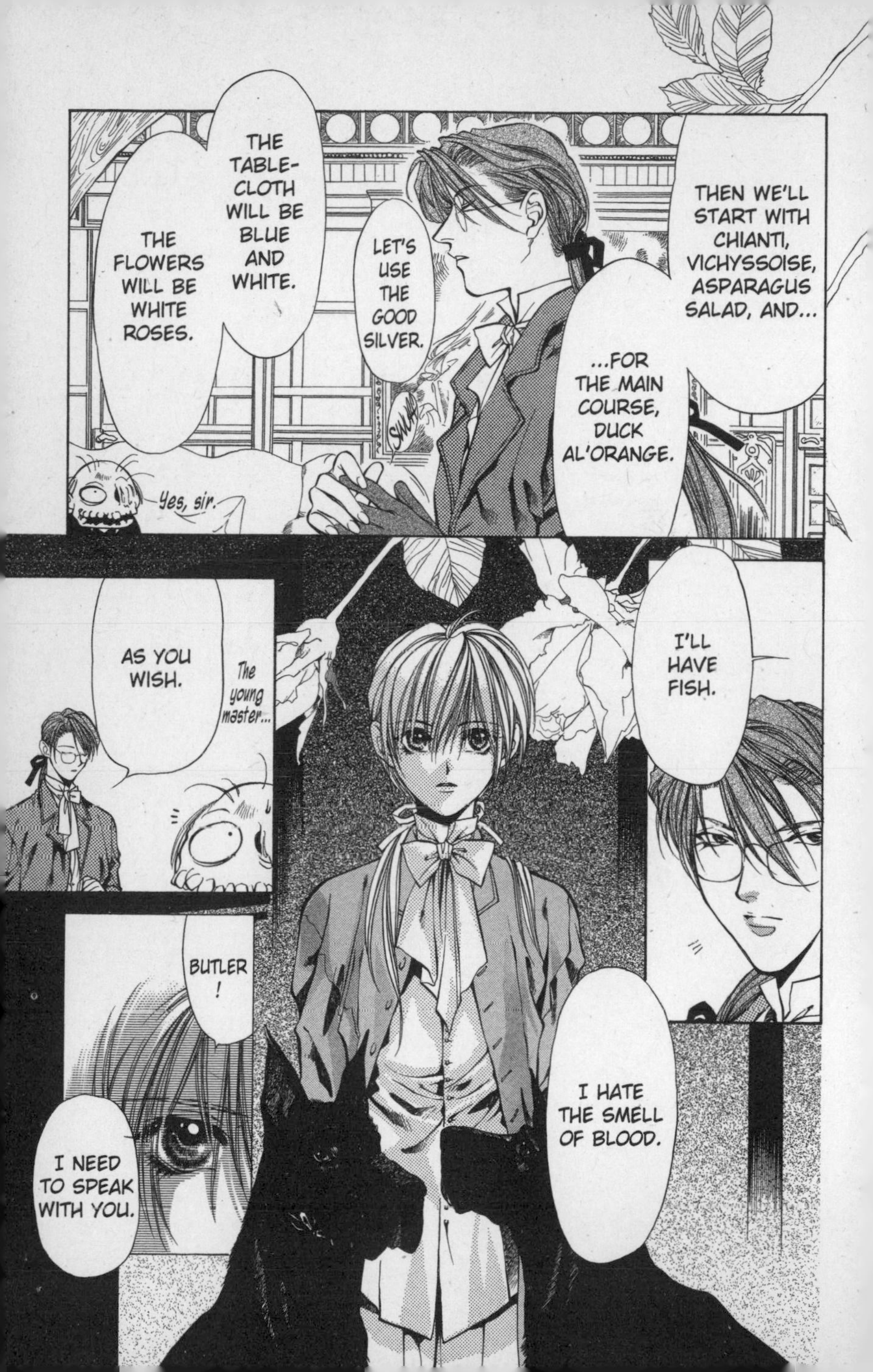
THEN WE'LL START WITH CHIANTI, VICHYSSOISE, ASPARAGUS SALAD, AND...
...FOR THE MAIN COURSE, DUCK AL'ORANGE.
LET'S USE THE GOOD SILVER.
THE TABLE-CLOTH WILL BE BLUE AND WHITE.
THE FLOWERS WILL BE WHITE ROSES.
Yes, sir.
I'LL HAVE FISH.
I HATE THE SMELL OF BLOOD.
AS YOU WISH.
The young master...
BUTLER!
I NEED TO SPEAK WITH YOU.

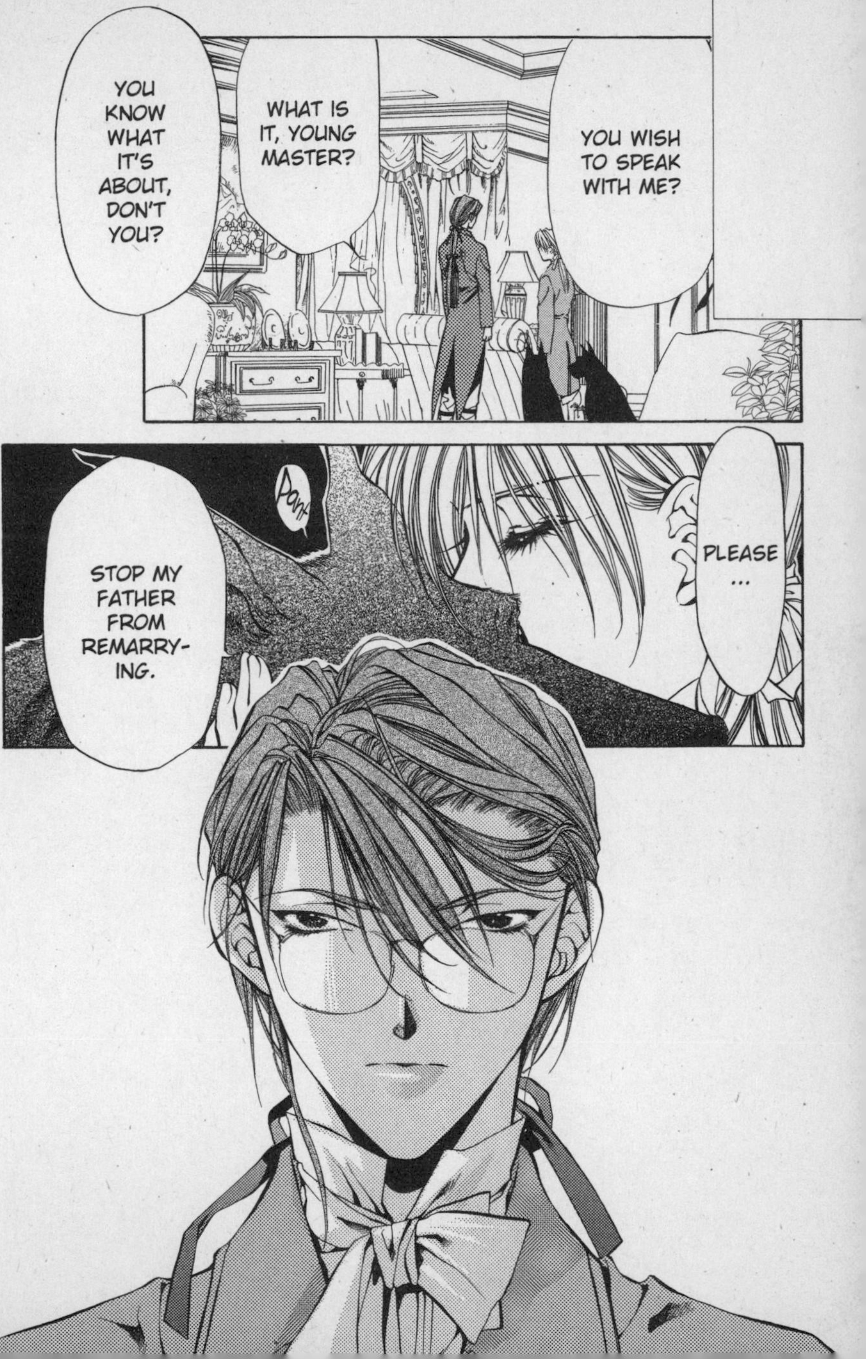
YOU WISH TO SPEAK WITH ME?
WHAT IS IT, YOUNG MASTER?
YOU KNOW WHAT IT'S ABOUT, DON'T YOU?
PLEASE ...
Pant
STOP MY FATHER FROM REMARRY-ING.

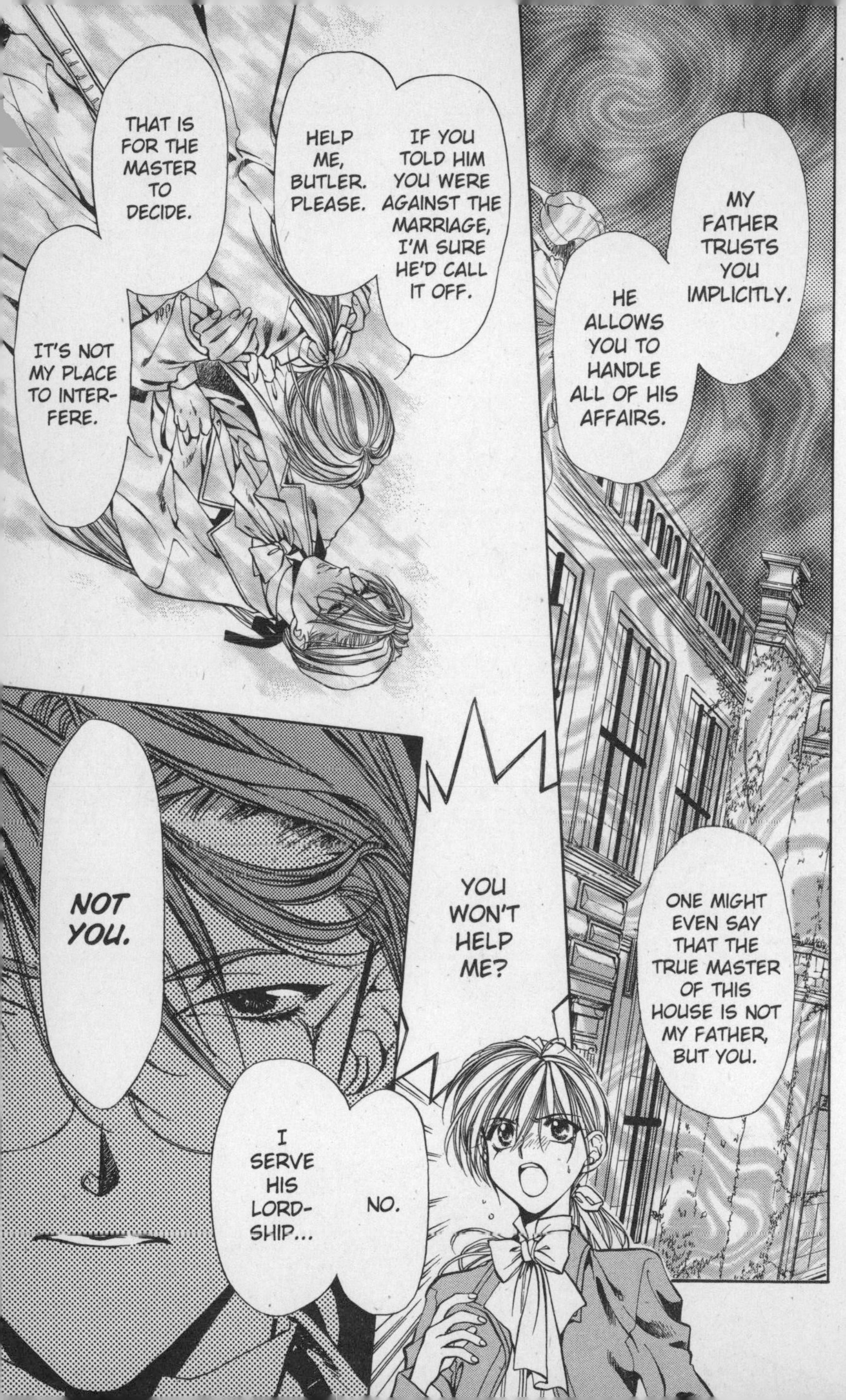
MY FATHER TRUSTS YOU IMPLICITLY.
HE ALLOWS YOU TO HANDLE ALL OF HIS AFFAIRS.
ONE MIGHT EVEN SAY THAT THE TRUE MASTER OF THIS HOUSE IS NOT MY FATHER, BUT YOU.
IF YOU TOLD HIM YOU WERE AGAINST THE MARRIAGE, I'M SURE HE'D CALL IT OFF.
HELP ME, BUTLER. PLEASE.
THAT IS FOR THE MASTER TO DECIDE.
IT'S NOT MY PLACE TO INTER-FERE.
YOU WON'T HELP ME?
NO.
I SERVE HIS LORDSHIP...
NOT YOU.

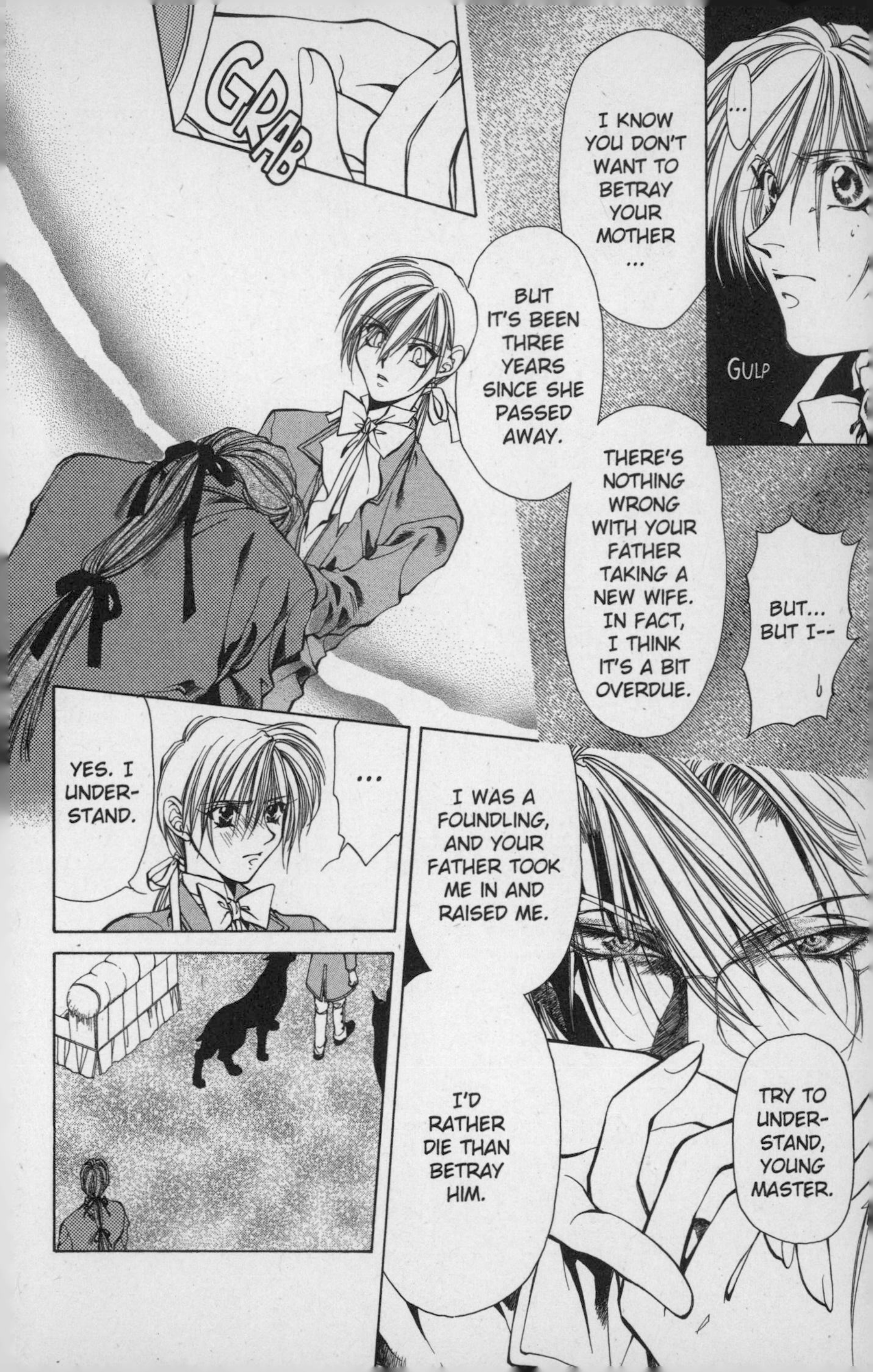
...
GULP
I KNOW YOU DON'T WANT TO BETRAY YOUR MOTHER ...
GRAB
BUT IT'S BEEN THREE YEARS SINCE SHE PASSED AWAY.
THERE'S NOTHING WRONG WITH YOUR FATHER TAKING A NEW WIFE. IN FACT, I THINK IT'S A BIT OVERDUE.
BUT... BUT I--
I WAS A FOUNDLING, AND YOUR FATHER TOOK ME IN AND RAISED ME.
TRY TO UNDER-STAND, YOUNG MASTER.
I'D RATHER DIE THAN BETRAY HIM.
...
YES. I UNDER-STAND.

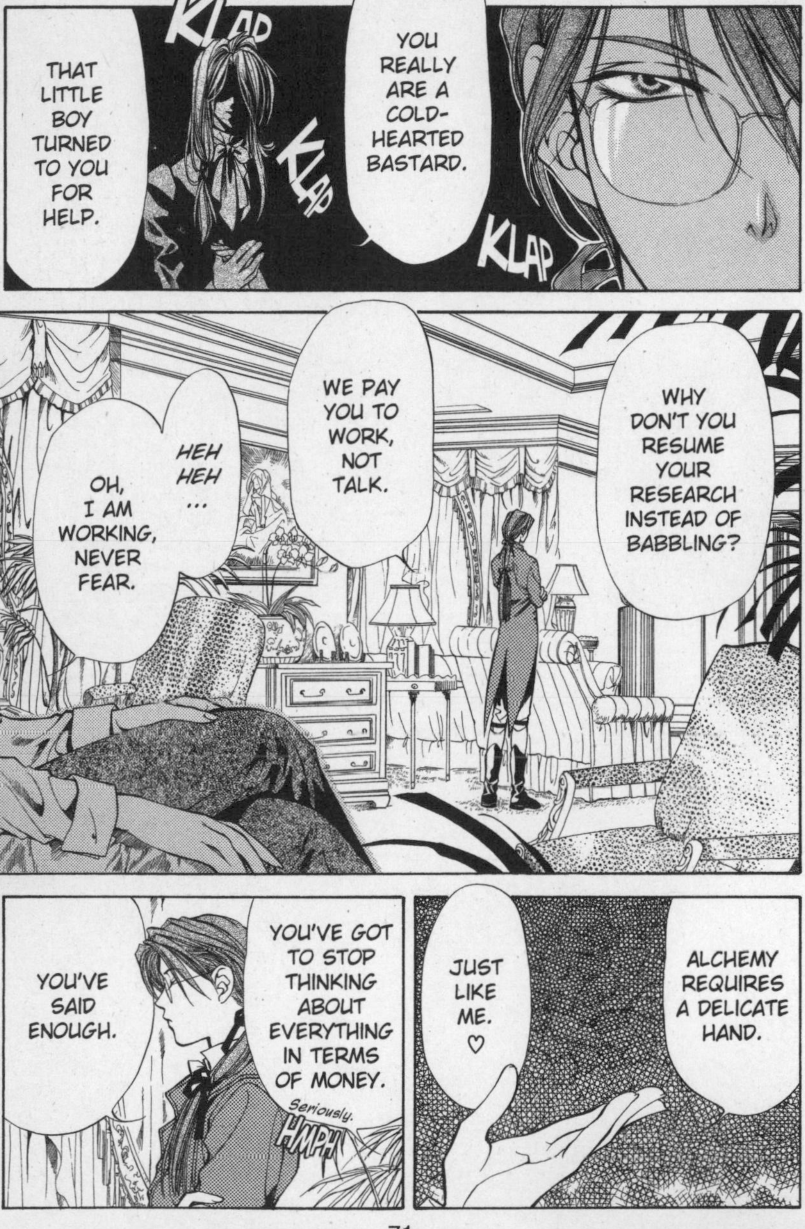
YOU REALLY ARE A COLD-HEARTED BASTARD.
THAT LITTLE BOY TURNED TO YOU FOR HELP.
KLAP
KLAP
KLAP
WHY DON'T YOU RESUME YOUR RESEARCH INSTEAD OF BABBLING?
WE PAY YOU TO WORK, NOT TALK.
HEH HEH ...
OH, I AM WORKING, NEVER FEAR.
ALCHEMY REQUIRES A DELICATE HAND.
JUST LIKE ME. ♡
YOU'VE GOT TO STOP THINKING ABOUT EVERYTHING IN TERMS OF MONEY.
Seriously.
HMPH
YOU'VE SAID ENOUGH.

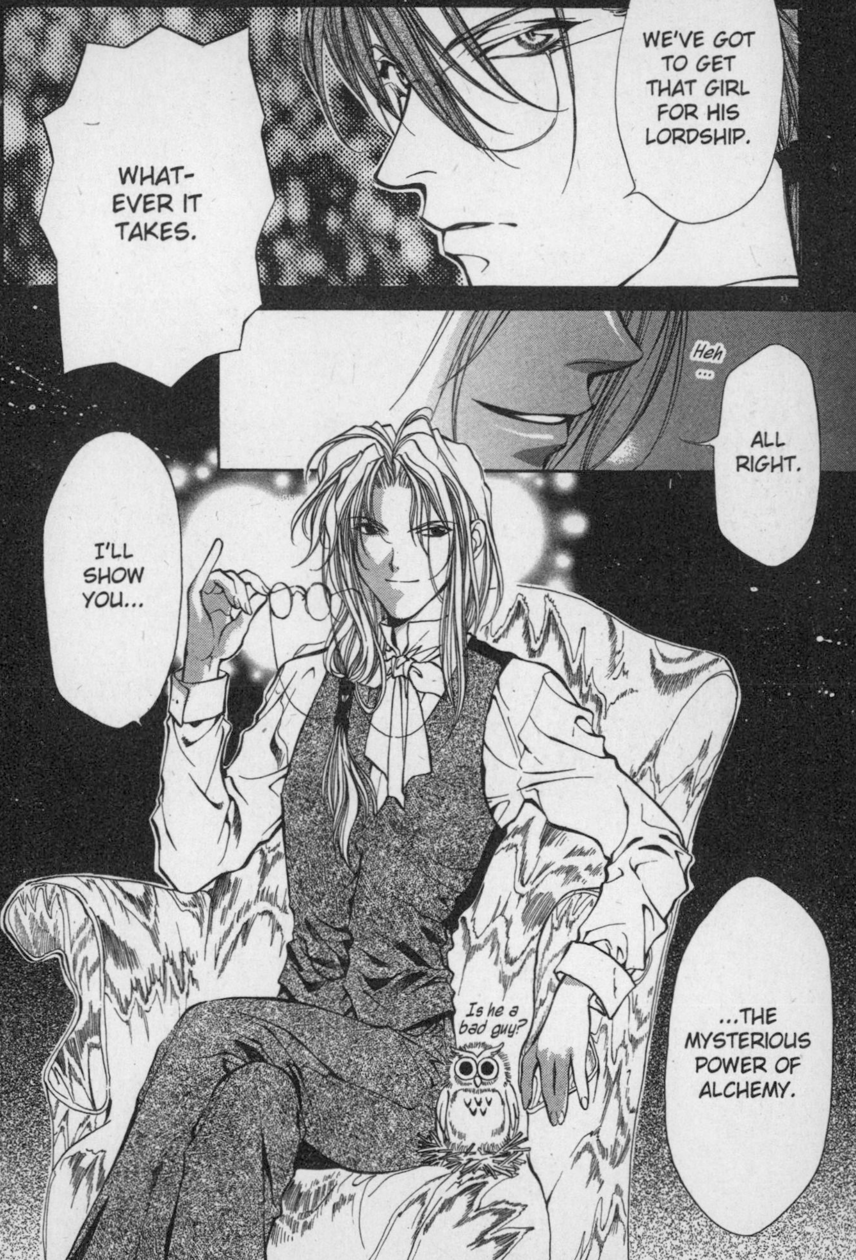
WE'VE GOT TO GET THAT GIRL FOR HIS LORDSHIP.
WHAT-EVER IT TAKES.
Heh...
ALL RIGHT.
I'LL SHOW YOU...
...THE MYSTERIOUS POWER OF ALCHEMY.
Is he a bad guy?

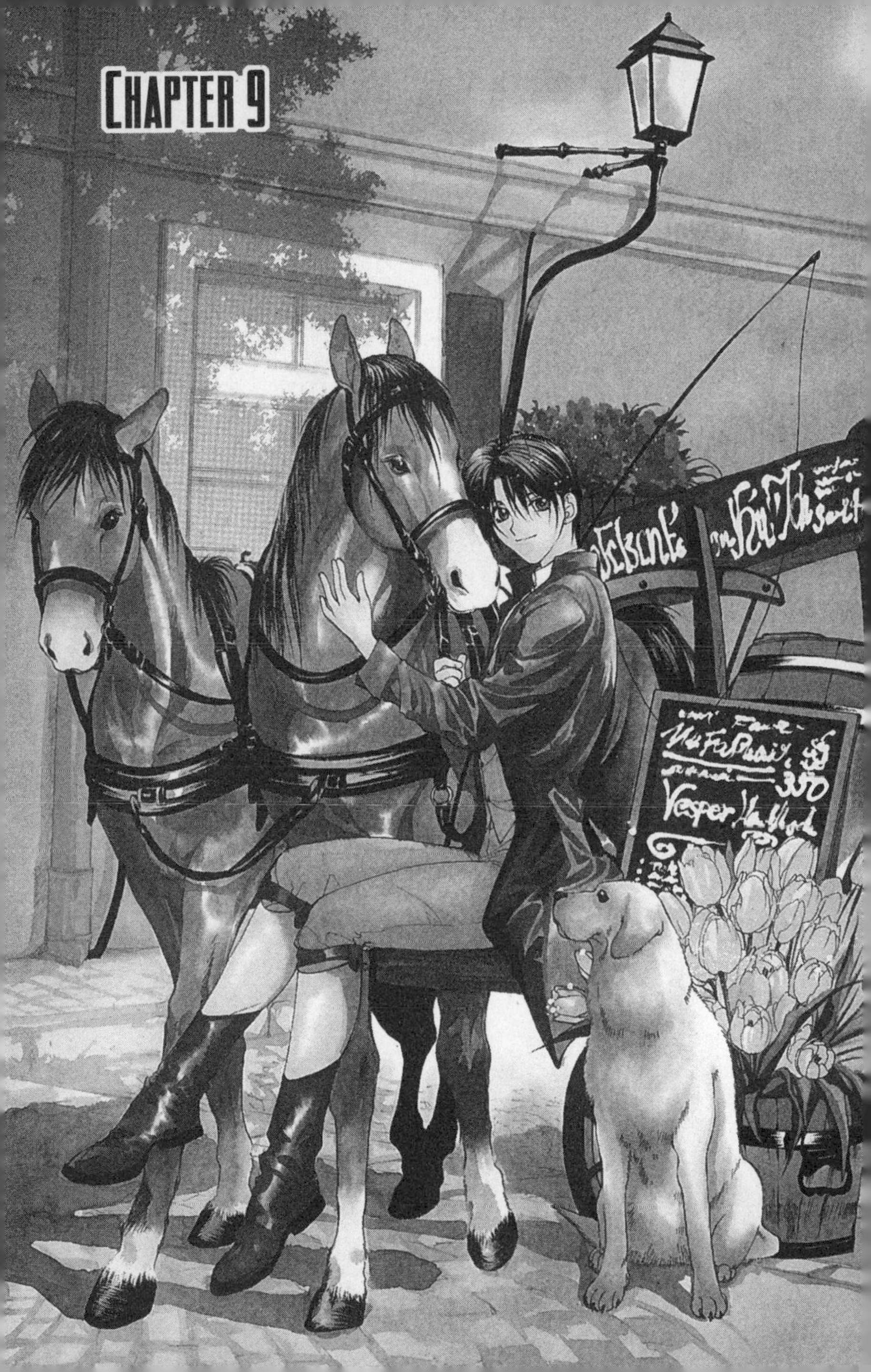
CHAPTER 9

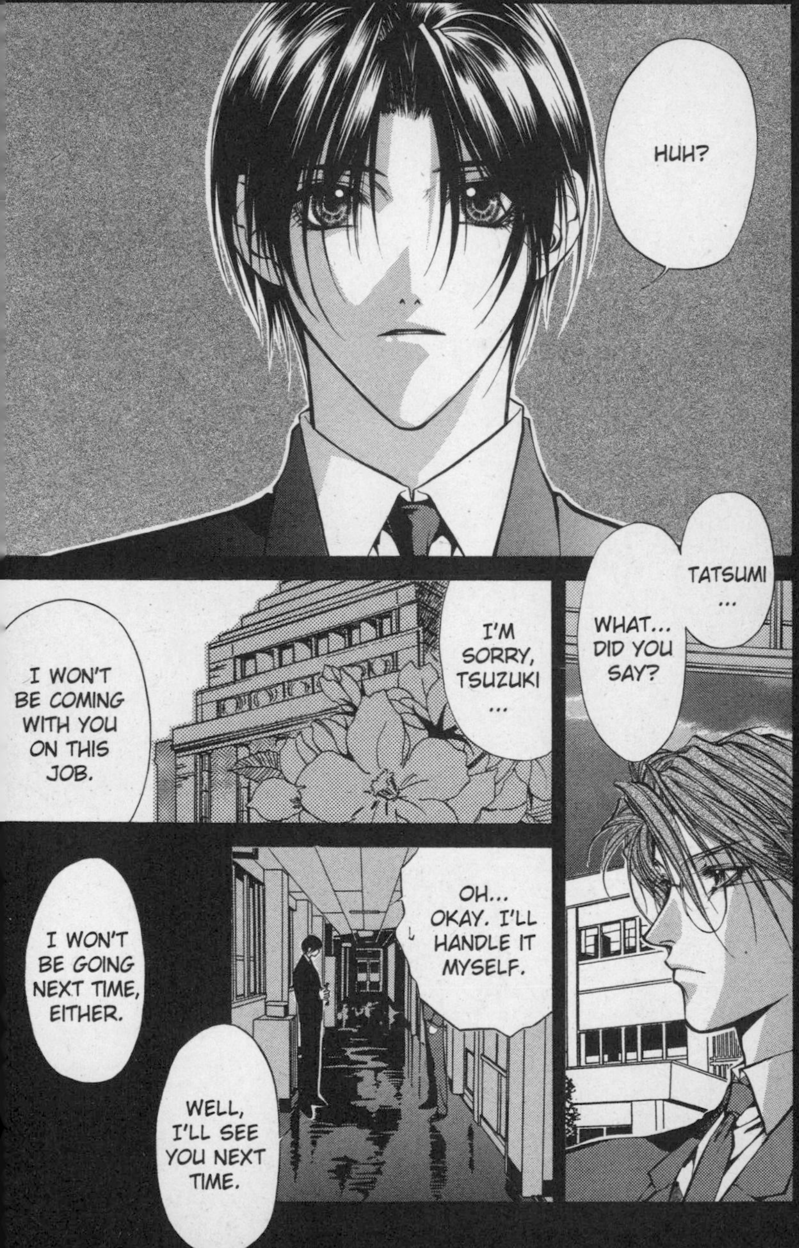
HUH?
TATSUMI ...
WHAT... DID YOU SAY?
I'M SORRY, TSUZUKI ...
I WON'T BE COMING WITH YOU ON THIS JOB.
OH... OKAY. I'LL HANDLE IT MYSELF.
I WON'T BE GOING NEXT TIME, EITHER.
WELL, I'LL SEE YOU NEXT TIME.

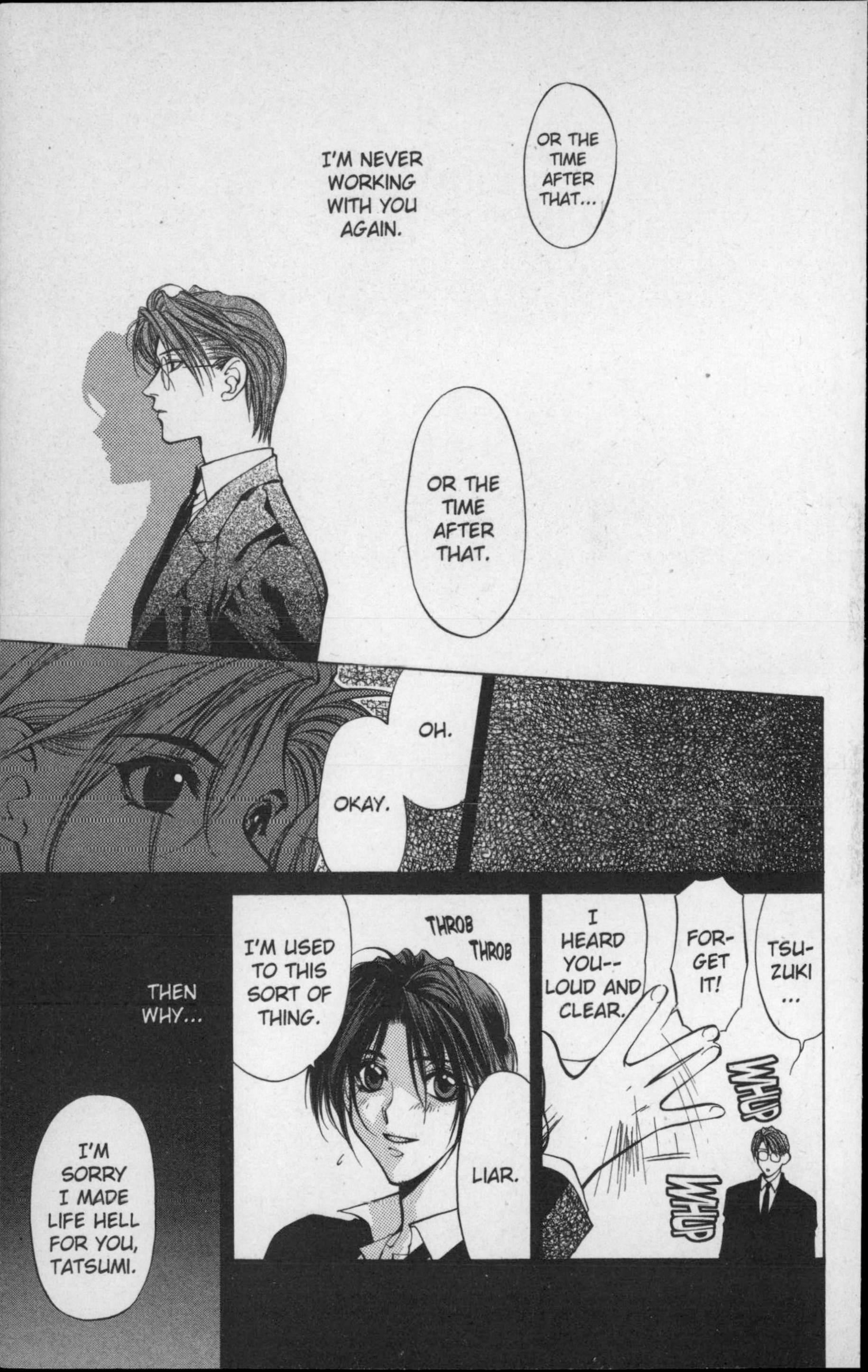
OR THE TIME AFTER THAT...
I'M NEVER WORKING WITH YOU AGAIN.
OR THE TIME AFTER THAT.
OH.
OKAY.
TSU-ZUKI...
FOR-GET IT!
I HEARD YOU-- LOUD AND CLEAR.
WHUP
WHUP
THROB
THROB
I'M USED TO THIS SORT OF THING.
LIAR.
THEN WHY...
I'M SORRY I MADE LIFE HELL FOR YOU, TATSUMI.

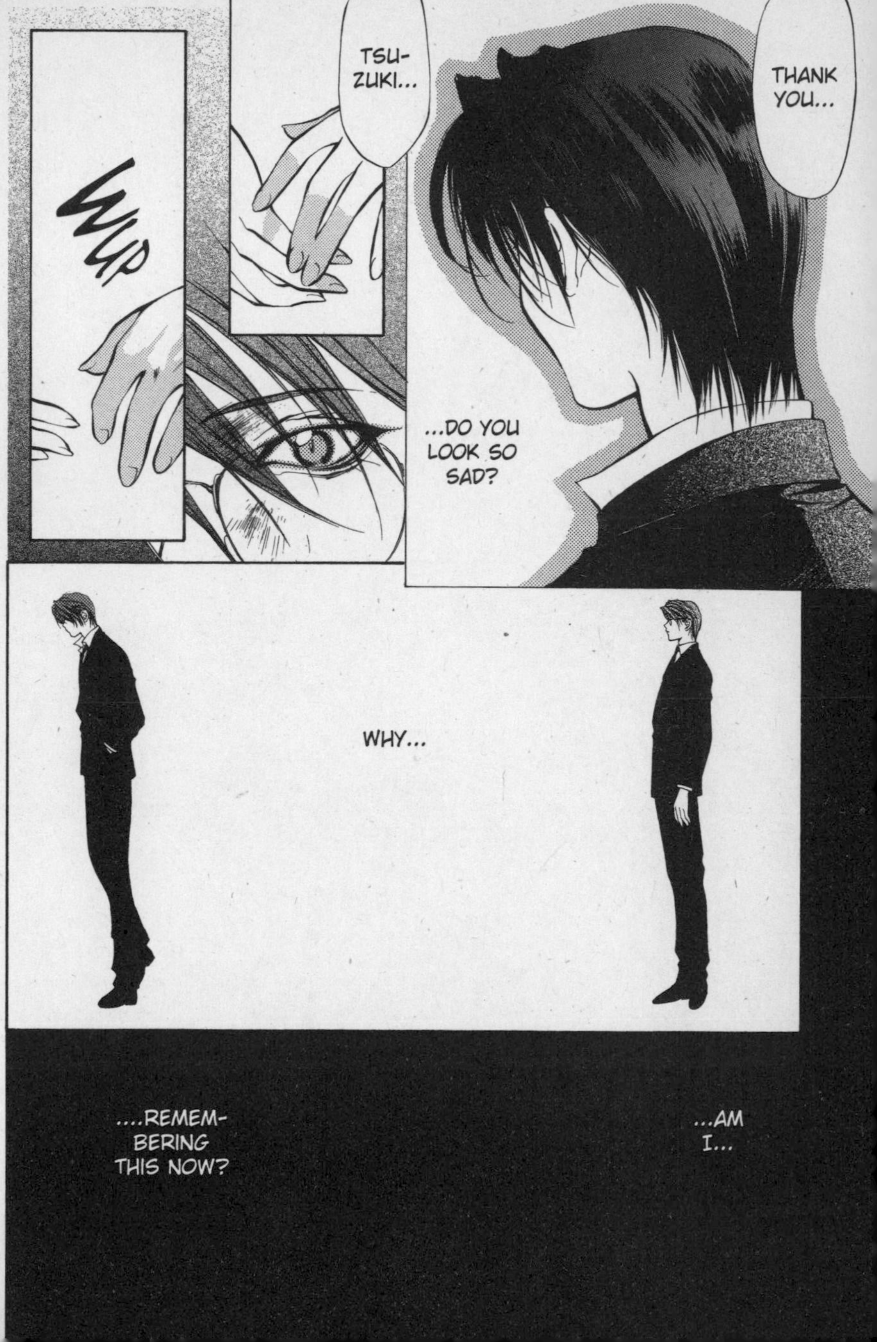
THANK YOU...
...DO YOU LOOK SO SAD?
TSU-ZUKI...
WUP
WHY...
...AM I...
....REMEM-BERING THIS NOW?

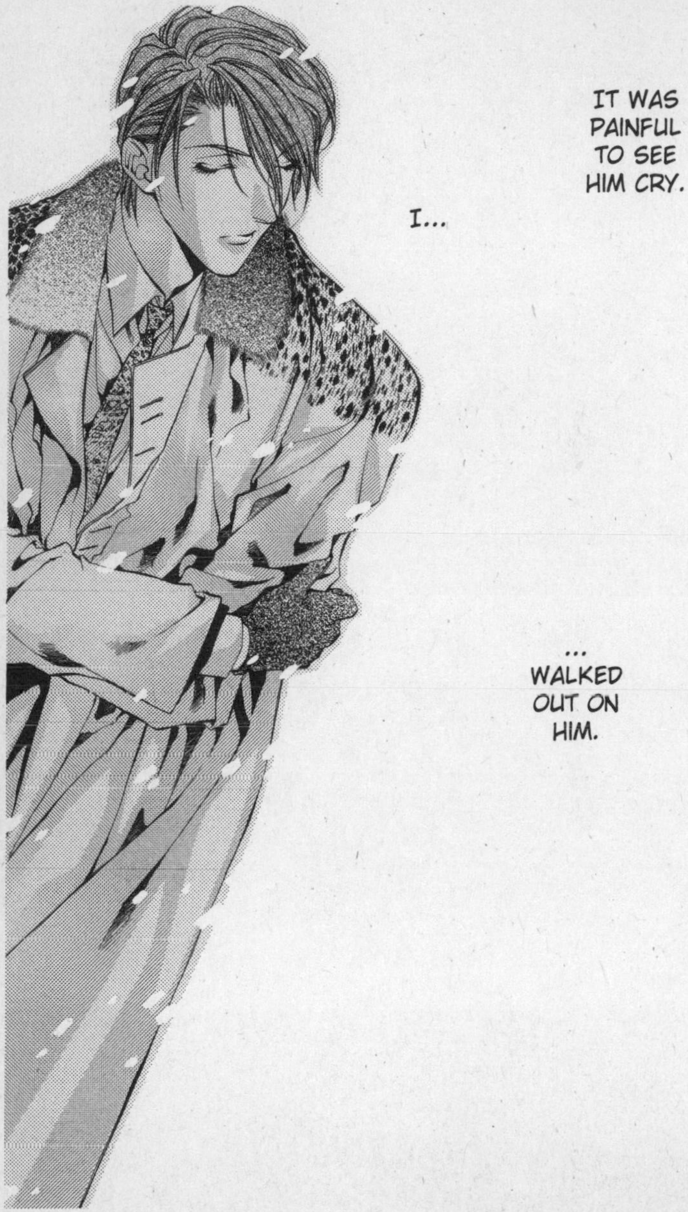
IT WAS PAINFUL TO SEE HIM CRY.
I...
...WALKED OUT ON HIM.

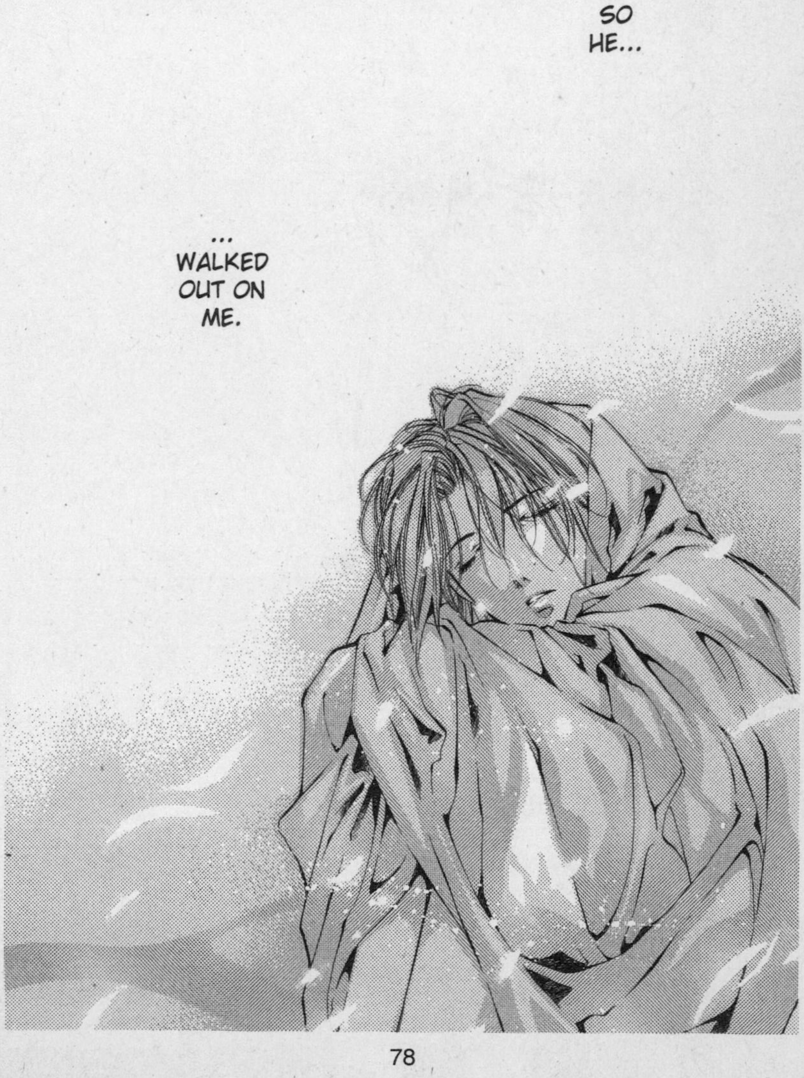
SO HE...
... WALKED OUT ON ME.

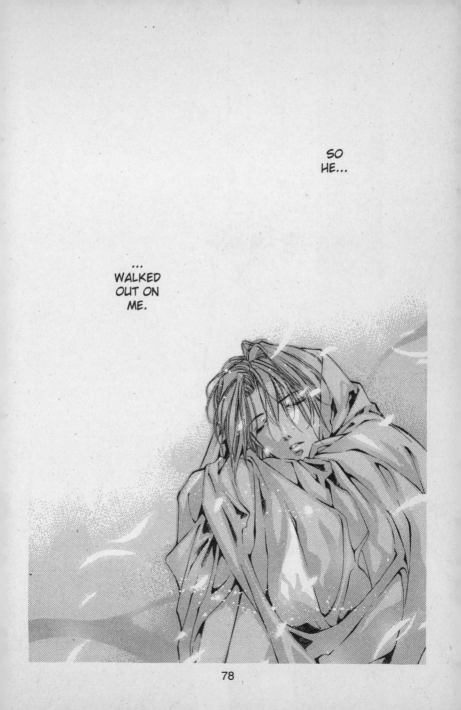

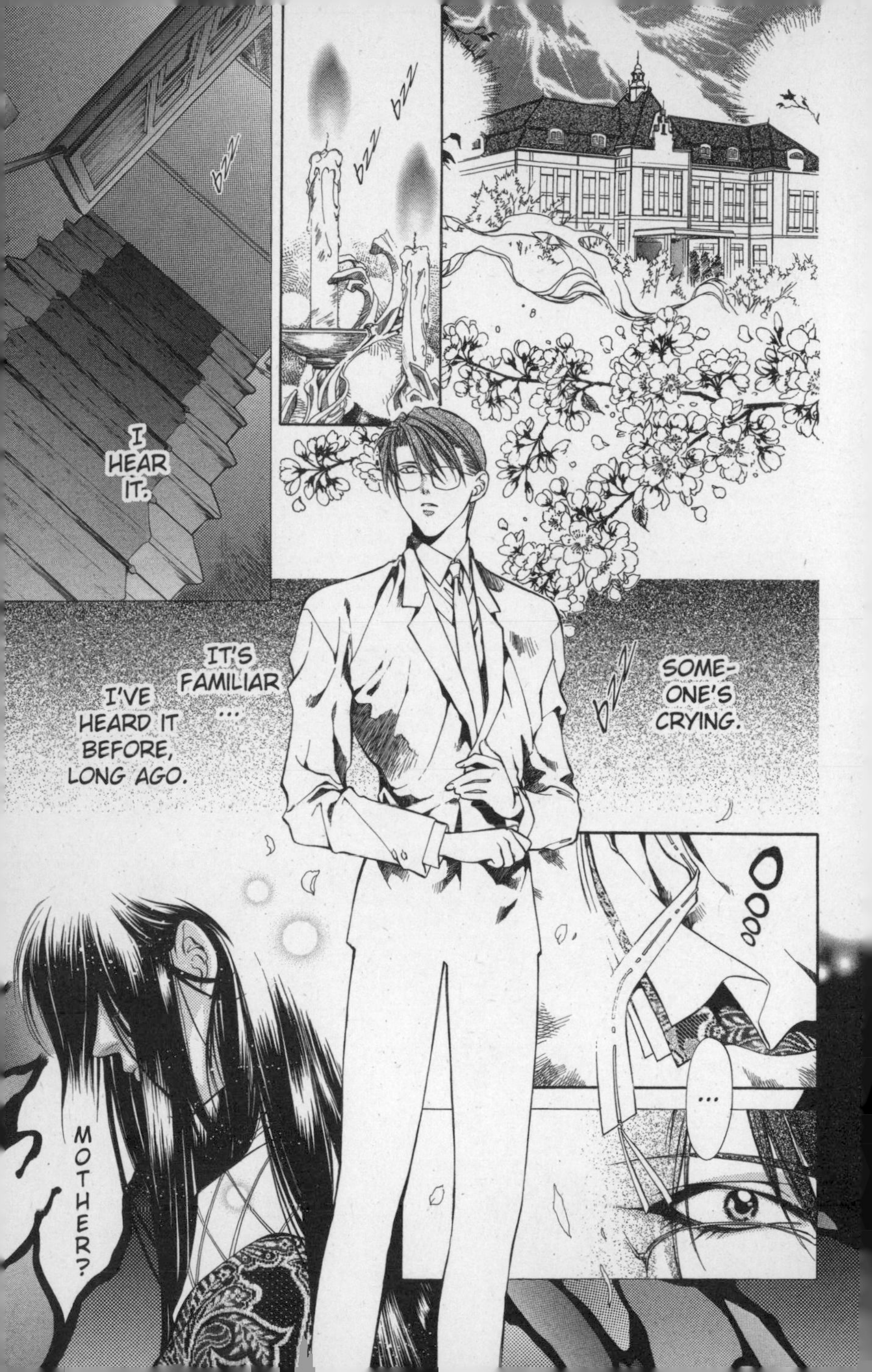

bzz
bzz
bzz
I HEAR IT.
SOME-ONE'S CRYING.
bzz
IT'S FAMILIAR ...
I'VE HEARD IT BEFORE, LONG AGO.
OOOO
...
MOTHER?

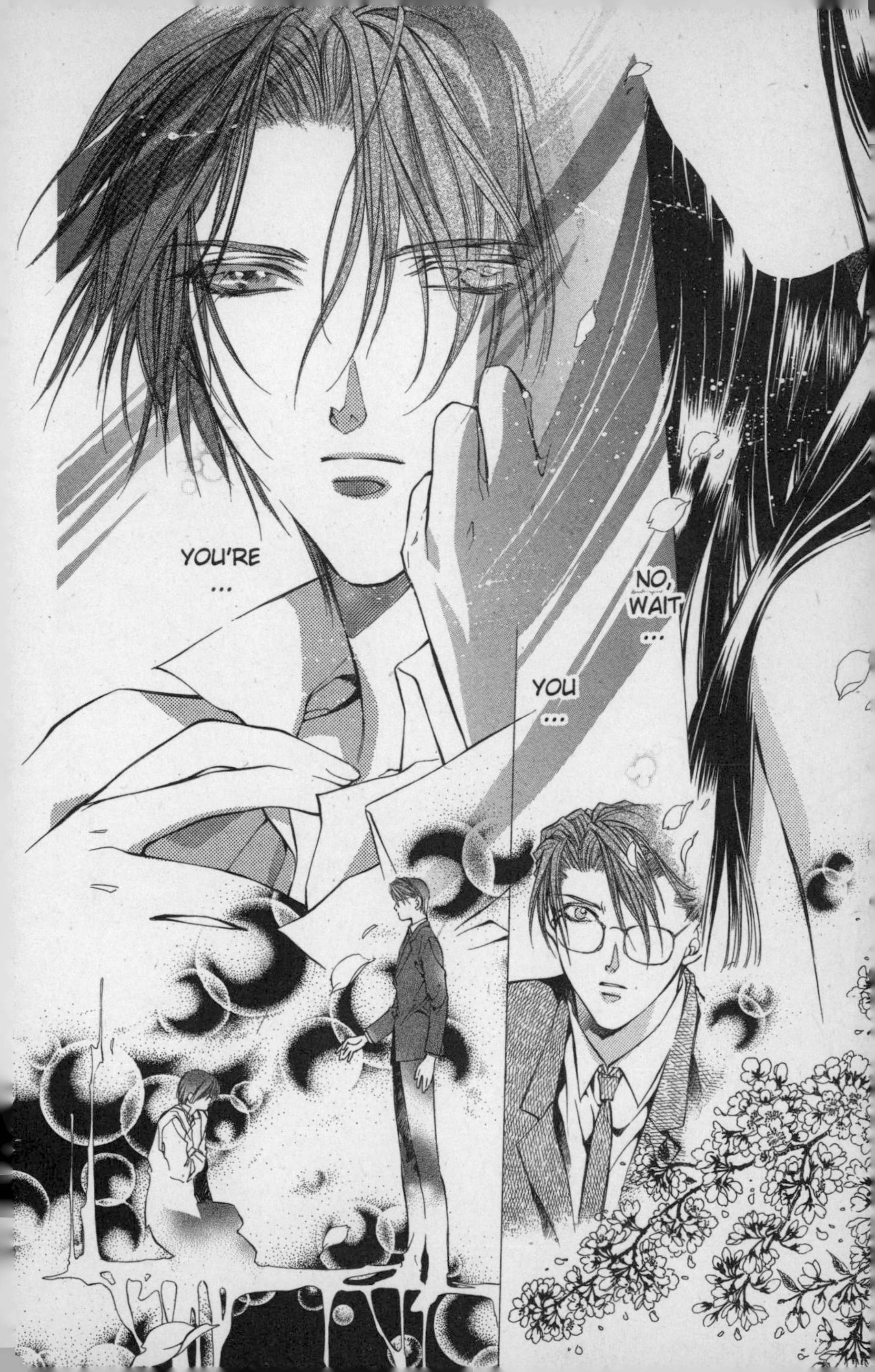
NO, WAIT ...
YOU ...
YOU'RE ...

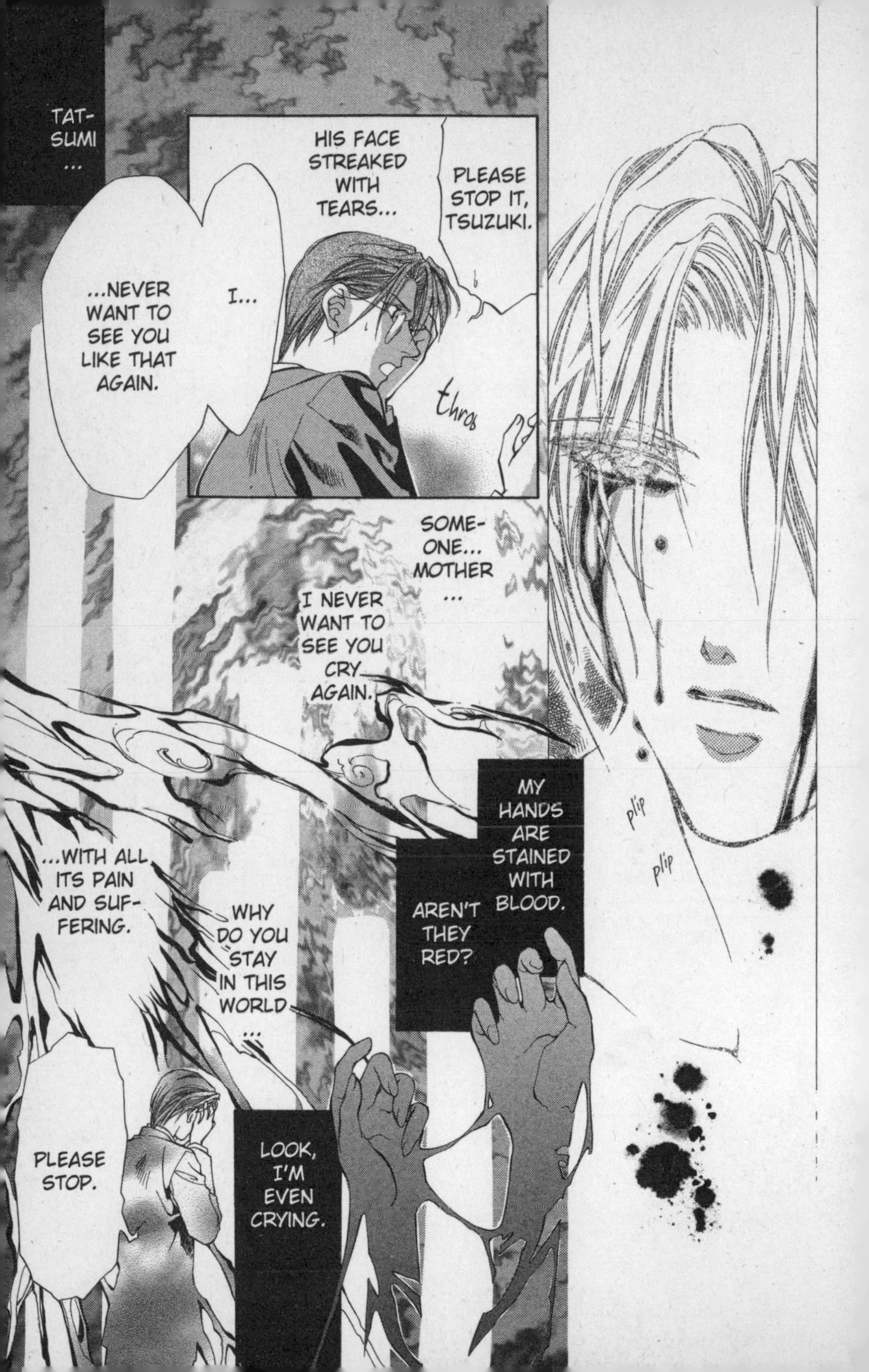
PLEASE STOP IT, TSUZUKI.
HIS FACE STREAKED WITH TEARS...
thros
I...
...NEVER WANT TO SEE YOU LIKE THAT AGAIN.
TAT-SUMI...
SOME-ONE... MOTHER...
I NEVER WANT TO SEE YOU CRY AGAIN.
plip
plip
MY HANDS ARE STAINED WITH BLOOD.
AREN'T THEY RED?
WHY DO YOU STAY IN THIS WORLD...
...WITH ALL ITS PAIN AND SUF-FERING.
LOOK, I'M EVEN CRYING.
PLEASE STOP.

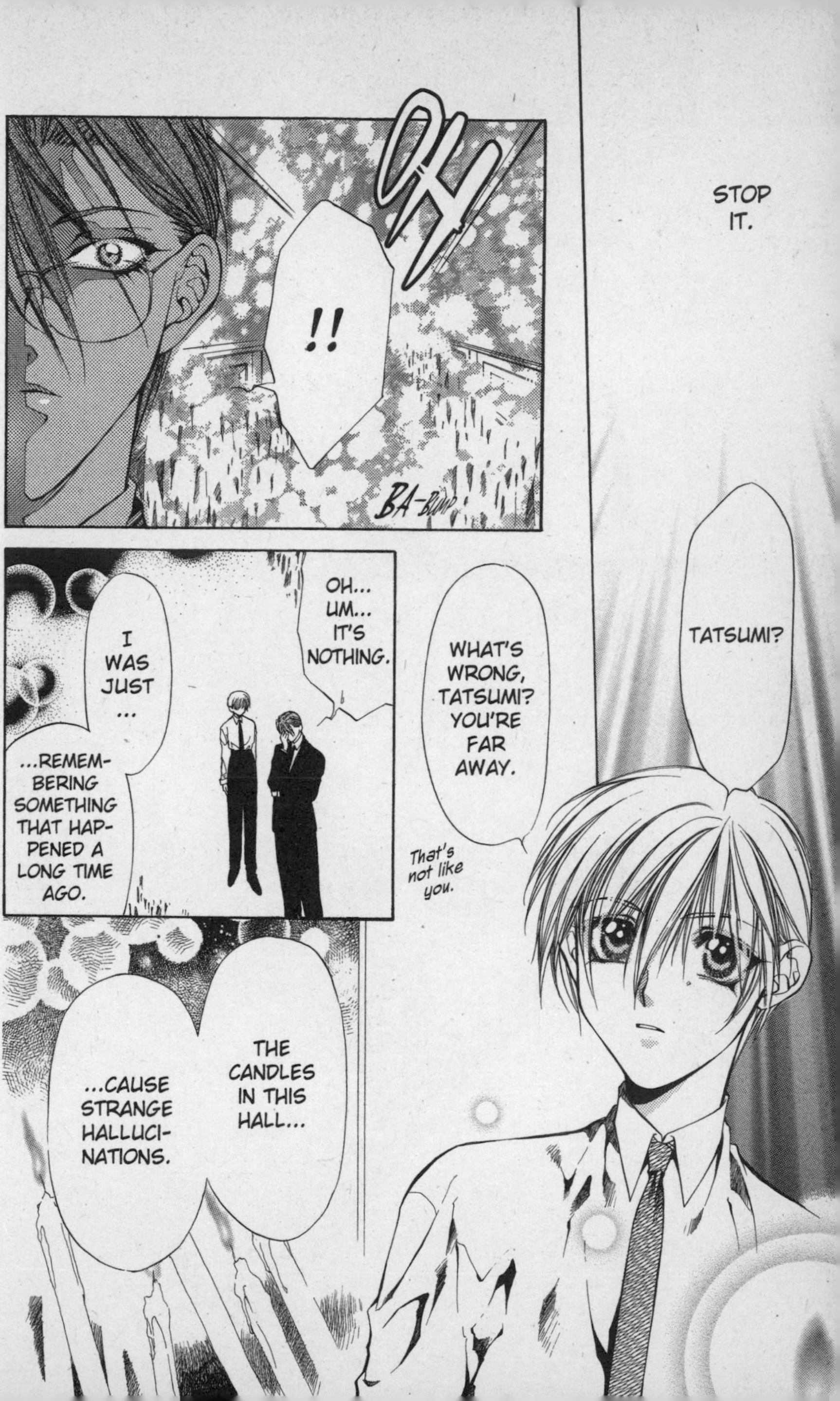
STOP IT.
TATSUMI?
WHAT'S WRONG, TATSUMI? YOU'RE FAR AWAY.
That's not like you.
!!
BA-BUMP
OH... UM... IT'S NOTHING.
I WAS JUST ...
...REMEMBERING SOMETHING THAT HAPPENED A LONG TIME AGO.
THE CANDLES IN THIS HALL...
...CAUSE STRANGE HALLUCINATIONS.

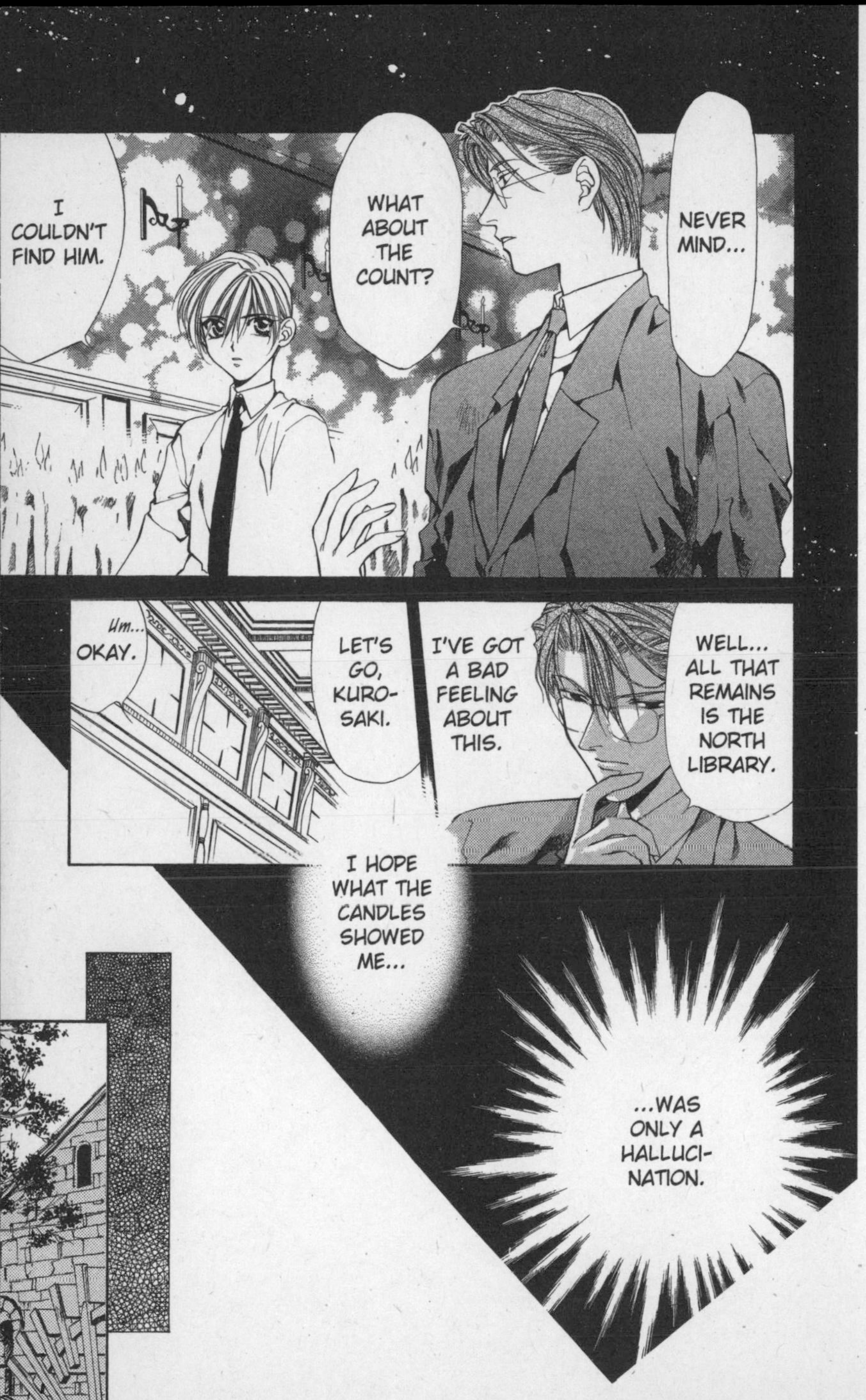
NEVER MIND...
WHAT ABOUT THE COUNT?
I COULDN'T FIND HIM.
WELL... ALL THAT REMAINS IS THE NORTH LIBRARY.
I'VE GOT A BAD FEELING ABOUT THIS.
LET'S GO, KURO-SAKI.
Um... OKAY.
I HOPE WHAT THE CANDLES SHOWED ME...
...WAS ONLY A HALLUCI-NATION.

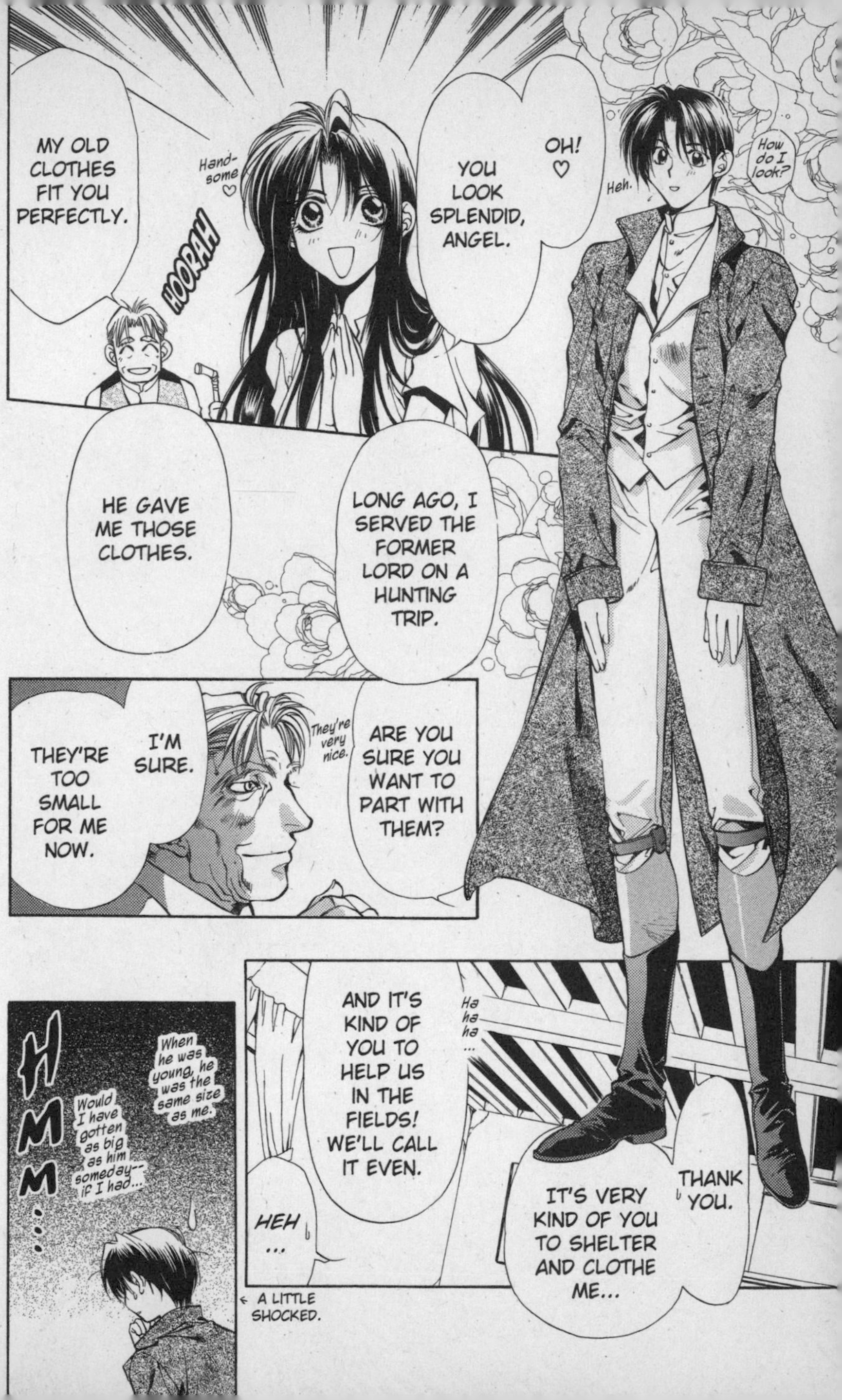
How do I look?
Heh.
OH! ♡
YOU LOOK SPLENDID, ANGEL.
Hand-some ♡
MY OLD CLOTHES FIT YOU PERFECTLY.
HOORAH
LONG AGO, I SERVED THE FORMER LORD ON A HUNTING TRIP.
HE GAVE ME THOSE CLOTHES.
They're very nice.
ARE YOU SURE YOU WANT TO PART WITH THEM?
I'M SURE.
THEY'RE TOO SMALL FOR ME NOW.
THANK YOU.
IT'S VERY KIND OF YOU TO SHELTER AND CLOTHE ME...
Ha ha ha...
AND IT'S KIND OF YOU TO HELP US IN THE FIELDS! WE'LL CALL IT EVEN.
HEH...
← A LITTLE SHOCKED.
When he was young, he was the same size as me.
Would I have gotten as big as him someday-- if I had...
HMM...

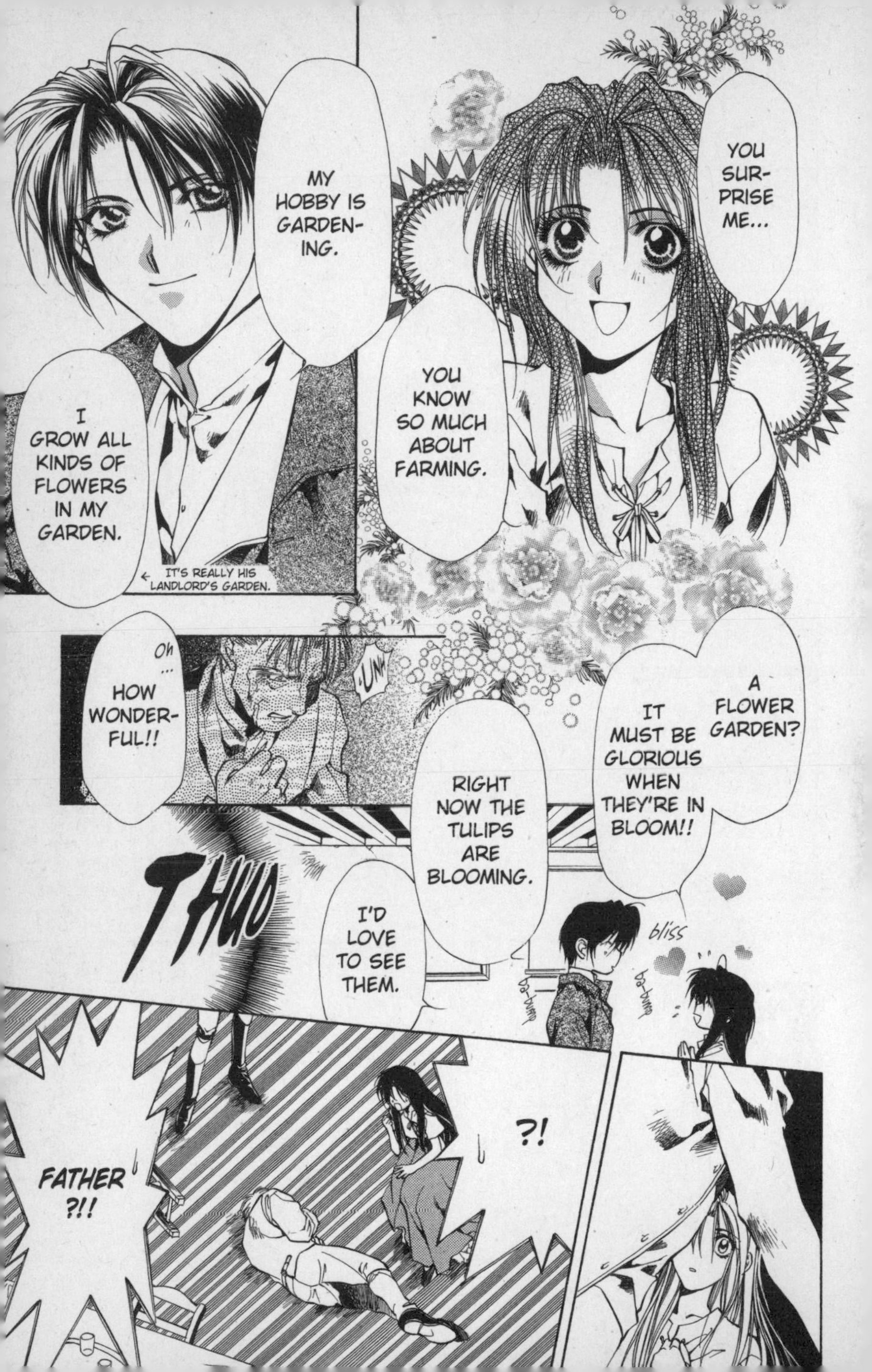
YOU SUR-PRISE ME...
YOU KNOW SO MUCH ABOUT FARMING.
MY HOBBY IS GARDEN-ING.
I GROW ALL KINDS OF FLOWERS IN MY GARDEN.
← IT'S REALLY HIS LANDLORD'S GARDEN.
A FLOWER GARDEN?
IT MUST BE GLORIOUS WHEN THEY'RE IN BLOOM!!
RIGHT NOW THE TULIPS ARE BLOOMING.
I'D LOVE TO SEE THEM.
bliss
Oh... HOW WONDER-FUL!!
THUD
?!
FATHER ?!!

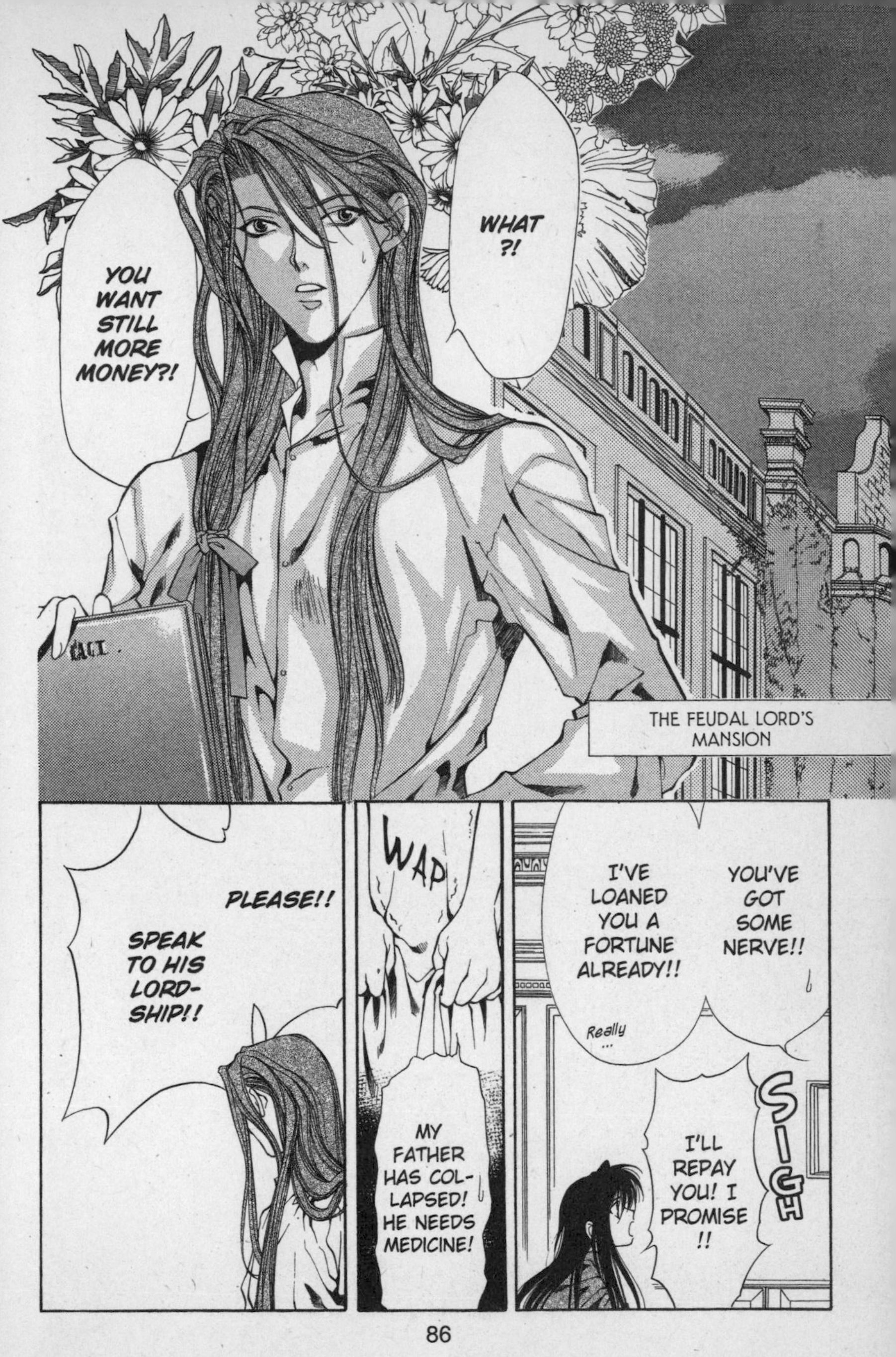
WHAT ?!
YOU WANT STILL MORE MONEY?!
THE FEUDAL LORD'S MANSION
YOU'VE GOT SOME NERVE!!
I'VE LOANED YOU A FORTUNE ALREADY!!
Really ...
SIGH
I'LL REPAY YOU! I PROMISE !!
WAP
MY FATHER HAS COL-LAPSED! HE NEEDS MEDICINE!
PLEASE!!
SPEAK TO HIS LORD-SHIP!!

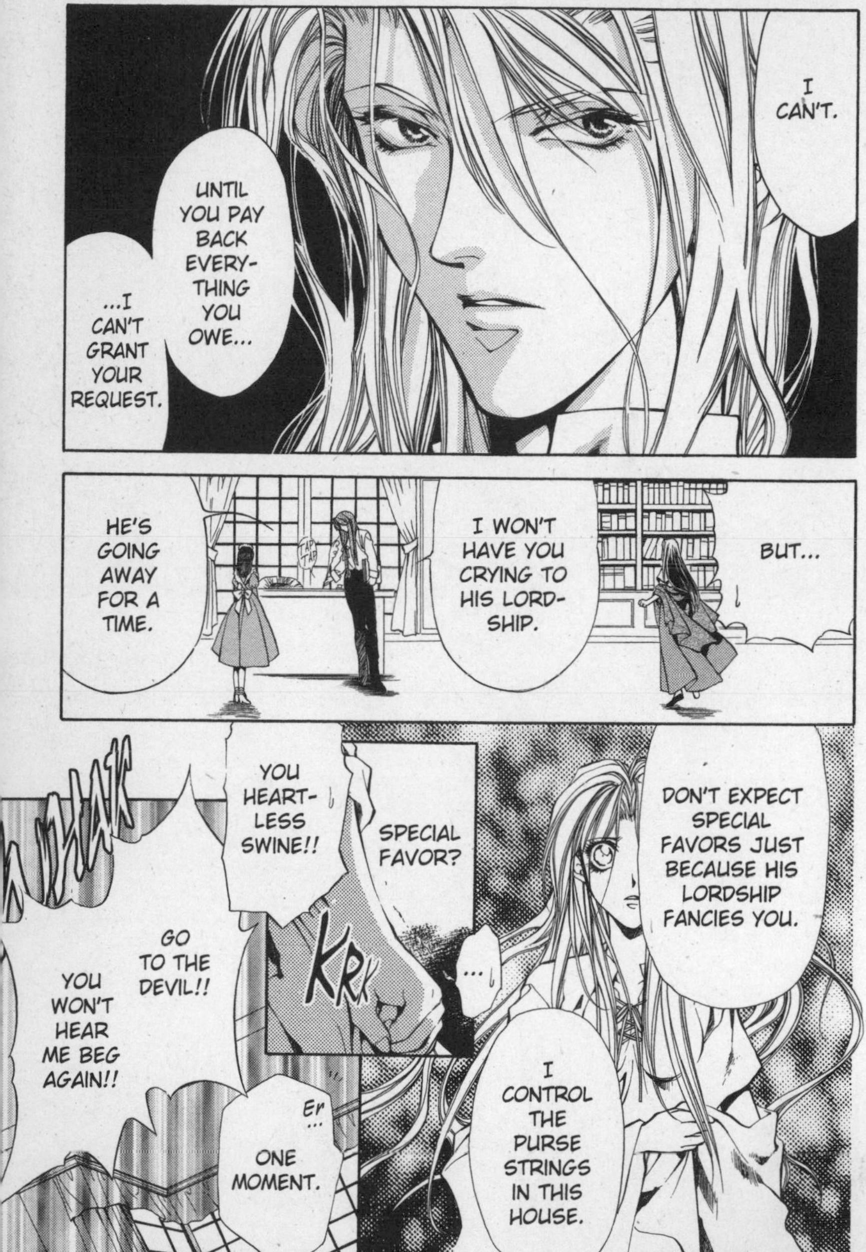
I CAN'T.
UNTIL YOU PAY BACK EVERY-THING YOU OWE...
...I CAN'T GRANT YOUR REQUEST.
BUT...
I WON'T HAVE YOU CRYING TO HIS LORD-SHIP.
HE'S GOING AWAY FOR A TIME.
TAP TAP
DON'T EXPECT SPECIAL FAVORS JUST BECAUSE HIS LORDSHIP FANCIES YOU.
...
I CONTROL THE PURSE STRINGS IN THIS HOUSE.
SPECIAL FAVOR?
KRK
YOU HEART-LESS SWINE!!
GO TO THE DEVIL!!
YOU WON'T HEAR ME BEG AGAIN!!
Er...
ONE MOMENT.

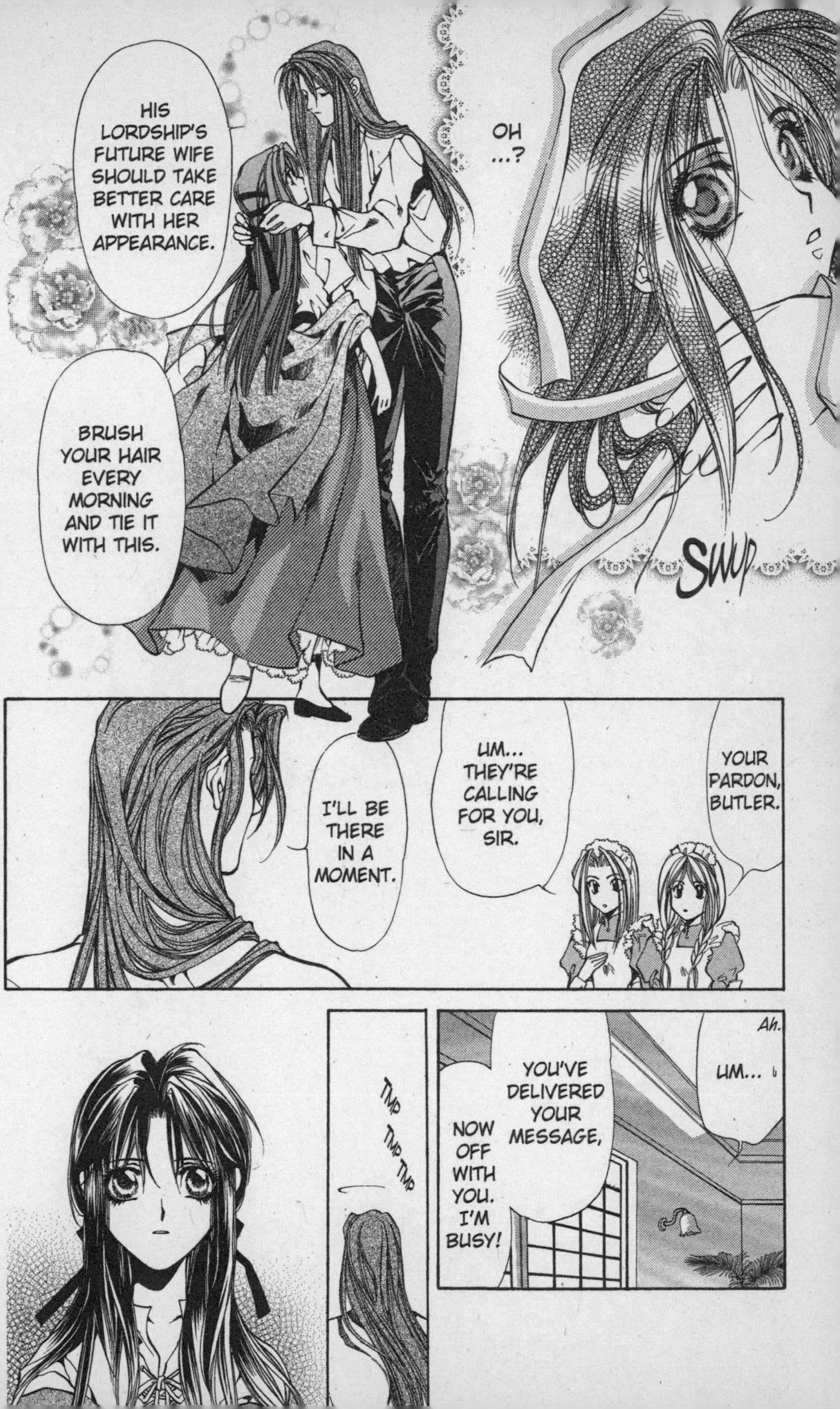
OH ...?
SWUP
HIS LORDSHIP'S FUTURE WIFE SHOULD TAKE BETTER CARE WITH HER APPEARANCE.
BRUSH YOUR HAIR EVERY MORNING AND TIE IT WITH THIS.
YOUR PARDON, BUTLER.
UM... THEY'RE CALLING FOR YOU, SIR.
I'LL BE THERE IN A MOMENT.
Ah.
UM...
YOU'VE DELIVERED YOUR MESSAGE,
NOW OFF WITH YOU. I'M BUSY!
TMP TMP TMP

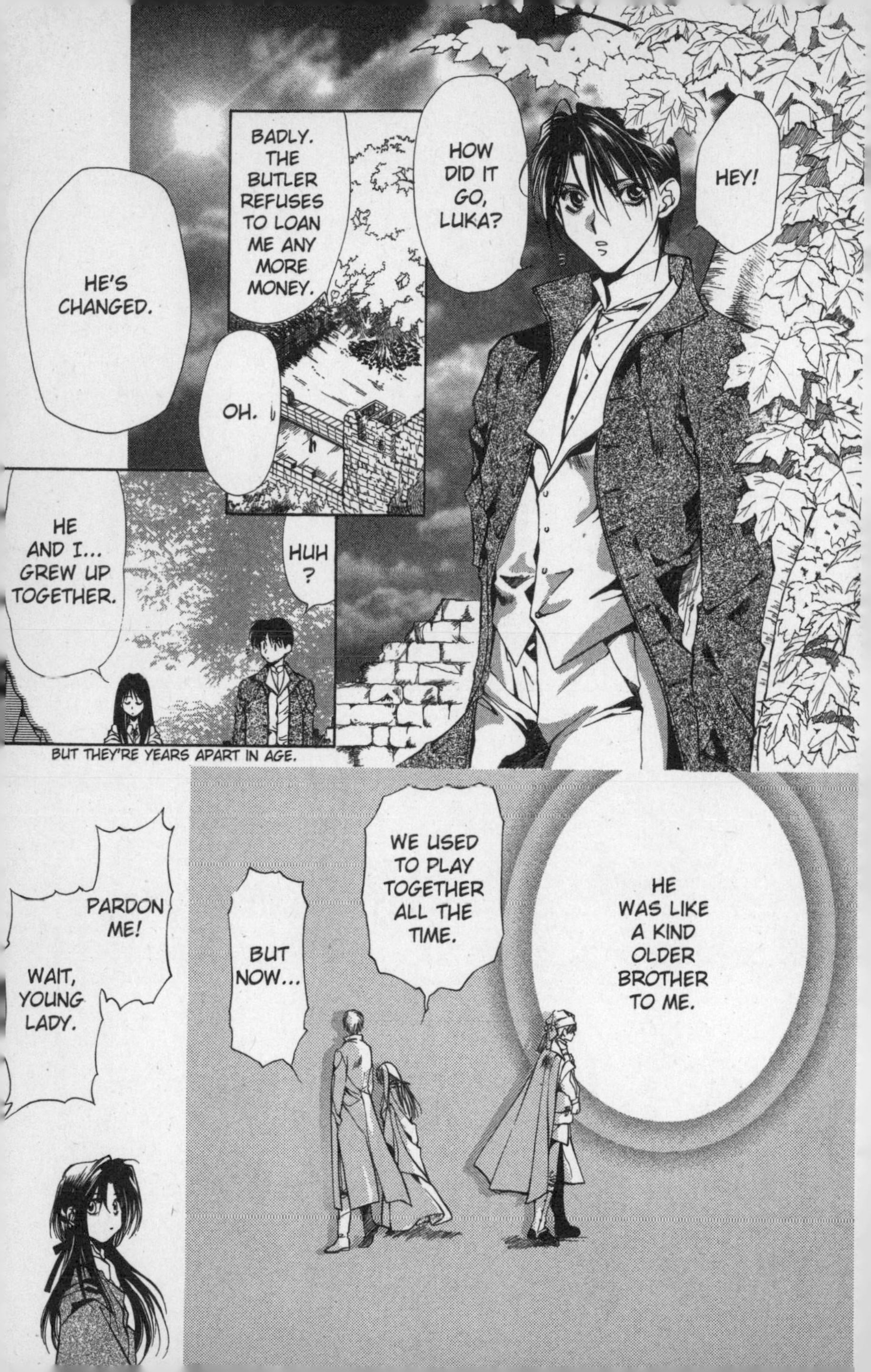
HEY!
HOW DID IT GO, LUKA?
BADLY. THE BUTLER REFUSES TO LOAN ME ANY MORE MONEY.
OH.
HE'S CHANGED.
HUH?
HE AND I... GREW UP TOGETHER.
BUT THEY'RE YEARS APART IN AGE.
HE WAS LIKE A KIND OLDER BROTHER TO ME.
WE USED TO PLAY TOGETHER ALL THE TIME.
BUT NOW...
PARDON ME!
WAIT, YOUNG LADY.

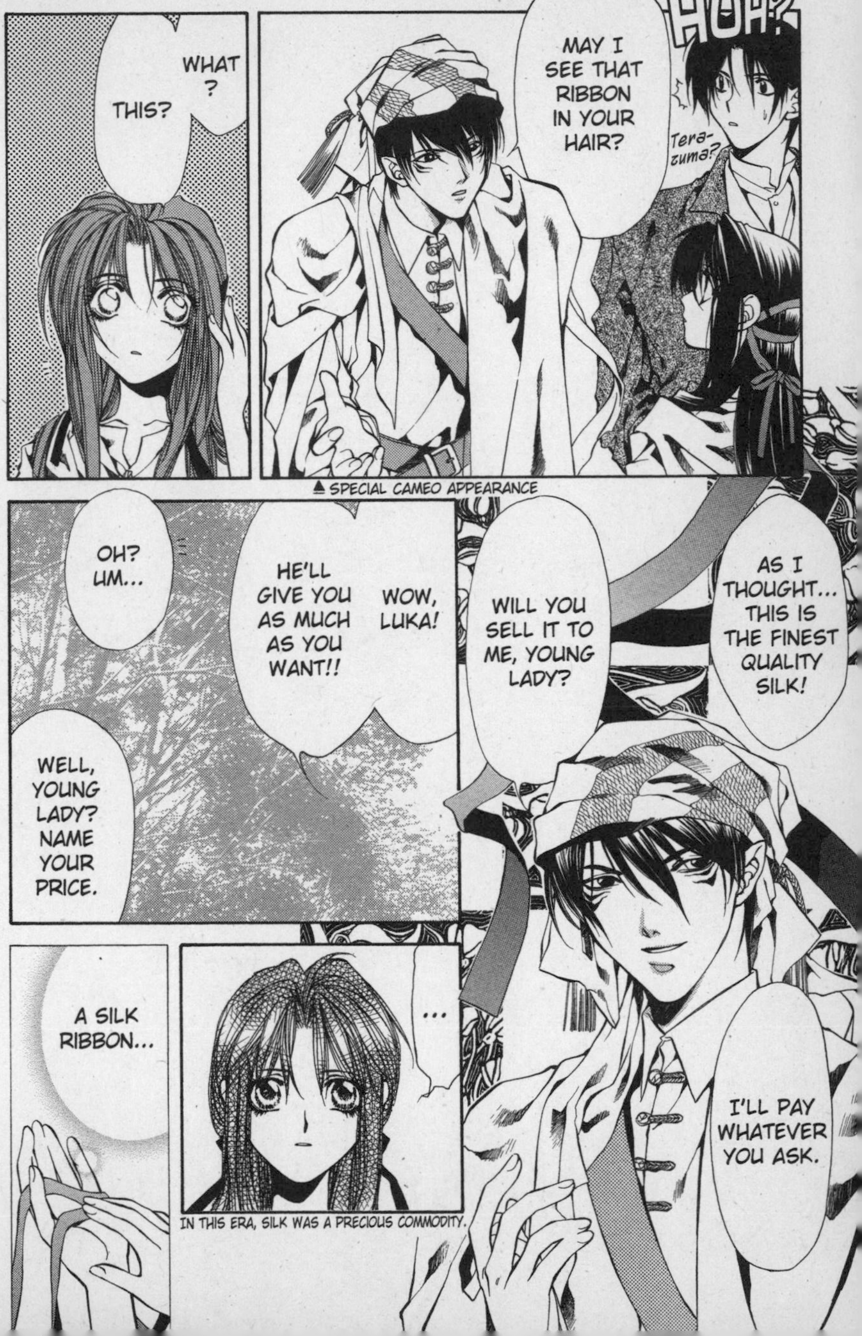
MAY I SEE THAT RIBBON IN YOUR HAIR?
HUH?
Tera-zuma?
WHAT?
THIS?
SPECIAL CAMEO APPEARANCE
AS I THOUGHT... THIS IS THE FINEST QUALITY SILK!
WILL YOU SELL IT TO ME, YOUNG LADY?
WOW, LUKA!
HE'LL GIVE YOU AS MUCH AS YOU WANT!!
OH? UM...
WELL, YOUNG LADY? NAME YOUR PRICE.
I'LL PAY WHATEVER YOU ASK.
...
IN THIS ERA, SILK WAS A PRECIOUS COMMODITY.
A SILK RIBBON...

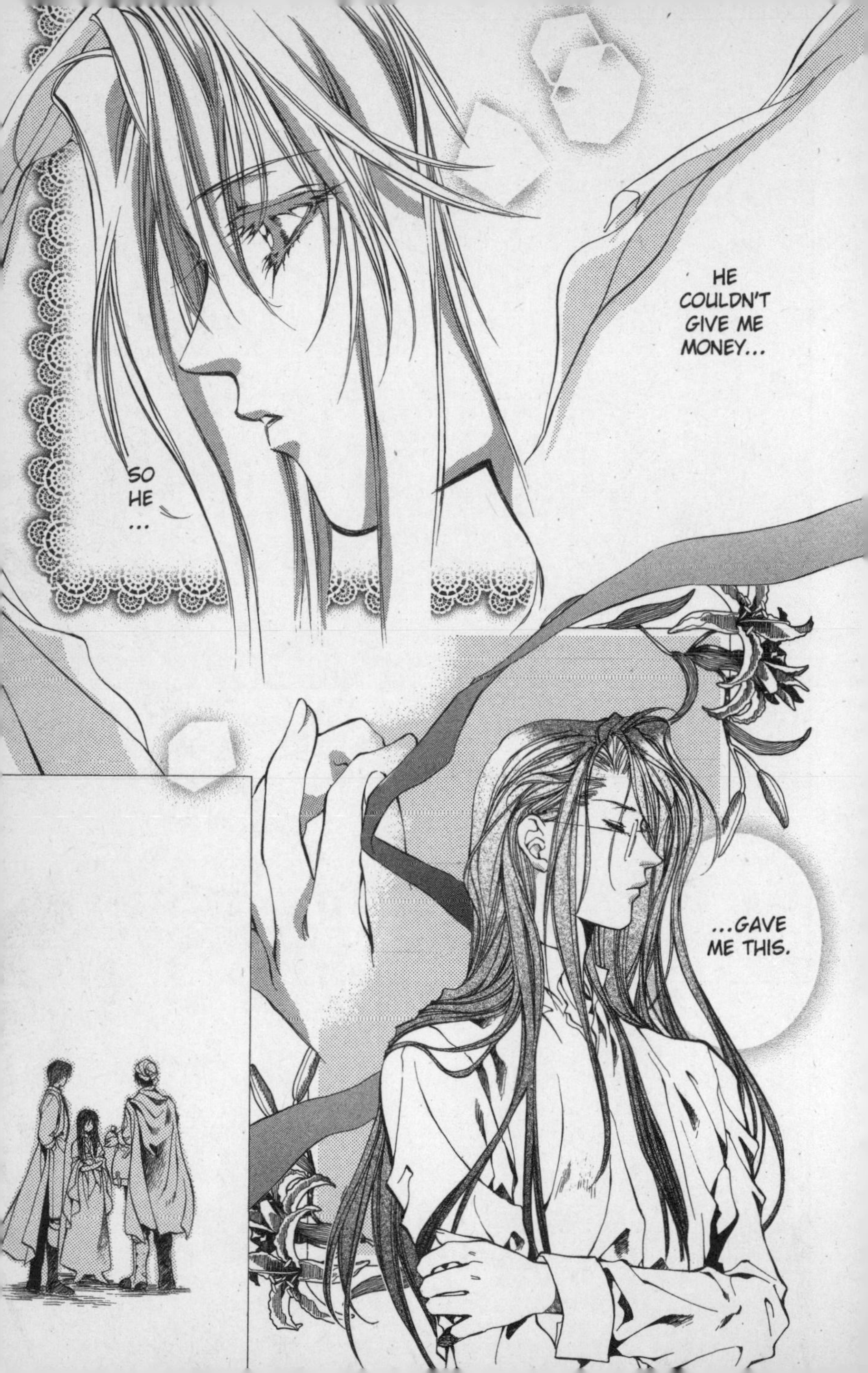
HE COULDN'T GIVE ME MONEY...
SO HE ...
...GAVE ME THIS.

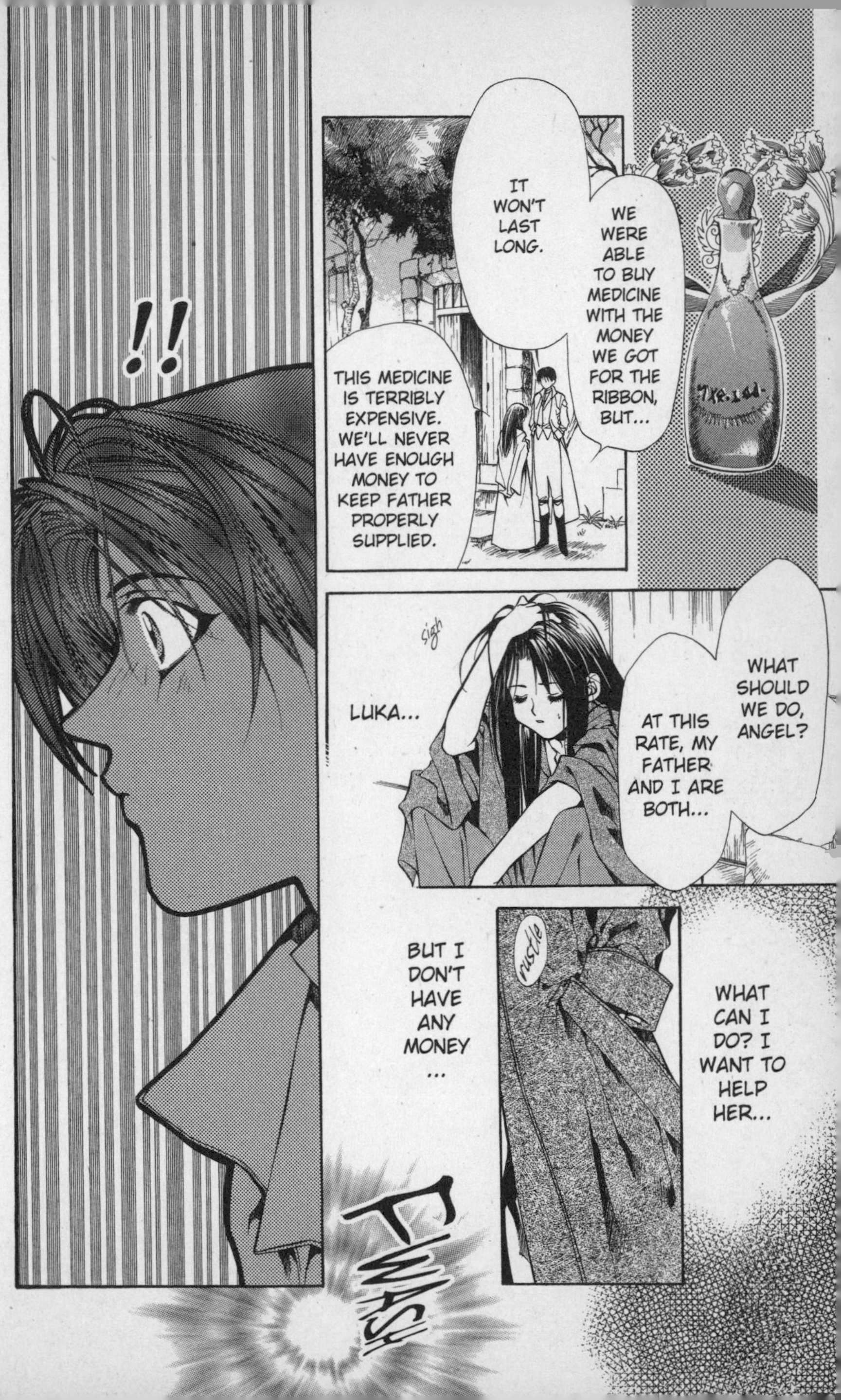
WE WERE ABLE TO BUY MEDICINE WITH THE MONEY WE GOT FOR THE RIBBON, BUT...
IT WON'T LAST LONG.
THIS MEDICINE IS TERRIBLY EXPENSIVE. WE'LL NEVER HAVE ENOUGH MONEY TO KEEP FATHER PROPERLY SUPPLIED.
WHAT SHOULD WE DO, ANGEL?
AT THIS RATE, MY FATHER AND I ARE BOTH...
sigh
LUKA...
WHAT CAN I DO? I WANT TO HELP HER...
rustle
BUT I DON'T HAVE ANY MONEY ...
!!
FWASH!

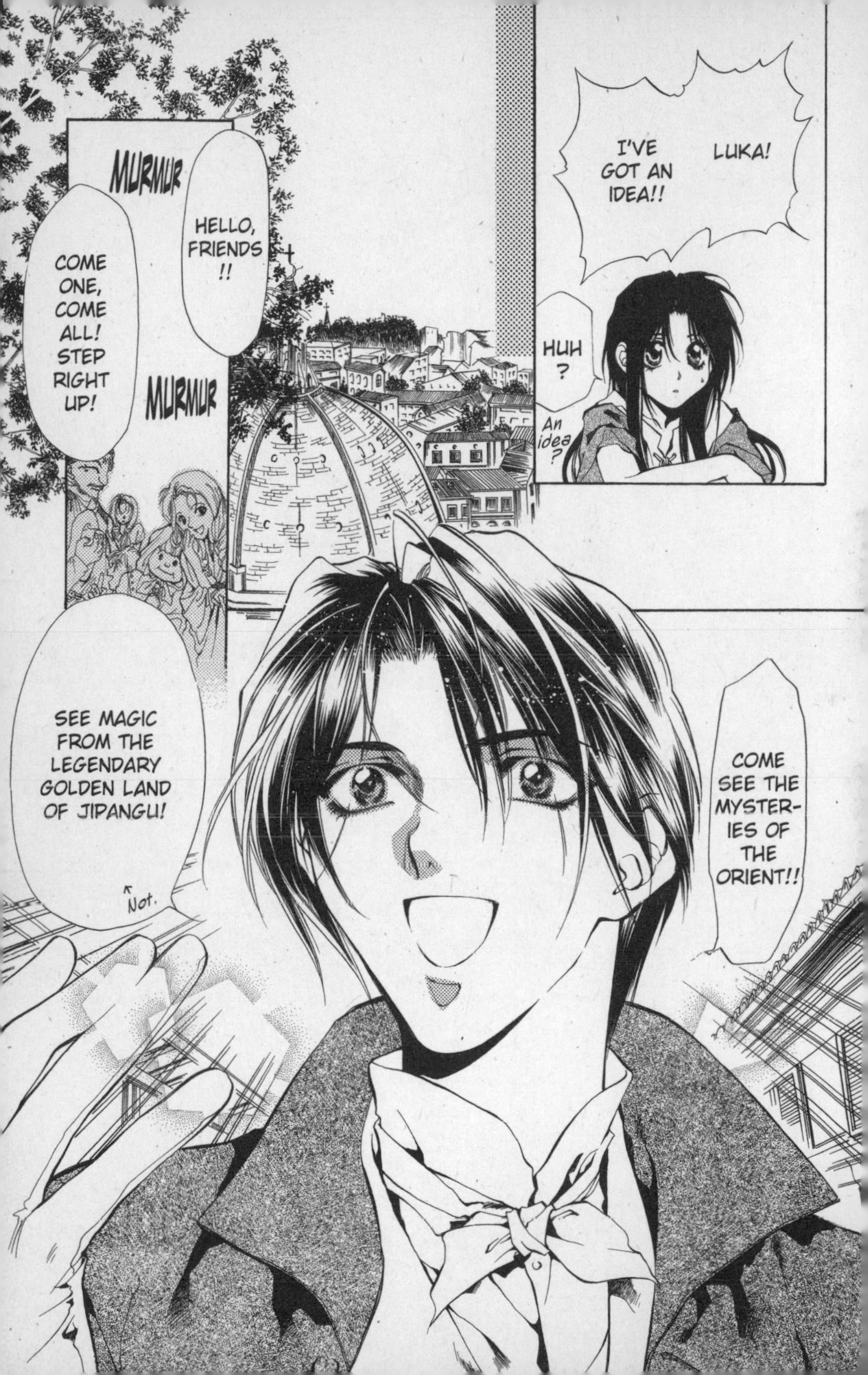
LUKA!
I'VE GOT AN IDEA!!
HUH?
An idea?
HELLO, FRIENDS!!
MURMUR
COME ONE, COME ALL! STEP RIGHT UP!
MURMUR
COME SEE THE MYSTERIES OF THE ORIENT!!
SEE MAGIC FROM THE LEGENDARY GOLDEN LAND OF JIPANGU!
Not.

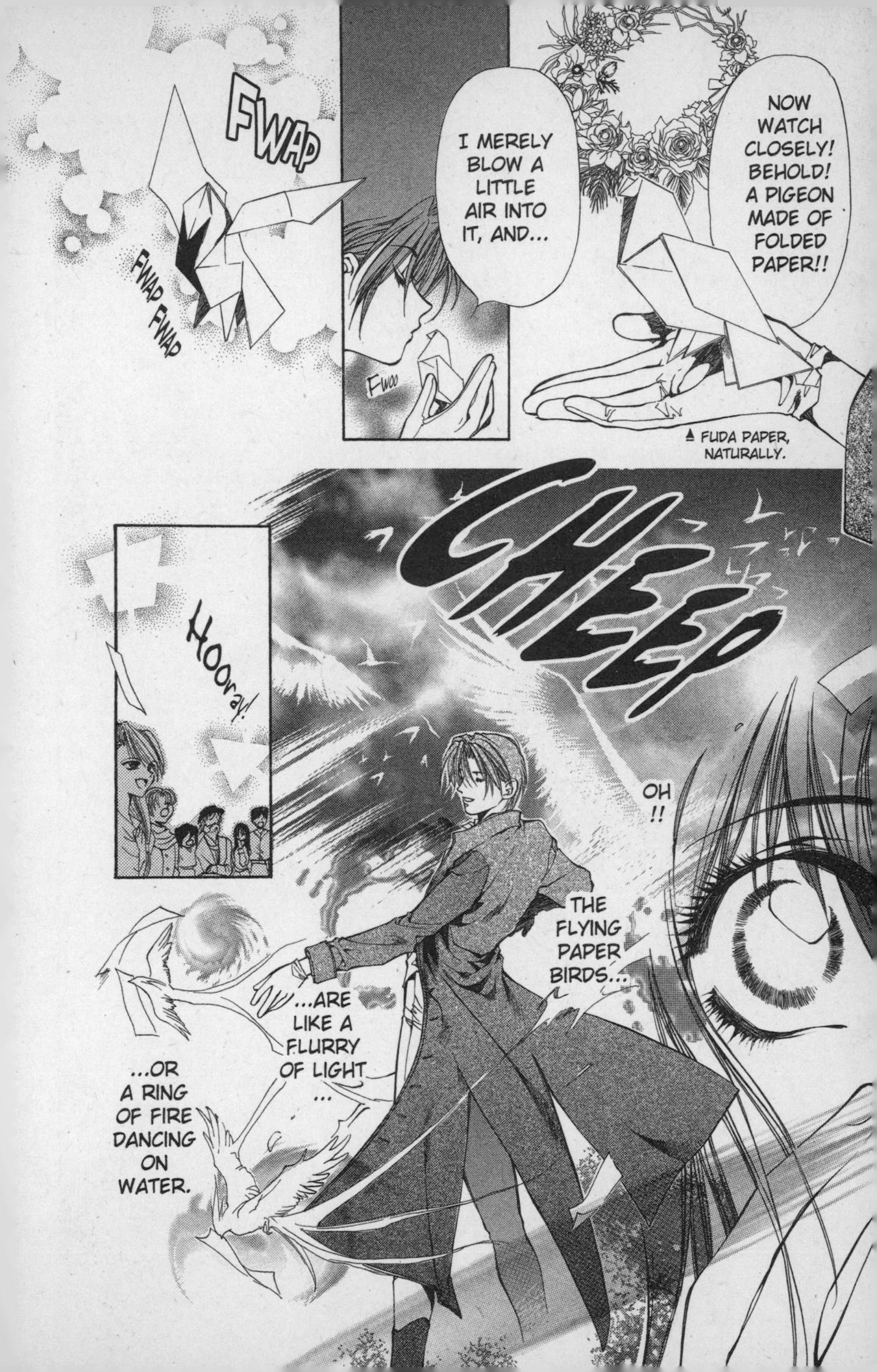
NOW WATCH CLOSELY! BEHOLD! A PIGEON MADE OF FOLDED PAPER!!
▲ FUDA PAPER, NATURALLY.
I MERELY BLOW A LITTLE AIR INTO IT, AND...
Fwoo
FWAP
FWAP FWAP
CHEEP
OH !!
HOOray!
THE FLYING PAPER BIRDS...
...ARE LIKE A FLURRY OF LIGHT ...
...OR A RING OF FIRE DANCING ON WATER.

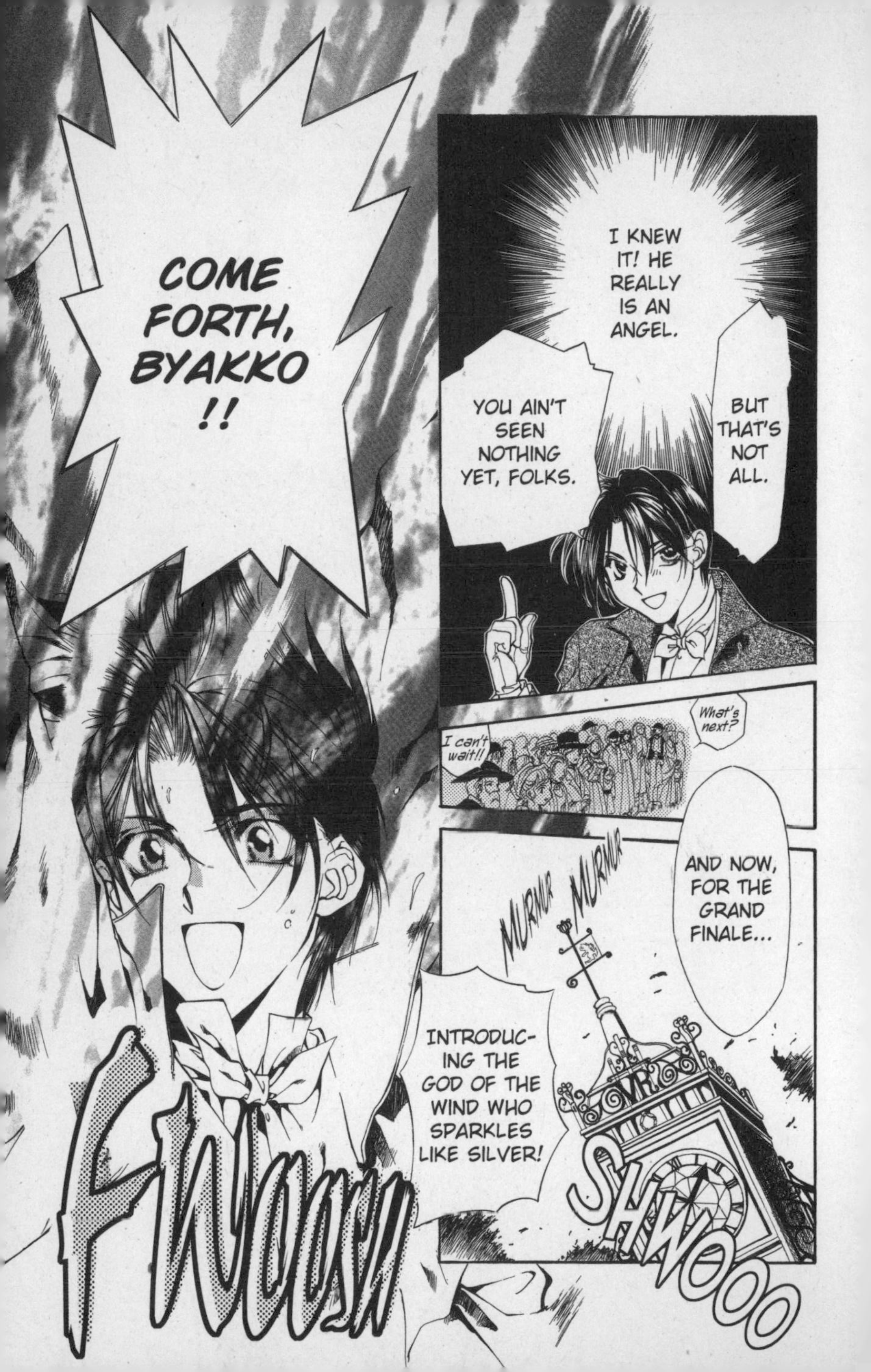
I KNEW IT! HE REALLY IS AN ANGEL.
BUT THAT'S NOT ALL.
YOU AIN'T SEEN NOTHING YET, FOLKS.
What's next?
I can't wait!!
AND NOW, FOR THE GRAND FINALE...
MURMUR MURMUR
INTRODUCING THE GOD OF THE WIND WHO SPARKLES LIKE SILVER!
SHWOOO
COME FORTH, BYAKKO!!
FWOOSH

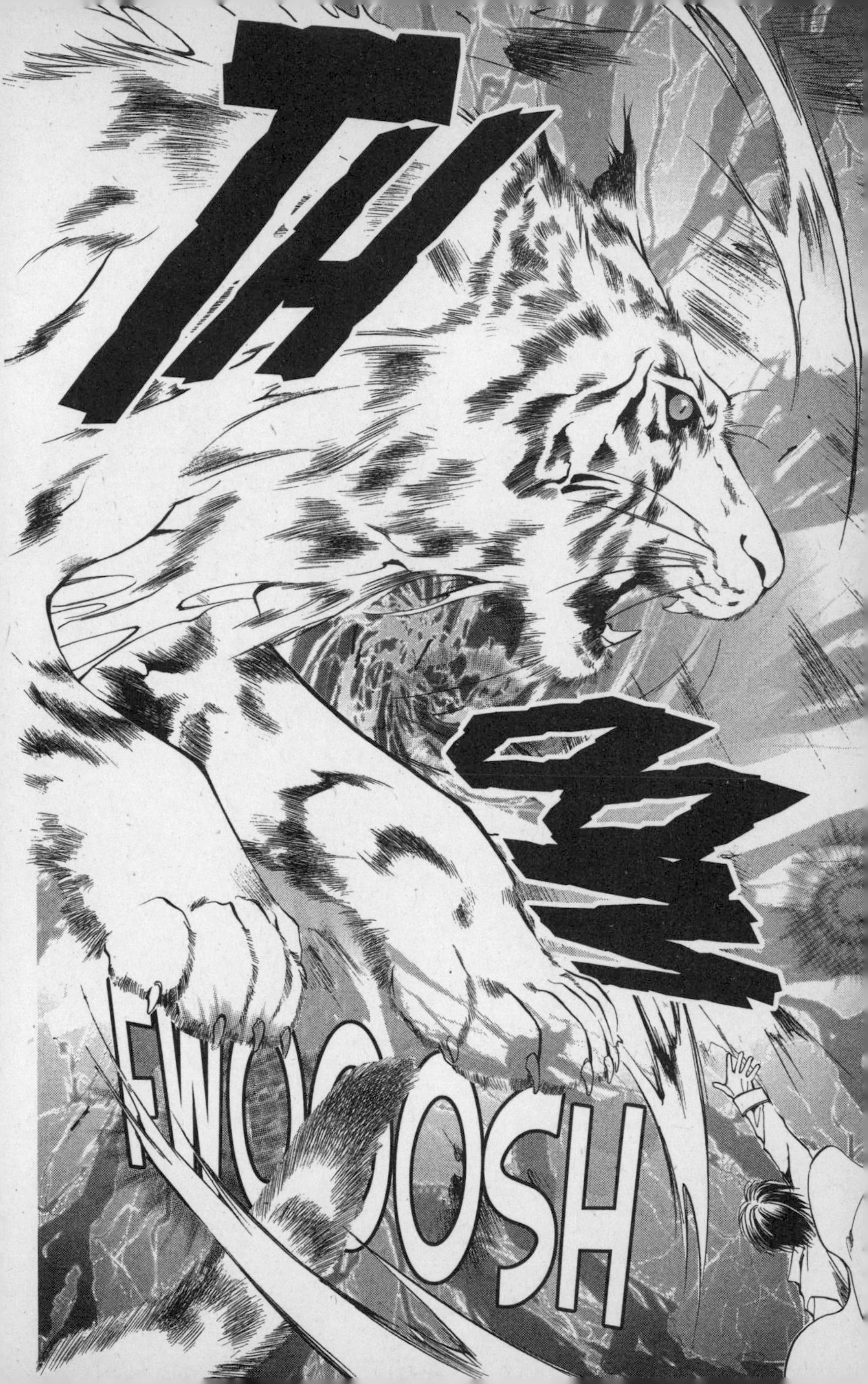
TH
FWOOSH

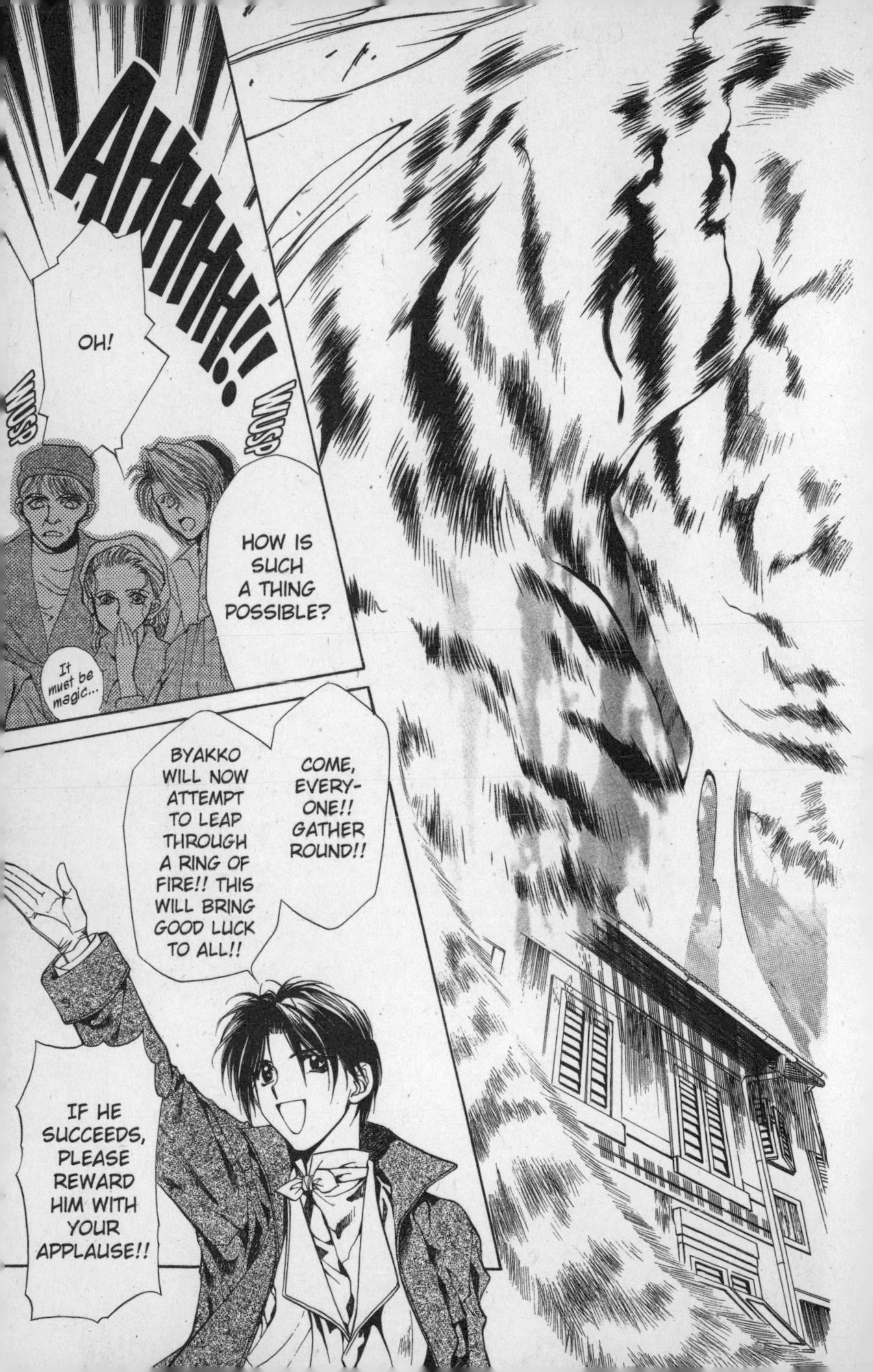
AHHHH!!
WUSP
HOW IS SUCH A THING POSSIBLE?
OH!
WUSP
It must be magic...
COME, EVERYONE!! GATHER ROUND!!
BYAKKO WILL NOW ATTEMPT TO LEAP THROUGH A RING OF FIRE!! THIS WILL BRING GOOD LUCK TO ALL!!
IF HE SUCCEEDS, PLEASE REWARD HIM WITH YOUR APPLAUSE!!

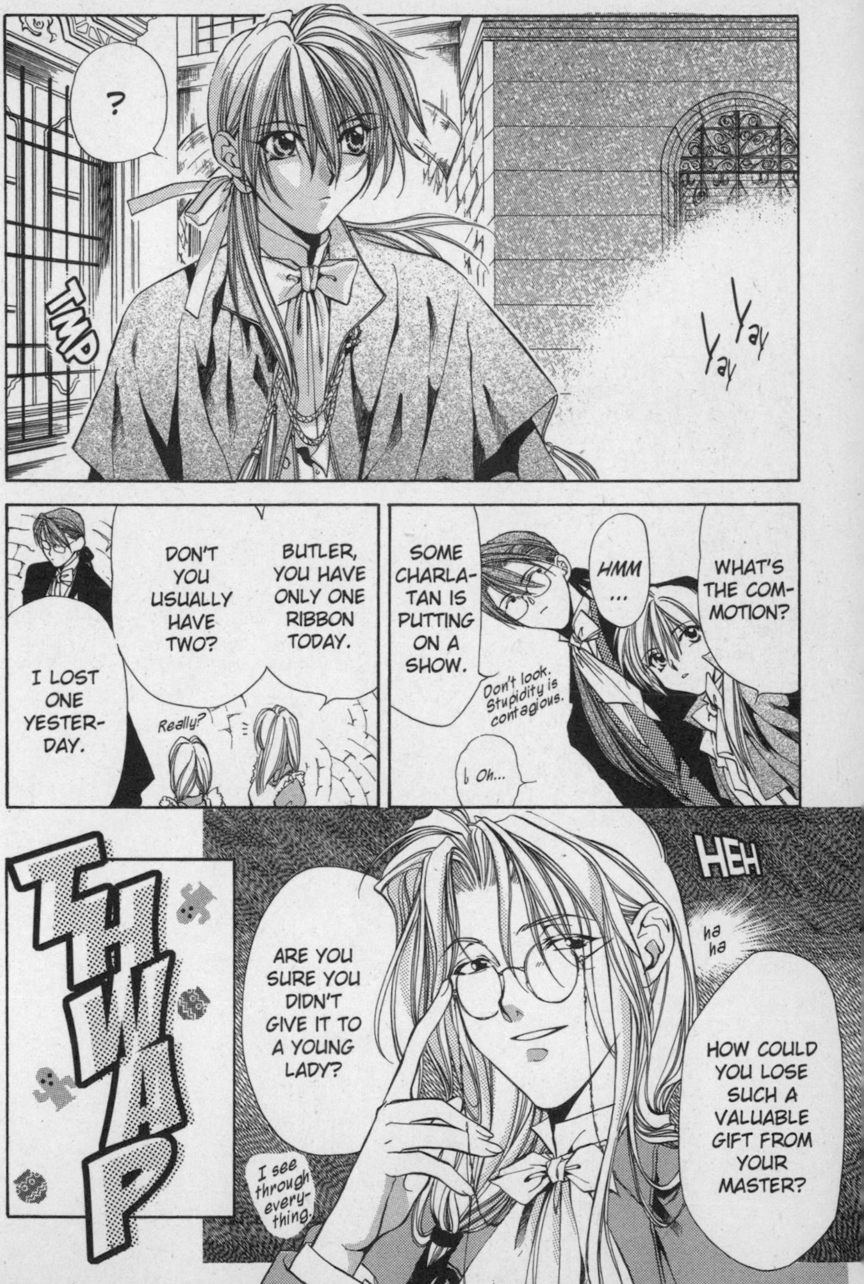
Yay Yay
?
TMP
WHAT'S THE COMMOTION?
HMM...
SOME CHARLATAN IS PUTTING ON A SHOW.
Don't look. Stupidity is contagious.
Oh...
BUTLER, YOU HAVE ONLY ONE RIBBON TODAY.
DON'T YOU USUALLY HAVE TWO?
Really?
I LOST ONE YESTERDAY.
HEH
ha ha
HOW COULD YOU LOSE SUCH A VALUABLE GIFT FROM YOUR MASTER?
ARE YOU SURE YOU DIDN'T GIVE IT TO A YOUNG LADY?
I see through everything.
THWAP

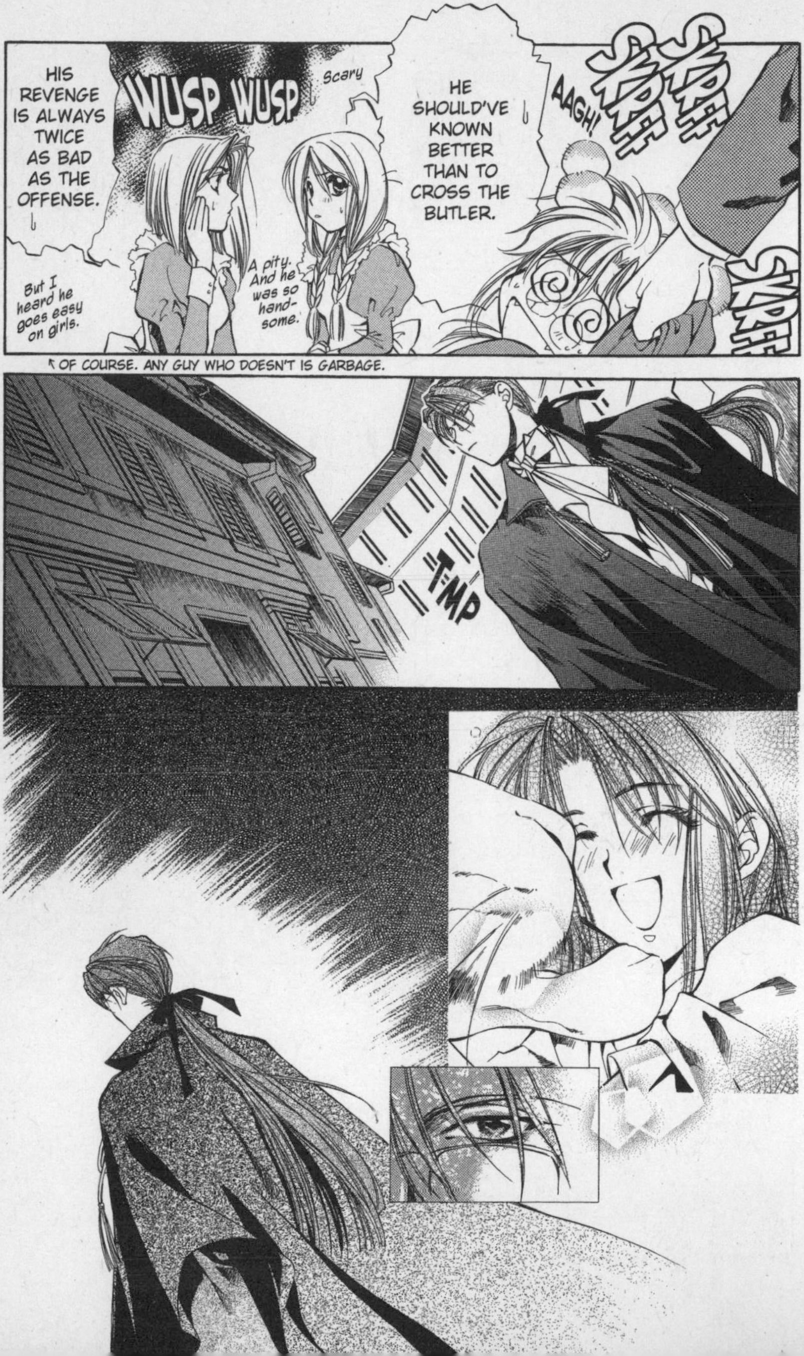
SKREE SKREE
AAGH!
HE SHOULD'VE KNOWN BETTER THAN TO CROSS THE BUTLER.
SKREE
Scary
WUSP WUSP
A pity. And he was so handsome.
HIS REVENGE IS ALWAYS TWICE AS BAD AS THE OFFENSE.
But I heard he goes easy on girls.
OF COURSE. ANY GUY WHO DOESN'T IS GARBAGE.
TMP

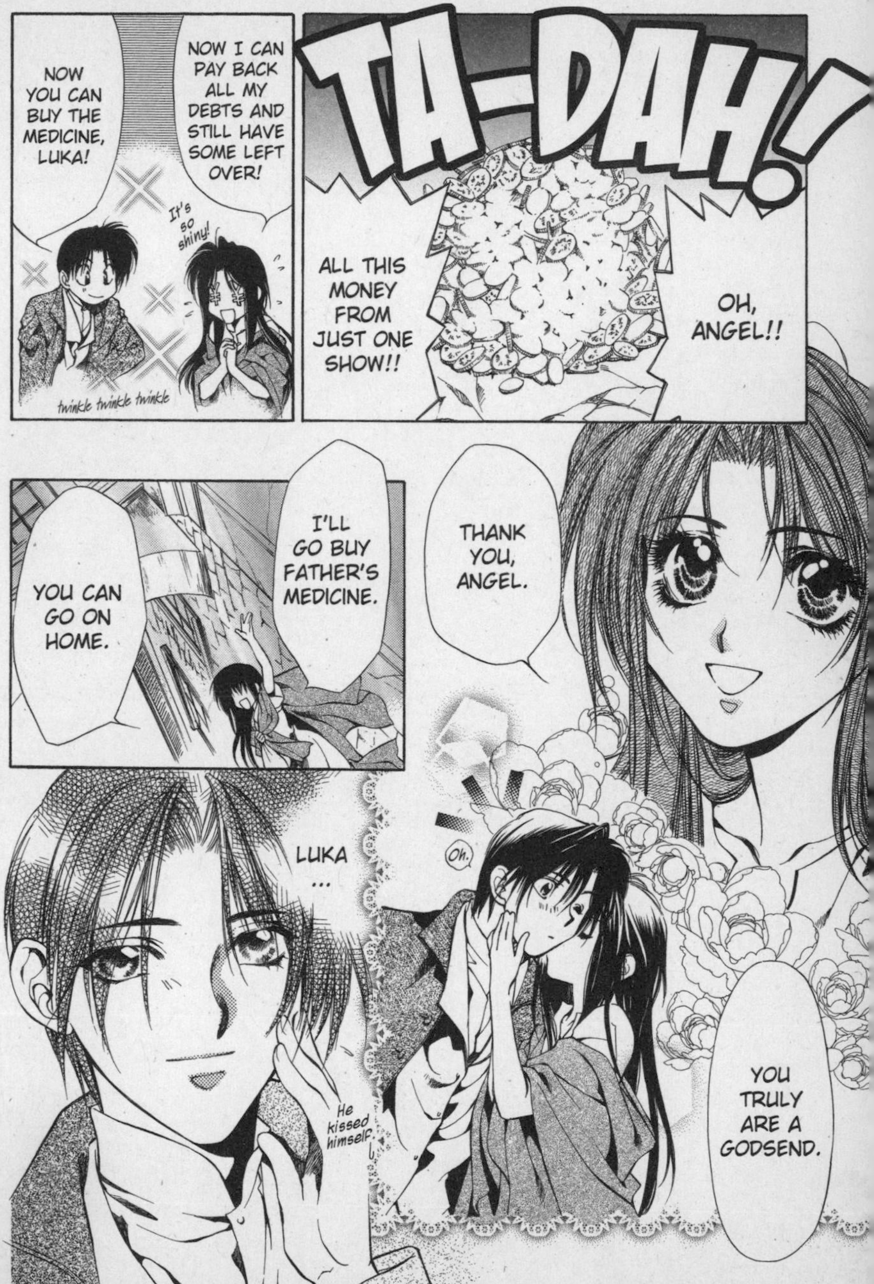
TA-DAH!
OH, ANGEL!!
ALL THIS MONEY FROM JUST ONE SHOW!!
NOW I CAN PAY BACK ALL MY DEBTS AND STILL HAVE SOME LEFT OVER!
NOW YOU CAN BUY THE MEDICINE, LUKA!
It's so shiny!
twinkle twinkle twinkle
THANK YOU, ANGEL.
YOU TRULY ARE A GODSEND.
I'LL GO BUY FATHER'S MEDICINE.
YOU CAN GO ON HOME.
LUKA ...
Oh.
He kissed himself.

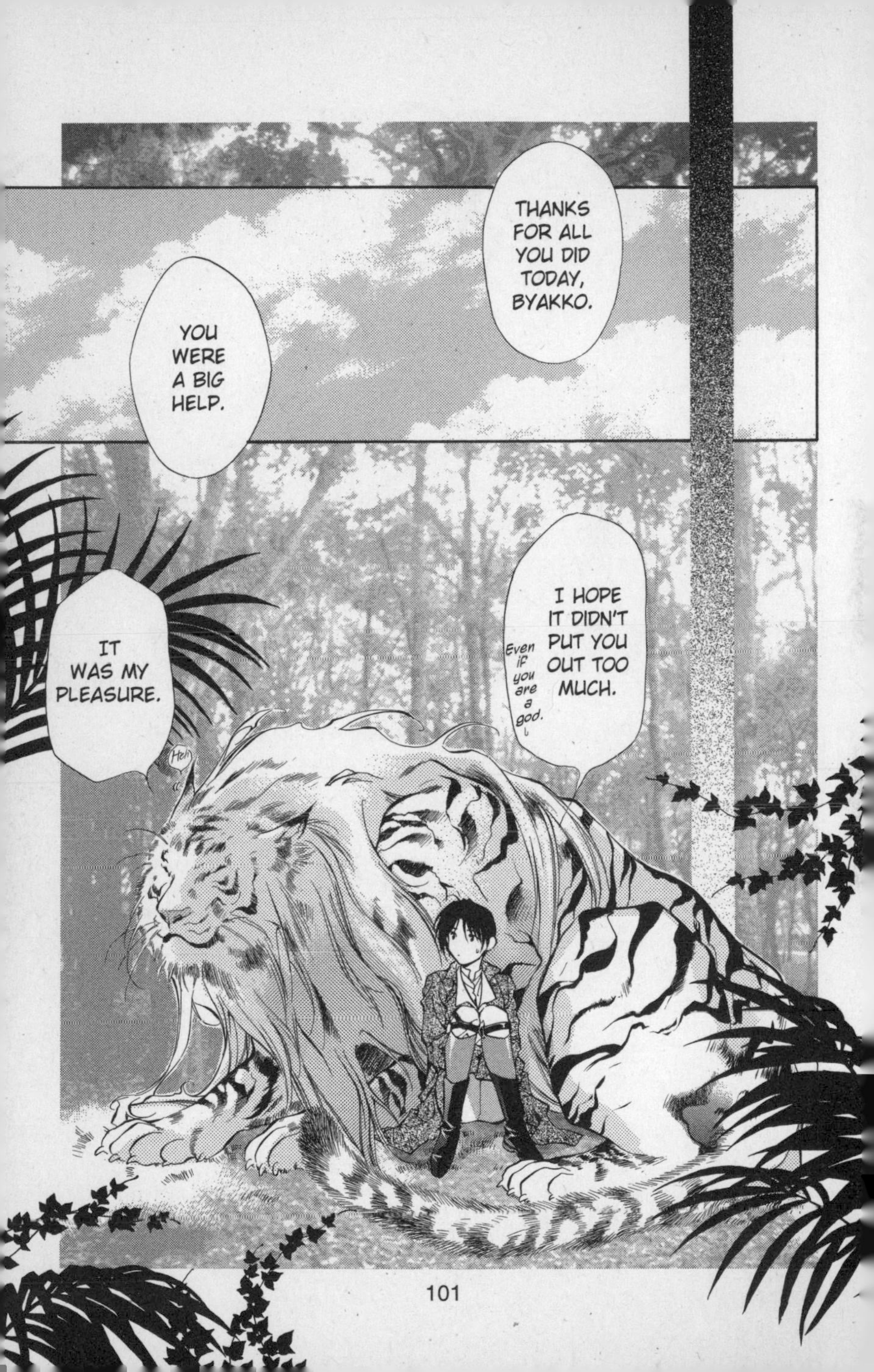
THANKS FOR ALL YOU DID TODAY, BYAKKO.
YOU WERE A BIG HELP.
I HOPE IT DIDN'T PUT YOU OUT TOO MUCH.
Even if you are a god.
IT WAS MY PLEASURE.
Heh

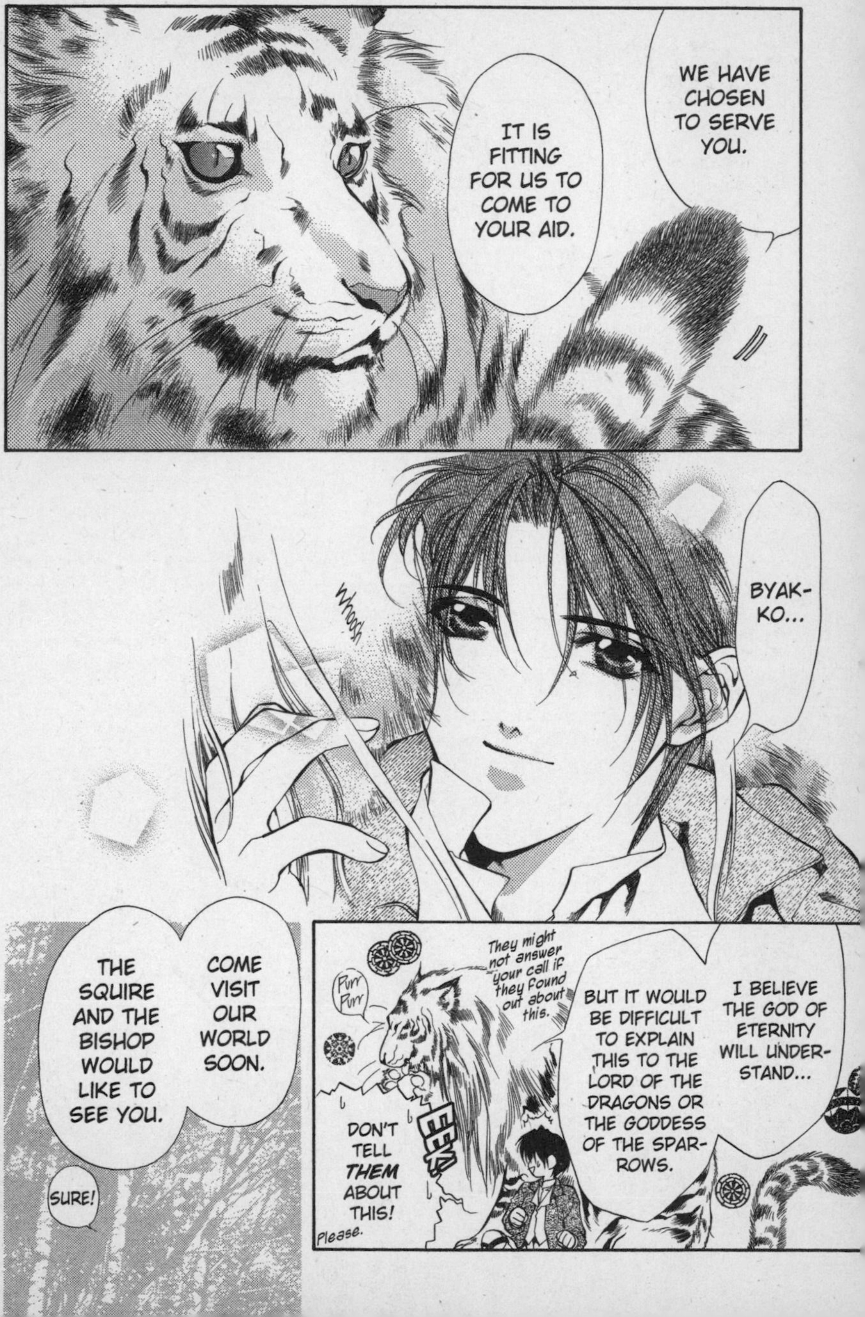
WE HAVE CHOSEN TO SERVE YOU.
IT IS FITTING FOR US TO COME TO YOUR AID.
BYAK-KO...
whoosh
I BELIEVE THE GOD OF ETERNITY WILL UNDER-STAND...
BUT IT WOULD BE DIFFICULT TO EXPLAIN THIS TO THE LORD OF THE DRAGONS OR THE GODDESS OF THE SPAR-ROWS.
They might not answer your call if they found out about this.
Purr Purr
EEK!
DON'T TELL THEM ABOUT THIS!
Please.
COME VISIT OUR WORLD SOON.
THE SQUIRE AND THE BISHOP WOULD LIKE TO SEE YOU.
SURE!

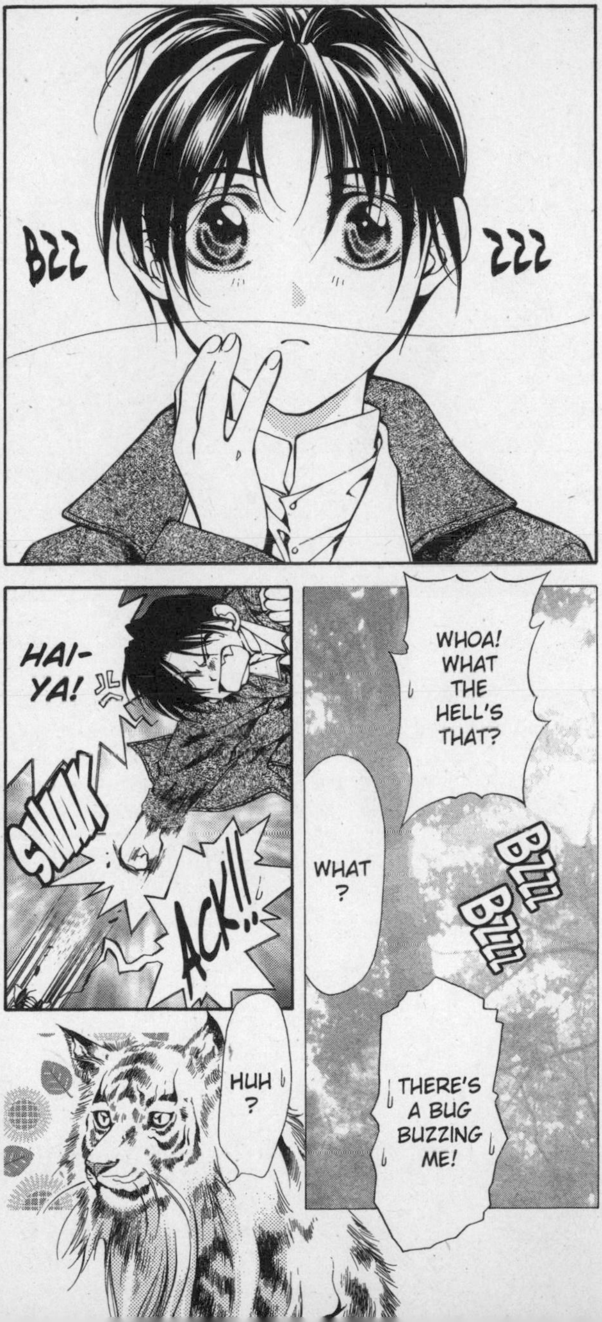
BZZ
ZZZ
WHOA! WHAT THE HELL'S THAT?
BZZZ BZZZ
WHAT?
THERE'S A BUG BUZZING ME!
HAI-YA!
SWAK
ACK!!
HUH?

I've got nothing ...

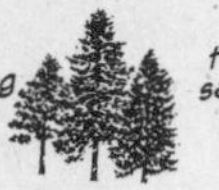

to say.

Lately, well...
ever since
I started writing
"Descendants of
Darkness," I've been
so busy I don't even
have time to go out.
I'm pretty stressed.
I don't have time to
read or watch TV,
so I have no idea
what's going on
in the world.
As a result,
I have nothing to
write about here.
Really. Nothing.
What should I write?

HMM, WAIT!
I'LL DO IT NEXT TIME!
(TO BE CONTINUED)

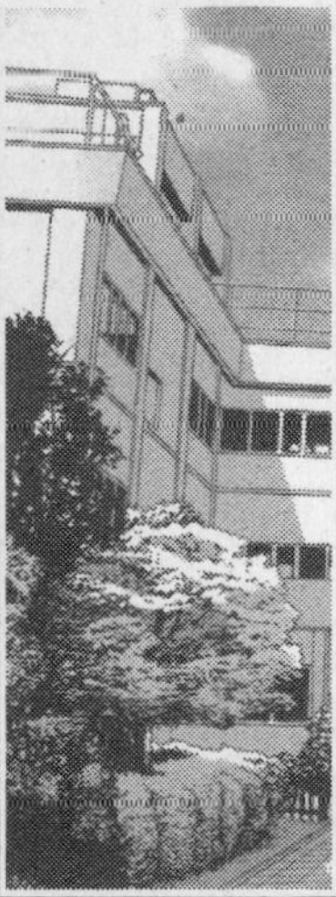

SURE...(HA!)

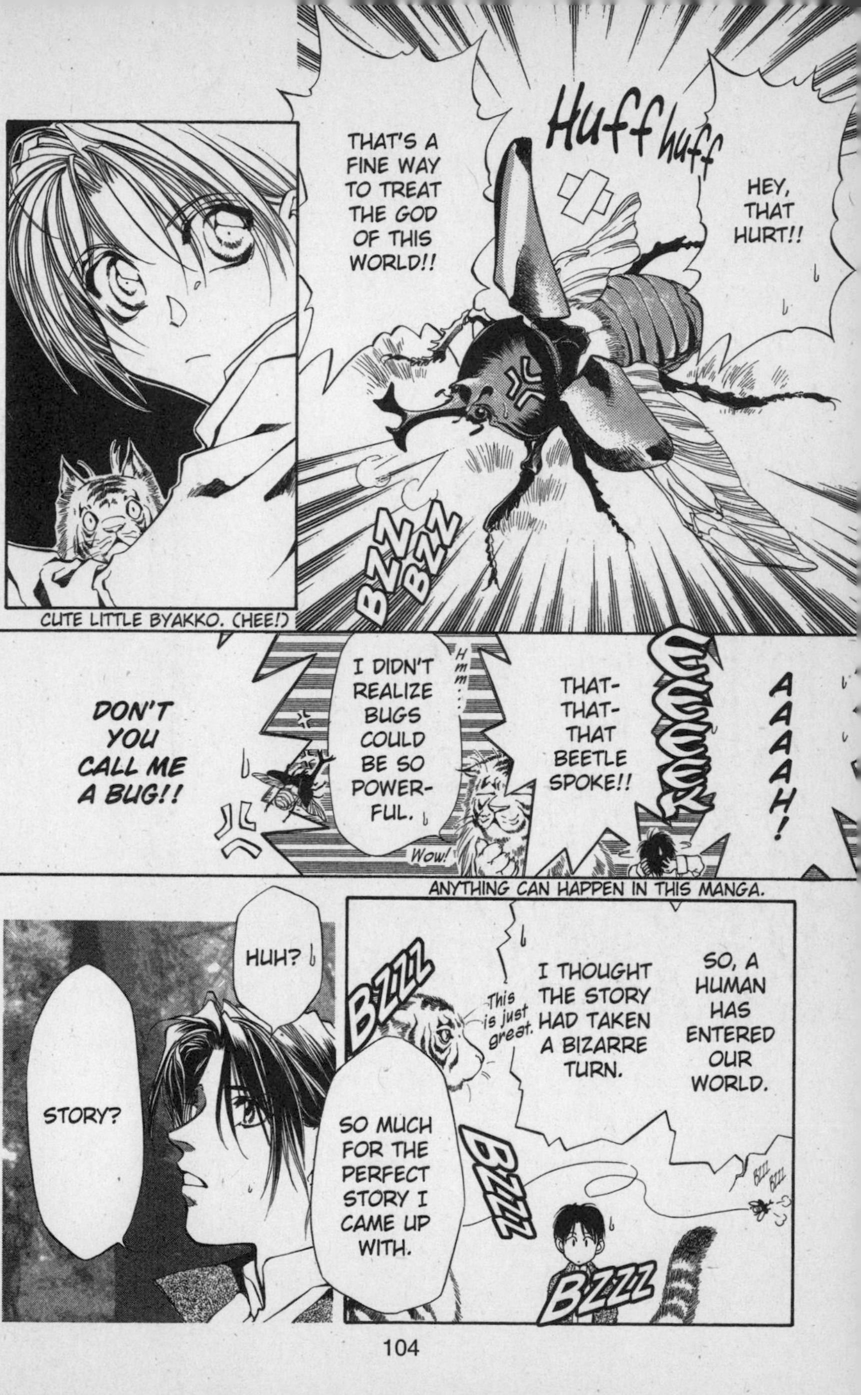
Huff huff
HEY, THAT HURT!!
THAT'S A FINE WAY TO TREAT THE GOD OF THIS WORLD!!
BZZZ BZZZ
CUTE LITTLE BYAKKO. (CHEE!)
AAAAAH!
THAT-THAT-THAT BEETLE SPOKE!!
Wow!
I DIDN'T REALIZE BUGS COULD BE SO POWERFUL.
Hmm...
DON'T YOU CALL ME A BUG!!
ANYTHING CAN HAPPEN IN THIS MANGA.
SO, A HUMAN HAS ENTERED OUR WORLD.
I THOUGHT THE STORY HAD TAKEN A BIZARRE TURN.
This is just great.
BZZZ
SO MUCH FOR THE PERFECT STORY I CAME UP WITH.
BZZZ
BZZZ
BZZZ BZZZ
HUH?
STORY?

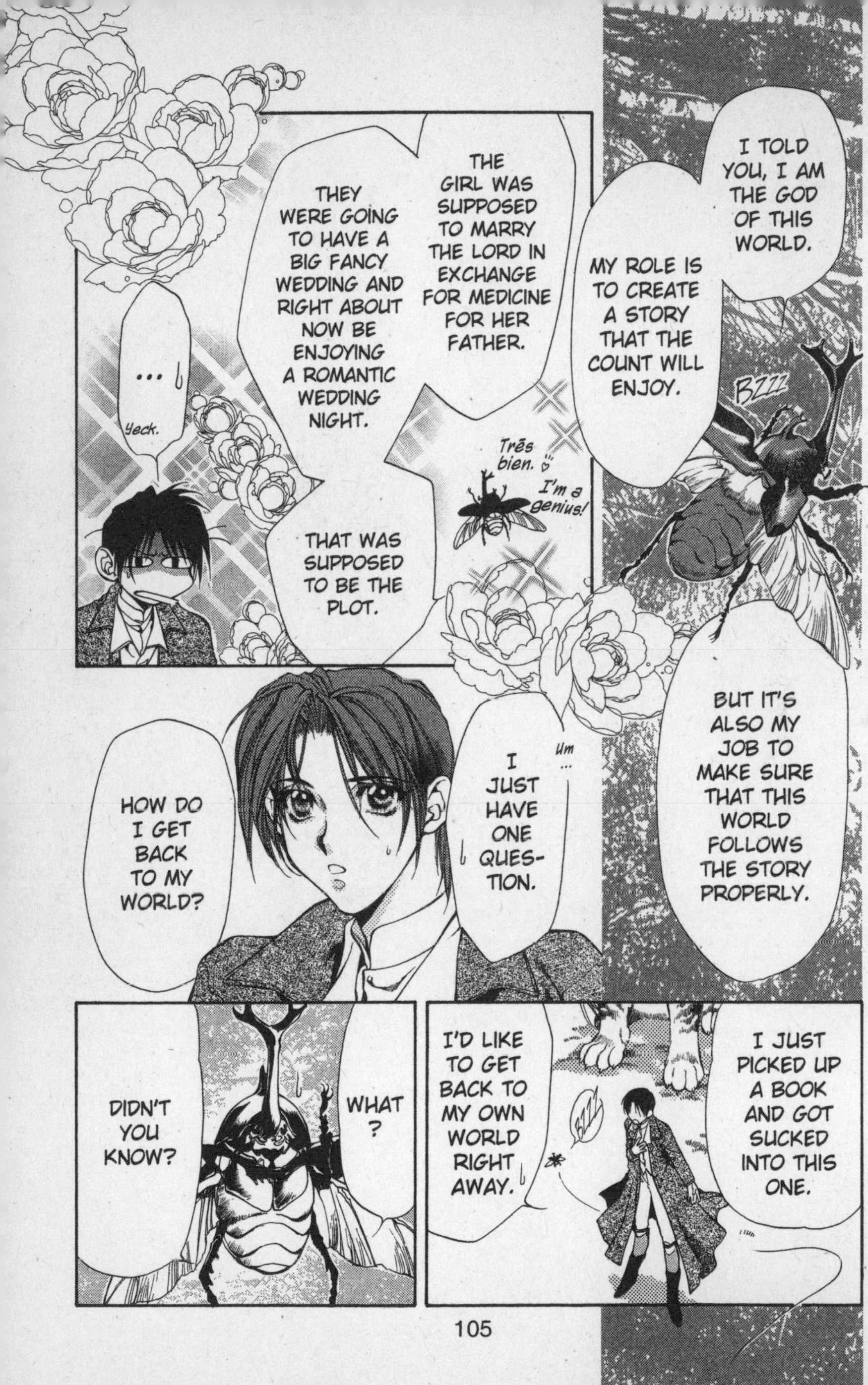
I TOLD YOU, I AM THE GOD OF THIS WORLD.
MY ROLE IS TO CREATE A STORY THAT THE COUNT WILL ENJOY.
BZZZ
THE GIRL WAS SUPPOSED TO MARRY THE LORD IN EXCHANGE FOR MEDICINE FOR HER FATHER.
THEY WERE GOING TO HAVE A BIG FANCY WEDDING AND RIGHT ABOUT NOW BE ENJOYING A ROMANTIC WEDDING NIGHT.
Três bien.
I'm a genius!
THAT WAS SUPPOSED TO BE THE PLOT.
...
Yeck.
BUT IT'S ALSO MY JOB TO MAKE SURE THAT THIS WORLD FOLLOWS THE STORY PROPERLY.
Um ...
I JUST HAVE ONE QUES-TION.
HOW DO I GET BACK TO MY WORLD?
I JUST PICKED UP A BOOK AND GOT SUCKED INTO THIS ONE.
I'D LIKE TO GET BACK TO MY OWN WORLD RIGHT AWAY.
WHAT ?
DIDN'T YOU KNOW?

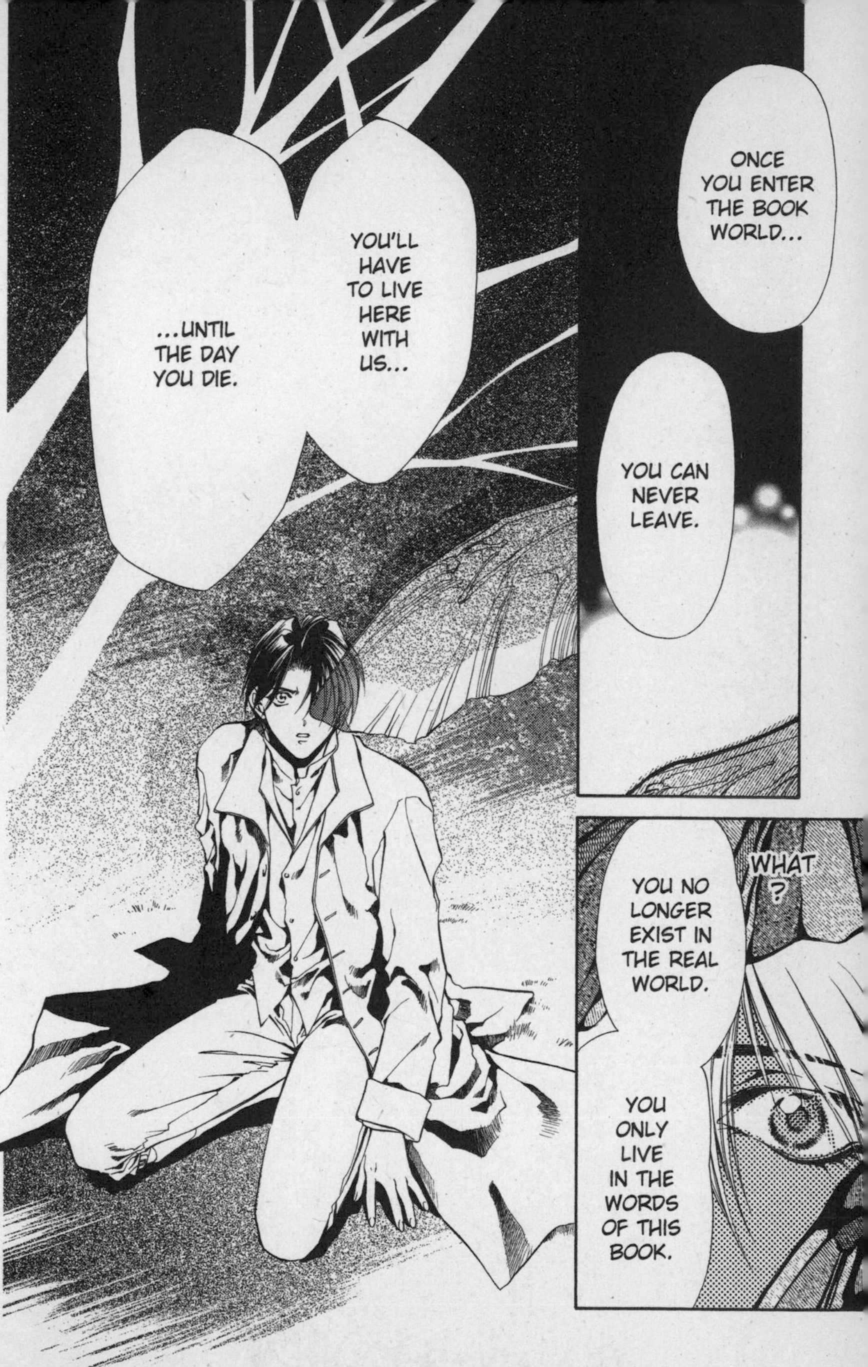
ONCE YOU ENTER THE BOOK WORLD...
YOU CAN NEVER LEAVE.
WHAT?
YOU NO LONGER EXIST IN THE REAL WORLD.
YOU ONLY LIVE IN THE WORDS OF THIS BOOK.
YOU'LL HAVE TO LIVE HERE WITH US...
...UNTIL THE DAY YOU DIE.

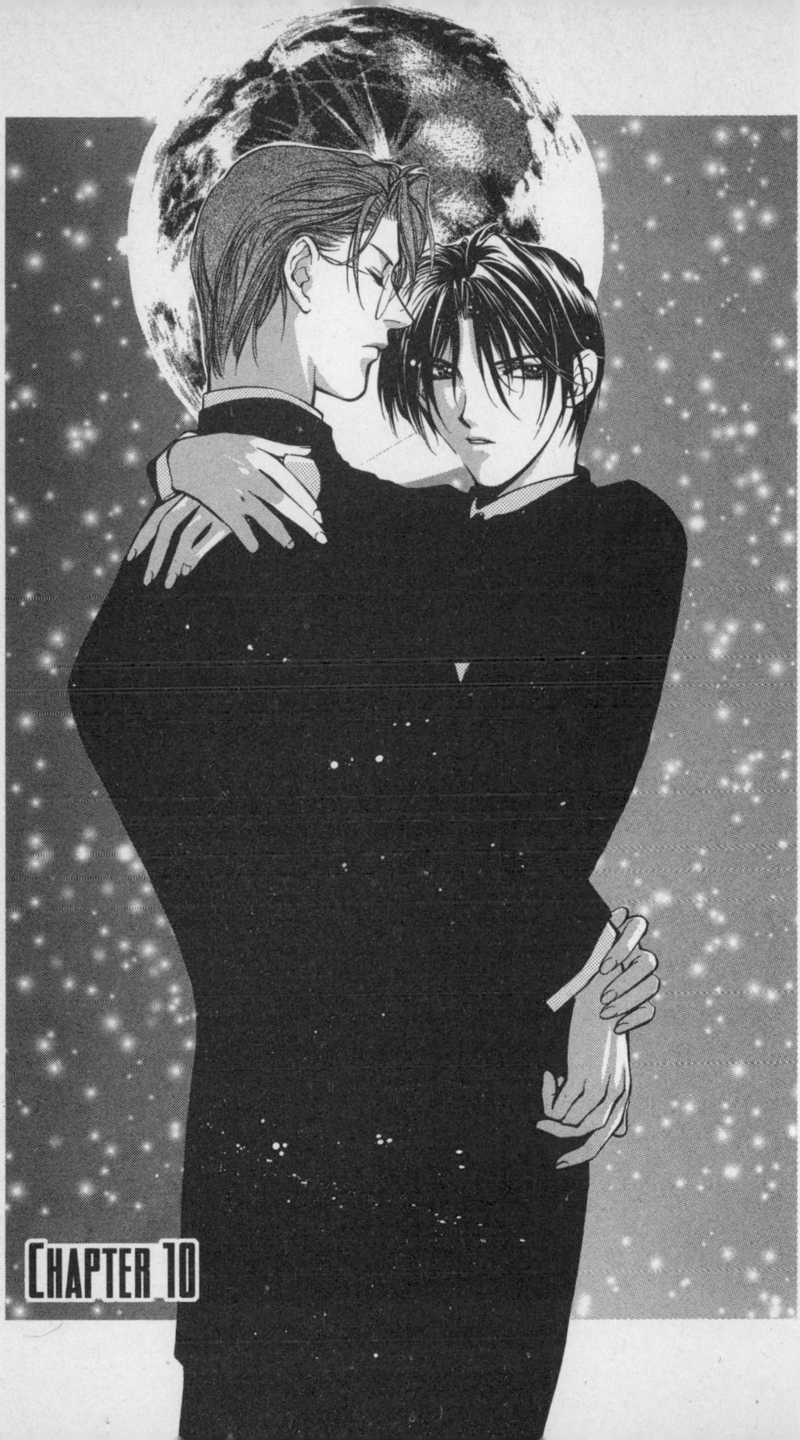
CHAPTER 10

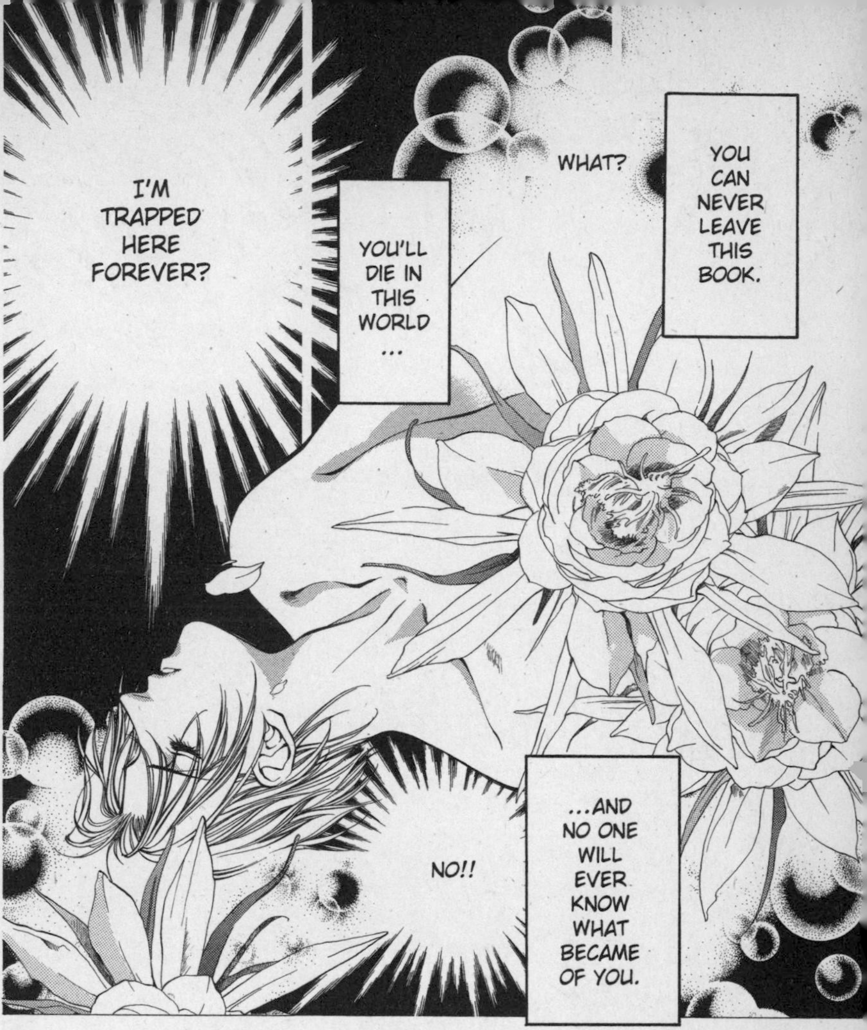
YOU CAN NEVER LEAVE THIS BOOK.
WHAT?
YOU'LL DIE IN THIS WORLD ...
I'M TRAPPED HERE FOREVER?
...AND NO ONE WILL EVER KNOW WHAT BECAME OF YOU.
NO!!

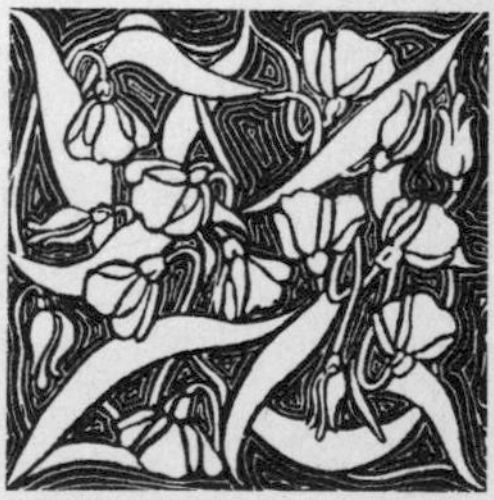

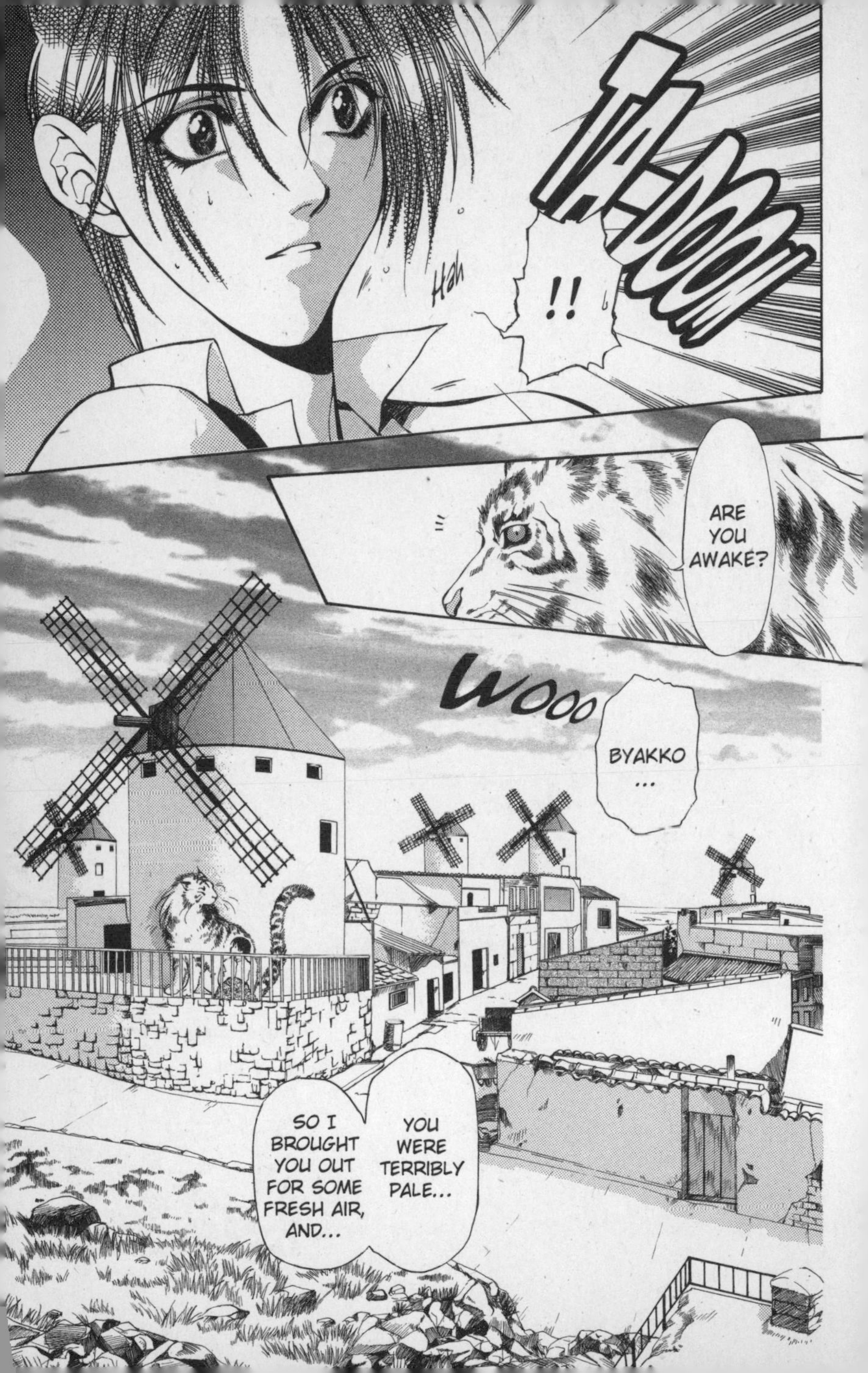
TA-DOOM
Hah
!!
ARE YOU AWAKE?
WOOO
BYAKKO ...
YOU WERE TERRIBLY PALE...
SO I BROUGHT YOU OUT FOR SOME FRESH AIR, AND...

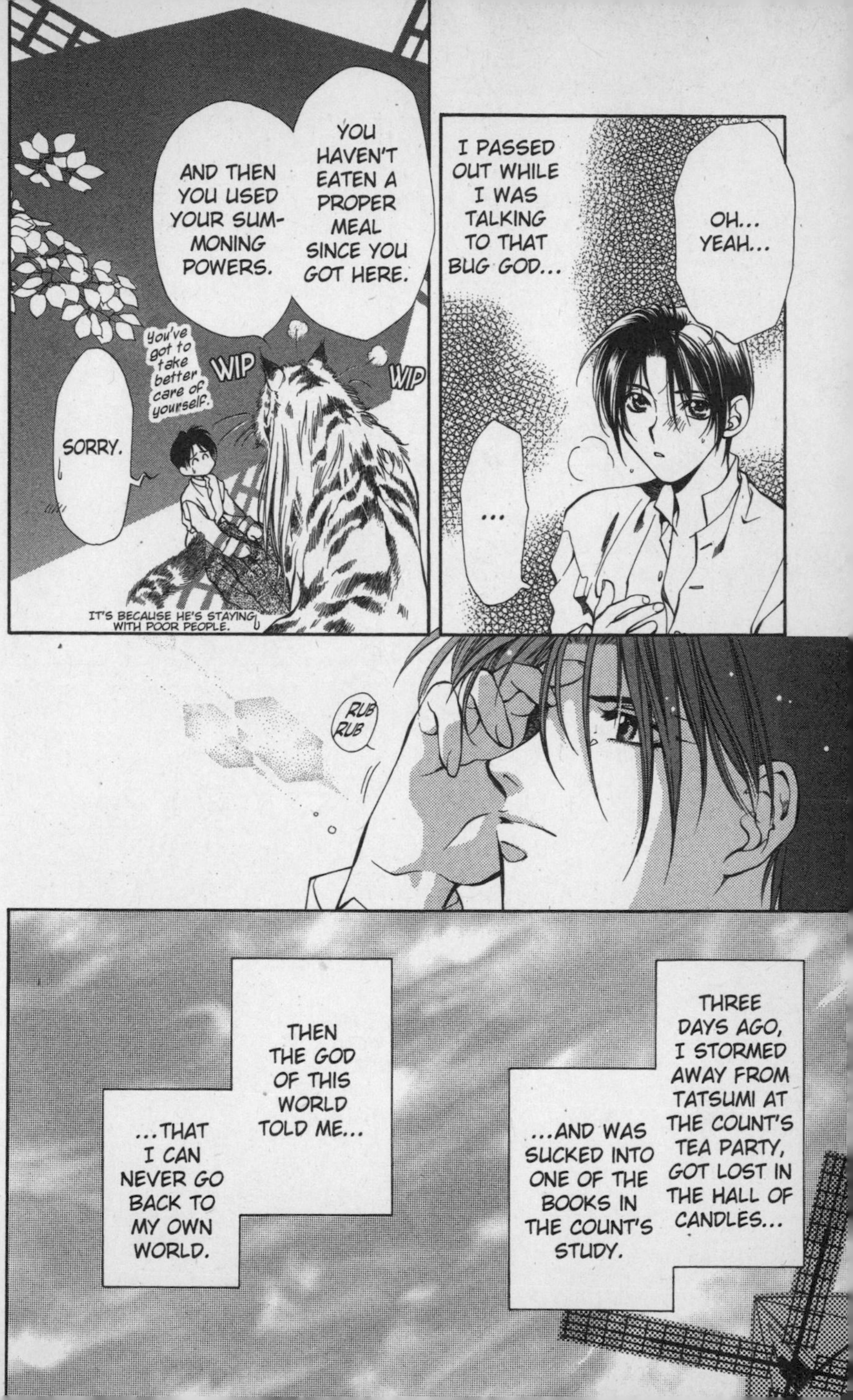
OH... YEAH...
I PASSED OUT WHILE I WAS TALKING TO THAT BUG GOD...
...
YOU HAVEN'T EATEN A PROPER MEAL SINCE YOU GOT HERE.
AND THEN YOU USED YOUR SUM-MONING POWERS.
WIP
WIP
You've got to take better care of yourself.
SORRY.
IT'S BECAUSE HE'S STAYING WITH POOR PEOPLE.
RUB RUB
THREE DAYS AGO, I STORMED AWAY FROM TATSUMI AT THE COUNT'S TEA PARTY, GOT LOST IN THE HALL OF CANDLES...
...AND WAS SUCKED INTO ONE OF THE BOOKS IN THE COUNT'S STUDY.
THEN THE GOD OF THIS WORLD TOLD ME...
...THAT I CAN NEVER GO BACK TO MY OWN WORLD.

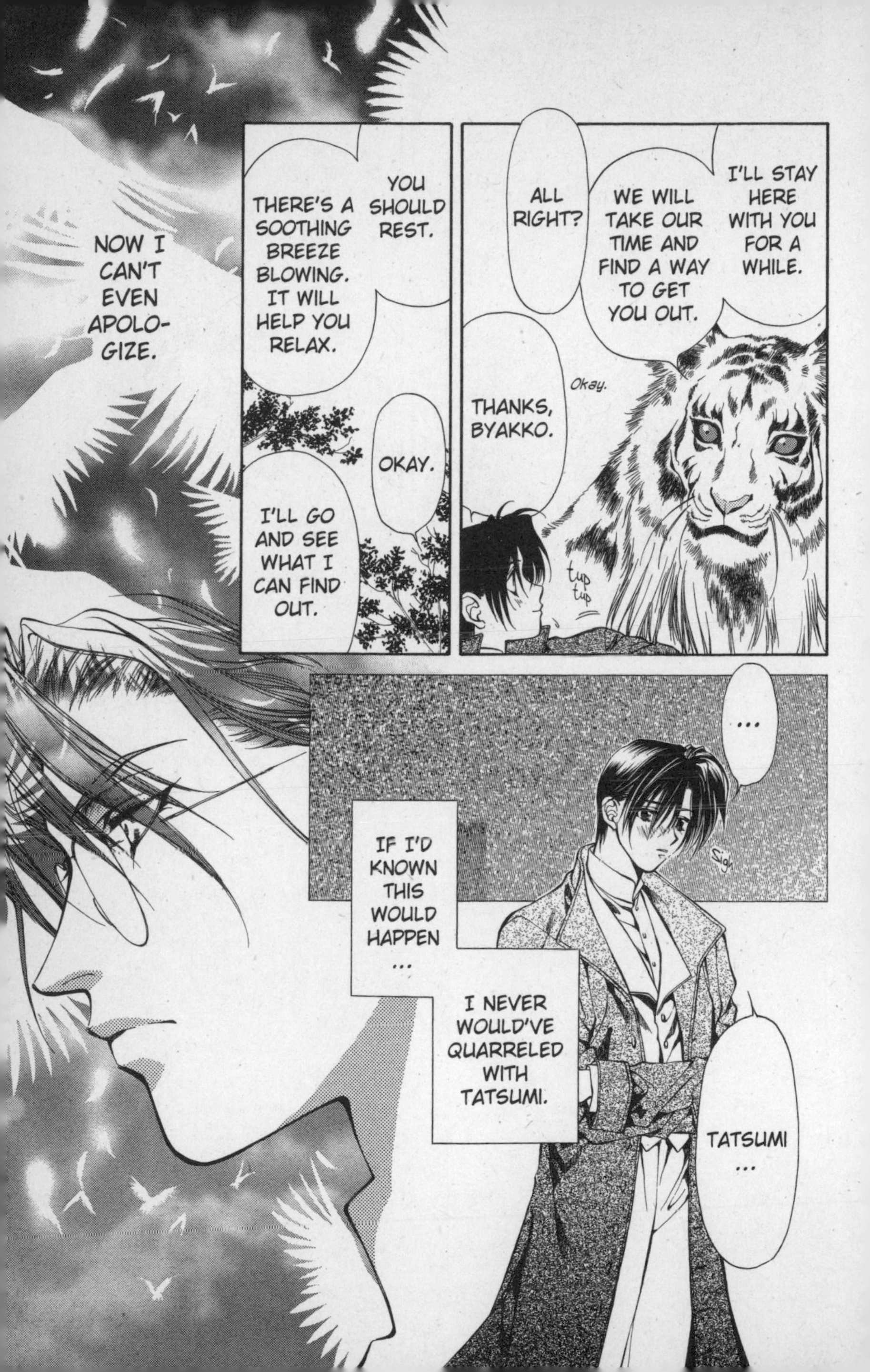
I'LL STAY HERE WITH YOU FOR A WHILE.
WE WILL TAKE OUR TIME AND FIND A WAY TO GET YOU OUT.
ALL RIGHT?
Okay.
THANKS, BYAKKO.
tup tup
YOU SHOULD REST.
THERE'S A SOOTHING BREEZE BLOWING. IT WILL HELP YOU RELAX.
OKAY.
I'LL GO AND SEE WHAT I CAN FIND OUT.
...
Sigh
IF I'D KNOWN THIS WOULD HAPPEN...
I NEVER WOULD'VE QUARRELED WITH TATSUMI.
TATSUMI...
NOW I CAN'T EVEN APOLOGIZE.

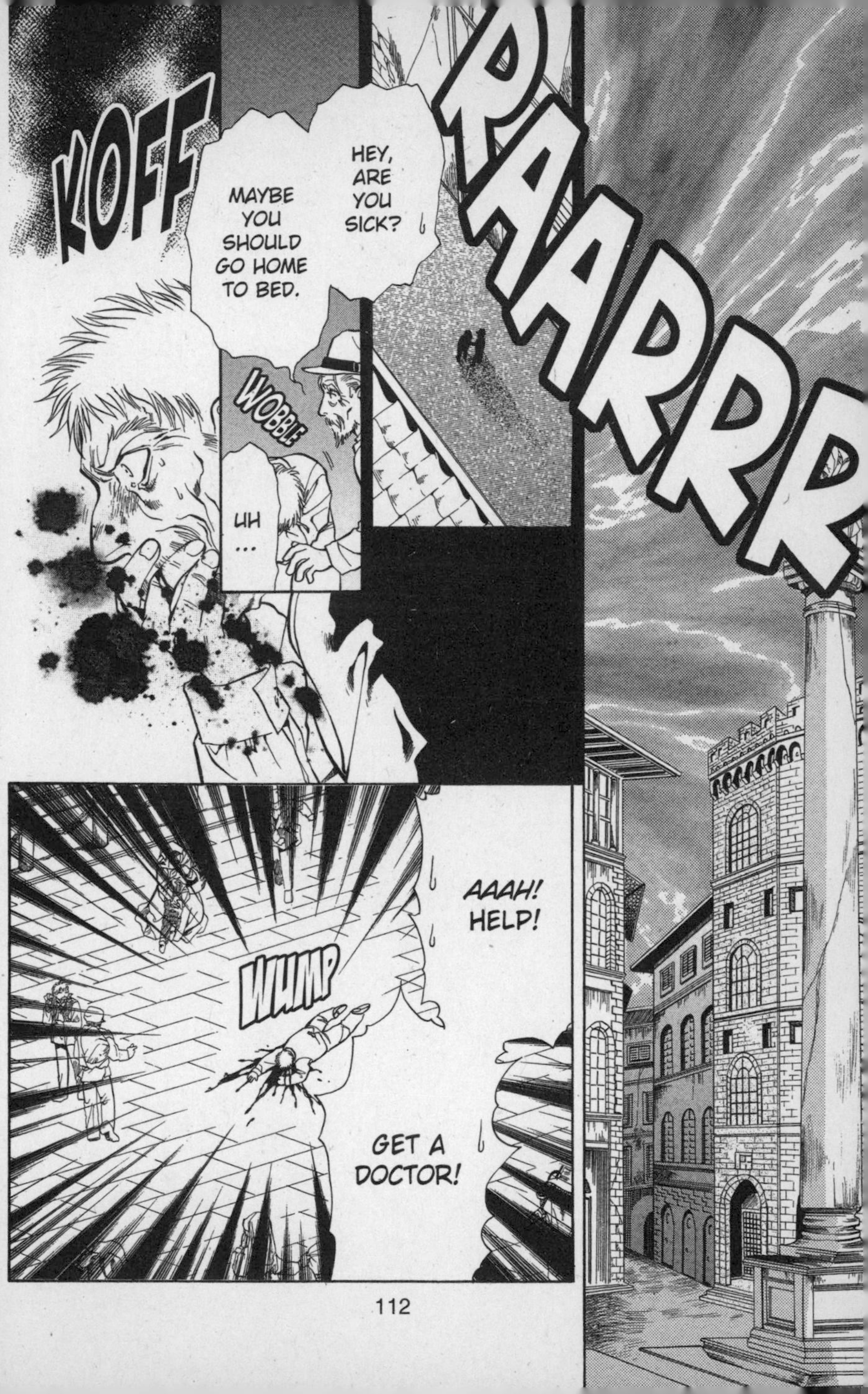
RAARRR
HEY, ARE YOU SICK?
MAYBE YOU SHOULD GO HOME TO BED.
KOFF
WOBBLE
UH ...
AAAH! HELP!
WHUMP
GET A DOCTOR!

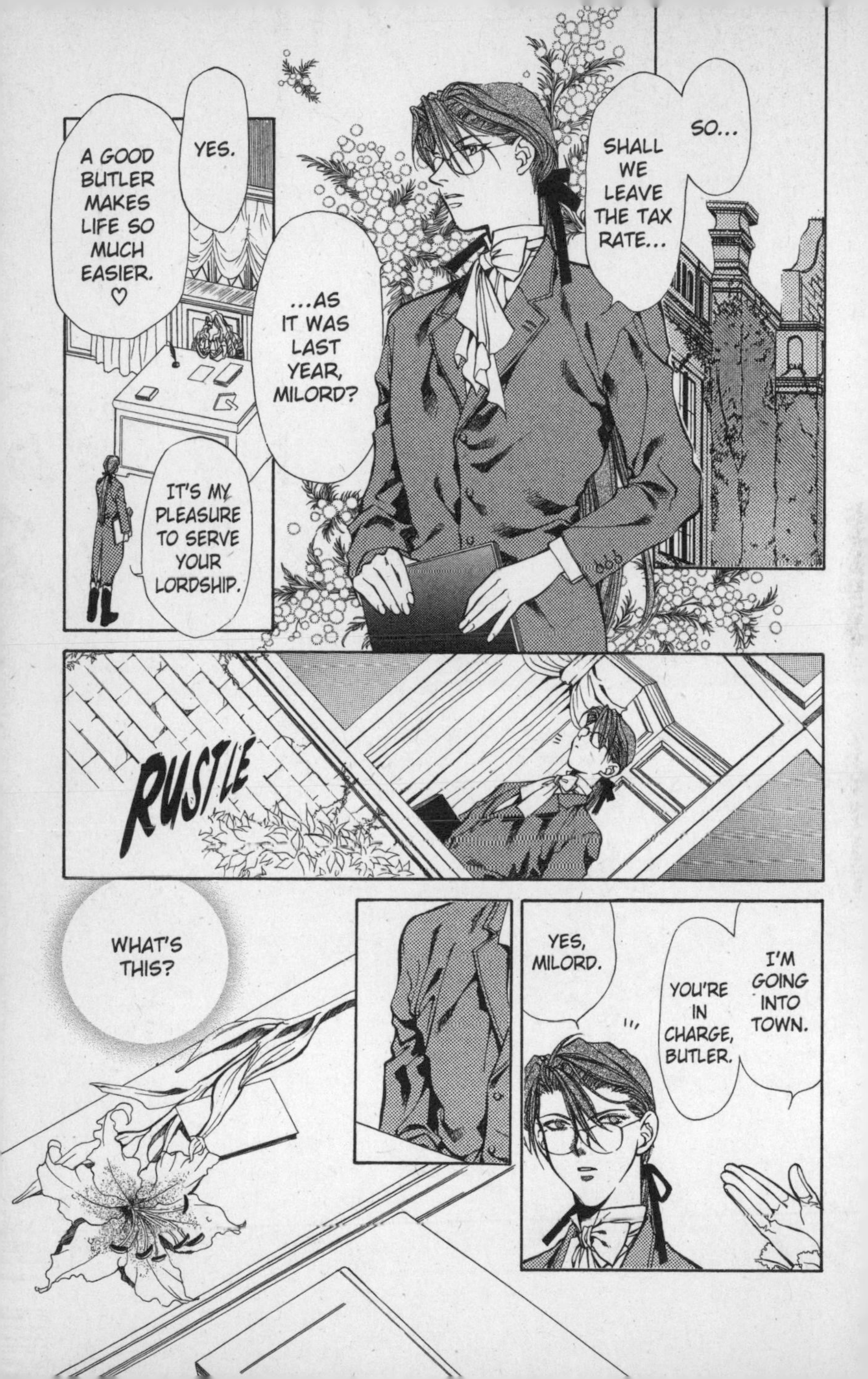
SO...
SHALL WE LEAVE THE TAX RATE...
...AS IT WAS LAST YEAR, MILORD?
YES.
A GOOD BUTLER MAKES LIFE SO MUCH EASIER. ♡
IT'S MY PLEASURE TO SERVE YOUR LORDSHIP.
RUSTLE
I'M GOING INTO TOWN.
YOU'RE IN CHARGE, BUTLER.
YES, MILORD.
WHAT'S THIS?

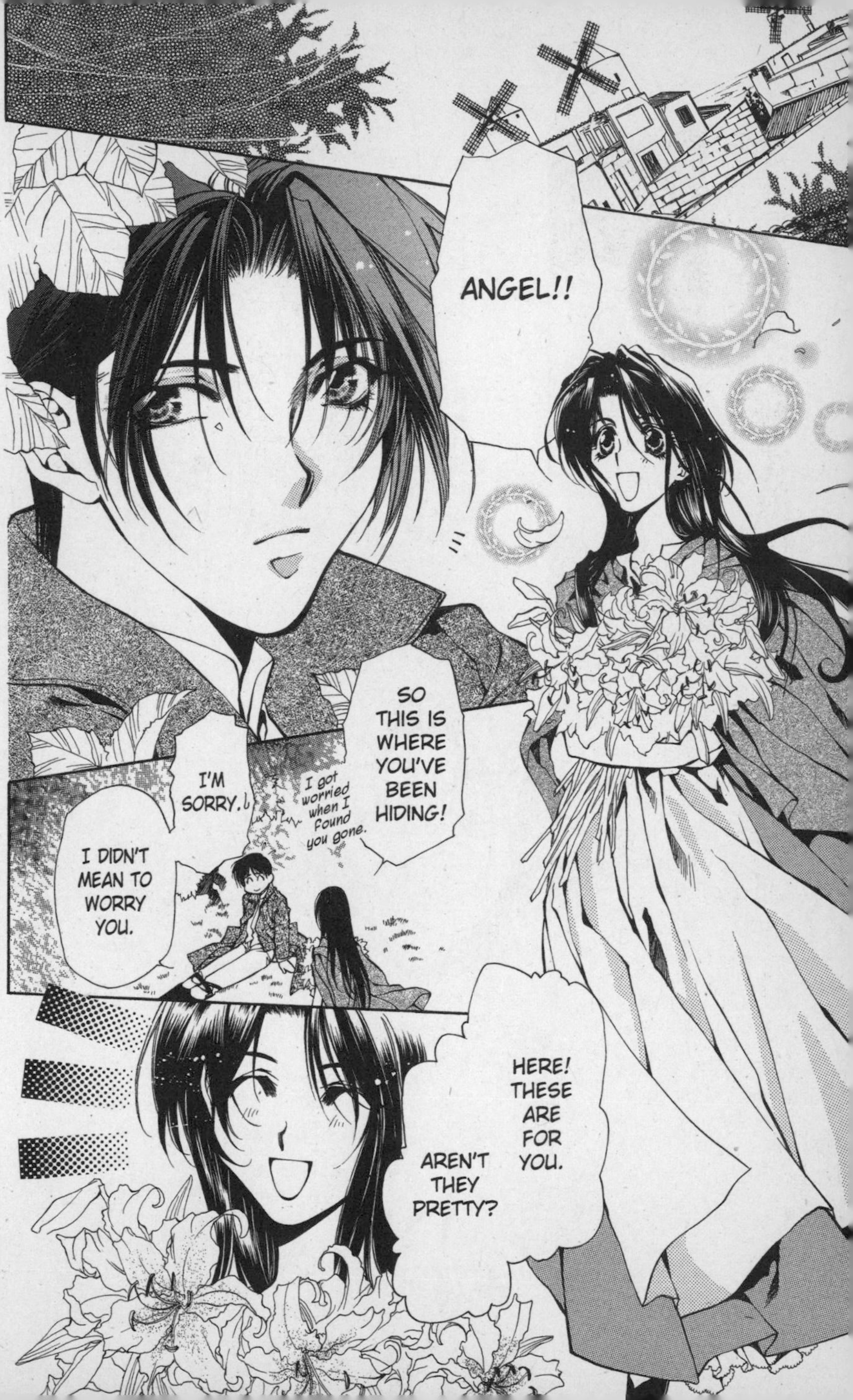
ANGEL!!
SO THIS IS WHERE YOU'VE BEEN HIDING!
I got worried when I found you gone.
I'M SORRY.
I DIDN'T MEAN TO WORRY YOU.
HERE! THESE ARE FOR YOU.
AREN'T THEY PRETTY?

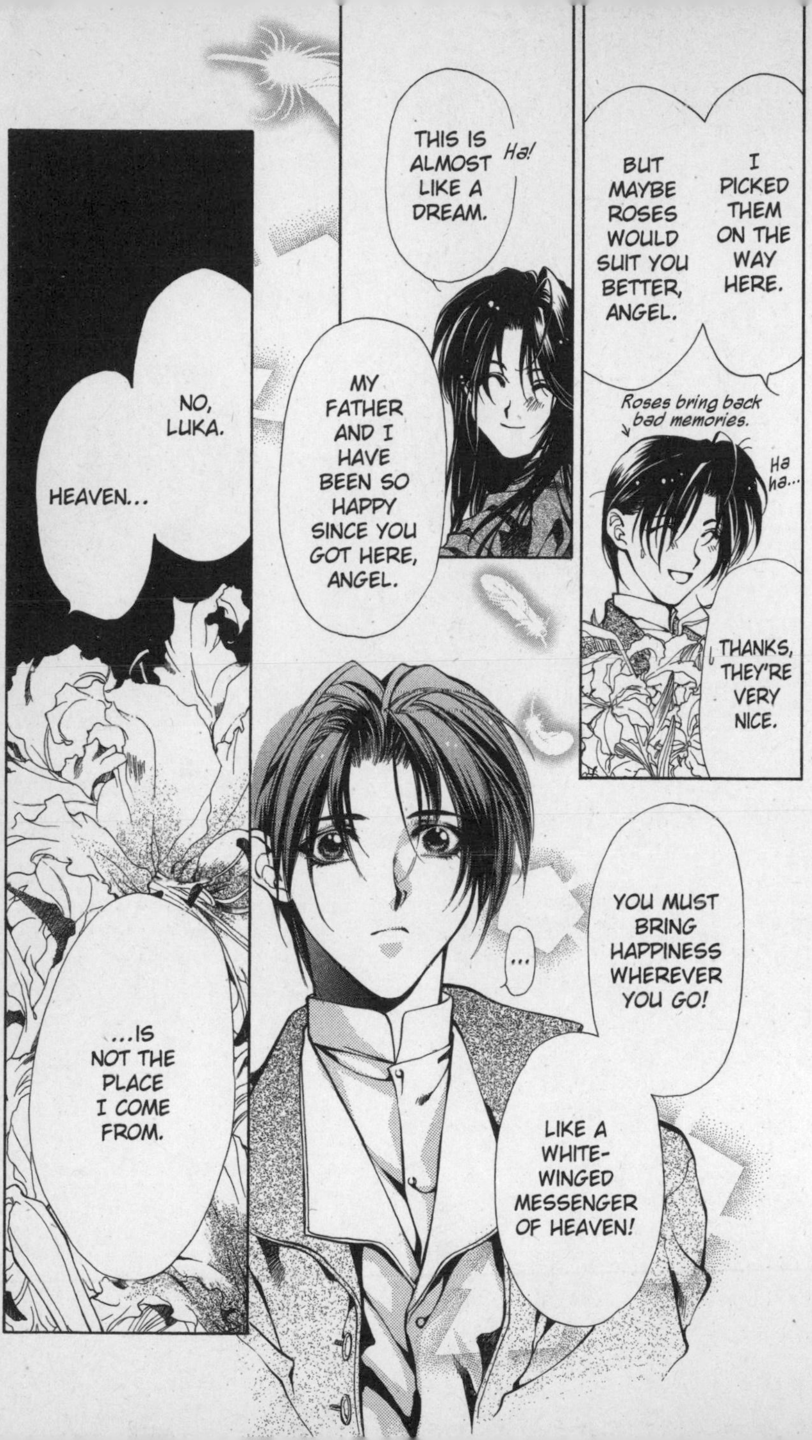
I PICKED THEM ON THE WAY HERE.
BUT MAYBE ROSES WOULD SUIT YOU BETTER, ANGEL.
Roses bring back bad memories.
Ha ha...
THANKS, THEY'RE VERY NICE.
Ha!
THIS IS ALMOST LIKE A DREAM.
MY FATHER AND I HAVE BEEN SO HAPPY SINCE YOU GOT HERE, ANGEL.
YOU MUST BRING HAPPINESS WHEREVER YOU GO!
LIKE A WHITE-WINGED MESSENGER OF HEAVEN!
...
NO, LUKA.
HEAVEN...
...IS NOT THE PLACE I COME FROM.

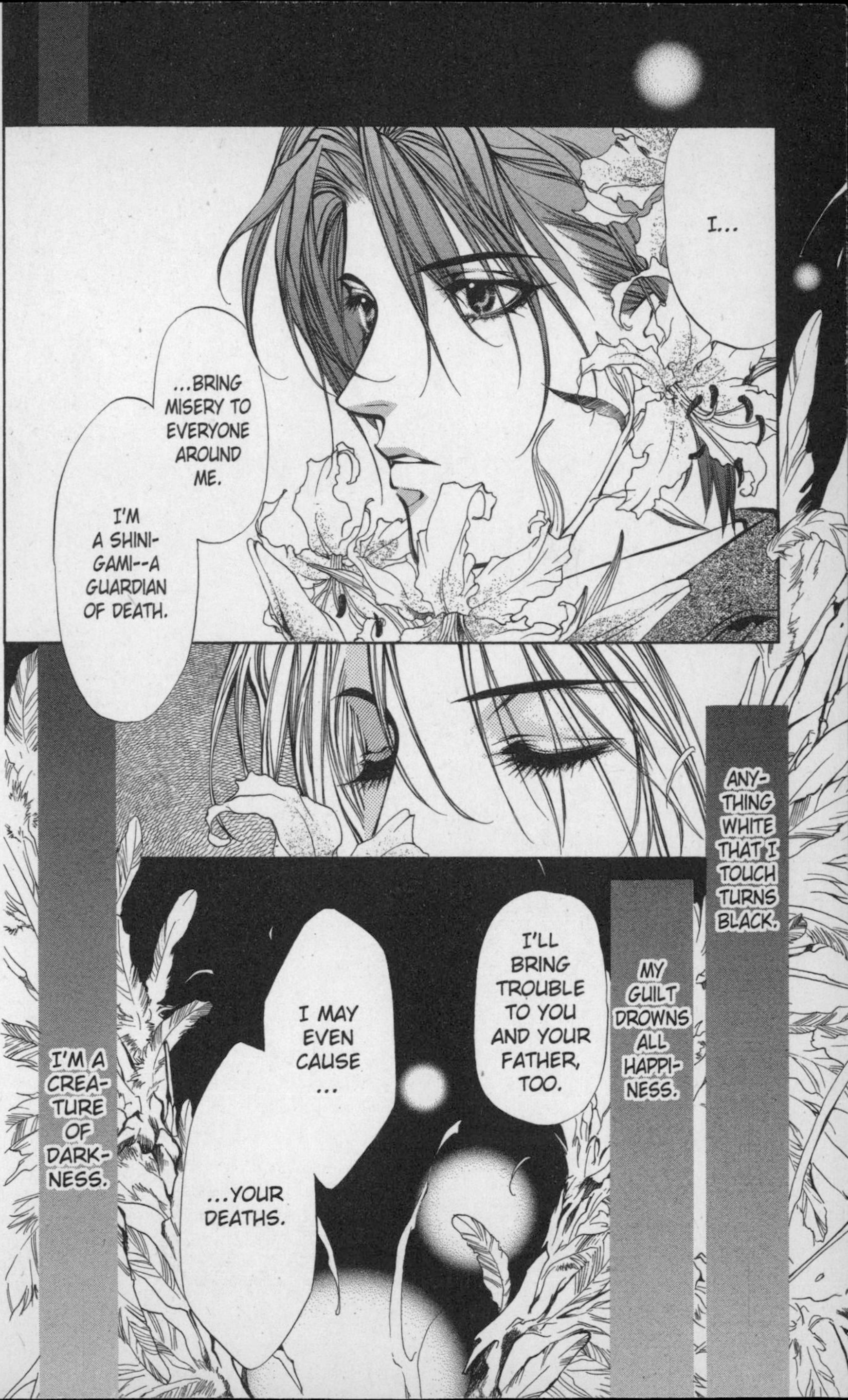
I...
...BRING MISERY TO EVERYONE AROUND ME.
I'M A SHINIGAMI--A GUARDIAN OF DEATH.
ANYTHING WHITE THAT I TOUCH TURNS BLACK.
MY GUILT DROWNS ALL HAPPINESS.
I'LL BRING TROUBLE TO YOU AND YOUR FATHER, TOO.
I MAY EVEN CAUSE ...
...YOUR DEATHS.
I'M A CREATURE OF DARKNESS.

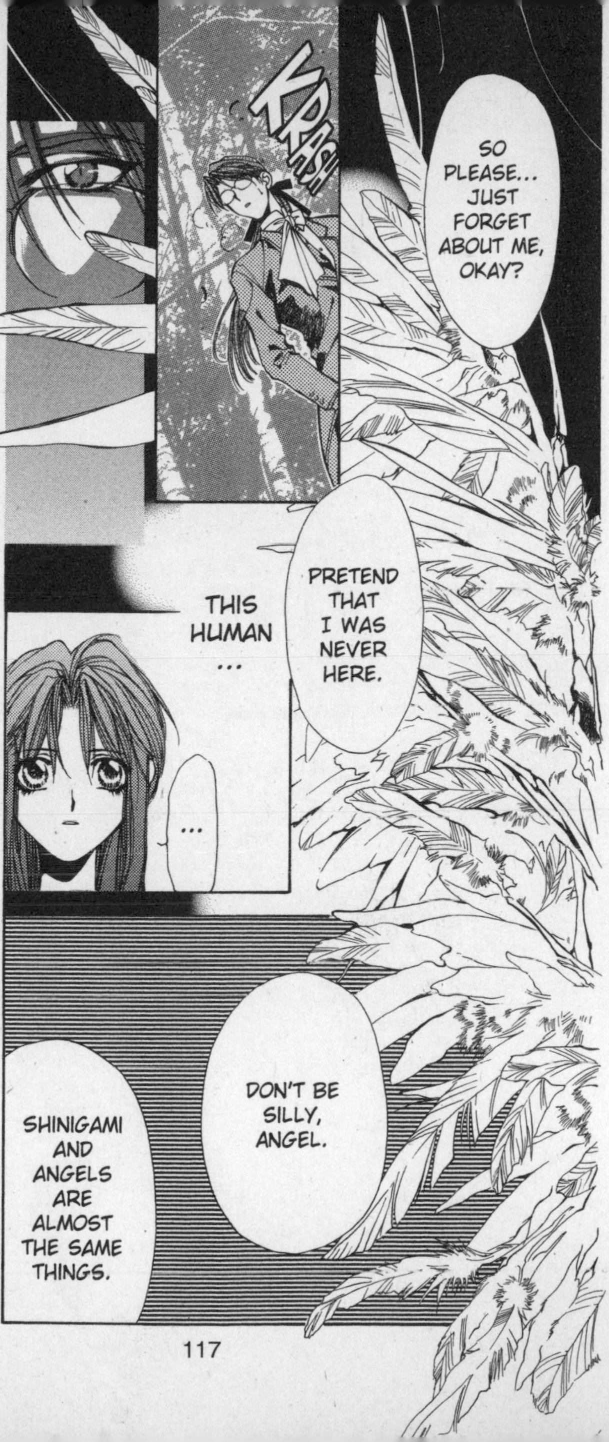
SO PLEASE... JUST FORGET ABOUT ME, OKAY?
KRASH
PRETEND THAT I WAS NEVER HERE.
THIS HUMAN ...
...
DON'T BE SILLY, ANGEL.
SHINIGAMI AND ANGELS ARE ALMOST THE SAME THINGS.

I don't have anything to write about, so I guess I'll write about the CD we've produced. I'll give you a behind-the-scenes look. Well... when I first heard about the project, I was so surprised that I kept asking my editor, "Am I really going to do this?" (Ha) I mean, this is my first series and it was still pretty new. (It still is.) I thought a title had to be super popular to rate a CD. But then I thought, why not? I started writing the story, casting the voice actors, and designing a color cover and a booklet for the CD, all at the same time. The three months I worked on it almost killed me (I had to do nine different color drawings). That's why there are so many basic drawings in this volume. I'm not happy about that, but hey...

PUT YOURSELF IN MY SHOES!!!

NEXT TIME I'LL WRITE ABOUT THE ACTORS.

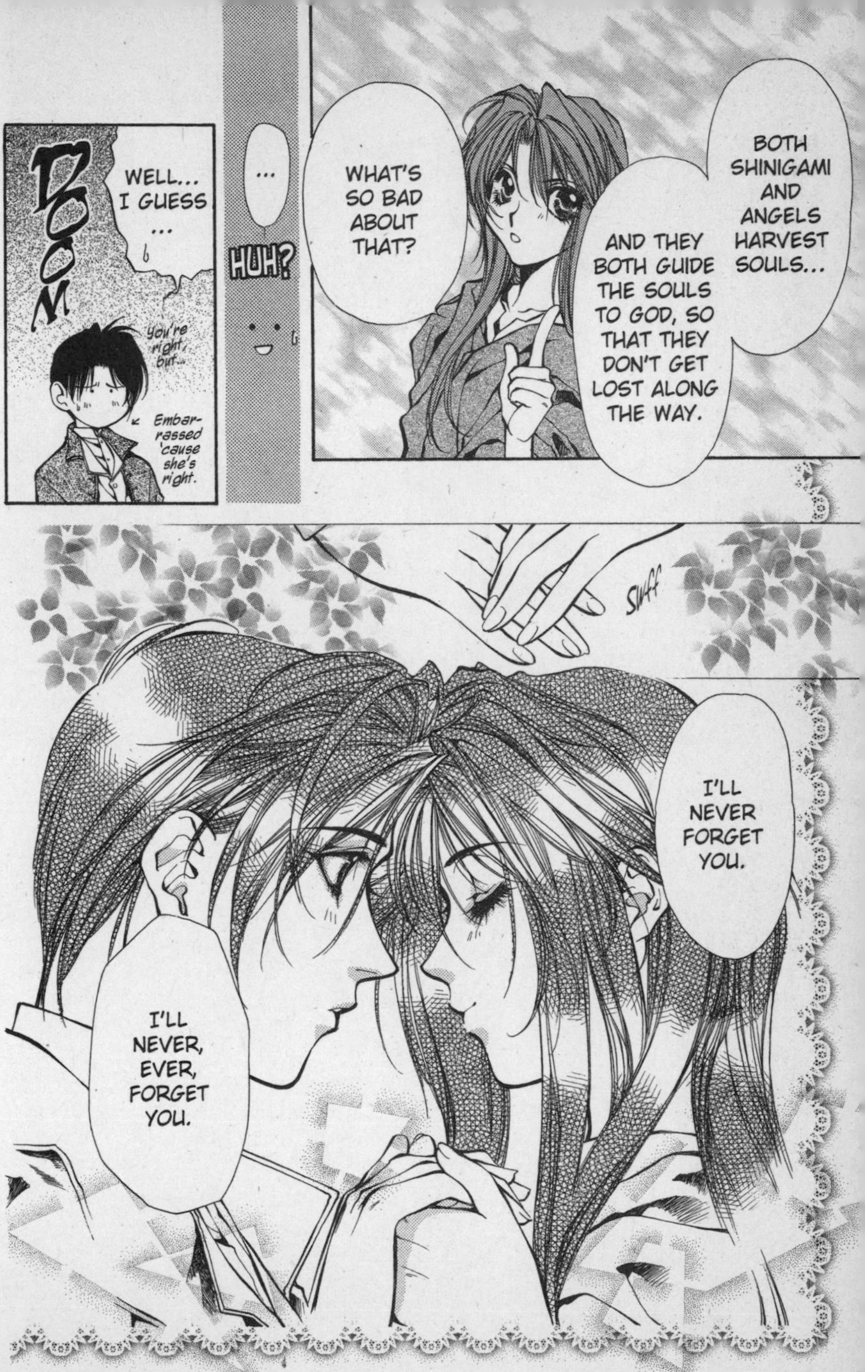
BOTH SHINIGAMI AND ANGELS HARVEST SOULS...
AND THEY BOTH GUIDE THE SOULS TO GOD, SO THAT THEY DON'T GET LOST ALONG THE WAY.
WHAT'S SO BAD ABOUT THAT?
...
HUH?
DOOM
WELL... I GUESS ...
You're right, but...
Embarrassed 'cause she's right.
SWFF
I'LL NEVER FORGET YOU.
I'LL NEVER, EVER, FORGET YOU.

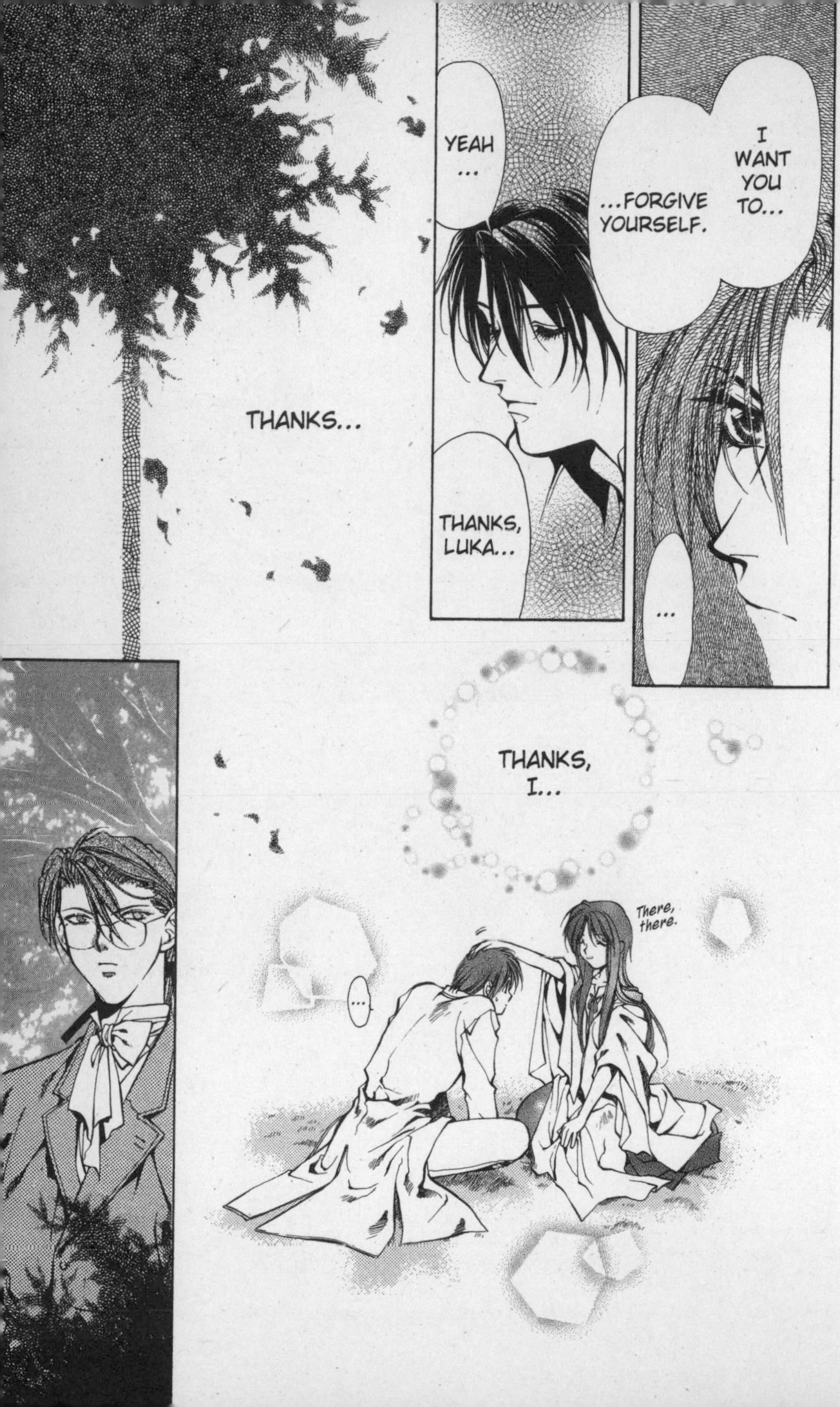
I WANT YOU TO...
...FORGIVE YOURSELF.
...
YEAH ...
THANKS, LUKA...
THANKS...
THANKS, I...
There, there.
...

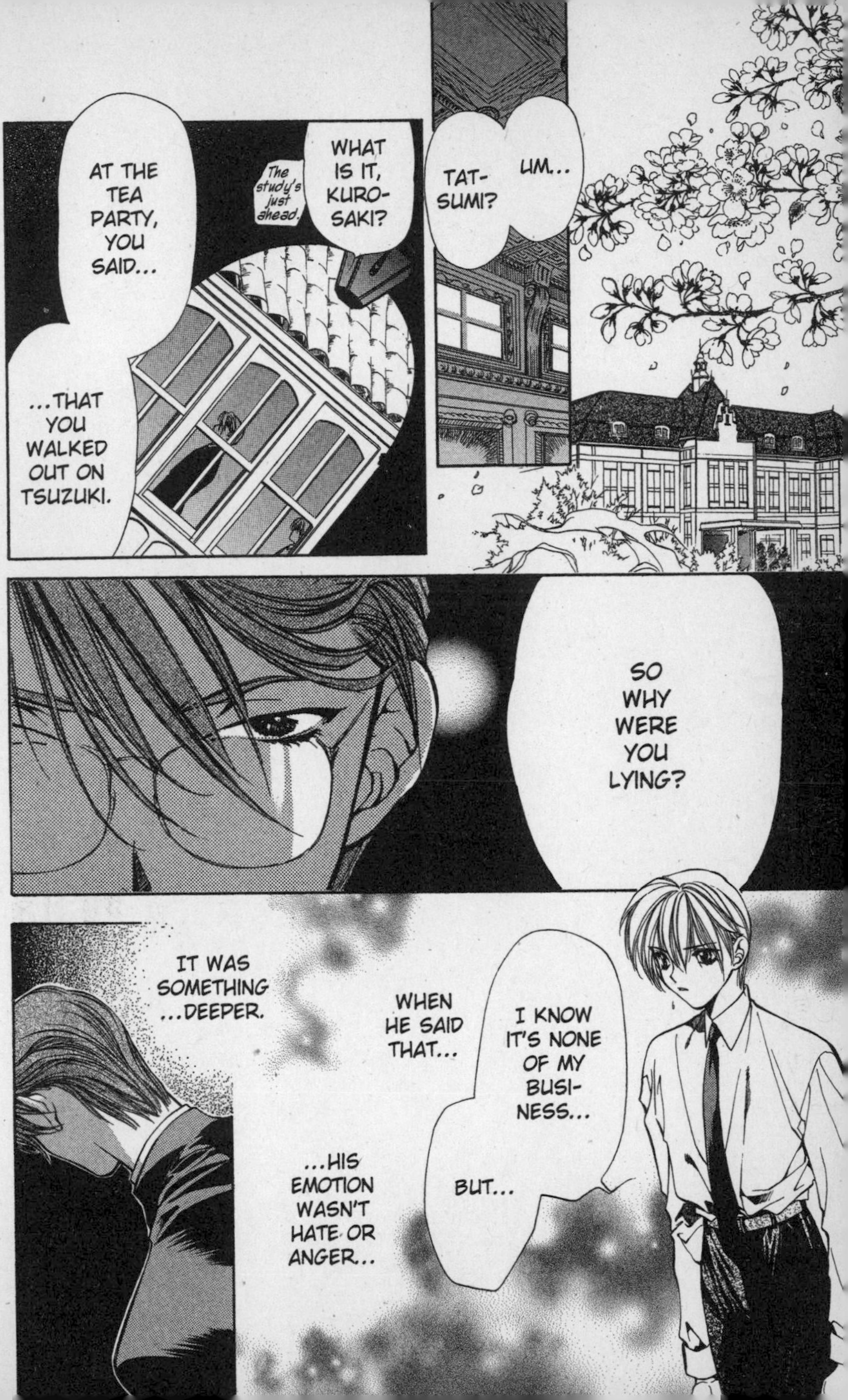
UM...
TAT-SUMI?
WHAT IS IT, KURO-SAKI?
The study's just ahead.
AT THE TEA PARTY, YOU SAID...
...THAT YOU WALKED OUT ON TSUZUKI.
SO WHY WERE YOU LYING?
I KNOW IT'S NONE OF MY BUSI-NESS...
BUT...
WHEN HE SAID THAT...
...HIS EMOTION WASN'T HATE OR ANGER...
IT WAS SOMETHING ...DEEPER.

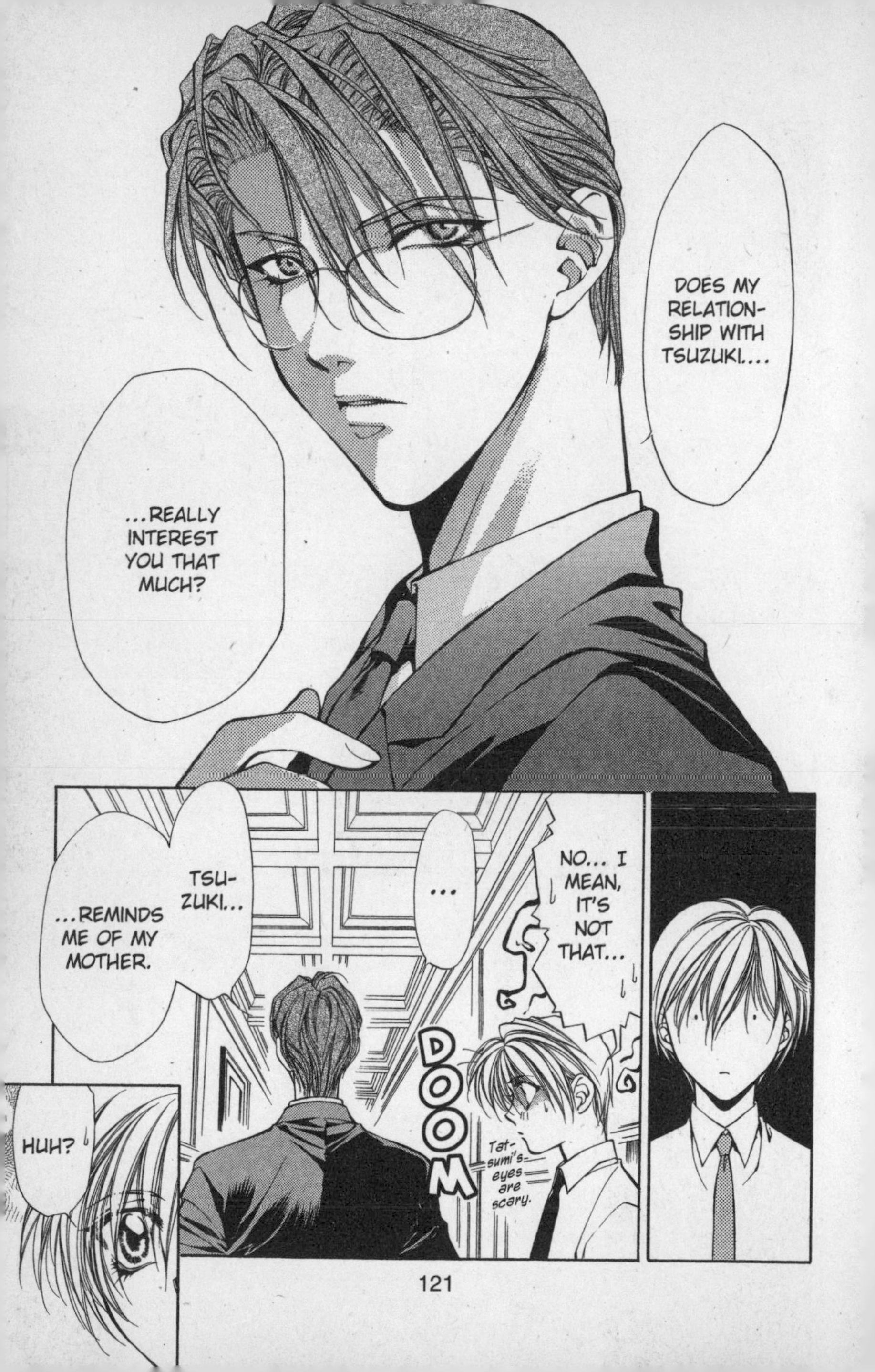
DOES MY RELATIONSHIP WITH TSUZUKI....
...REALLY INTEREST YOU THAT MUCH?
NO... I MEAN, IT'S NOT THAT...
DOOM
Tatsumi's eyes are scary.
...
TSUZUKI...
...REMINDS ME OF MY MOTHER.
HUH?

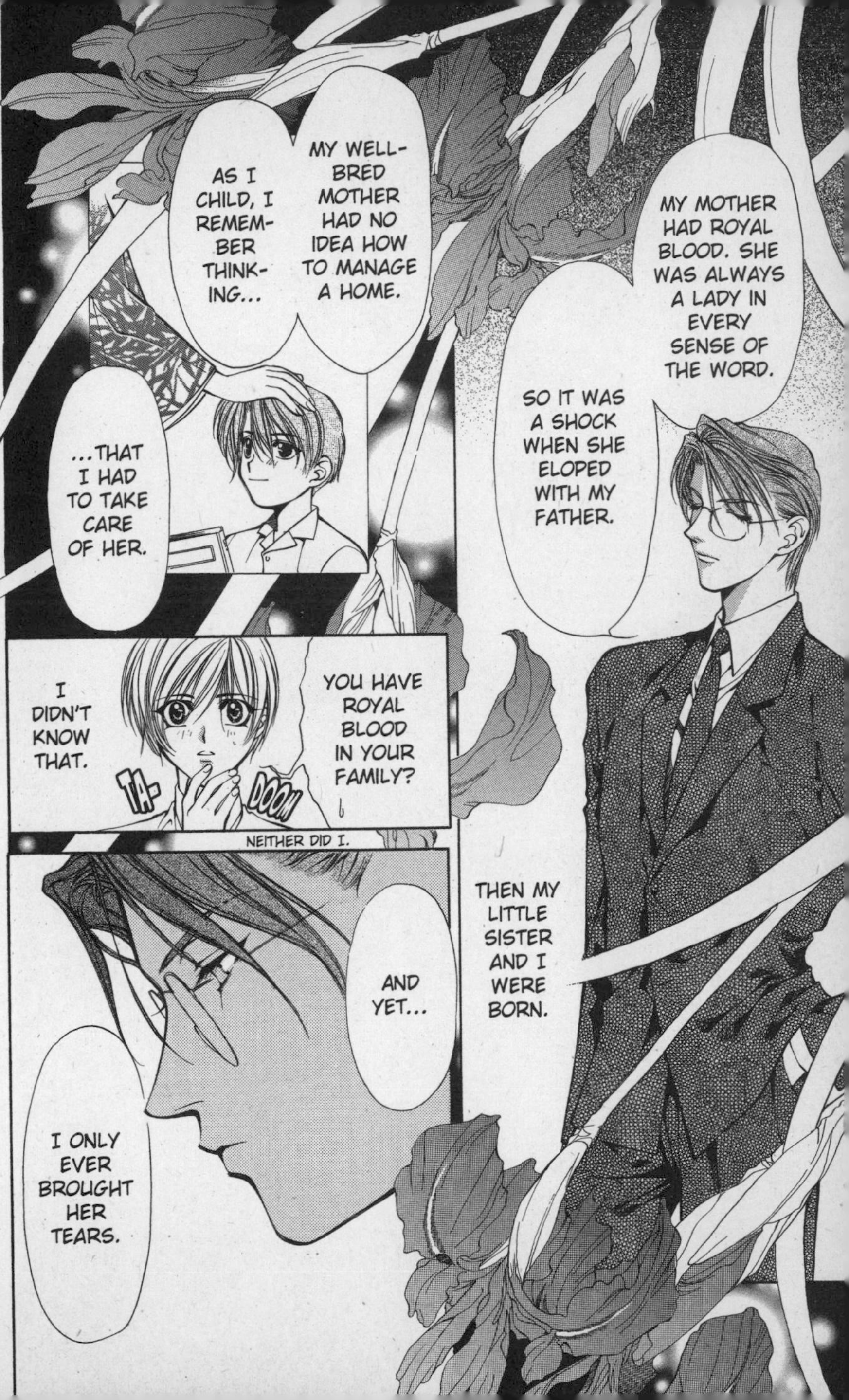
MY MOTHER HAD ROYAL BLOOD. SHE WAS ALWAYS A LADY IN EVERY SENSE OF THE WORD.
SO IT WAS A SHOCK WHEN SHE ELOPED WITH MY FATHER.
THEN MY LITTLE SISTER AND I WERE BORN.
MY WELL-BRED MOTHER HAD NO IDEA HOW TO MANAGE A HOME.
AS I CHILD, I REMEMBER THINKING...
...THAT I HAD TO TAKE CARE OF HER.
YOU HAVE ROYAL BLOOD IN YOUR FAMILY?
I DIDN'T KNOW THAT.
TA-DOOM
NEITHER DID I.
AND YET...
I ONLY EVER BROUGHT HER TEARS.

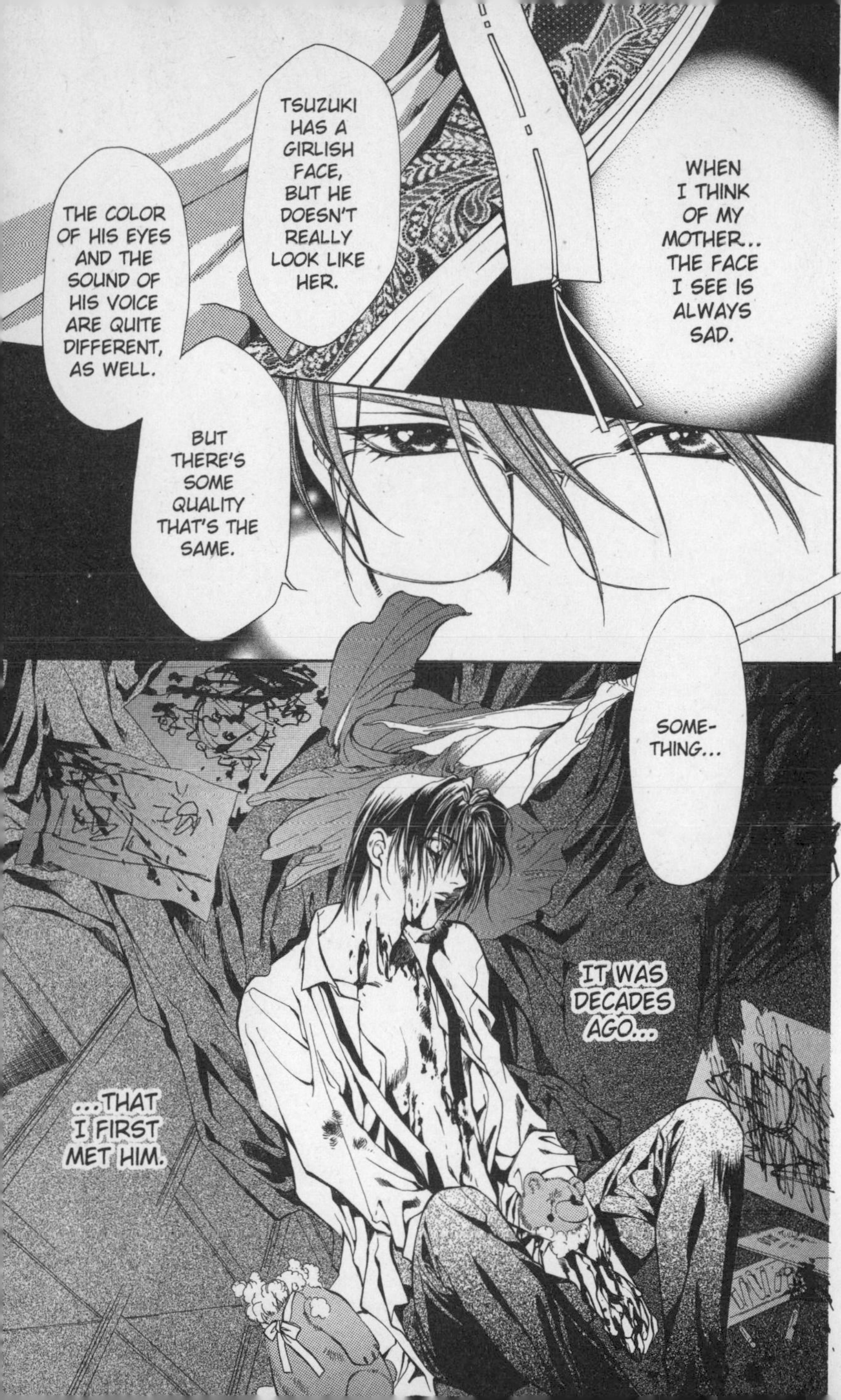
WHEN I THINK OF MY MOTHER... THE FACE I SEE IS ALWAYS SAD.
TSUZUKI HAS A GIRLISH FACE, BUT HE DOESN'T REALLY LOOK LIKE HER.
THE COLOR OF HIS EYES AND THE SOUND OF HIS VOICE ARE QUITE DIFFERENT, AS WELL.
BUT THERE'S SOME QUALITY THAT'S THE SAME.
SOME-THING...
IT WAS DECADES AGO...
...THAT I FIRST MET HIM.

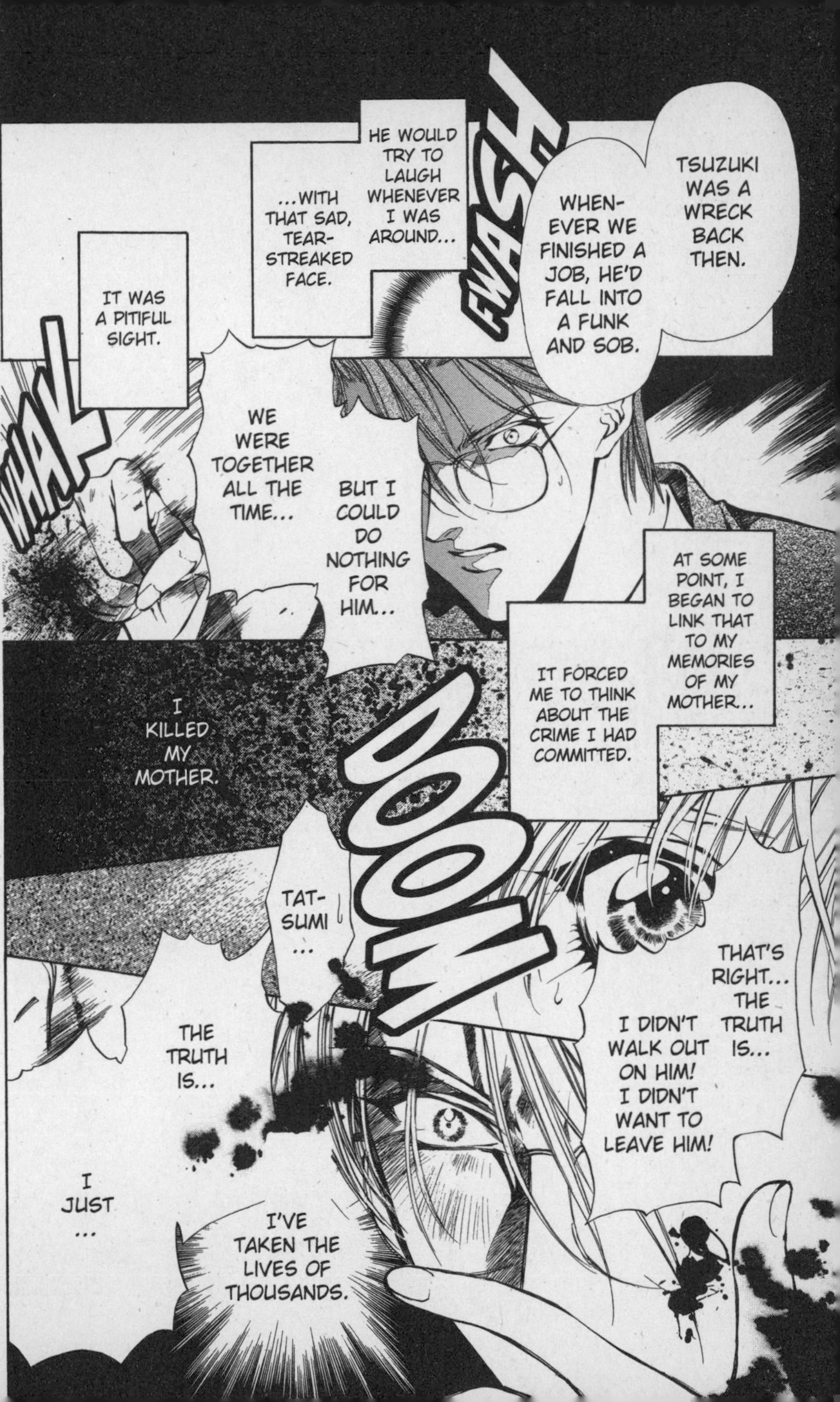
TSUZUKI WAS A WRECK BACK THEN.
WHEN-EVER WE FINISHED A JOB, HE'D FALL INTO A FUNK AND SOB.
FWASH
HE WOULD TRY TO LAUGH WHENEVER I WAS AROUND...
...WITH THAT SAD, TEAR-STREAKED FACE.
IT WAS A PITIFUL SIGHT.
WHAK
WE WERE TOGETHER ALL THE TIME...
BUT I COULD DO NOTHING FOR HIM...
AT SOME POINT, I BEGAN TO LINK THAT TO MY MEMORIES OF MY MOTHER...
IT FORCED ME TO THINK ABOUT THE CRIME I HAD COMMITTED.
I KILLED MY MOTHER.
DOOOOM
TAT-SUMI ...
THAT'S RIGHT... THE TRUTH IS...
I DIDN'T WALK OUT ON HIM! I DIDN'T WANT TO LEAVE HIM!
THE TRUTH IS...
I'VE TAKEN THE LIVES OF THOUSANDS.
I JUST ...

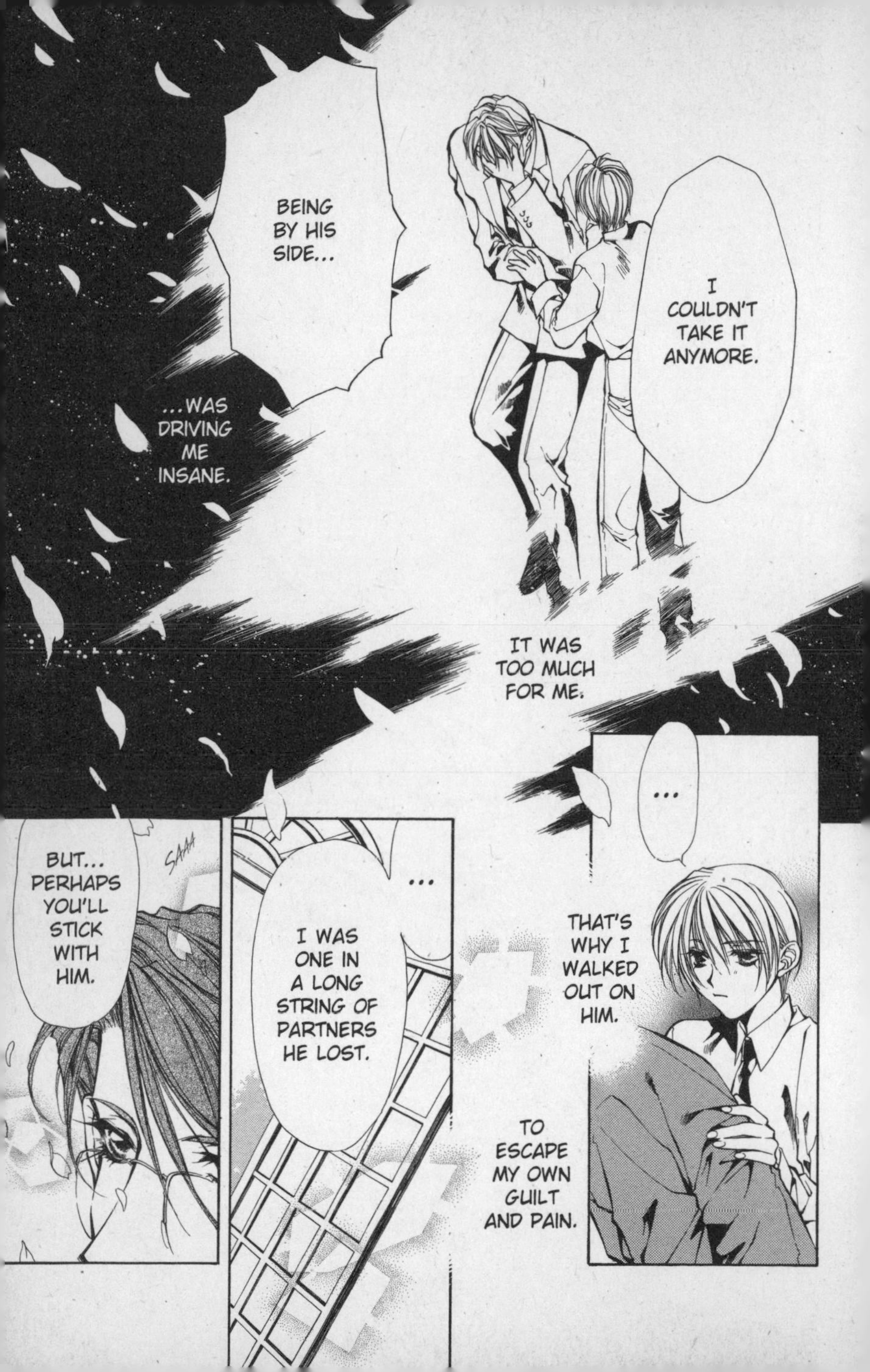
I COULDN'T TAKE IT ANYMORE.
BEING BY HIS SIDE...
...WAS DRIVING ME INSANE.
IT WAS TOO MUCH FOR ME.
...
THAT'S WHY I WALKED OUT ON HIM.
TO ESCAPE MY OWN GUILT AND PAIN.
...
I WAS ONE IN A LONG STRING OF PARTNERS HE LOST.
SAAA
BUT... PERHAPS YOU'LL STICK WITH HIM.

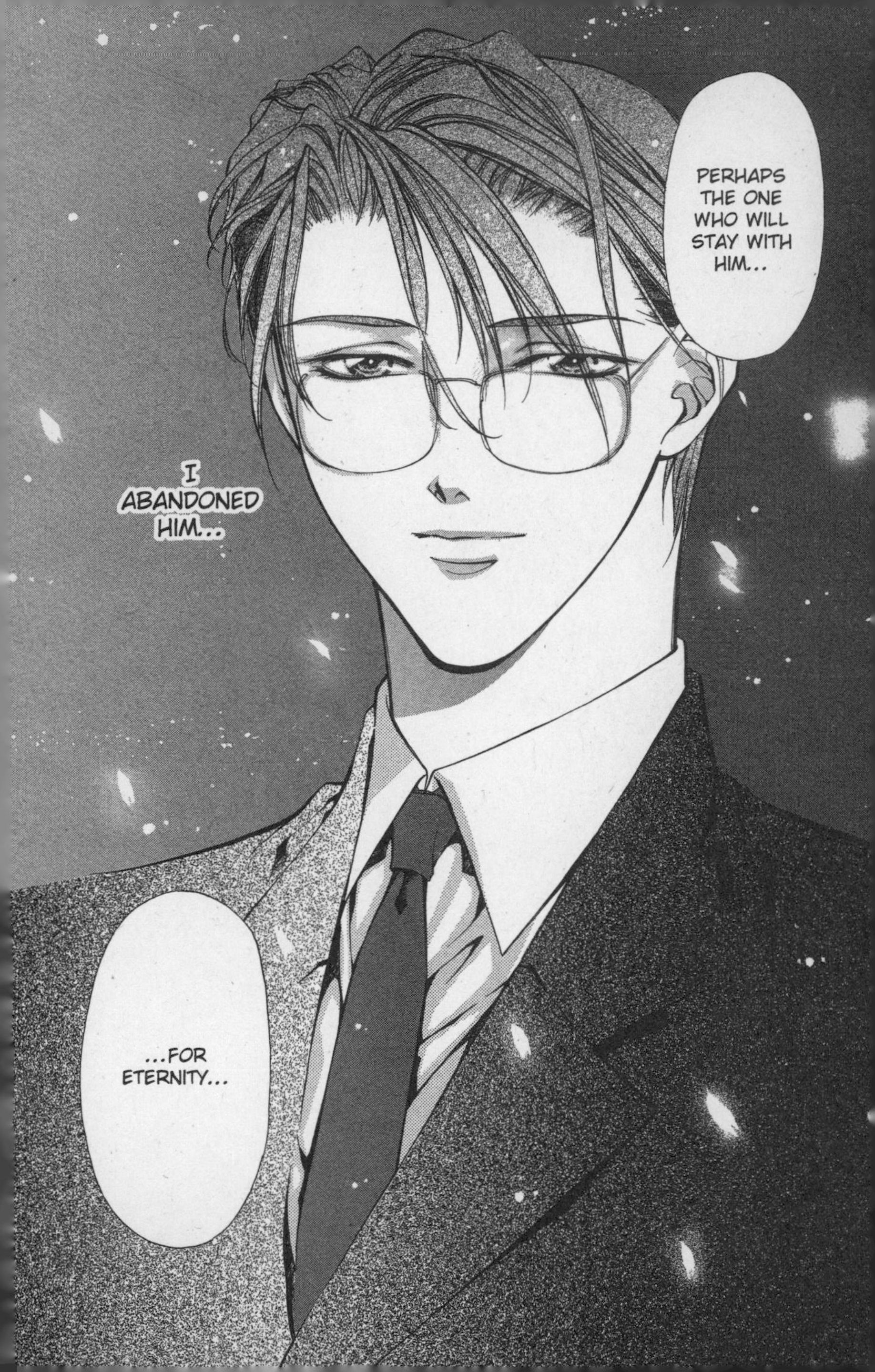
PERHAPS THE ONE WHO WILL STAY WITH HIM...
I ABANDONED HIM...
...FOR ETERNITY...

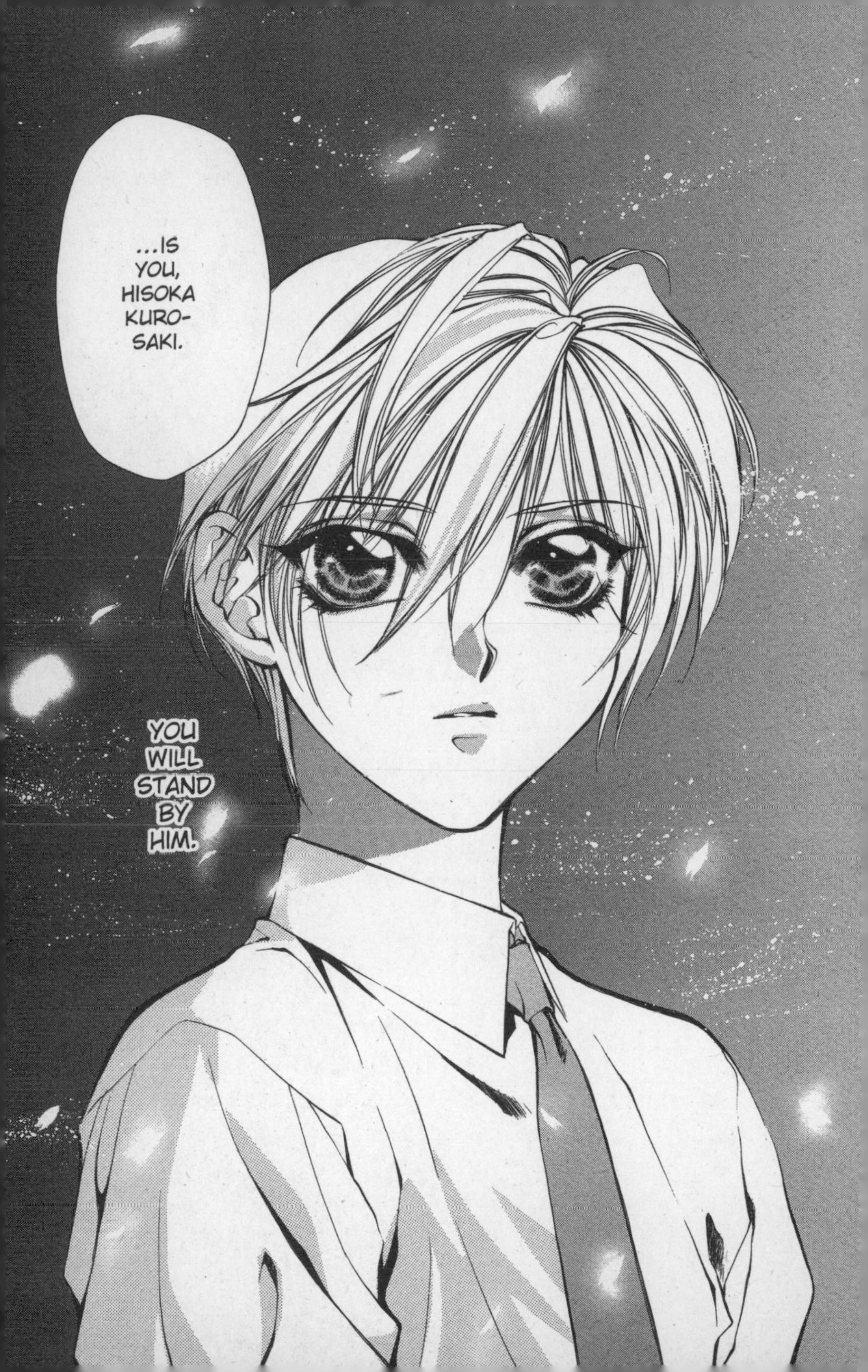
...IS YOU, HISOKA KURO-SAKI.
YOU WILL STAND BY HIM.

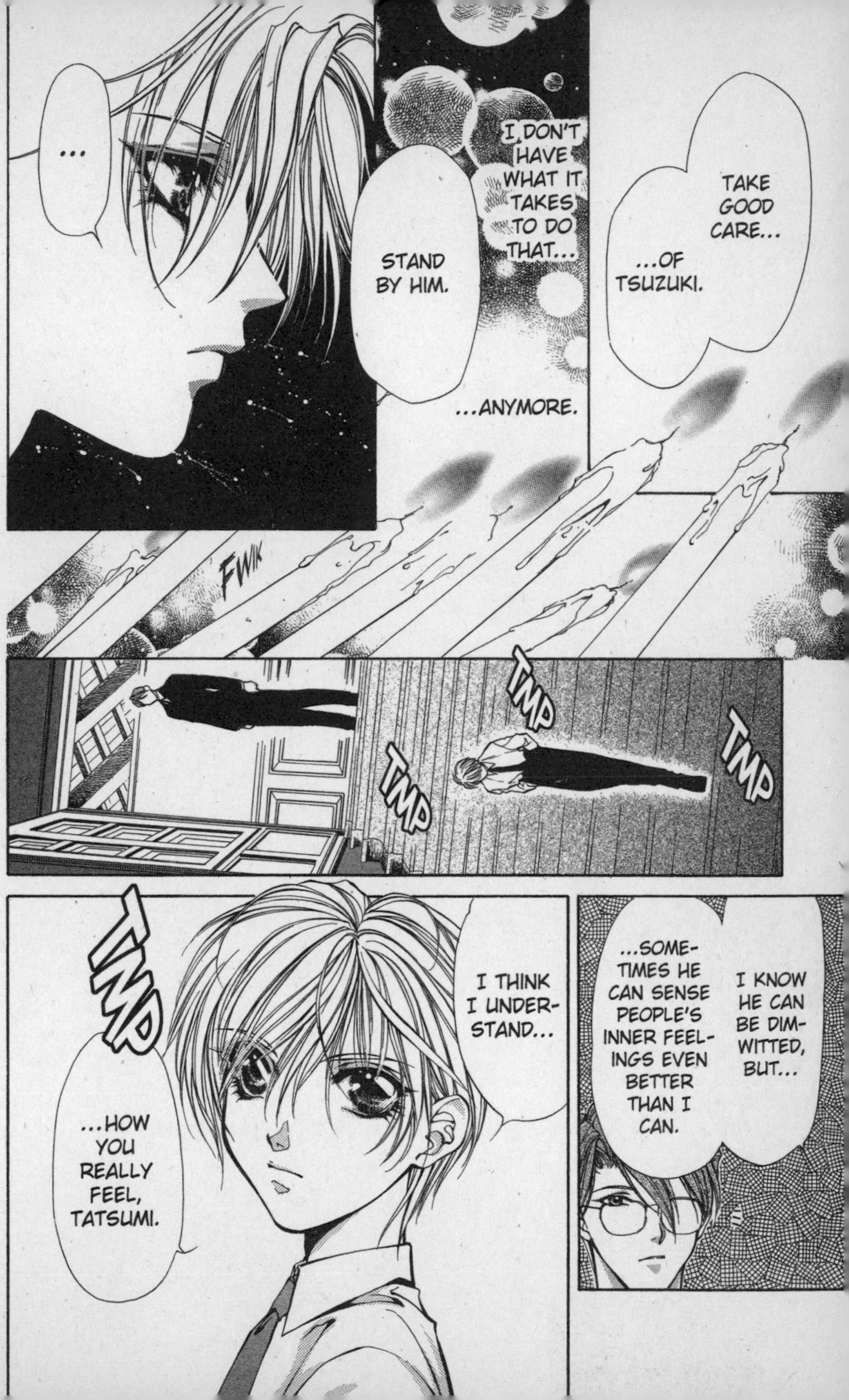
TAKE GOOD CARE...
...OF TSUZUKI.
I DON'T HAVE WHAT IT TAKES TO DO THAT...
STAND BY HIM.
...ANYMORE.
...
FWIK
TMP
TMP
TMP
I KNOW HE CAN BE DIM-WITTED, BUT...
...SOME-TIMES HE CAN SENSE PEOPLE'S INNER FEEL-INGS EVEN BETTER THAN I CAN.
TMP
I THINK I UNDER-STAND...
...HOW YOU REALLY FEEL, TATSUMI.

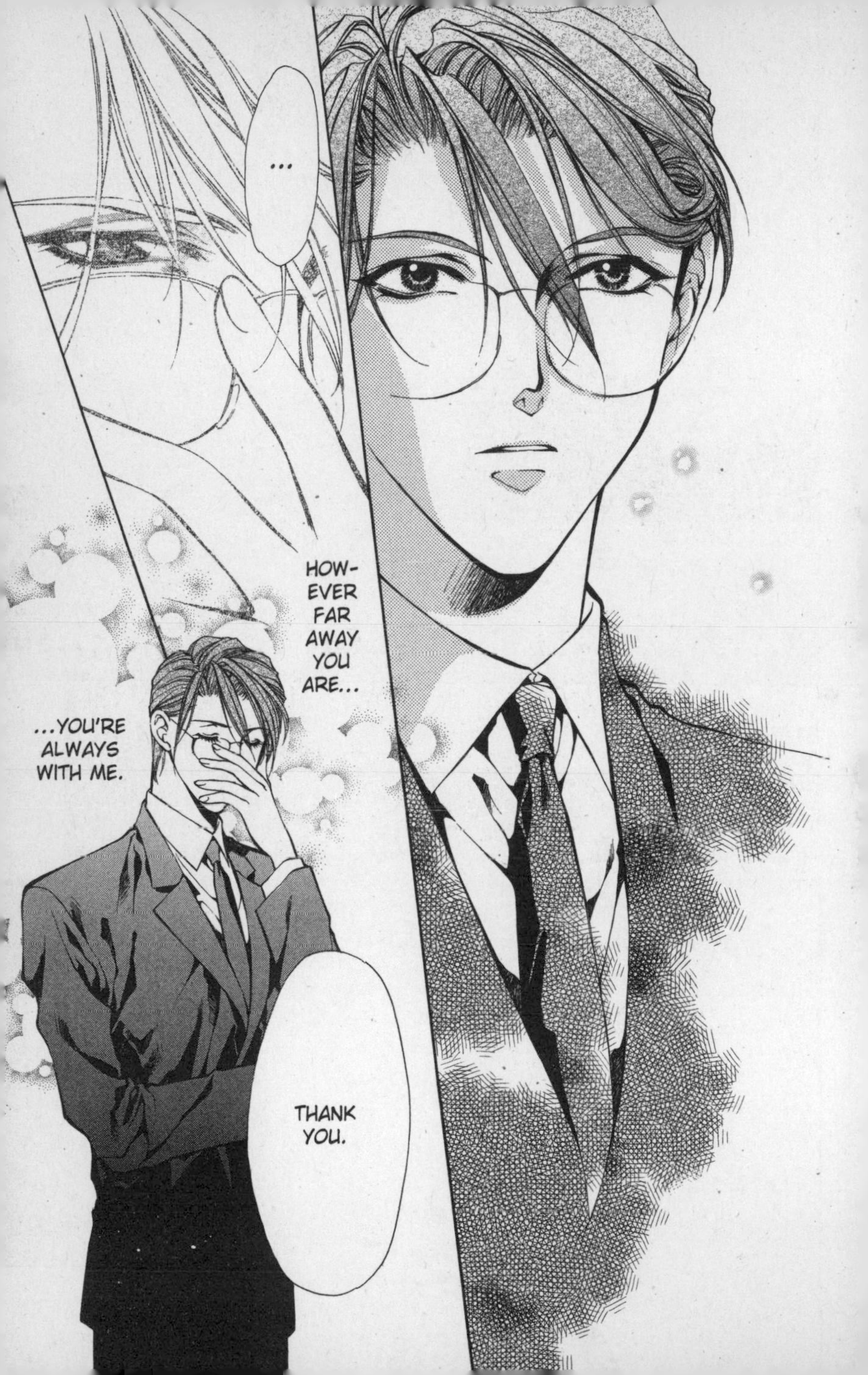
...
HOW-EVER FAR AWAY YOU ARE...
...YOU'RE ALWAYS WITH ME.
THANK YOU.

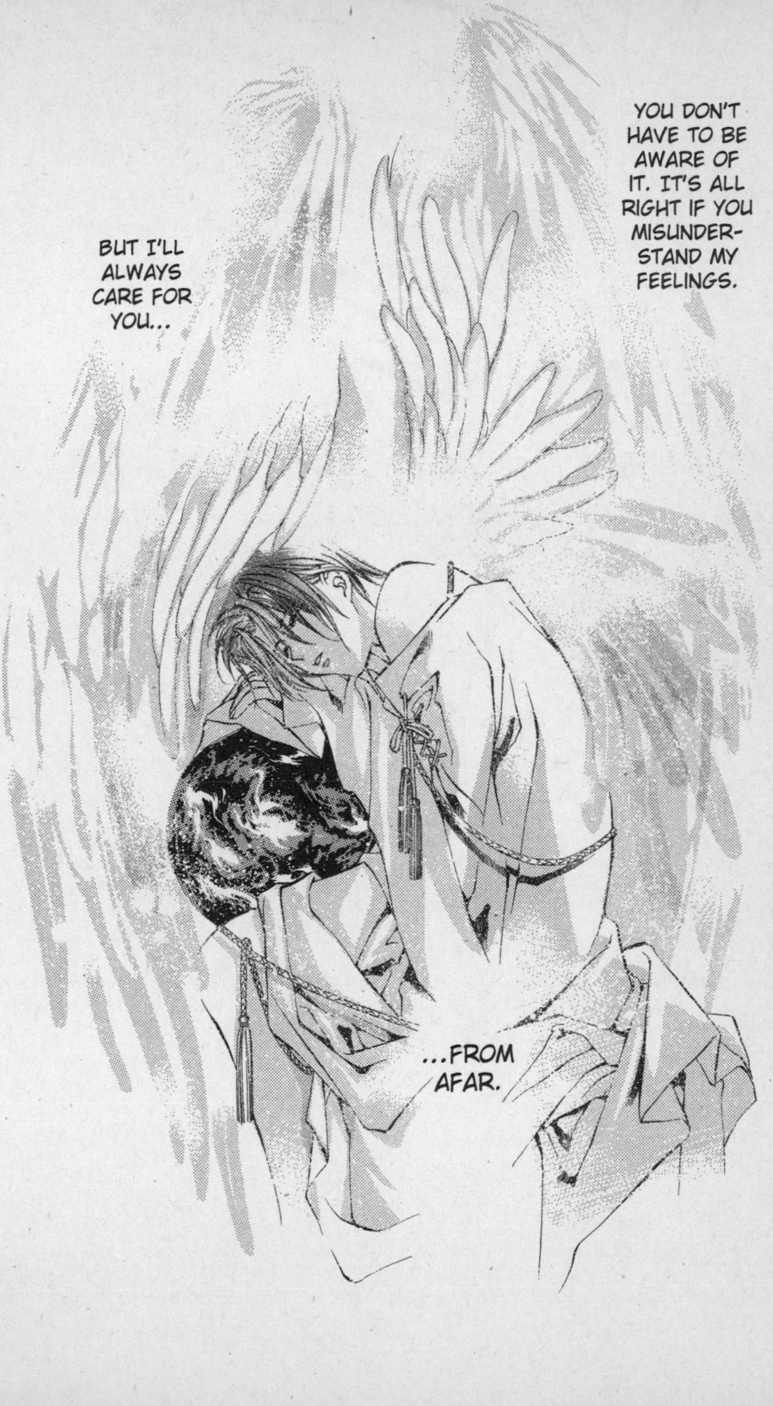
YOU DON'T HAVE TO BE AWARE OF IT. IT'S ALL RIGHT IF YOU MISUNDER-STAND MY FEELINGS.
BUT I'LL ALWAYS CARE FOR YOU...
...FROM AFAR.

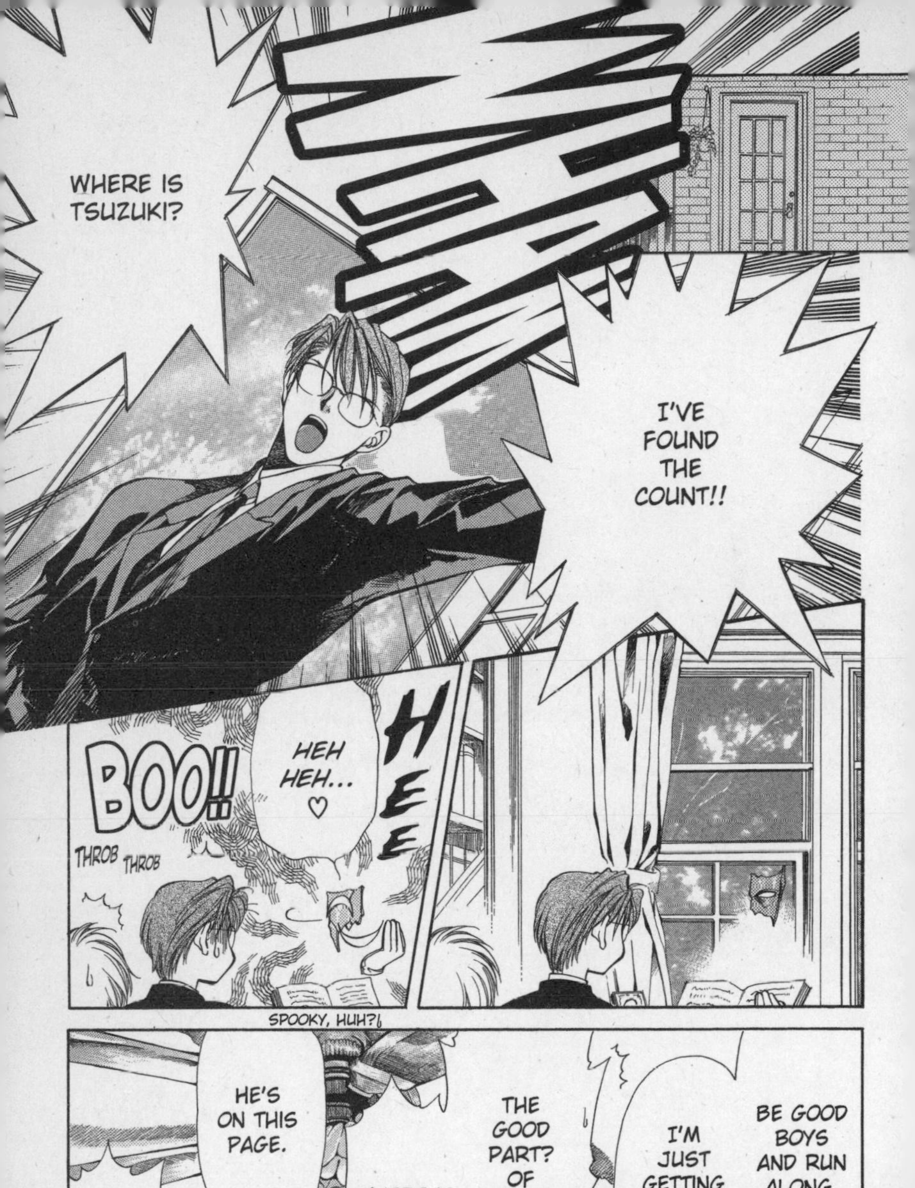
I'VE FOUND THE COUNT!!
WHERE IS TSUZUKI?
HEE
HEH HEH... ♡
BOO!!
THROB THROB
SPOOKY, HUH?
BE GOOD BOYS AND RUN ALONG.
I'M JUST GETTING TO THE GOOD PART.
THE GOOD PART? OF WHAT?
WHERE IS TSUZUKI?
HE'S ON THIS PAGE.
HUH?
On the Page?

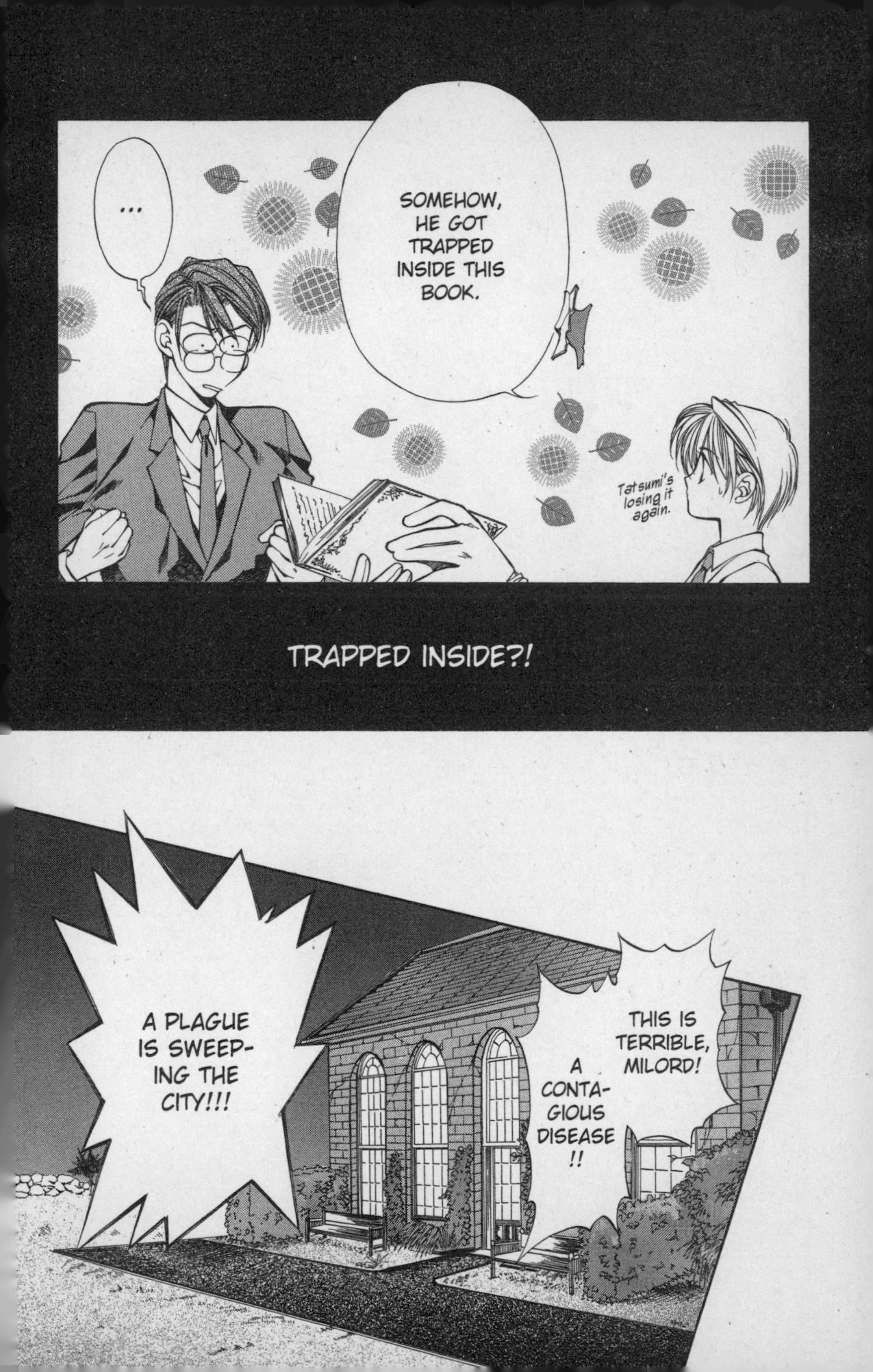
SOMEHOW, HE GOT TRAPPED INSIDE THIS BOOK.
...
Tatsumi's losing it again.
TRAPPED INSIDE?!
THIS IS TERRIBLE, MILORD!
A CONTA-GIOUS DISEASE !!
A PLAGUE IS SWEEP-ING THE CITY!!!

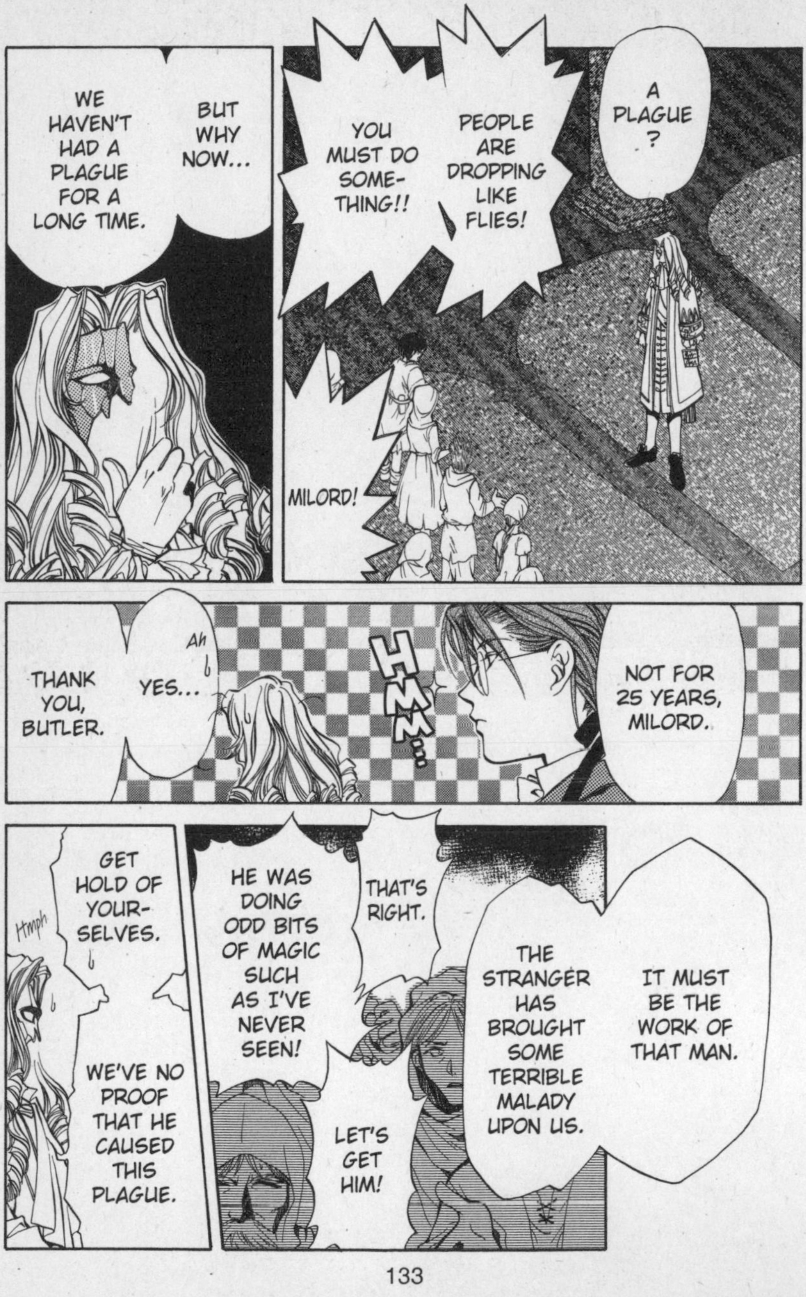
A PLAGUE?
PEOPLE ARE DROPPING LIKE FLIES!
YOU MUST DO SOME-THING!!
MILORD!
BUT WHY NOW...
WE HAVEN'T HAD A PLAGUE FOR A LONG TIME.
NOT FOR 25 YEARS, MILORD.
HMM...
Ah
YES...
THANK YOU, BUTLER.
IT MUST BE THE WORK OF THAT MAN.
THE STRANGER HAS BROUGHT SOME TERRIBLE MALADY UPON US.
THAT'S RIGHT.
HE WAS DOING ODD BITS OF MAGIC SUCH AS I'VE NEVER SEEN!
LET'S GET HIM!
GET HOLD OF YOUR-SELVES.
Hmph
WE'VE NO PROOF THAT HE CAUSED THIS PLAGUE.

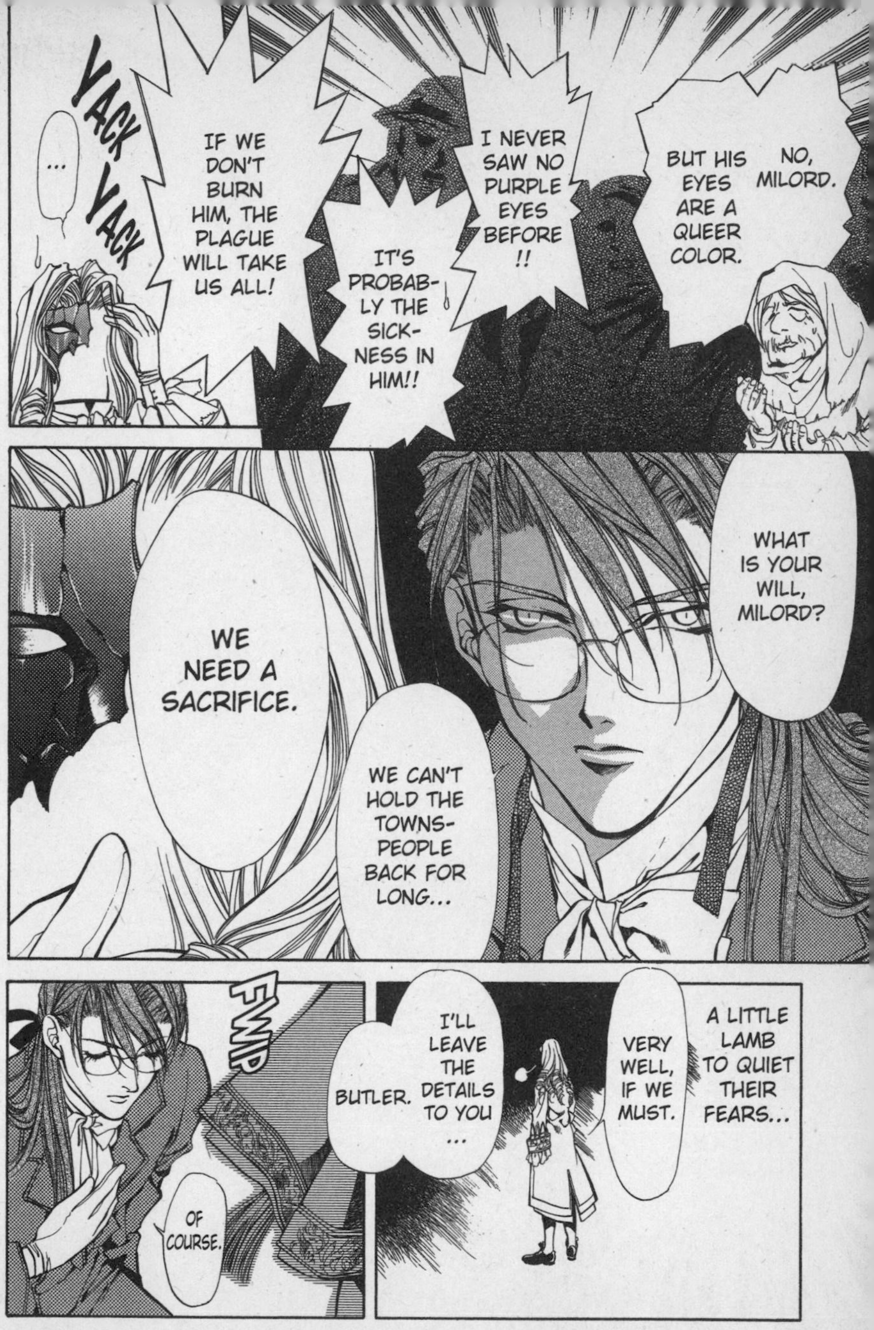
NO, MILORD.
BUT HIS EYES ARE A QUEER COLOR.
I NEVER SAW NO PURPLE EYES BEFORE!!
IT'S PROBAB-LY THE SICK-NESS IN HIM!!
IF WE DON'T BURN HIM, THE PLAGUE WILL TAKE US ALL!
YACK YACK
...
WHAT IS YOUR WILL, MILORD?
WE CAN'T HOLD THE TOWNS-PEOPLE BACK FOR LONG...
WE NEED A SACRIFICE.
A LITTLE LAMB TO QUIET THEIR FEARS...
VERY WELL, IF WE MUST.
I'LL LEAVE THE DETAILS TO YOU...
BUTLER.
FWIP
OF COURSE.

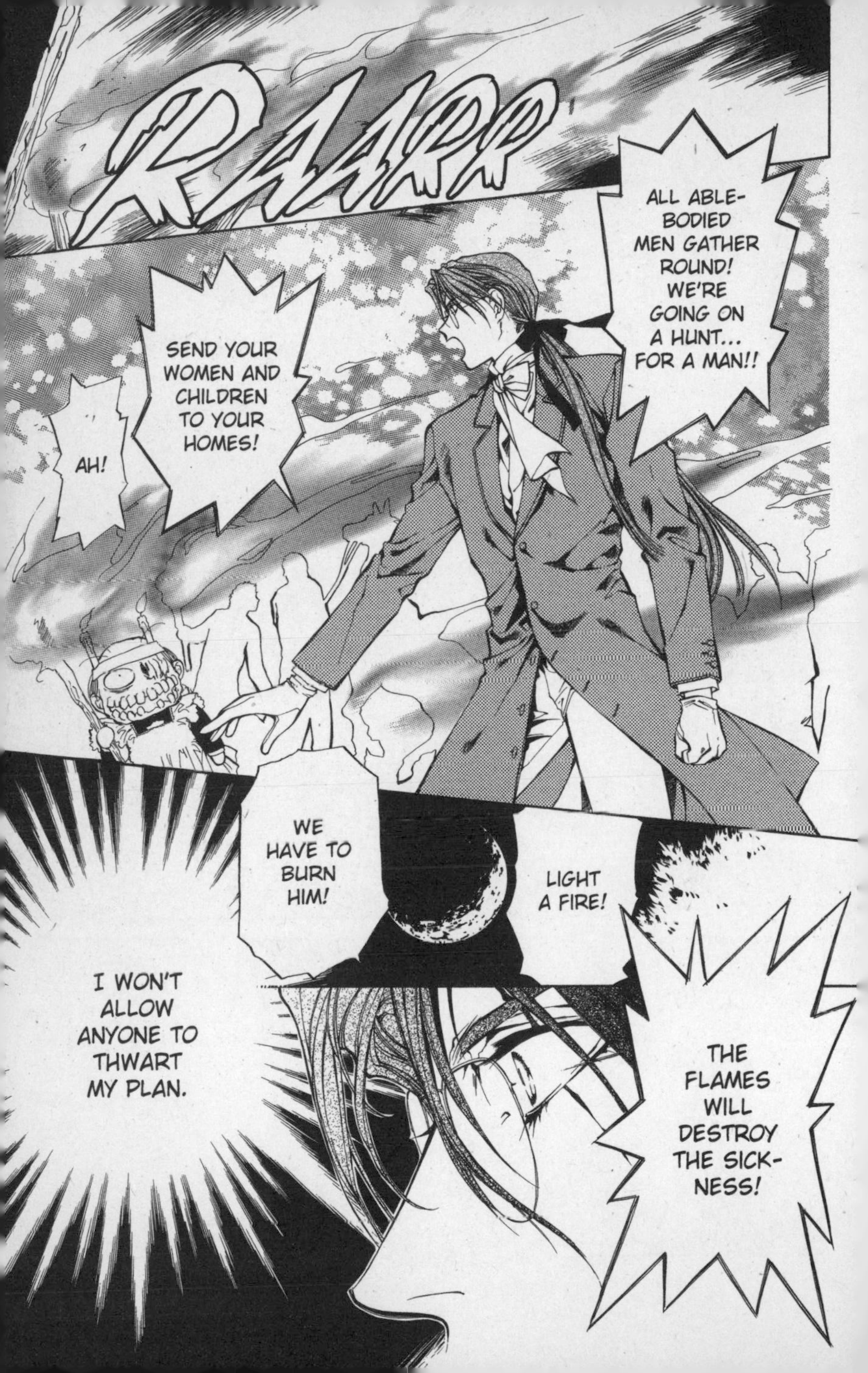
RAARR
ALL ABLE-BODIED MEN GATHER ROUND! WE'RE GOING ON A HUNT... FOR A MAN!!
SEND YOUR WOMEN AND CHILDREN TO YOUR HOMES!
AH!
LIGHT A FIRE!
WE HAVE TO BURN HIM!
THE FLAMES WILL DESTROY THE SICK-NESS!
I WON'T ALLOW ANYONE TO THWART MY PLAN.

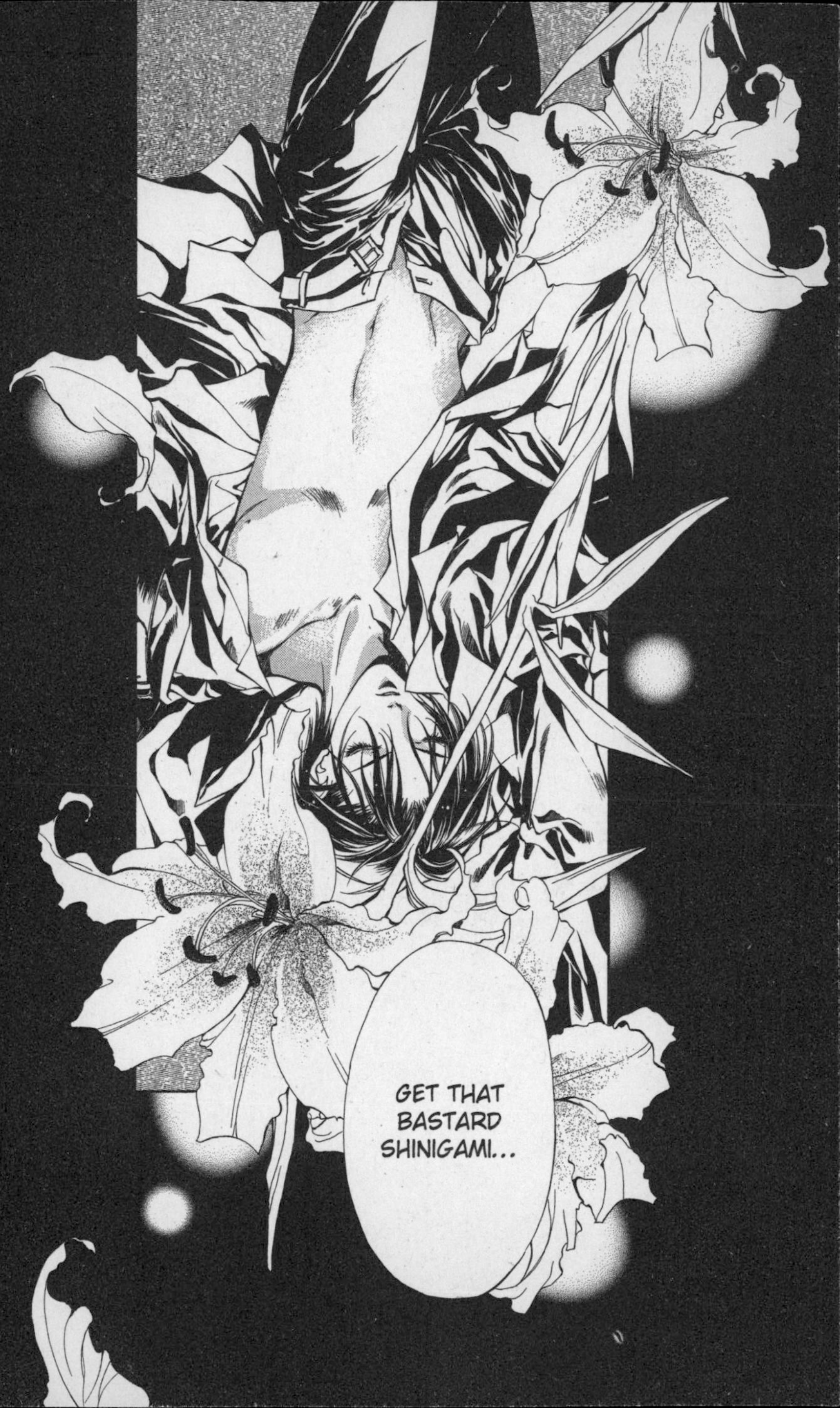
GET THAT BASTARD SHINIGAMI...

CHAPTER 11

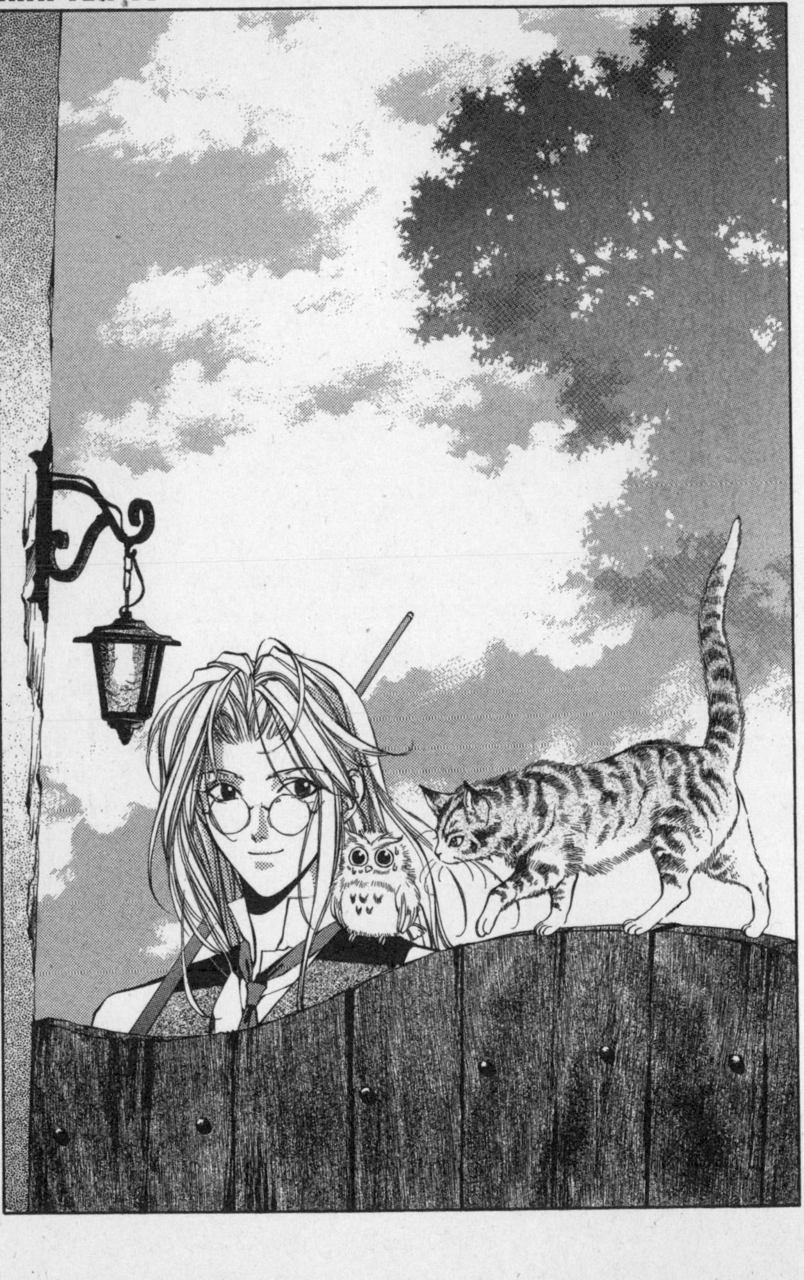

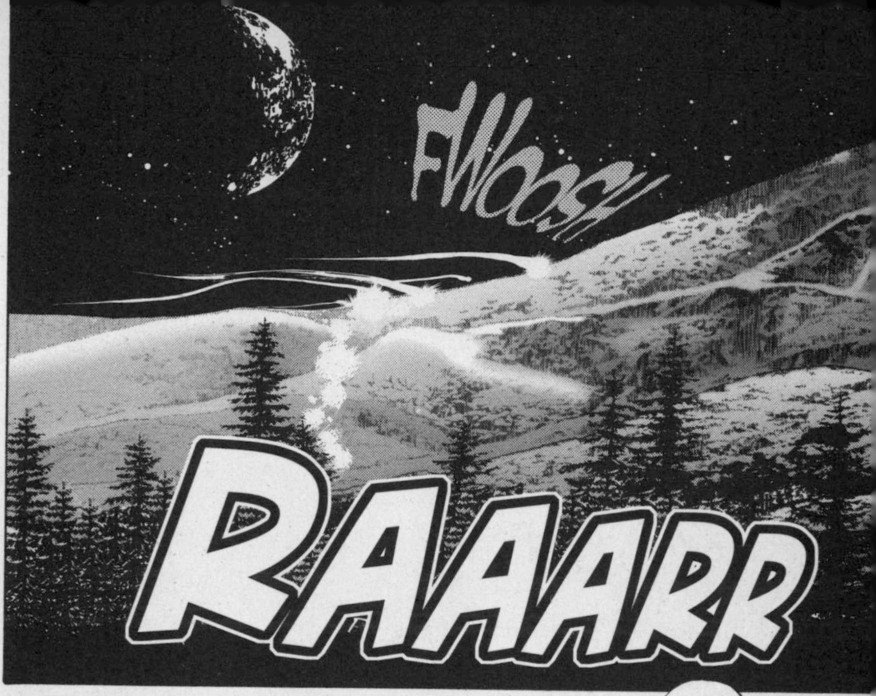
FWOOSH
RAAARR

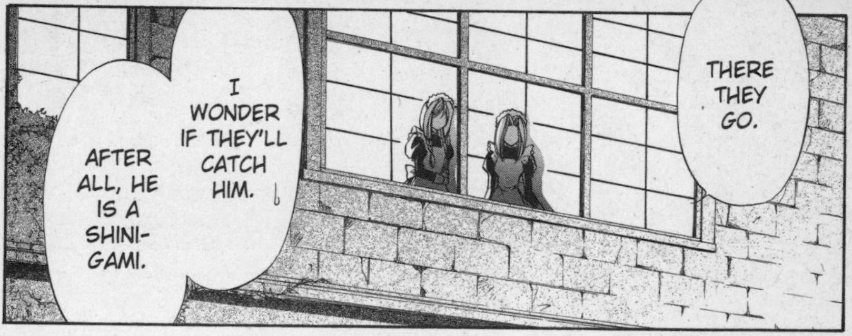
THERE THEY GO.
I WONDER IF THEY'LL CATCH HIM.
AFTER ALL, HE IS A SHINI-GAMI.

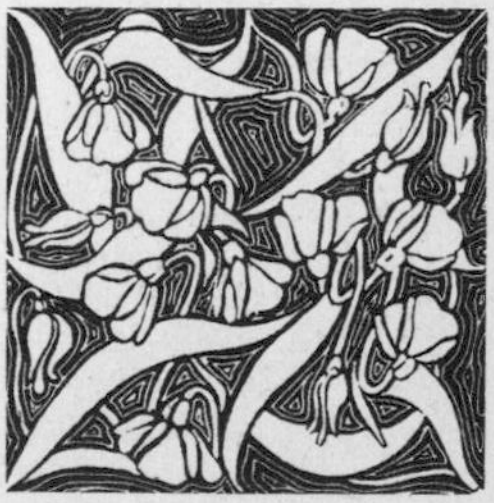

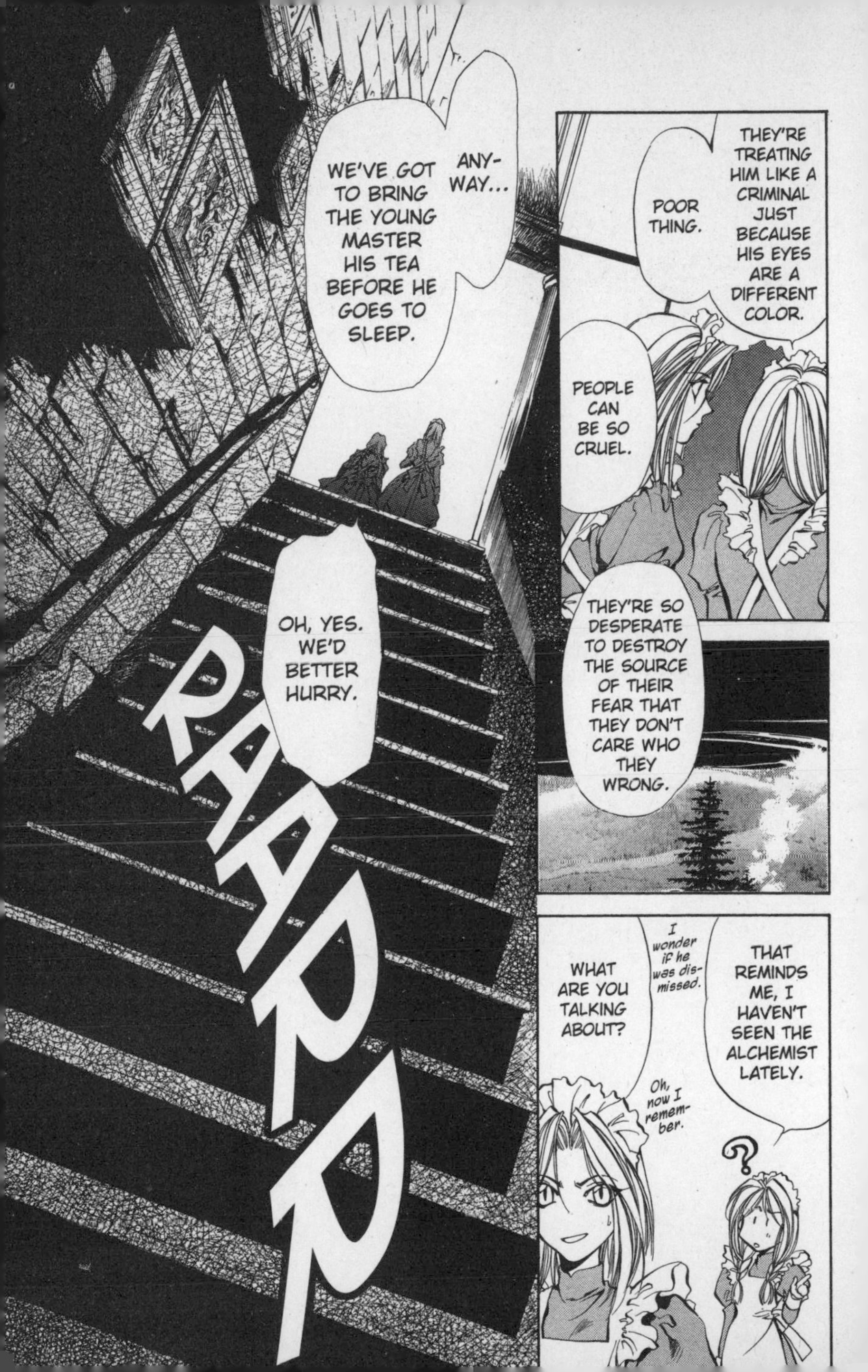
THEY'RE TREATING HIM LIKE A CRIMINAL JUST BECAUSE HIS EYES ARE A DIFFERENT COLOR.
POOR THING.
PEOPLE CAN BE SO CRUEL.
THEY'RE SO DESPERATE TO DESTROY THE SOURCE OF THEIR FEAR THAT THEY DON'T CARE WHO THEY WRONG.
THAT REMINDS ME, I HAVEN'T SEEN THE ALCHEMIST LATELY.
I wonder if he was dis-missed.
WHAT ARE YOU TALKING ABOUT?
Oh, now I remem-ber.
ANY-WAY...
WE'VE GOT TO BRING THE YOUNG MASTER HIS TEA BEFORE HE GOES TO SLEEP.
OH, YES. WE'D BETTER HURRY.
RAAPP

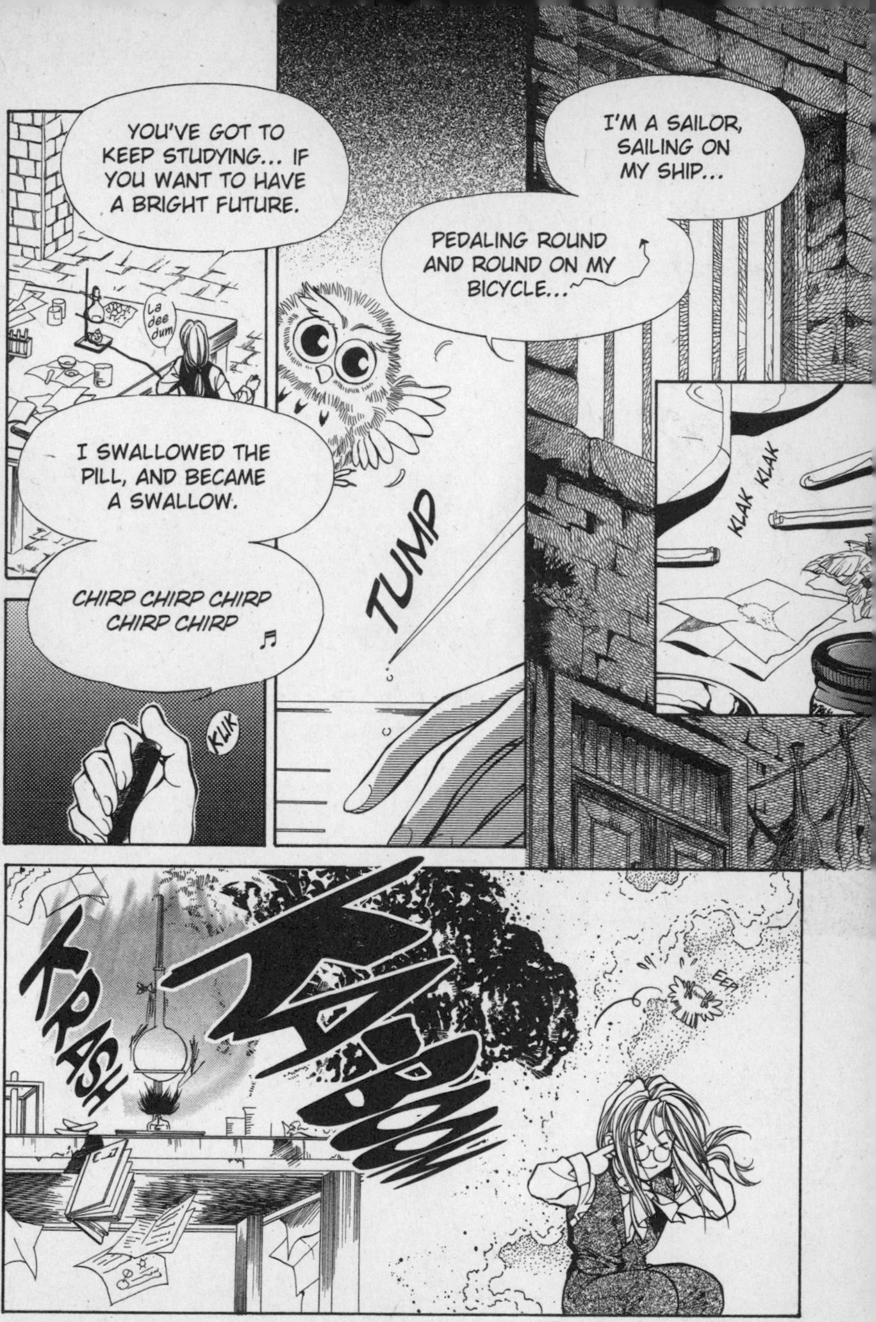
I'M A SAILOR, SAILING ON MY SHIP...
PEDALING ROUND AND ROUND ON MY BICYCLE...
KLAK KLAK
TUMP
YOU'VE GOT TO KEEP STUDYING... IF YOU WANT TO HAVE A BRIGHT FUTURE.
La dee dum
I SWALLOWED THE PILL, AND BECAME A SWALLOW.
CHIRP CHIRP CHIRP CHIRP CHIRP ♪
KLUK
EEP
KRASH

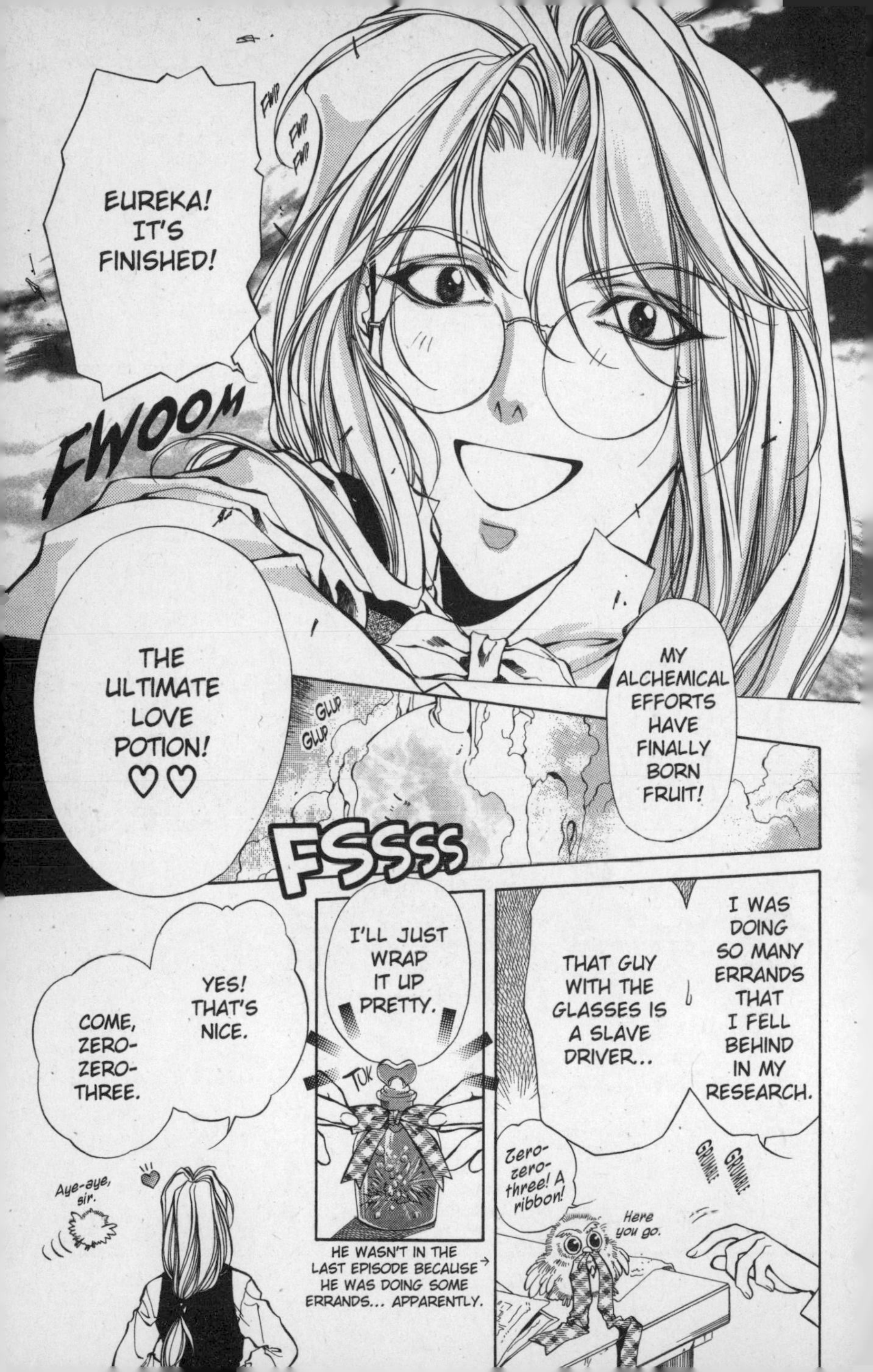
FWIP
FWIP FWIP
EUREKA! IT'S FINISHED!
FWOOM
MY ALCHEMICAL EFFORTS HAVE FINALLY BORN FRUIT!
THE ULTIMATE LOVE POTION! ♡♡
GLUP GLUP
FSSSS
I WAS DOING SO MANY ERRANDS THAT I FELL BEHIND IN MY RESEARCH.
THAT GUY WITH THE GLASSES IS A SLAVE DRIVER...
GRUMBLE GRUMBLE
Here you go.
Zero-zero-three! A ribbon!
I'LL JUST WRAP IT UP PRETTY.
TOK
HE WASN'T IN THE LAST EPISODE BECAUSE HE WAS DOING SOME ERRANDS... APPARENTLY.
YES! THAT'S NICE.
COME, ZERO-ZERO-THREE.
Aye-aye, sir.

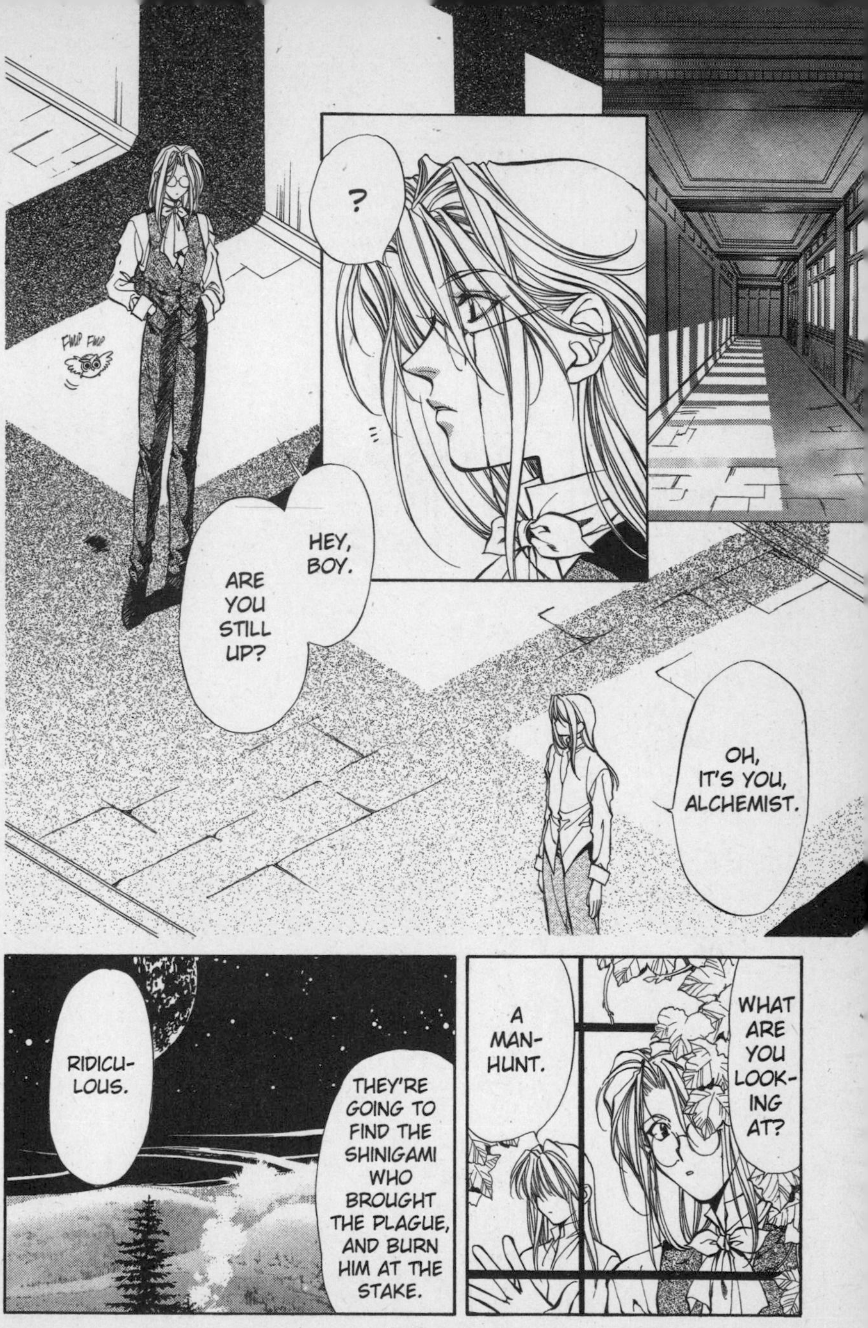
?
FWIP FWIP
HEY, BOY. ARE YOU STILL UP?
OH, IT'S YOU, ALCHEMIST.
WHAT ARE YOU LOOKING AT?
A MAN-HUNT.
THEY'RE GOING TO FIND THE SHINIGAMI WHO BROUGHT THE PLAGUE, AND BURN HIM AT THE STAKE.
RIDICU-LOUS.

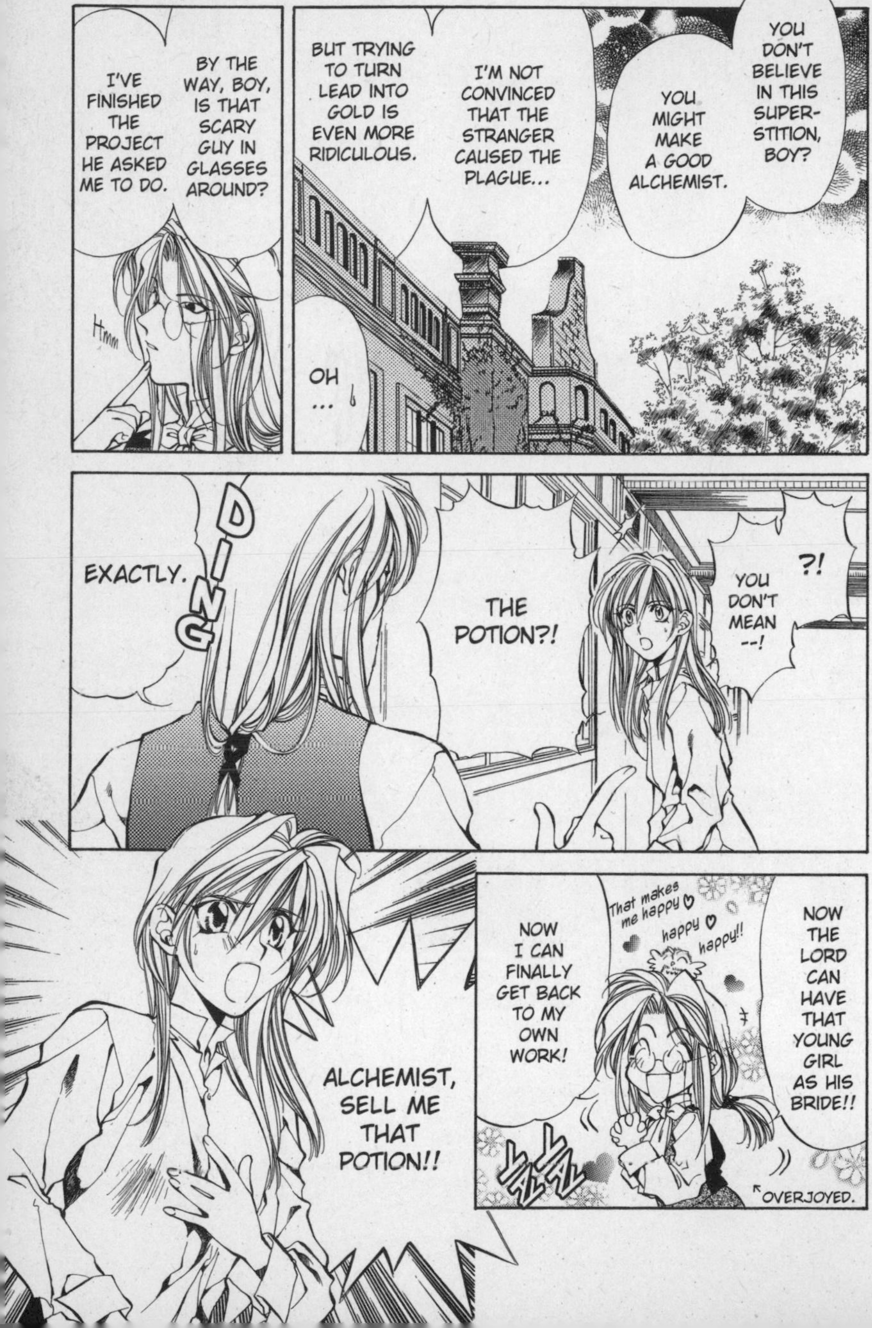
YOU DON'T BELIEVE IN THIS SUPER-STITION, BOY?
YOU MIGHT MAKE A GOOD ALCHEMIST.
I'M NOT CONVINCED THAT THE STRANGER CAUSED THE PLAGUE...
BUT TRYING TO TURN LEAD INTO GOLD IS EVEN MORE RIDICULOUS.
OH ...
BY THE WAY, BOY, IS THAT SCARY GUY IN GLASSES AROUND?
I'VE FINISHED THE PROJECT HE ASKED ME TO DO.
Hmm
?!
YOU DON'T MEAN --!
THE POTION?!
DING
EXACTLY.
NOW THE LORD CAN HAVE THAT YOUNG GIRL AS HIS BRIDE!!
That makes me happy ♡ happy ♡ happy!!
NOW I CAN FINALLY GET BACK TO MY OWN WORK!
OVERJOYED.
ALCHEMIST, SELL ME THAT POTION!!

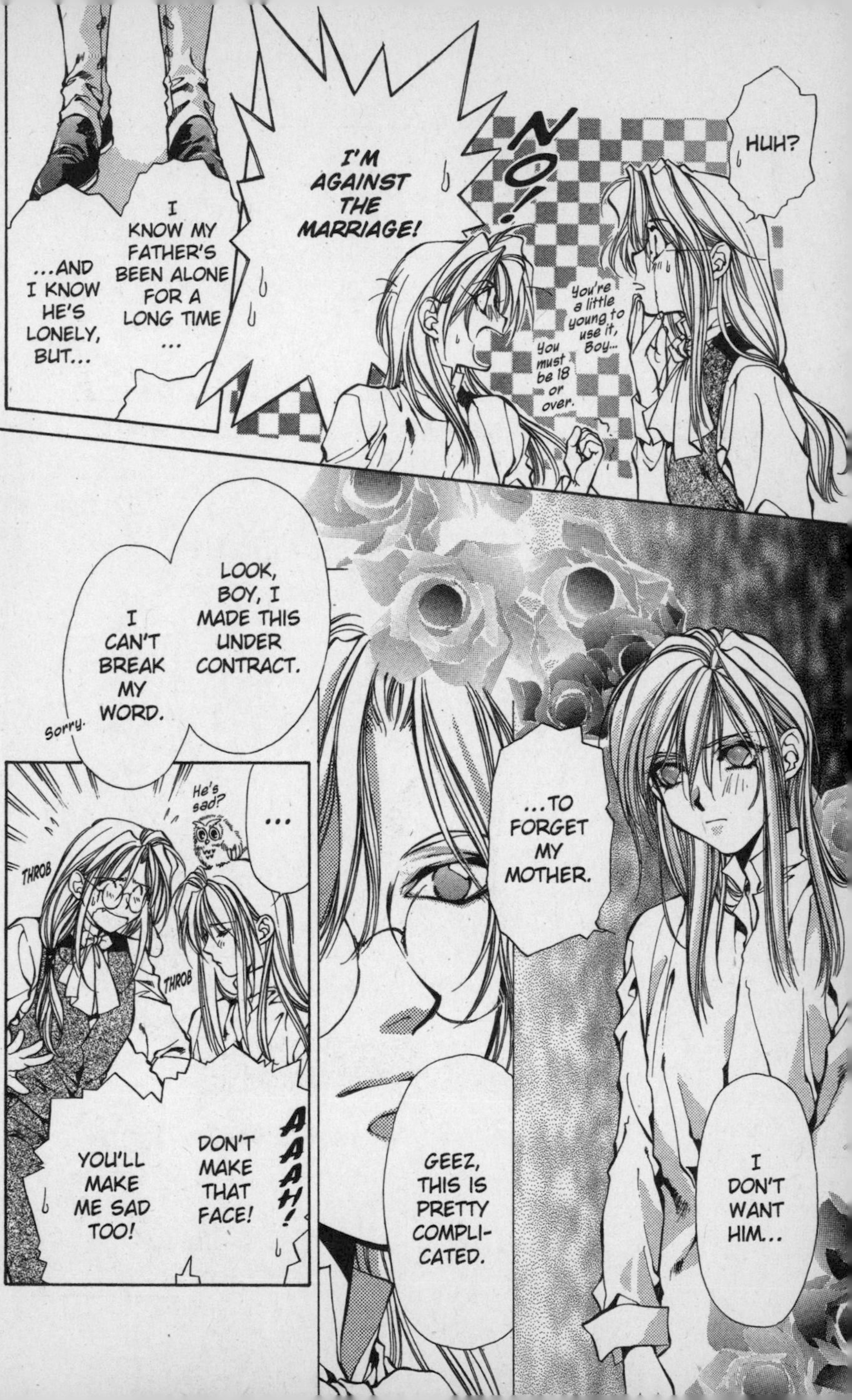

NO!
I'M AGAINST THE MARRIAGE!
HUH?
You're a little young to use it, Boy...
You must be 18 or over.
I KNOW MY FATHER'S BEEN ALONE FOR A LONG TIME...
...AND I KNOW HE'S LONELY, BUT...
I DON'T WANT HIM...
...TO FORGET MY MOTHER.
GEEZ, THIS IS PRETTY COMPLI-CATED.
LOOK, BOY, I MADE THIS UNDER CONTRACT.
I CAN'T BREAK MY WORD.
Sorry.
...
He's sad?
DON'T MAKE THAT FACE!
AAAAH!
YOU'LL MAKE ME SAD TOO!
THROB
THROB

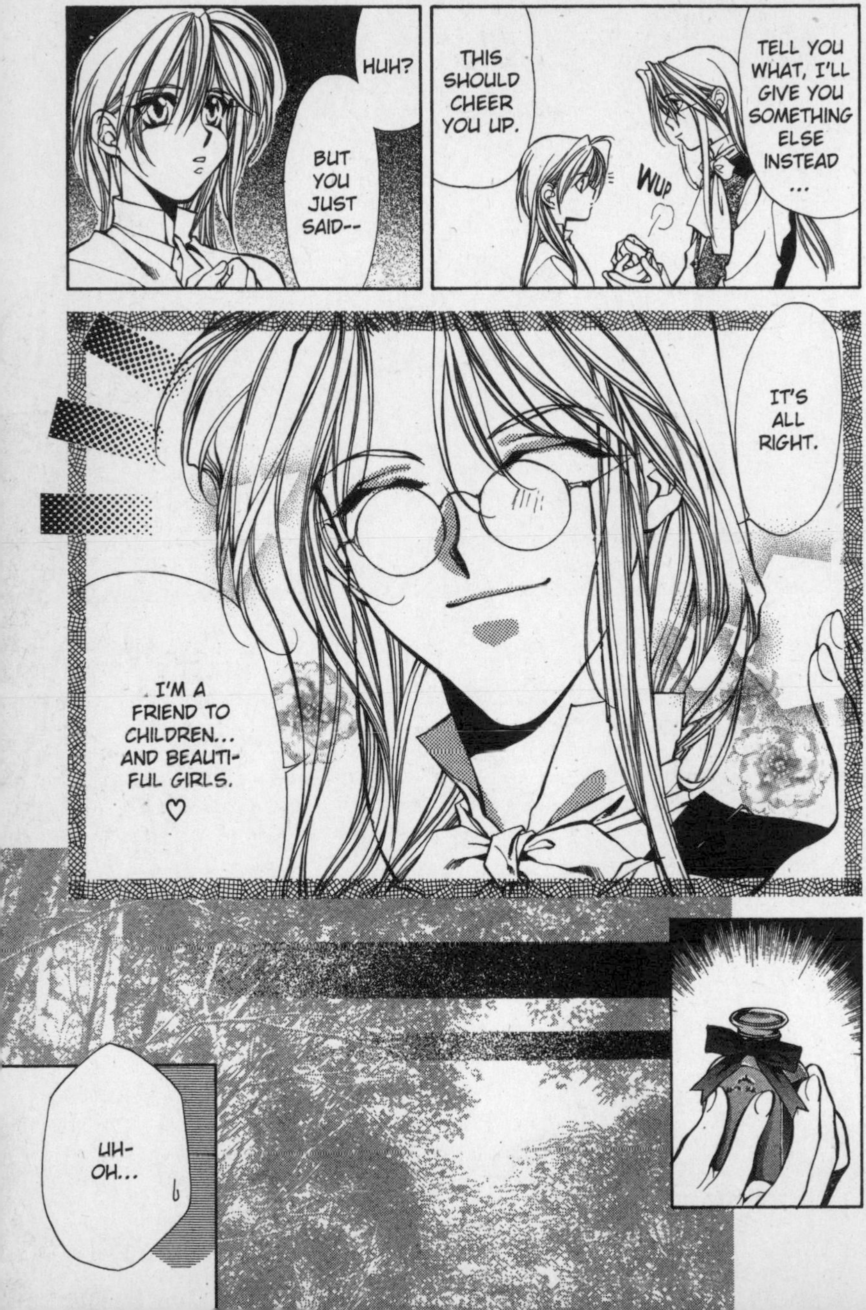
TELL YOU WHAT, I'LL GIVE YOU SOMETHING ELSE INSTEAD ...
THIS SHOULD CHEER YOU UP.
WUP
HUH?
BUT YOU JUST SAID--
IT'S ALL RIGHT.
I'M A FRIEND TO CHILDREN... AND BEAUTI-FUL GIRLS. ♡
UH-OH...

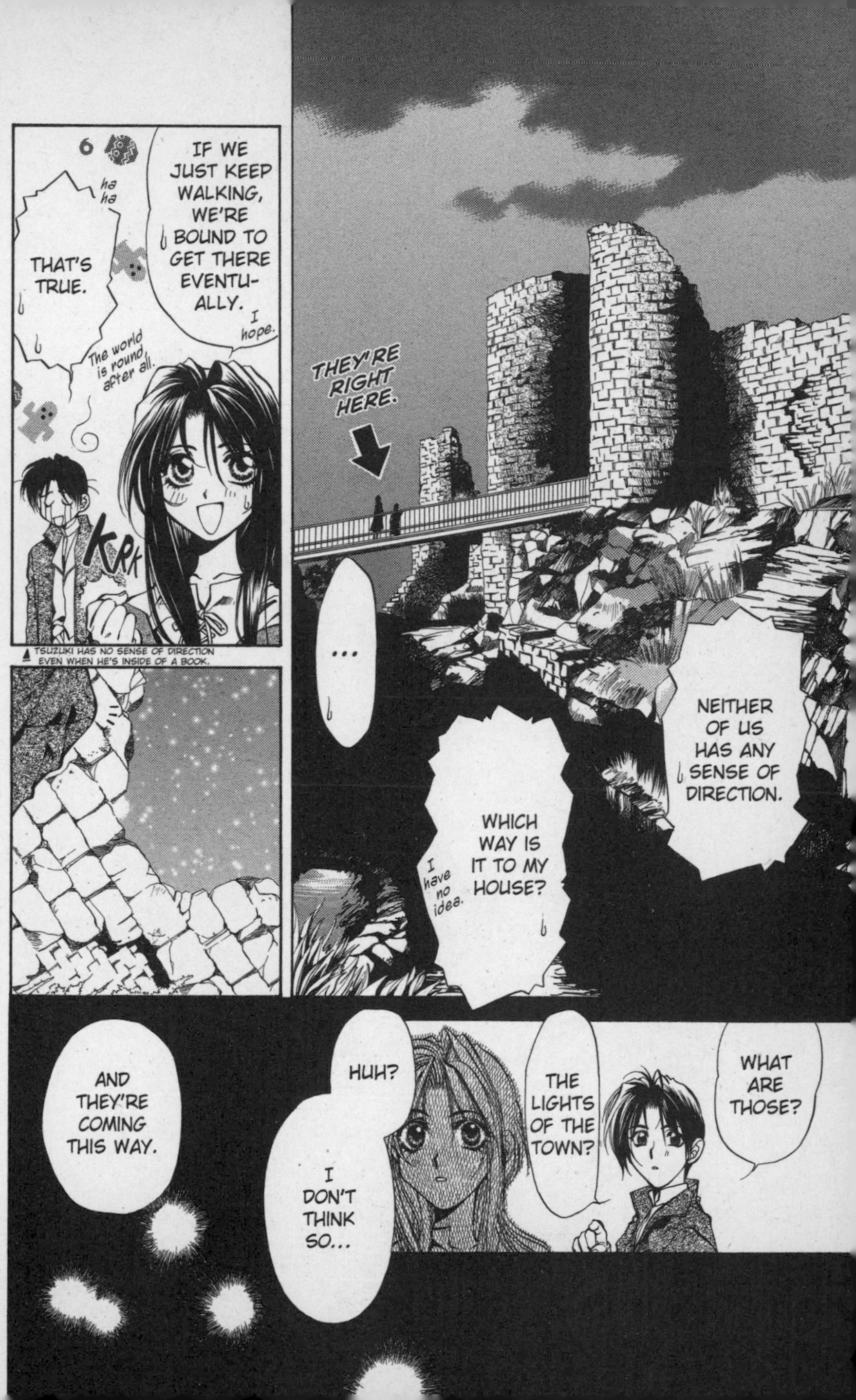
THEY'RE RIGHT HERE.
NEITHER OF US HAS ANY SENSE OF DIRECTION.
...
WHICH WAY IS IT TO MY HOUSE?
I have no idea.
IF WE JUST KEEP WALKING, WE'RE BOUND TO GET THERE EVENTUALLY.
I hope.
The world is round, after all.
ha ha
THAT'S TRUE.
KRK
6
TSUZUKI HAS NO SENSE OF DIRECTION EVEN WHEN HE'S INSIDE OF A BOOK.
WHAT ARE THOSE?
THE LIGHTS OF THE TOWN?
HUH?
I DON'T THINK SO...
AND THEY'RE COMING THIS WAY.

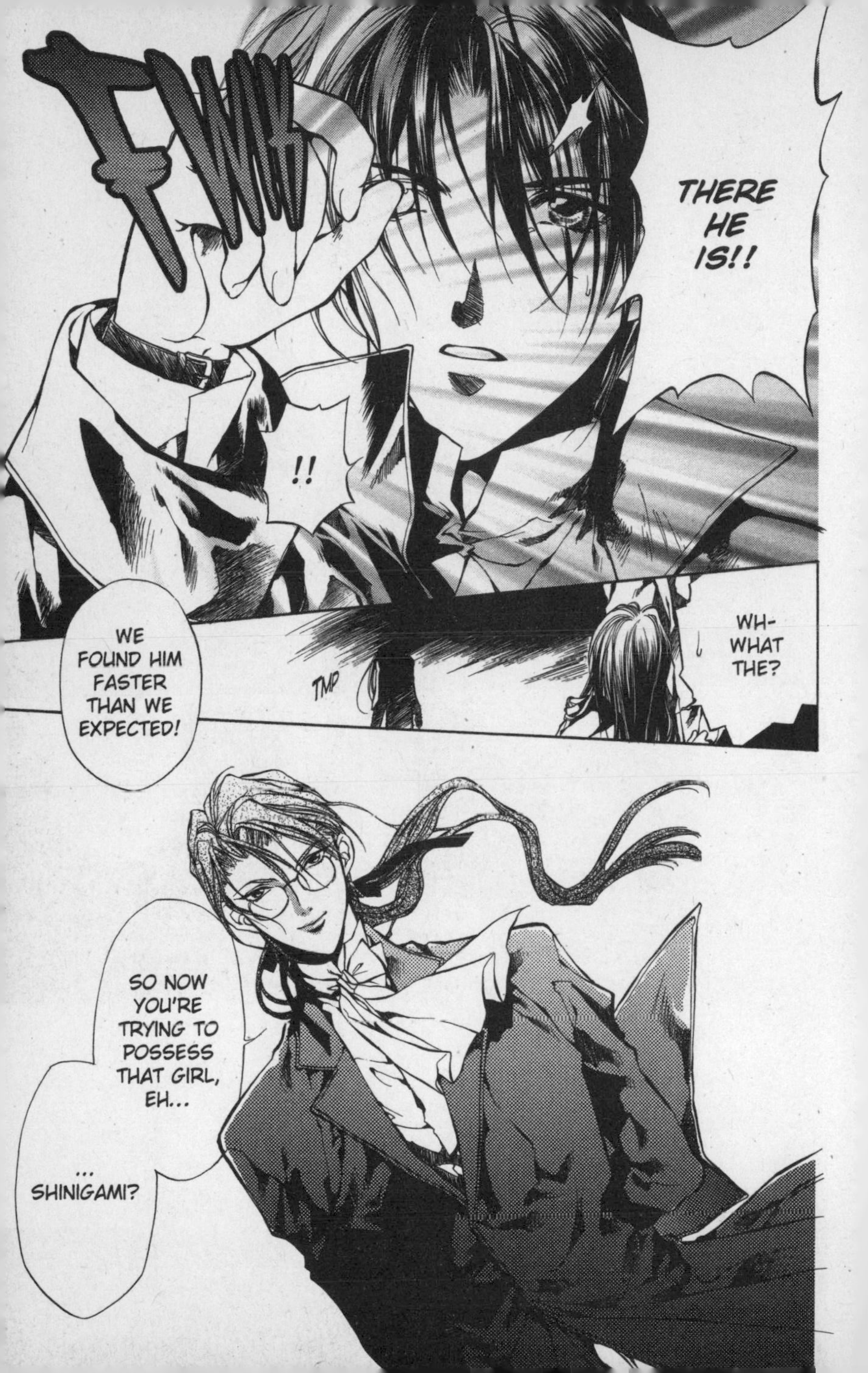
THERE HE IS!!
!!
WH- WHAT THE?
TMP
WE FOUND HIM FASTER THAN WE EXPECTED!
SO NOW YOU'RE TRYING TO POSSESS THAT GIRL, EH...
... SHINIGAMI?

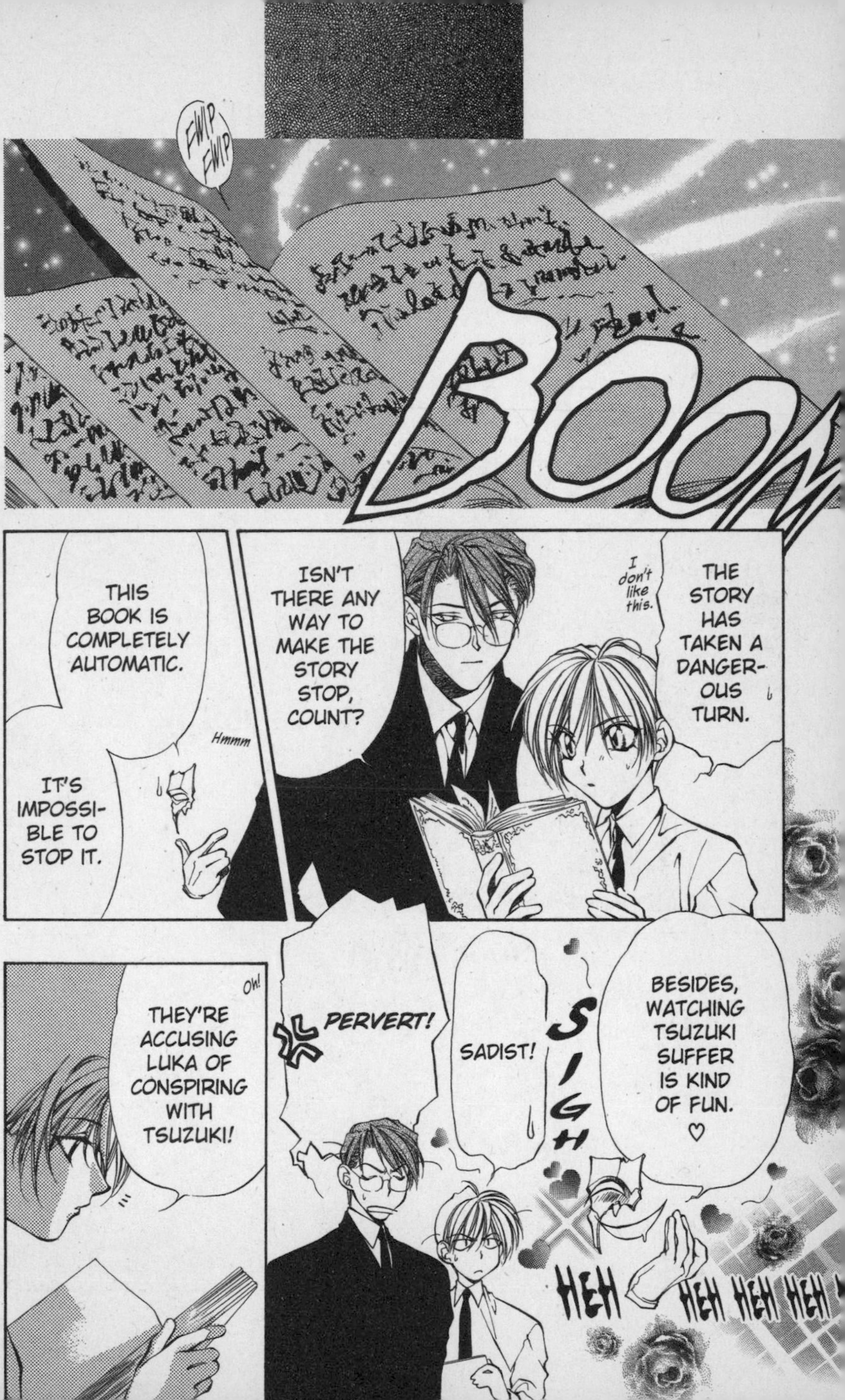
FWIP FWIP
BOOM
I don't like this.
THE STORY HAS TAKEN A DANGER-OUS TURN.
ISN'T THERE ANY WAY TO MAKE THE STORY STOP, COUNT?
THIS BOOK IS COMPLETELY AUTOMATIC.
Hmmm
IT'S IMPOSSI-BLE TO STOP IT.
BESIDES, WATCHING TSUZUKI SUFFER IS KIND OF FUN. ♡
SIGH
SADIST!
PERVERT!
HEH HEH HEH HEH
Oh!
THEY'RE ACCUSING LUKA OF CONSPIRING WITH TSUZUKI!

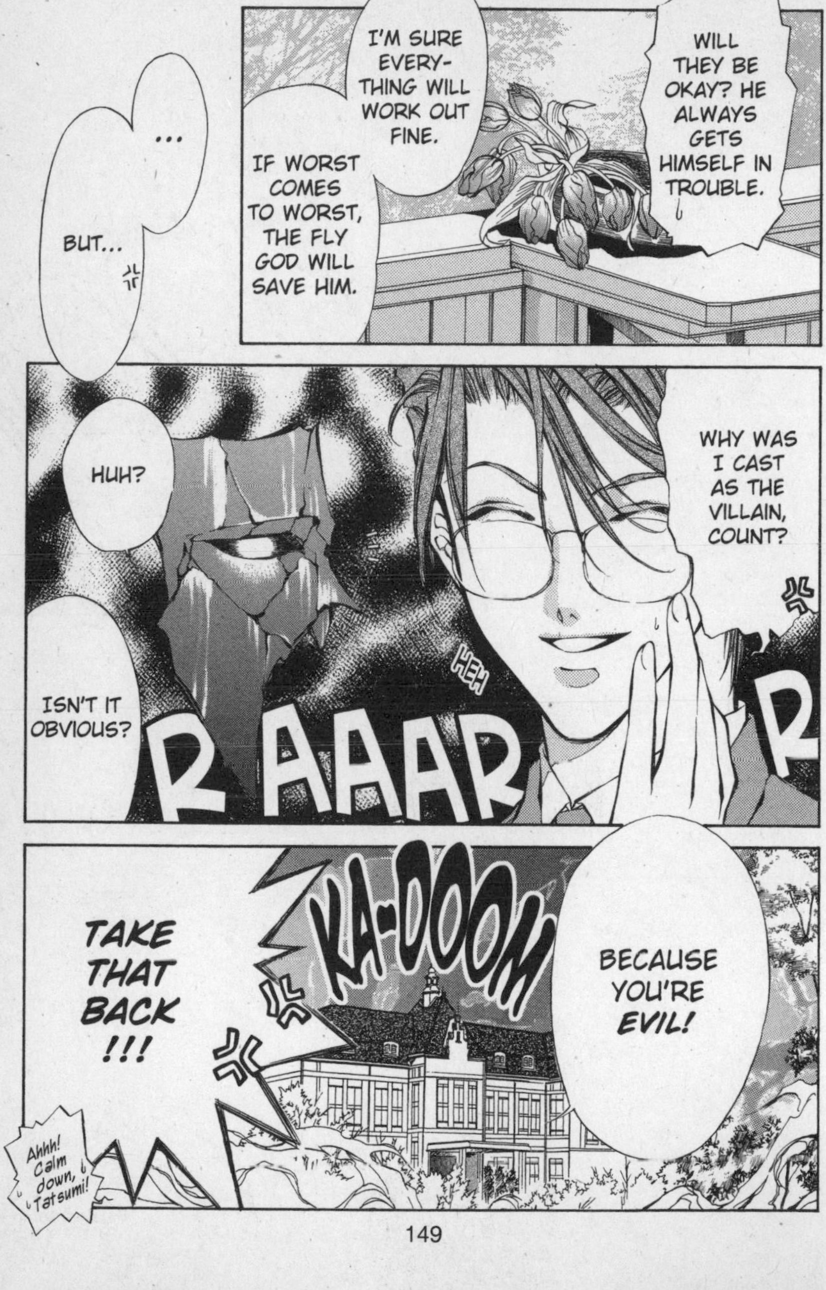
WILL THEY BE OKAY? HE ALWAYS GETS HIMSELF IN TROUBLE.
I'M SURE EVERY-THING WILL WORK OUT FINE.
IF WORST COMES TO WORST, THE FLY GOD WILL SAVE HIM.
...
BUT...
WHY WAS I CAST AS THE VILLAIN, COUNT?
HEH
HUH?
ISN'T IT OBVIOUS?
R AAAR R
BECAUSE YOU'RE *EVIL!*
KA-DOOM
TAKE THAT BACK!!!
Ahhh! Calm down, Tatsumi!

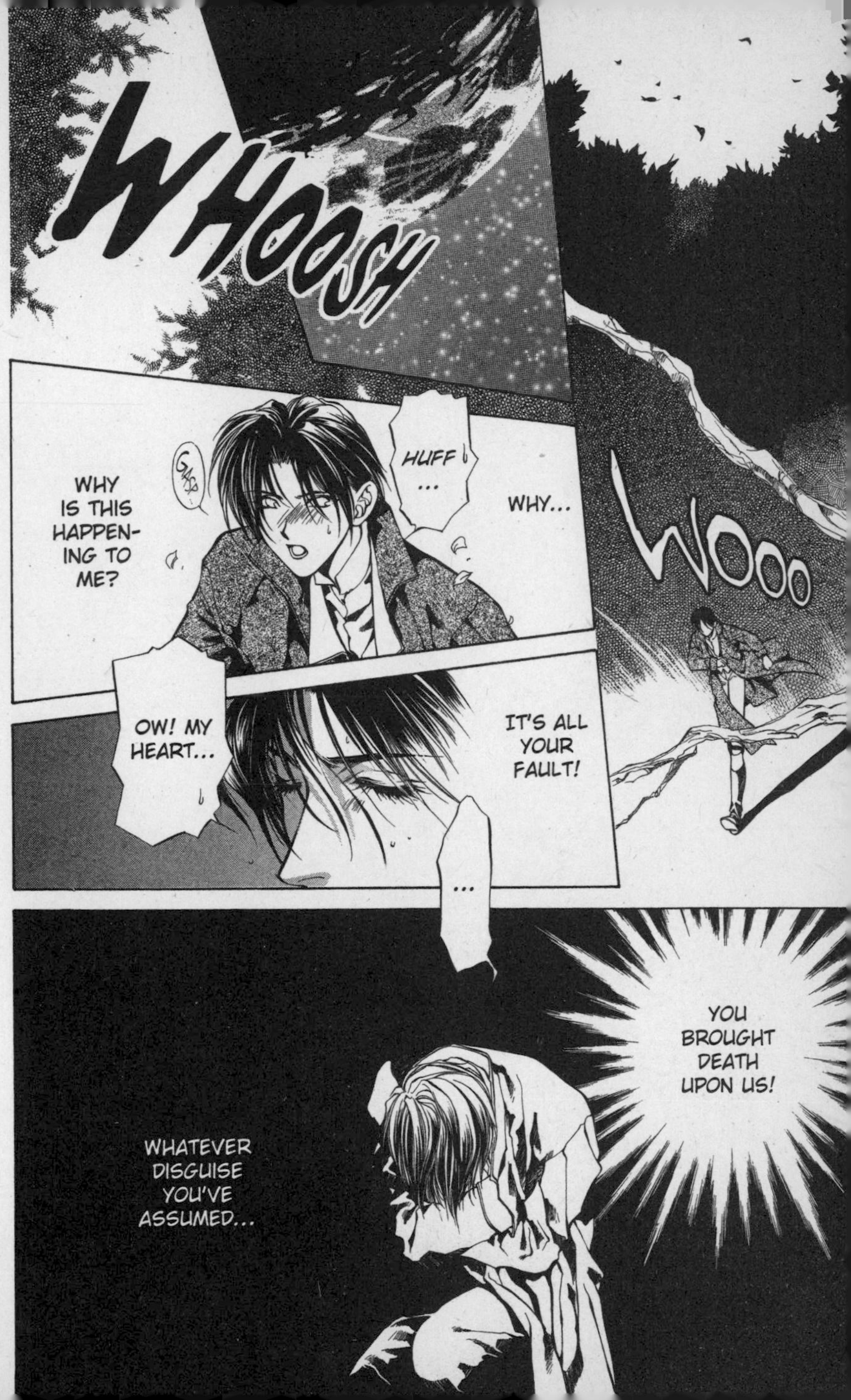
WOOO
WHOOSH
HUFF ...
WHY...
GASP
WHY IS THIS HAPPENING TO ME?
IT'S ALL YOUR FAULT!
OW! MY HEART...
...
YOU BROUGHT DEATH UPON US!
WHATEVER DISGUISE YOU'VE ASSUMED...

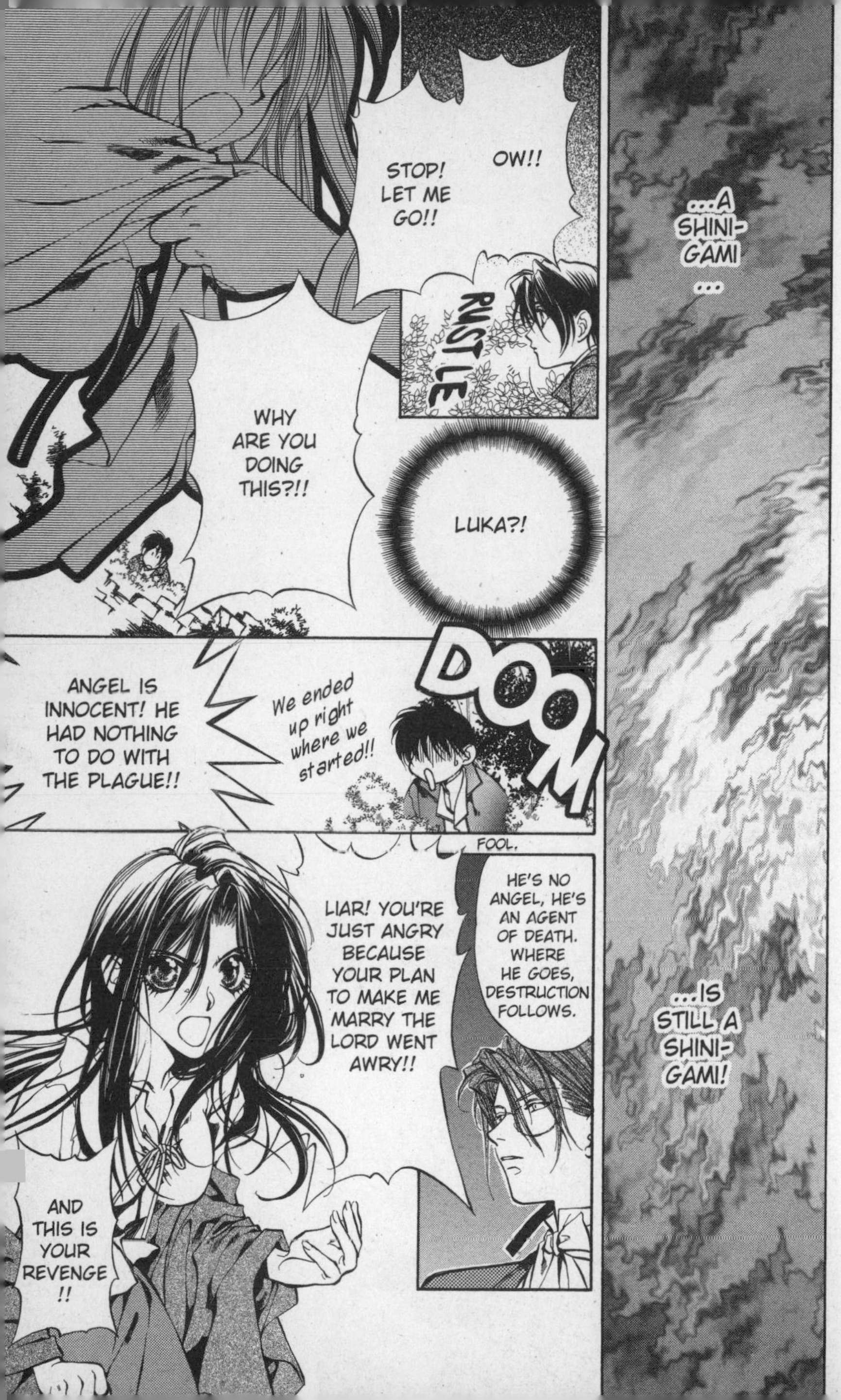
...A SHINI-GAMI ...
...IS STILL A SHINI-GAMI!
OW!!
STOP! LET ME GO!!
RUST LE
WHY ARE YOU DOING THIS?!!
LUKA?!
DOOM
We ended up right where we started!!
ANGEL IS INNOCENT! HE HAD NOTHING TO DO WITH THE PLAGUE!!
FOOL.
HE'S NO ANGEL, HE'S AN AGENT OF DEATH. WHERE HE GOES, DESTRUCTION FOLLOWS.
LIAR! YOU'RE JUST ANGRY BECAUSE YOUR PLAN TO MAKE ME MARRY THE LORD WENT AWRY!!
AND THIS IS YOUR REVENGE !!

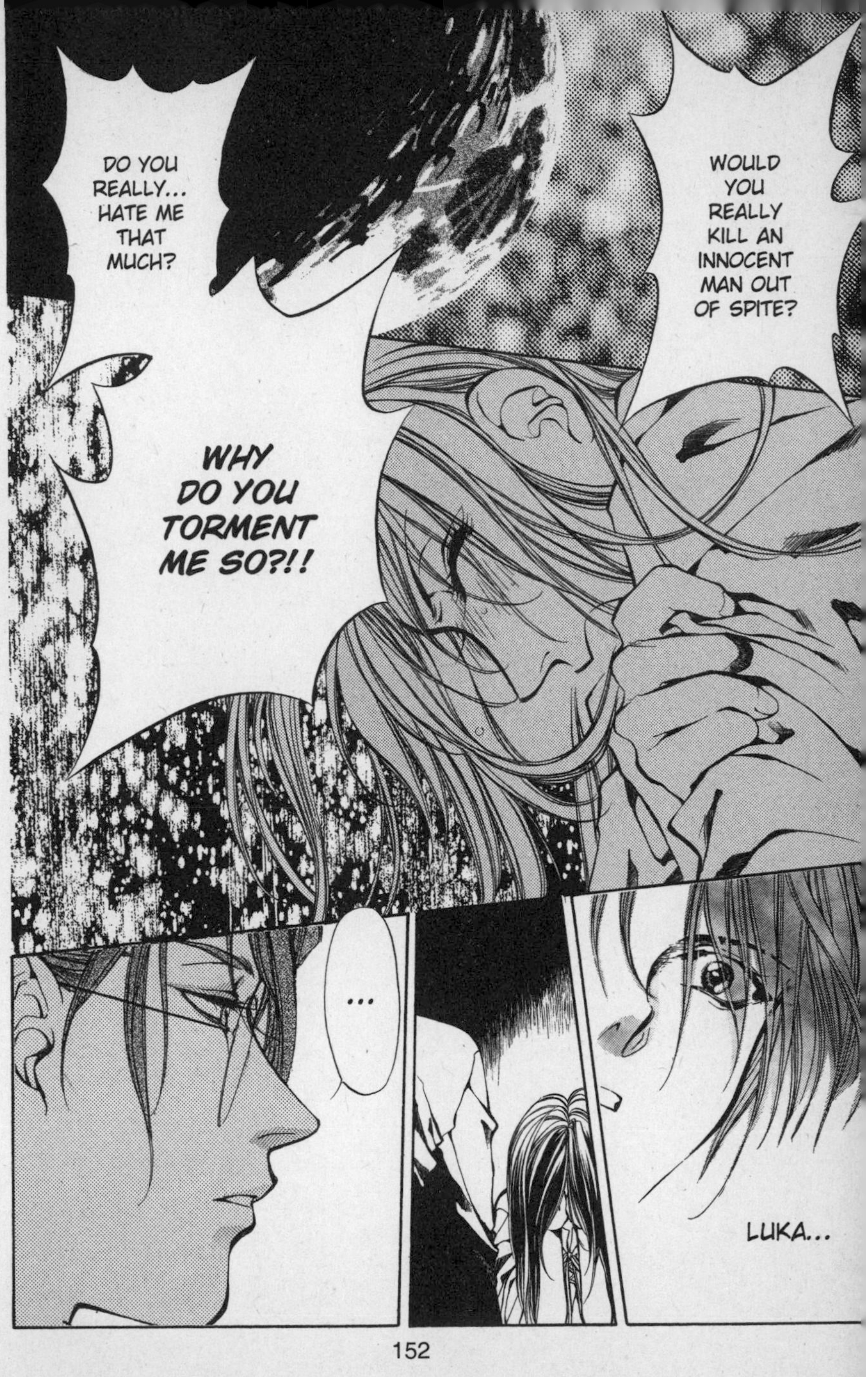
WOULD YOU REALLY KILL AN INNOCENT MAN OUT OF SPITE?
DO YOU REALLY... HATE ME THAT MUCH?
WHY DO YOU TORMENT ME SO?!!
LUKA...
...

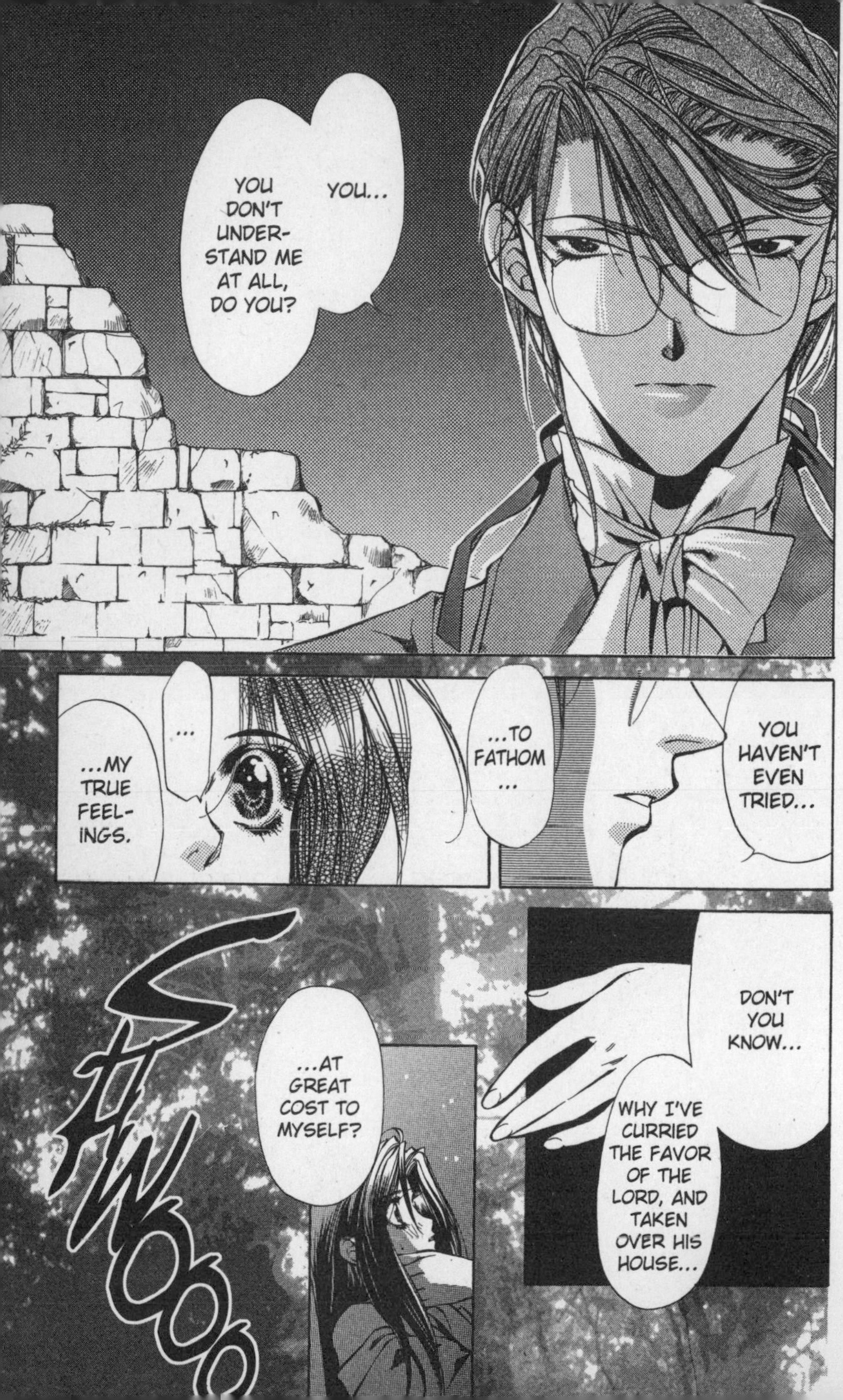
YOU...
YOU DON'T UNDER-STAND ME AT ALL, DO YOU?
YOU HAVEN'T EVEN TRIED...
...TO FATHOM ...
...
...MY TRUE FEEL-INGS.
DON'T YOU KNOW...
WHY I'VE CURRIED THE FAVOR OF THE LORD, AND TAKEN OVER HIS HOUSE...
...AT GREAT COST TO MYSELF?
SHWOOO

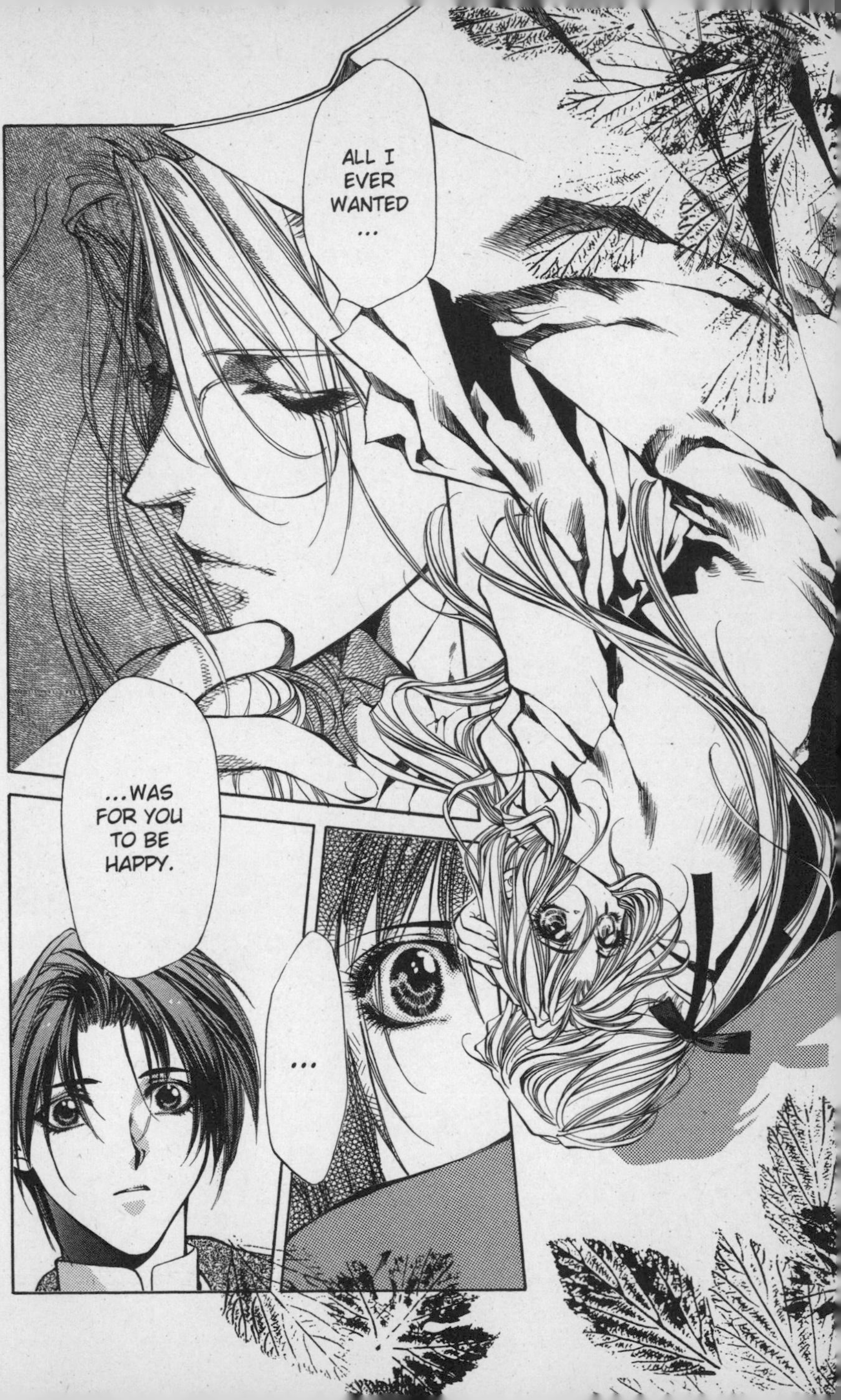
ALL I EVER WANTED ...
...WAS FOR YOU TO BE HAPPY.
...

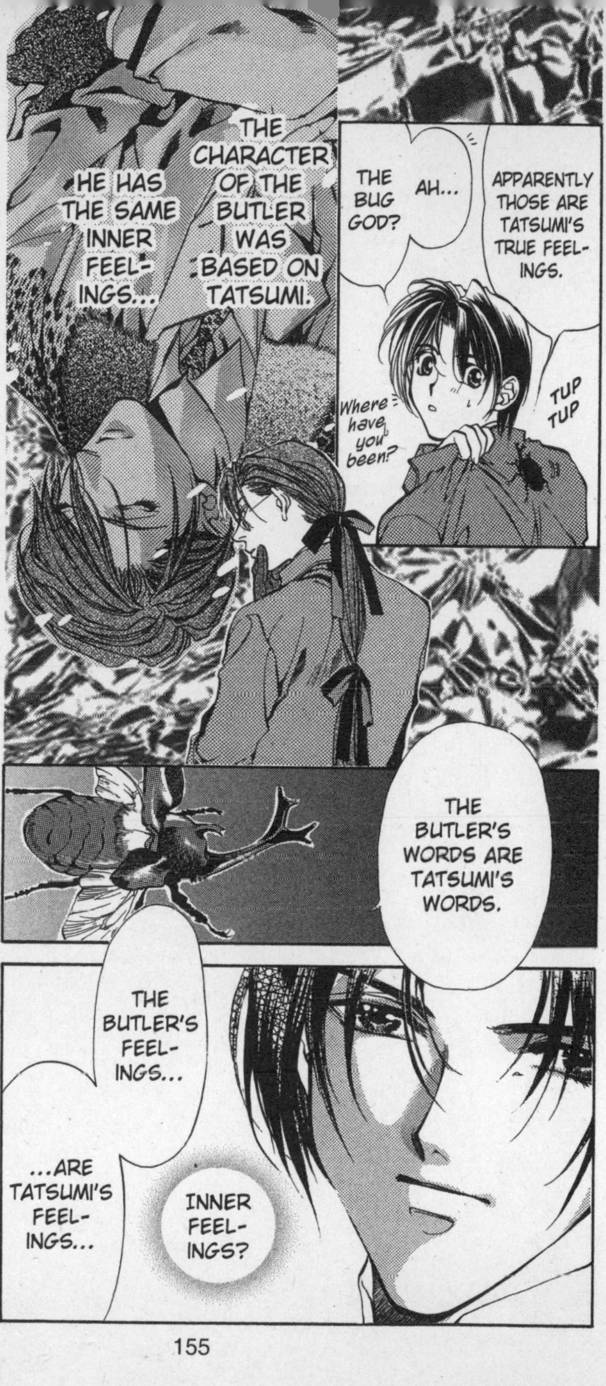
APPARENTLY THOSE ARE TATSUMI'S TRUE FEEL-INGS.
AH...
THE BUG GOD?
TUP TUP
Where have you been?
THE CHARACTER OF THE BUTLER WAS BASED ON TATSUMI.
HE HAS THE SAME INNER FEEL-INGS...
THE BUTLER'S WORDS ARE TATSUMI'S WORDS.
THE BUTLER'S FEEL-INGS...
...ARE TATSUMI'S FEEL-INGS...
INNER FEEL-INGS?

I was raised by the television, so I'm picky when it comes to voice actors. The first one I chose was Shou Hayami who did the voice of Muraki. I just really love his voice. I actually imagined his voice as I was creating Muraki, that's how perfect he was. And he did a great job. We even made the recording schedule around Hayami's schedule! (Ha) This CD was meant for him.

Before I decided on the actor's who would play the two main characters, I cast Toshiyuki Morikawa as Tatsumi and Toshihiko Seki as Watari. Their voices are just my type--totally sexy. I asked the editing department not to scrimp on the budget for the voice actors. I learned that Morikawa used to work for the police department (I didn't know that--pathetic, huh?) and that he was also a chief researcher before he became a successful voice actor. (Hee) I'd seen Seki before on the kids' show *The Singing Flute*. I absolutely love him. So I decided on those guys right away.

TO BE CONTINUED...

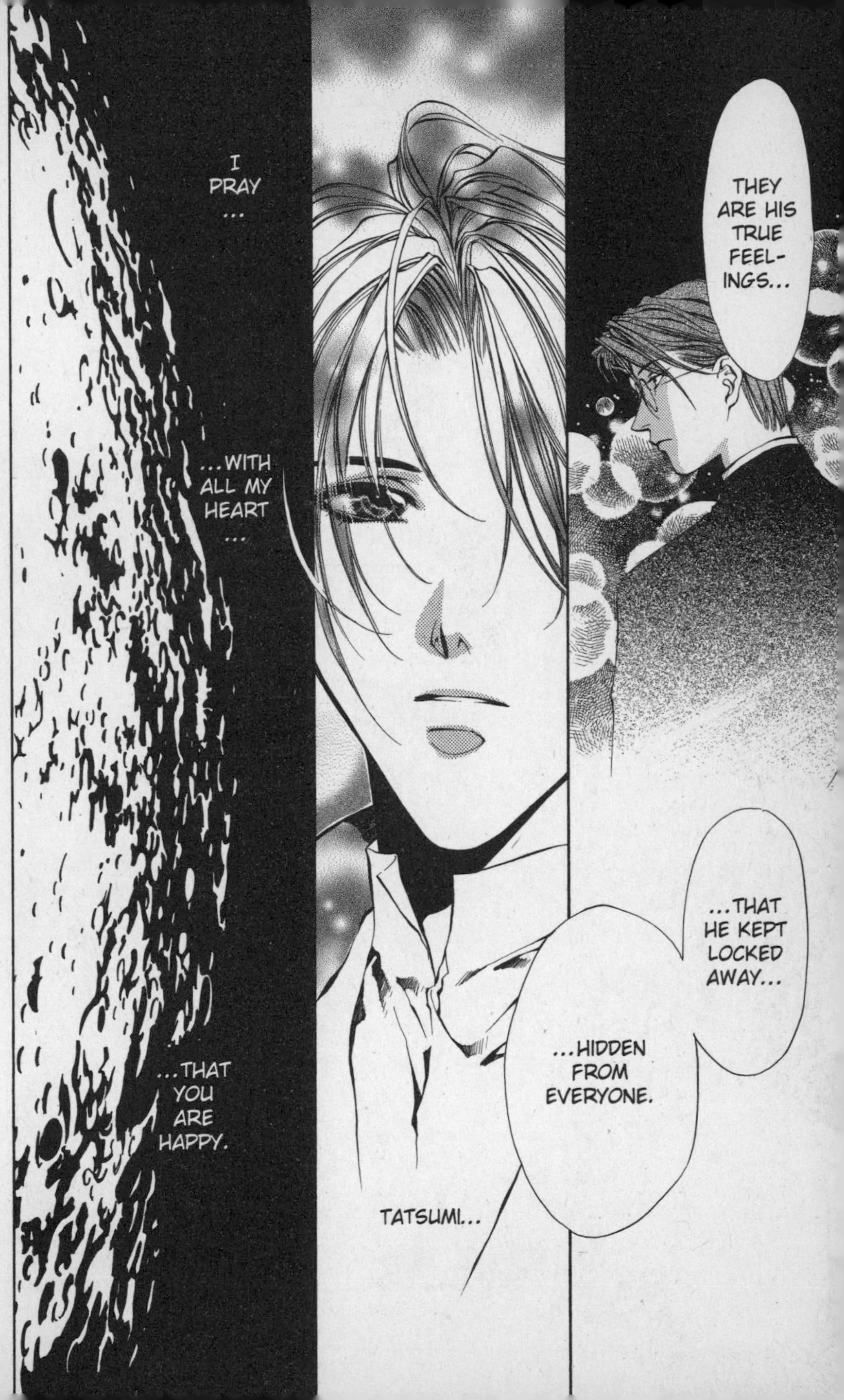
THEY ARE HIS TRUE FEEL- INGS...
...THAT HE KEPT LOCKED AWAY...
...HIDDEN FROM EVERYONE.
TATSUMI...
I PRAY ...
...WITH ALL MY HEART ...
...THAT YOU ARE HAPPY.

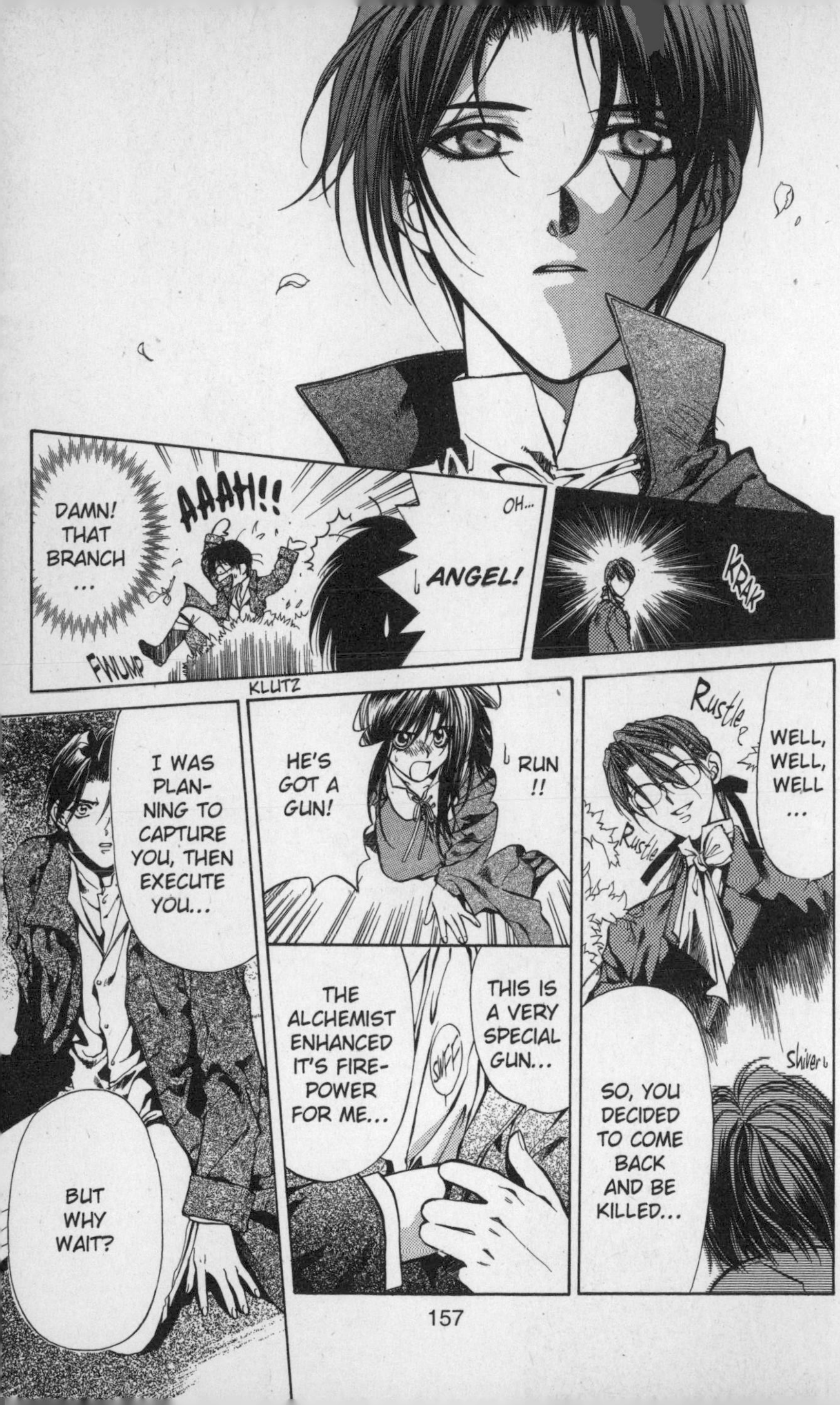
KRAK
OH...
ANGEL!
AAAH!!
DAMN! THAT BRANCH...
FWUMP
KLUTZ
Rustle
WELL, WELL, WELL...
Rustle
Shiver
SO, YOU DECIDED TO COME BACK AND BE KILLED...
RUN!!
HE'S GOT A GUN!
THIS IS A VERY SPECIAL GUN...
SWFF
THE ALCHEMIST ENHANCED IT'S FIRE-POWER FOR ME...
I WAS PLAN-NING TO CAPTURE YOU, THEN EXECUTE YOU...
BUT WHY WAIT?

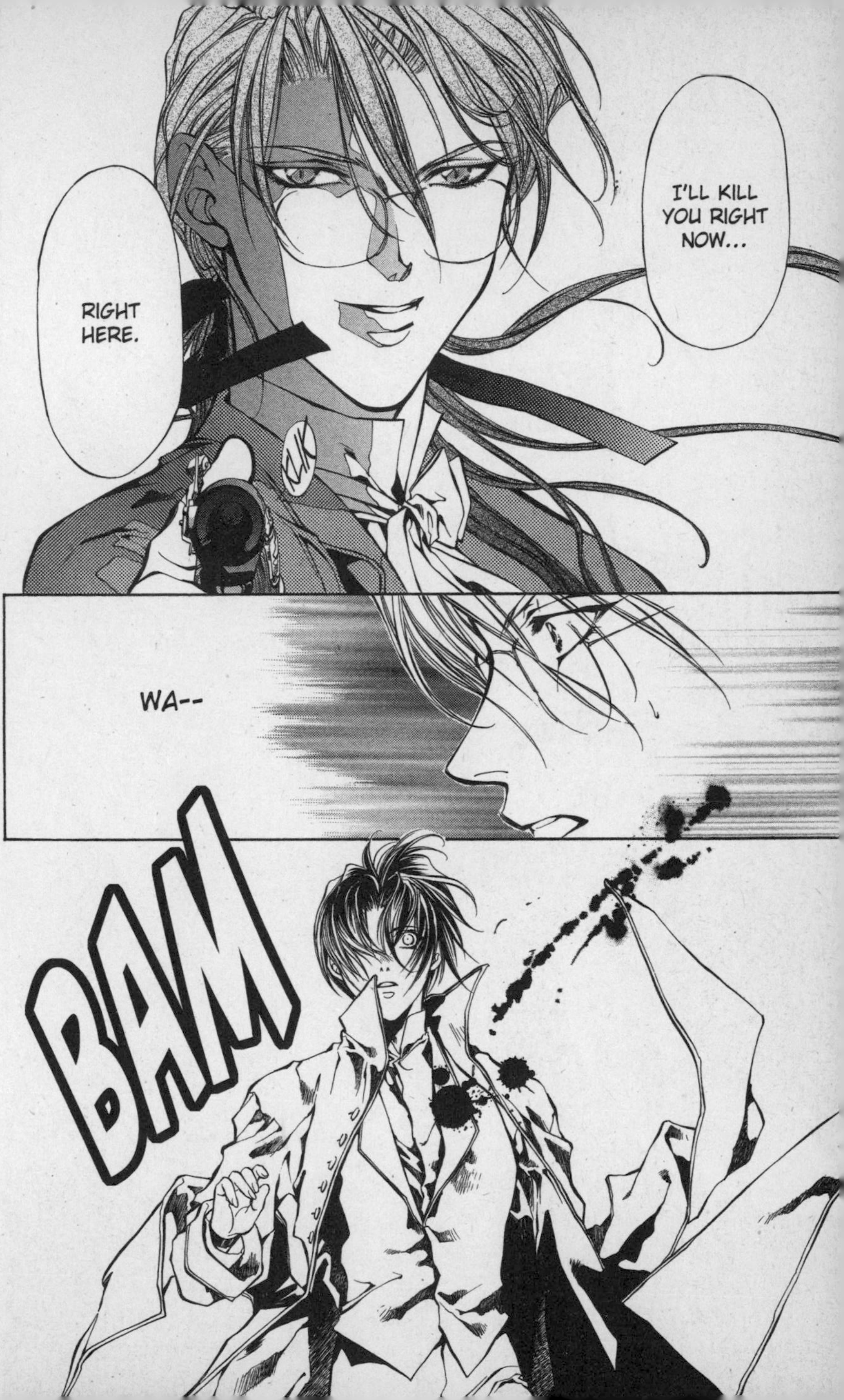
I'LL KILL YOU RIGHT NOW...
RIGHT HERE.
KLIK
WA--
BAM

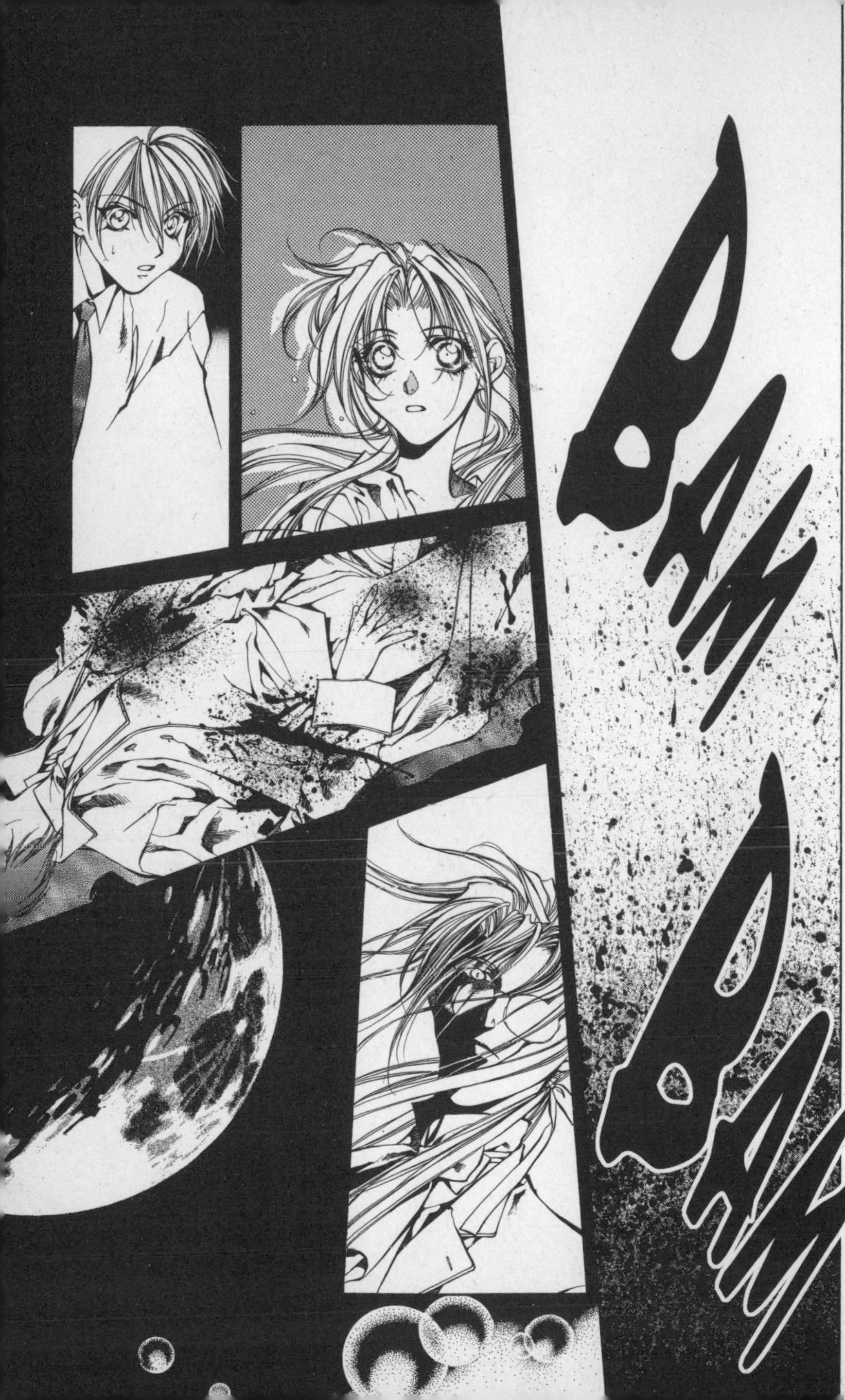
BAM BAM

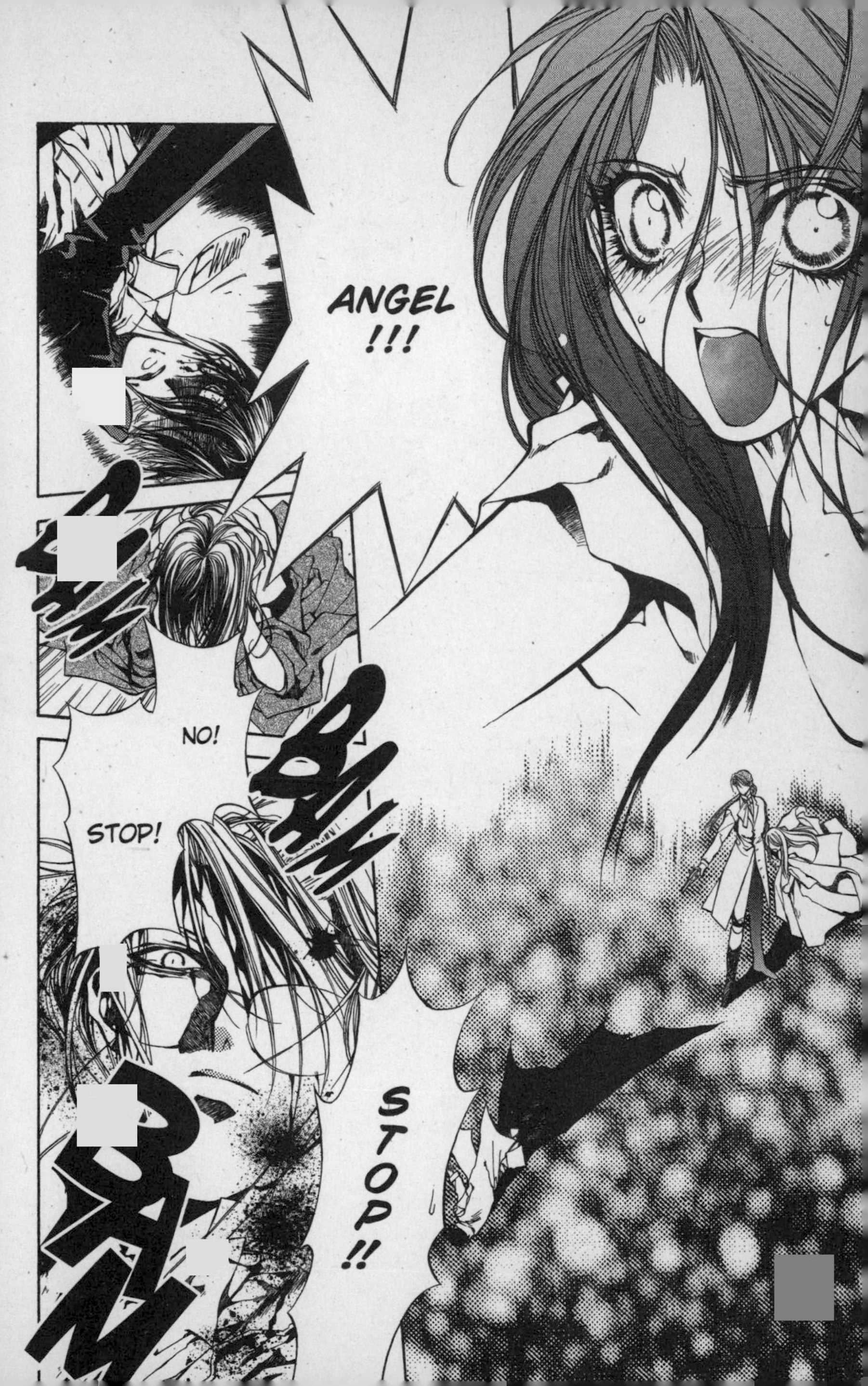
ANGEL !!!
STOP!!
BAM
NO!
STOP!
BAM
BAM

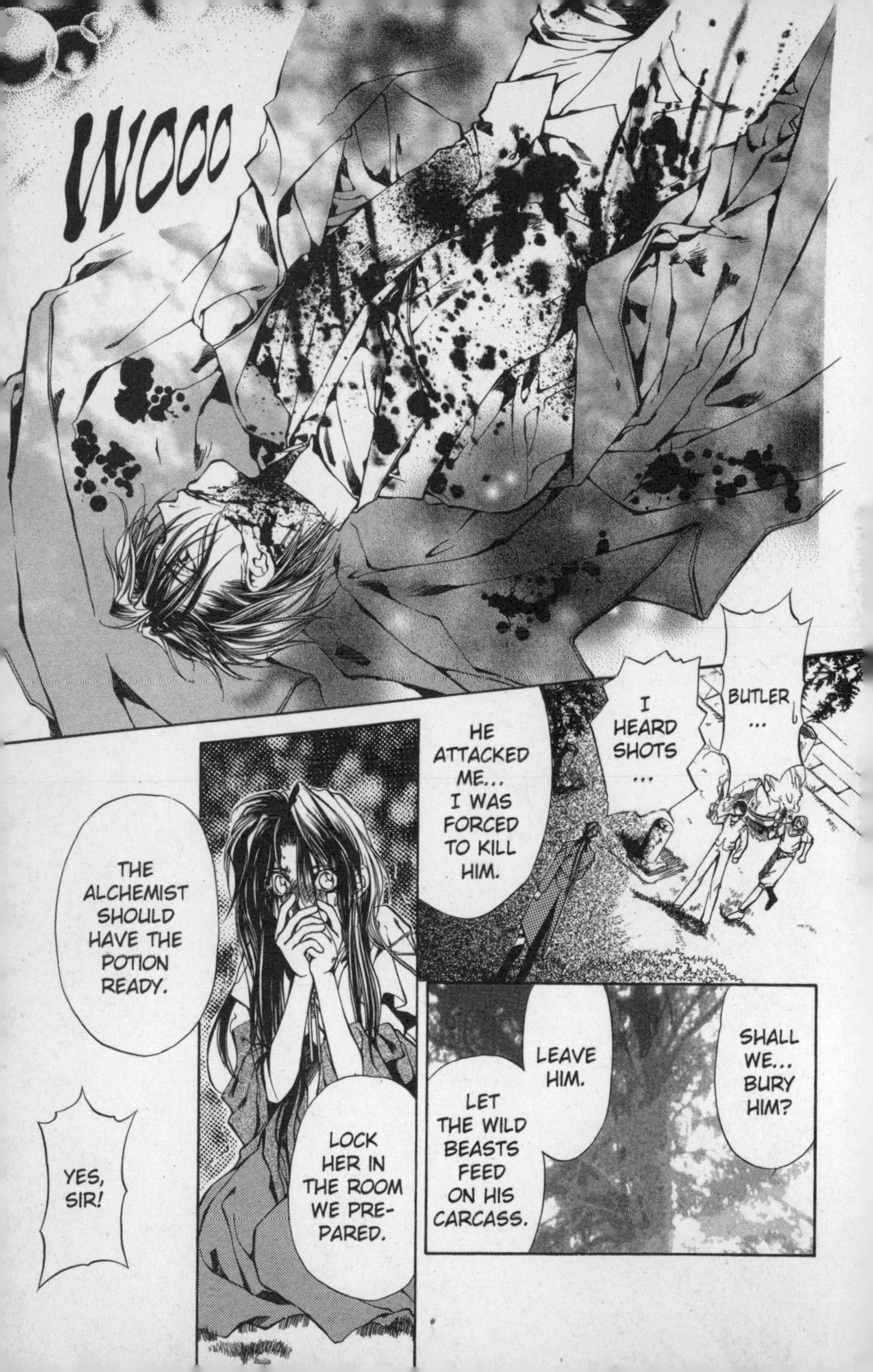
WOOO
BUTLER ...
I HEARD SHOTS ...
HE ATTACKED ME... I WAS FORCED TO KILL HIM.
SHALL WE... BURY HIM?
LEAVE HIM.
LET THE WILD BEASTS FEED ON HIS CARCASS.
THE ALCHEMIST SHOULD HAVE THE POTION READY.
LOCK HER IN THE ROOM WE PRE-PARED.
YES, SIR!

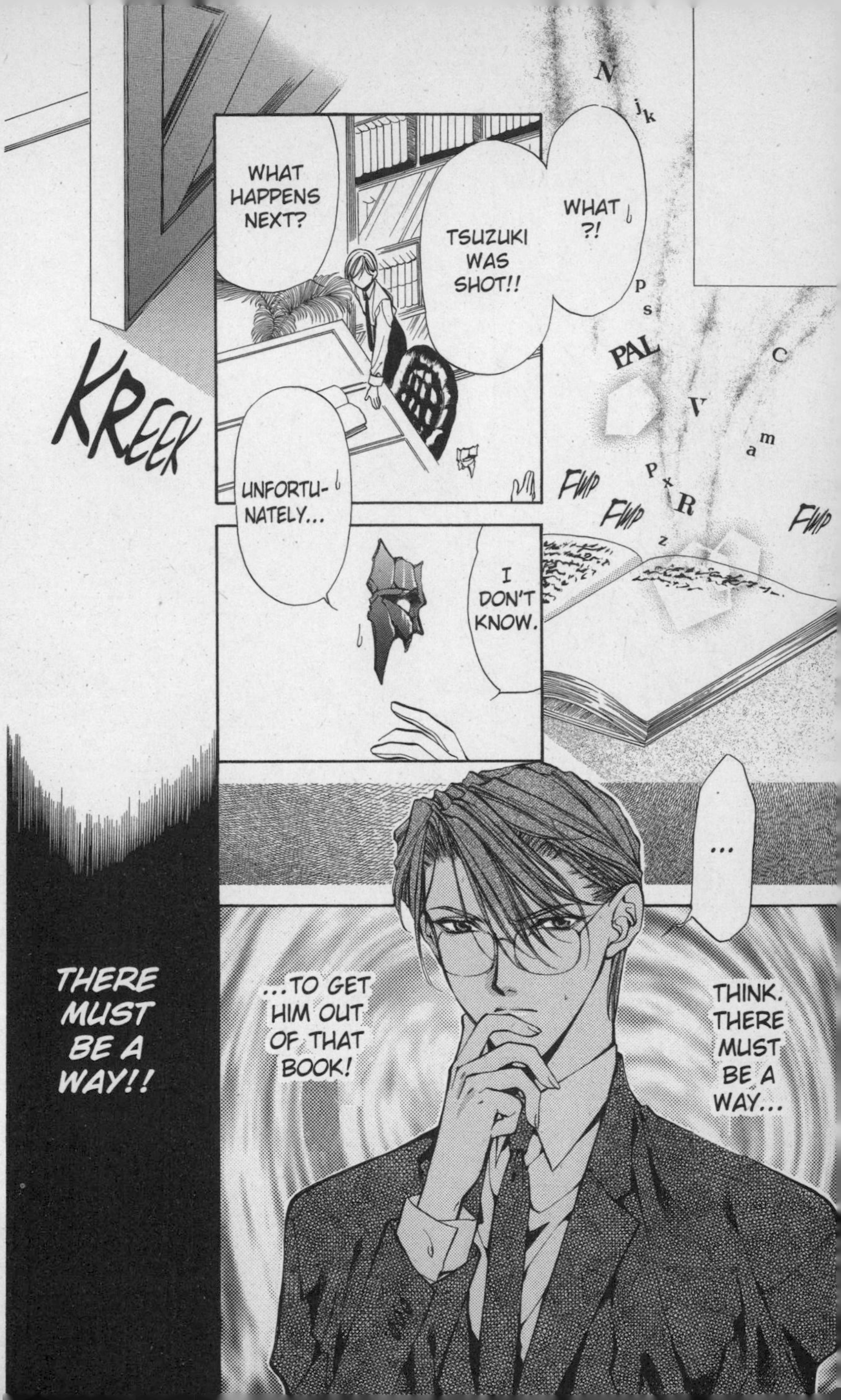
WHAT ?!
TSUZUKI WAS SHOT!!
WHAT HAPPENS NEXT?
UNFORTU-NATELY...
KREEK
I DON'T KNOW.
FWP
FWP
FWP
...
THINK. THERE MUST BE A WAY...
...TO GET HIM OUT OF THAT BOOK!
THERE MUST BE A WAY!!

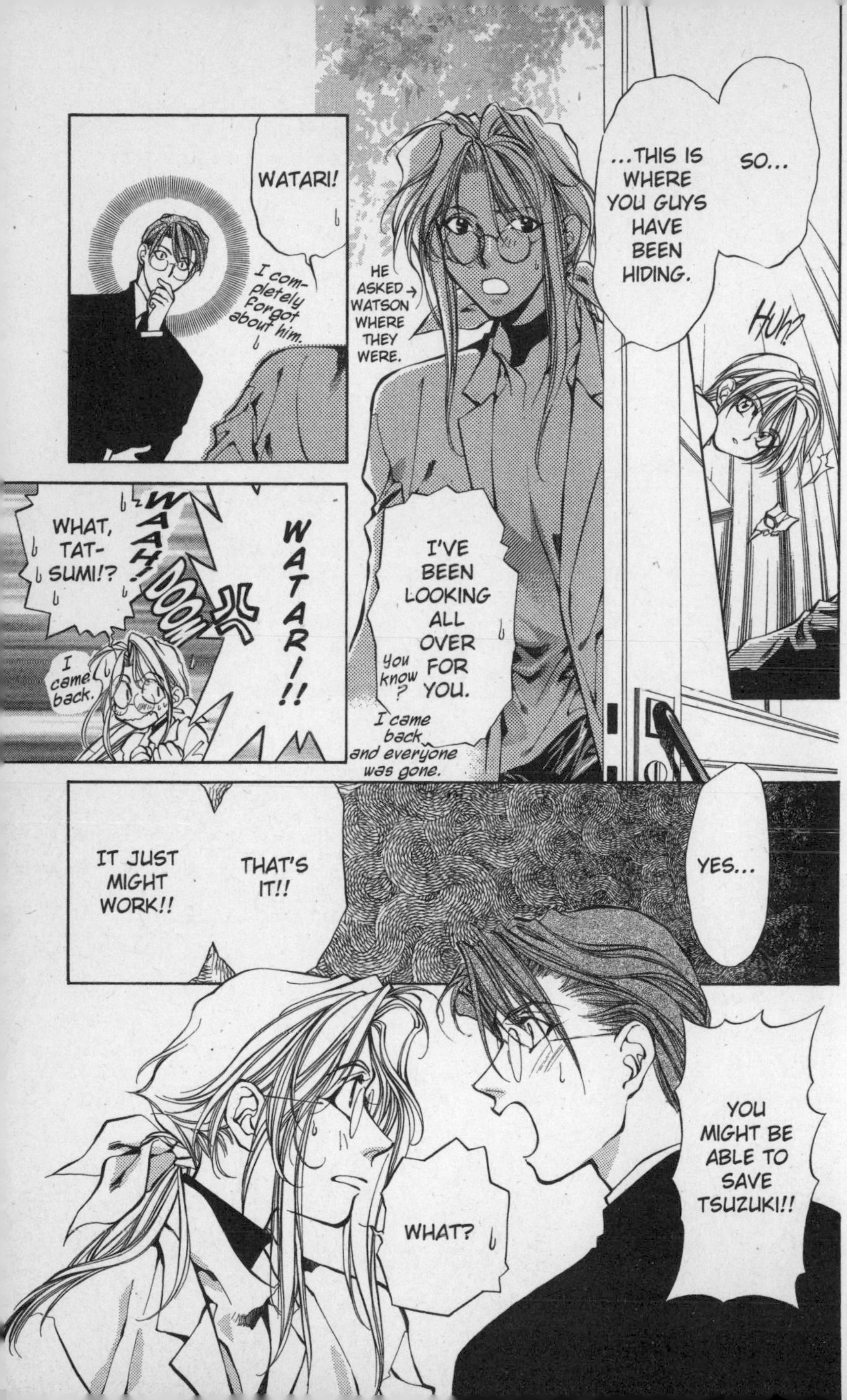
SO...
...THIS IS WHERE YOU GUYS HAVE BEEN HIDING.
Huh?
I'VE BEEN LOOKING ALL OVER FOR YOU.
You know?
I came back and everyone was gone.
HE ASKED → WATSON WHERE THEY WERE.
WATARI!
I completely forgot about him.
WATARI!!
WAAH!
DOOM
WHAT, TAT-SUMI!?
I came back.
YES...
THAT'S IT!!
IT JUST MIGHT WORK!!
YOU MIGHT BE ABLE TO SAVE TSUZUKI!!
WHAT?

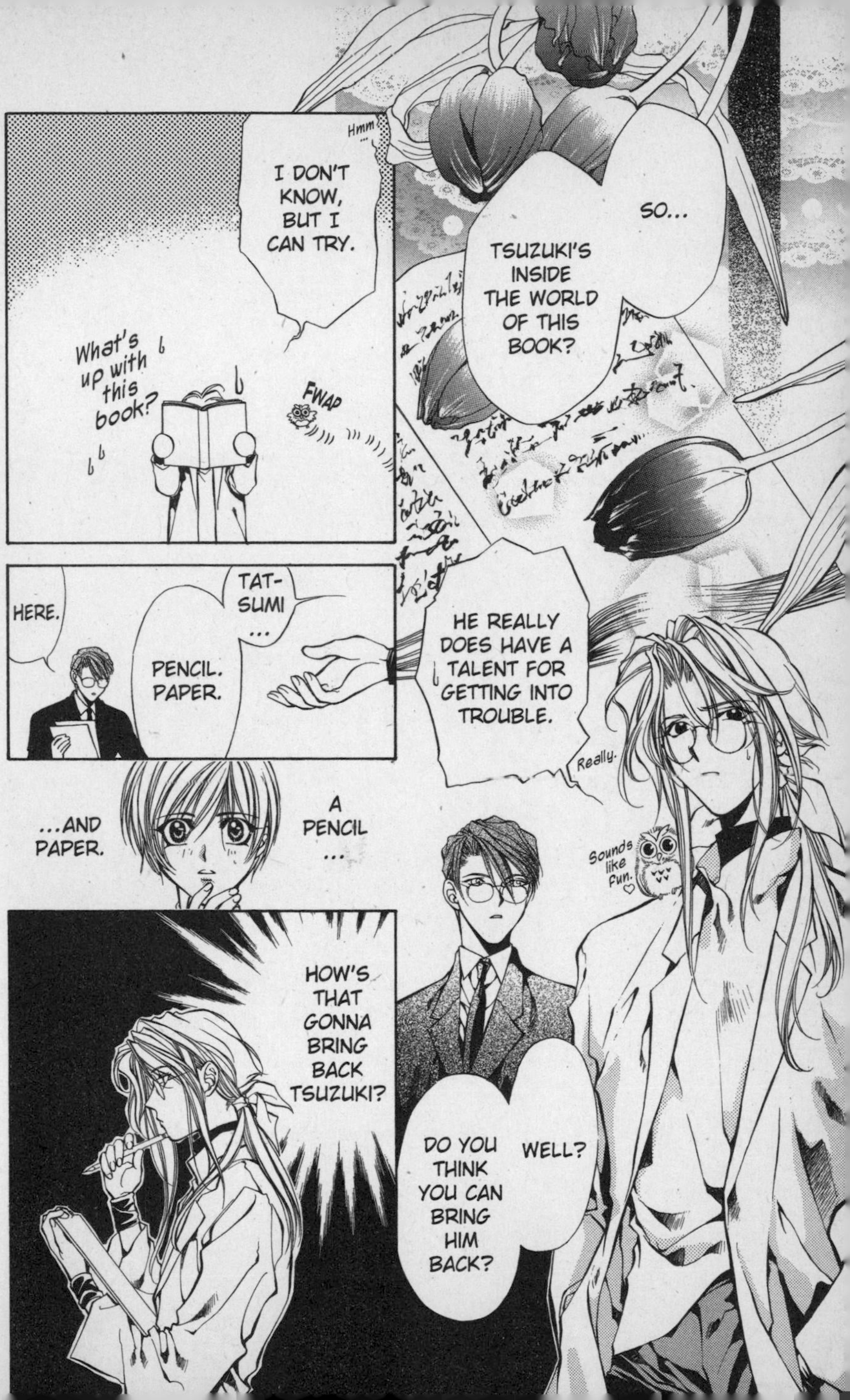
SO...
TSUZUKI'S INSIDE THE WORLD OF THIS BOOK?
HE REALLY DOES HAVE A TALENT FOR GETTING INTO TROUBLE.
Really.
Sounds like fun. ♡
WELL?
DO YOU THINK YOU CAN BRING HIM BACK?
Hmm...
I DON'T KNOW, BUT I CAN TRY.
What's up with this book?
FWAP
TAT-SUMI...
PENCIL. PAPER.
HERE.
A PENCIL...
...AND PAPER.
HOW'S THAT GONNA BRING BACK TSUZUKI?

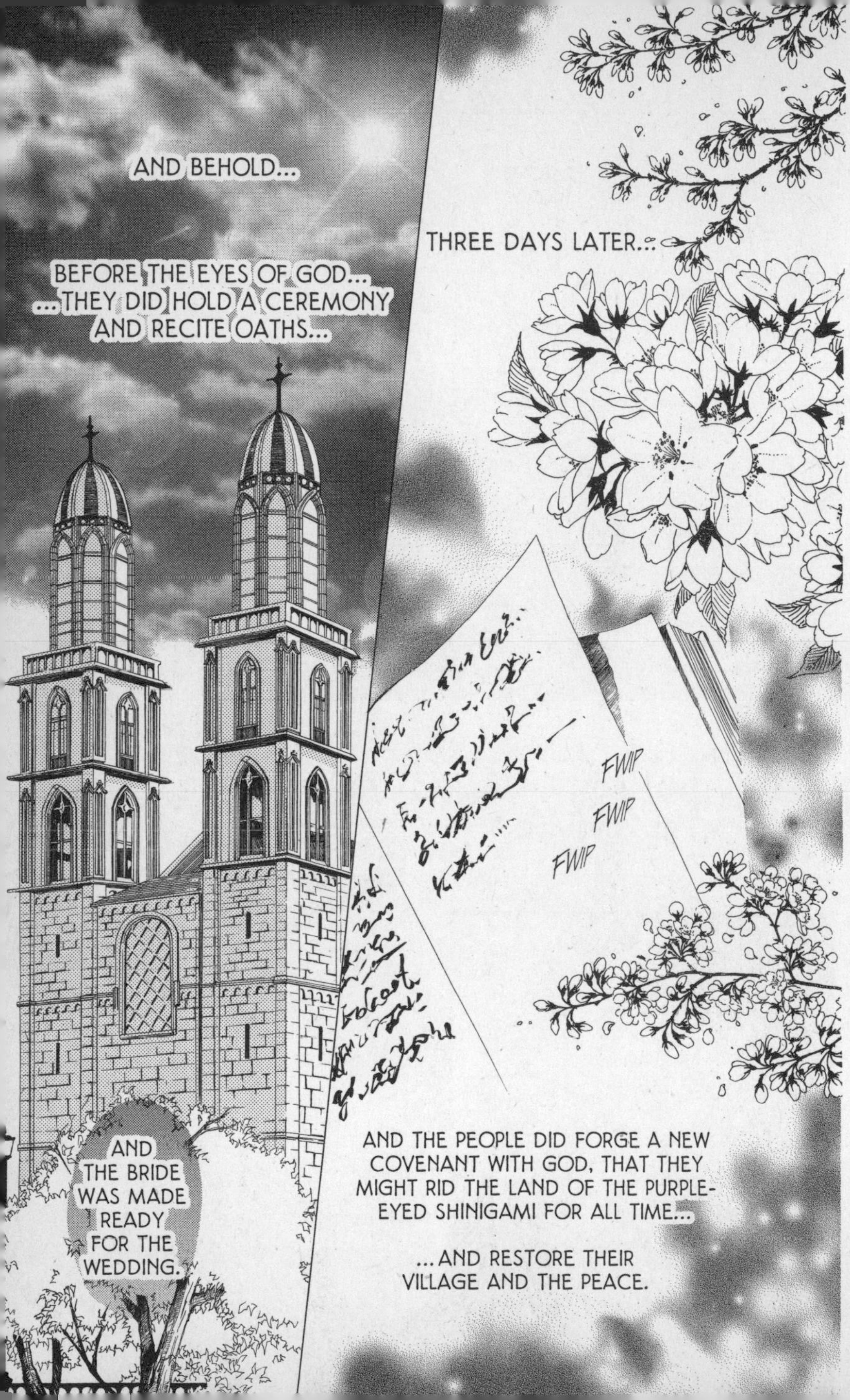
THREE DAYS LATER...
FWIP
FWIP
FWIP
AND THE PEOPLE DID FORGE A NEW COVENANT WITH GOD, THAT THEY MIGHT RID THE LAND OF THE PURPLE-EYED SHINIGAMI FOR ALL TIME...
...AND RESTORE THEIR VILLAGE AND THE PEACE.
AND BEHOLD...
BEFORE THE EYES OF GOD... ...THEY DID HOLD A CEREMONY AND RECITE OATHS...
AND THE BRIDE WAS MADE READY FOR THE WEDDING.

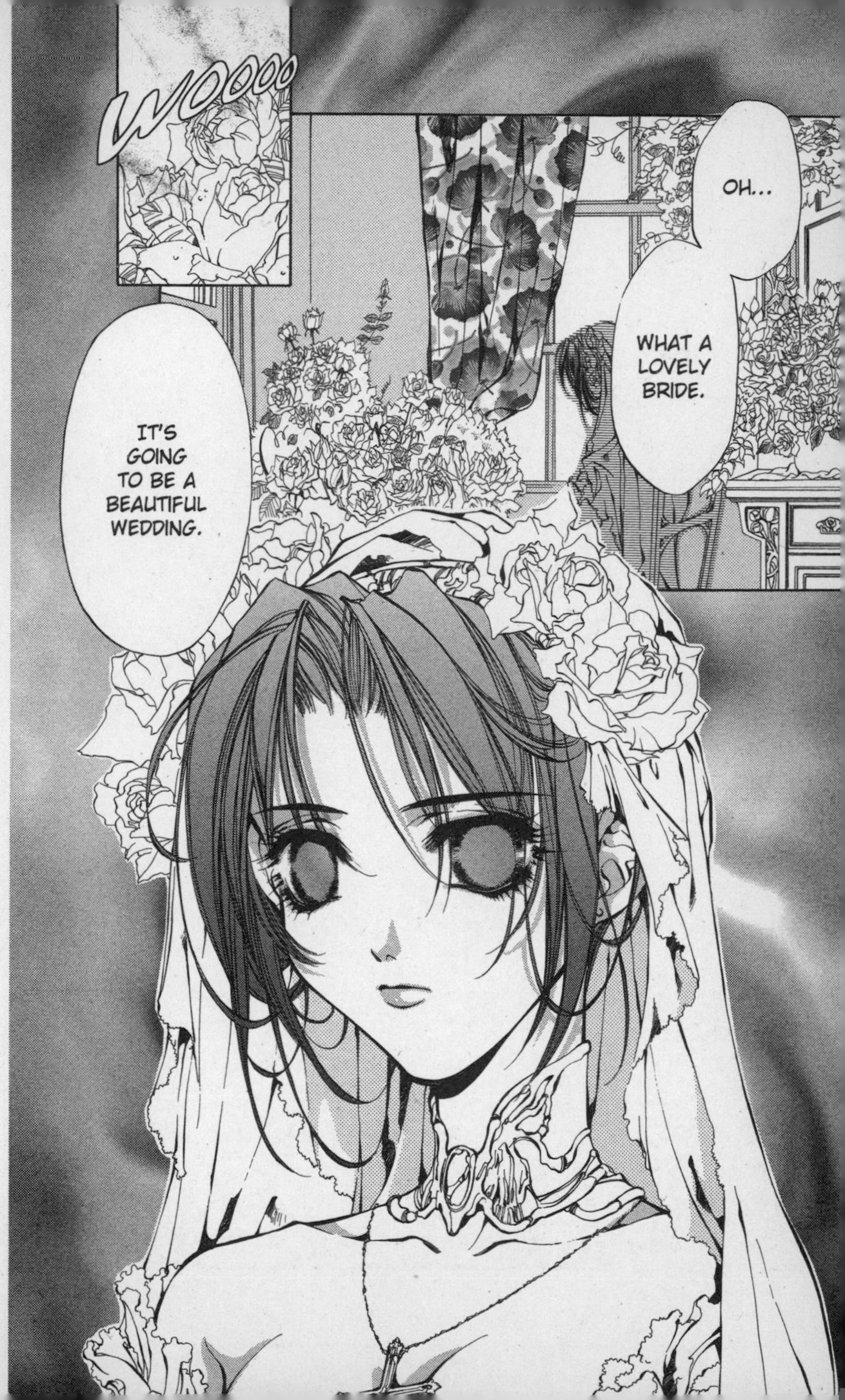
OH...
WHAT A LOVELY BRIDE.
WOOOO
IT'S GOING TO BE A BEAUTIFUL WEDDING.

CHAPTER 12

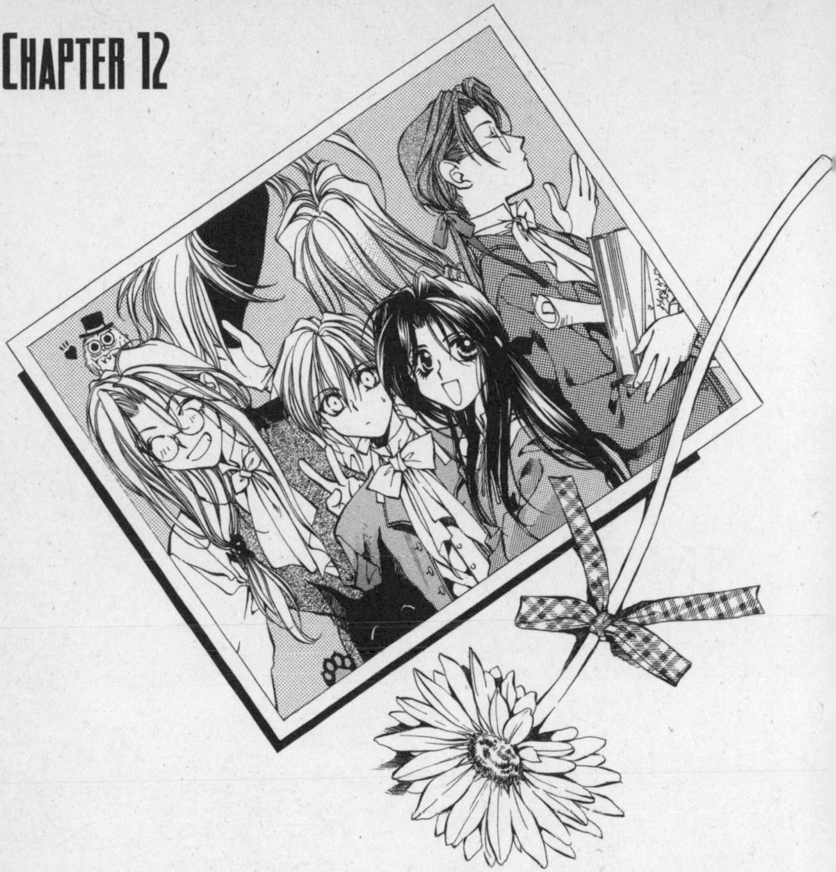

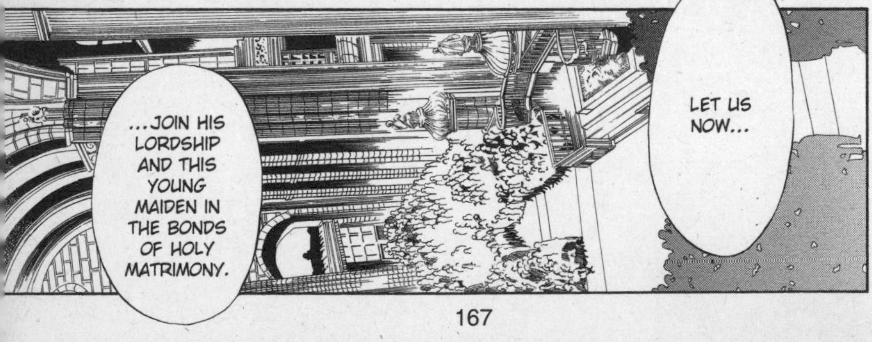
LET US NOW...
...JOIN HIS LORDSHIP AND THIS YOUNG MAIDEN IN THE BONDS OF HOLY MATRIMONY.

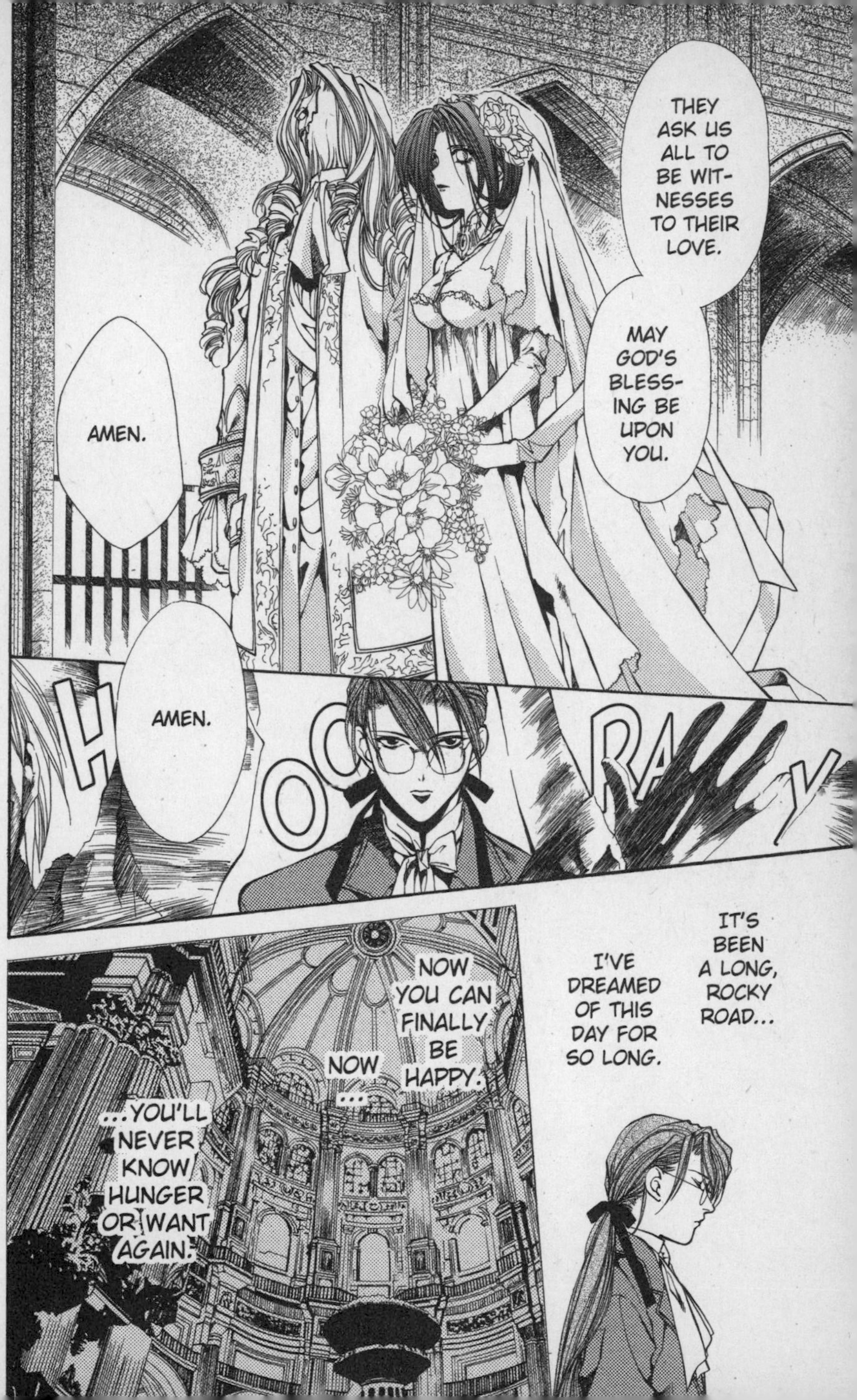
THEY ASK US ALL TO BE WITNESSES TO THEIR LOVE.
MAY GOD'S BLESSING BE UPON YOU.
AMEN.
AMEN.
HOORAY
IT'S BEEN A LONG, ROCKY ROAD...
I'VE DREAMED OF THIS DAY FOR SO LONG.
NOW YOU CAN FINALLY BE HAPPY.
NOW...
...YOU'LL NEVER KNOW HUNGER OR WANT AGAIN.

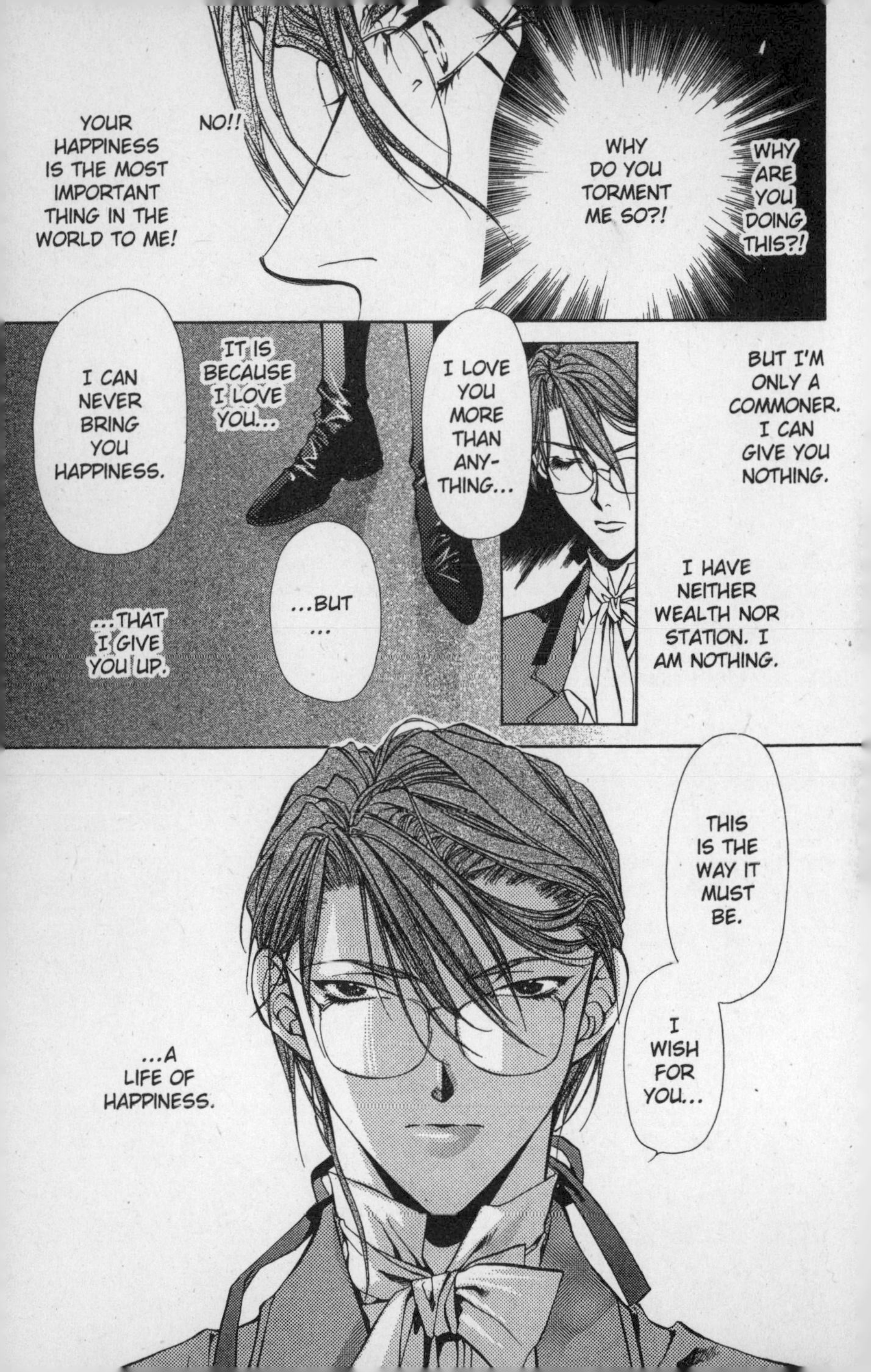
WHY ARE YOU DOING THIS?!
WHY DO YOU TORMENT ME SO?!
NO!!
YOUR HAPPINESS IS THE MOST IMPORTANT THING IN THE WORLD TO ME!
BUT I'M ONLY A COMMONER. I CAN GIVE YOU NOTHING.
I HAVE NEITHER WEALTH NOR STATION. I AM NOTHING.
I LOVE YOU MORE THAN ANY-THING...
...BUT ...
IT IS BECAUSE I LOVE YOU...
...THAT I GIVE YOU UP.
I CAN NEVER BRING YOU HAPPINESS.
THIS IS THE WAY IT MUST BE.
I WISH FOR YOU...
...A LIFE OF HAPPINESS.

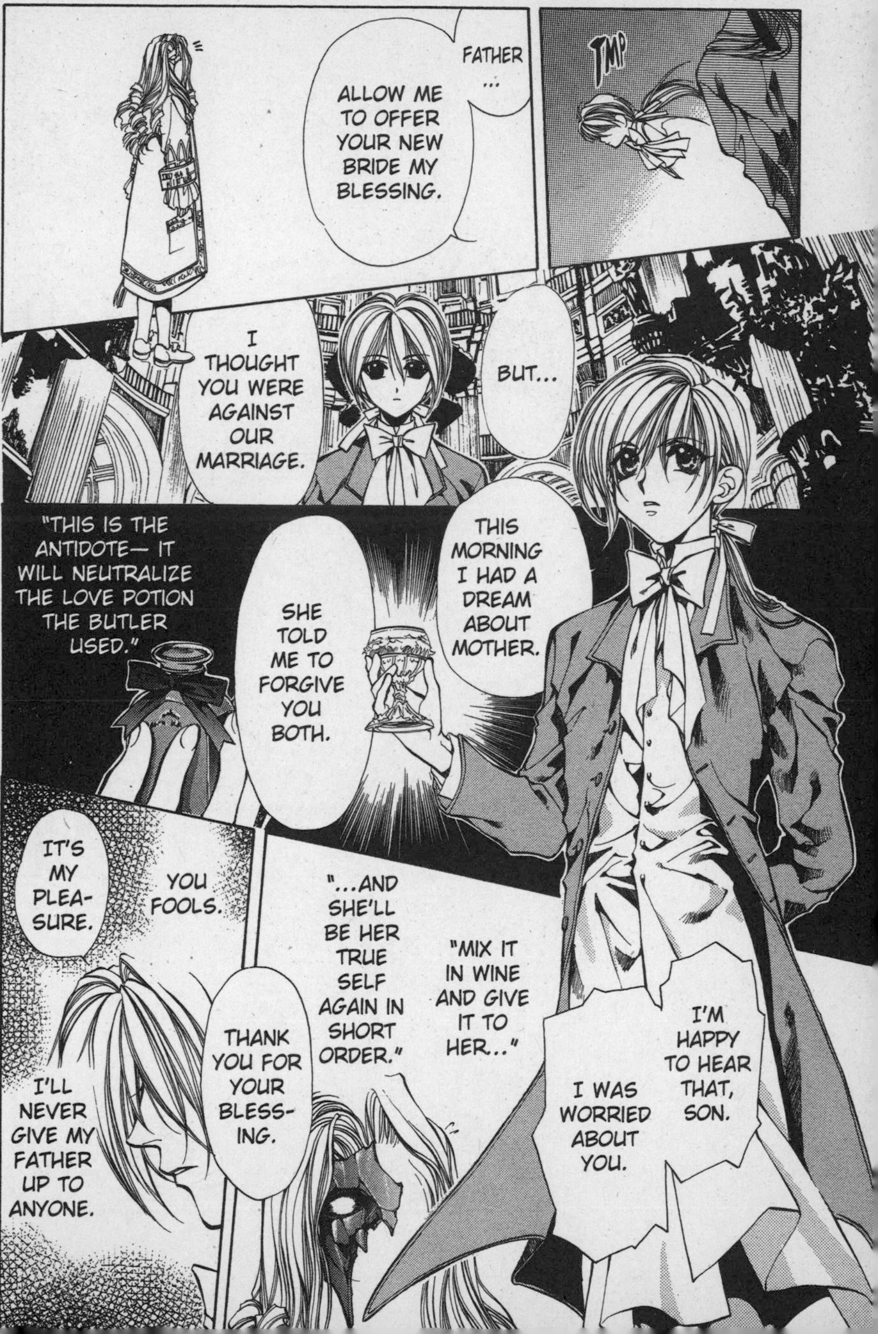
TMP
FATHER...
ALLOW ME TO OFFER YOUR NEW BRIDE MY BLESSING.
BUT...
I THOUGHT YOU WERE AGAINST OUR MARRIAGE.
THIS MORNING I HAD A DREAM ABOUT MOTHER.
SHE TOLD ME TO FORGIVE YOU BOTH.
"THIS IS THE ANTIDOTE— IT WILL NEUTRALIZE THE LOVE POTION THE BUTLER USED."
I'M HAPPY TO HEAR THAT, SON.
I WAS WORRIED ABOUT YOU.
"MIX IT IN WINE AND GIVE IT TO HER..."
"...AND SHE'LL BE HER TRUE SELF AGAIN IN SHORT ORDER."
THANK YOU FOR YOUR BLESS-ING.
YOU FOOLS.
IT'S MY PLEA-SURE.
I'LL NEVER GIVE MY FATHER UP TO ANYONE.

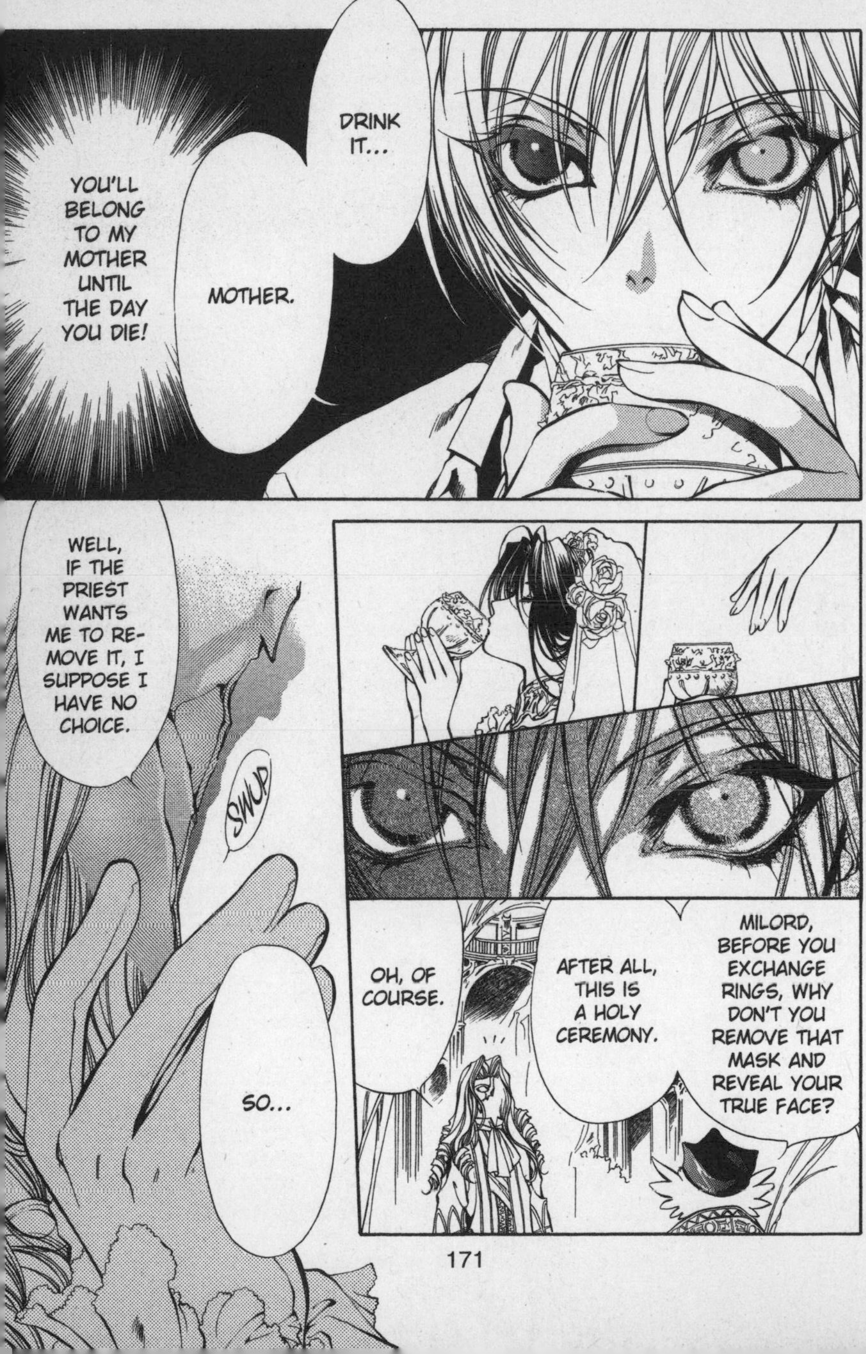
DRINK IT...
MOTHER.
YOU'LL BELONG TO MY MOTHER UNTIL THE DAY YOU DIE!
MILORD, BEFORE YOU EXCHANGE RINGS, WHY DON'T YOU REMOVE THAT MASK AND REVEAL YOUR TRUE FACE?
AFTER ALL, THIS IS A HOLY CEREMONY.
OH, OF COURSE.
WELL, IF THE PRIEST WANTS ME TO RE-MOVE IT, I SUPPOSE I HAVE NO CHOICE.
SWUP
SO...

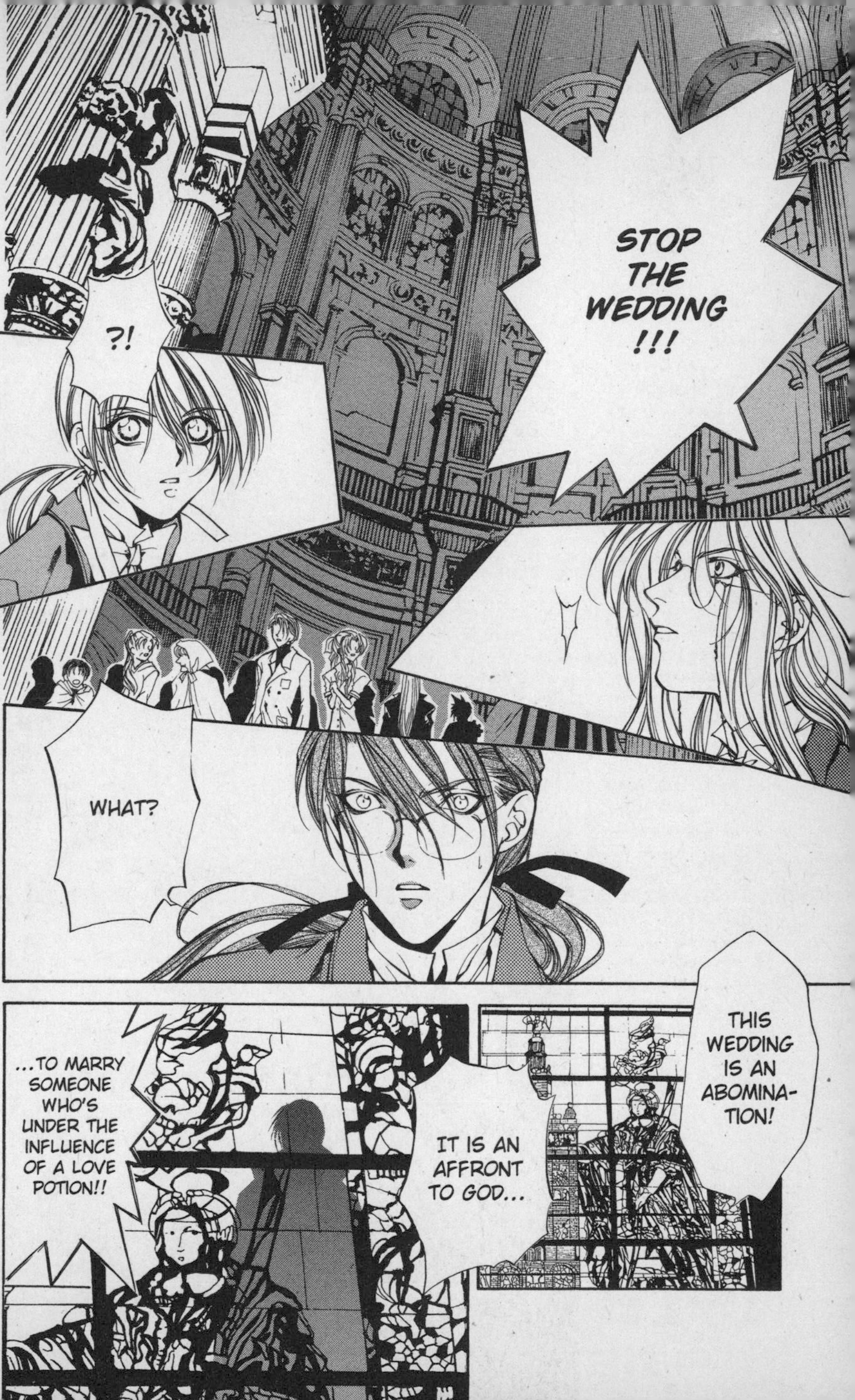
STOP THE WEDDING!!!
?!
WHAT?
THIS WEDDING IS AN ABOMINATION!
IT IS AN AFFRONT TO GOD...
...TO MARRY SOMEONE WHO'S UNDER THE INFLUENCE OF A LOVE POTION!!

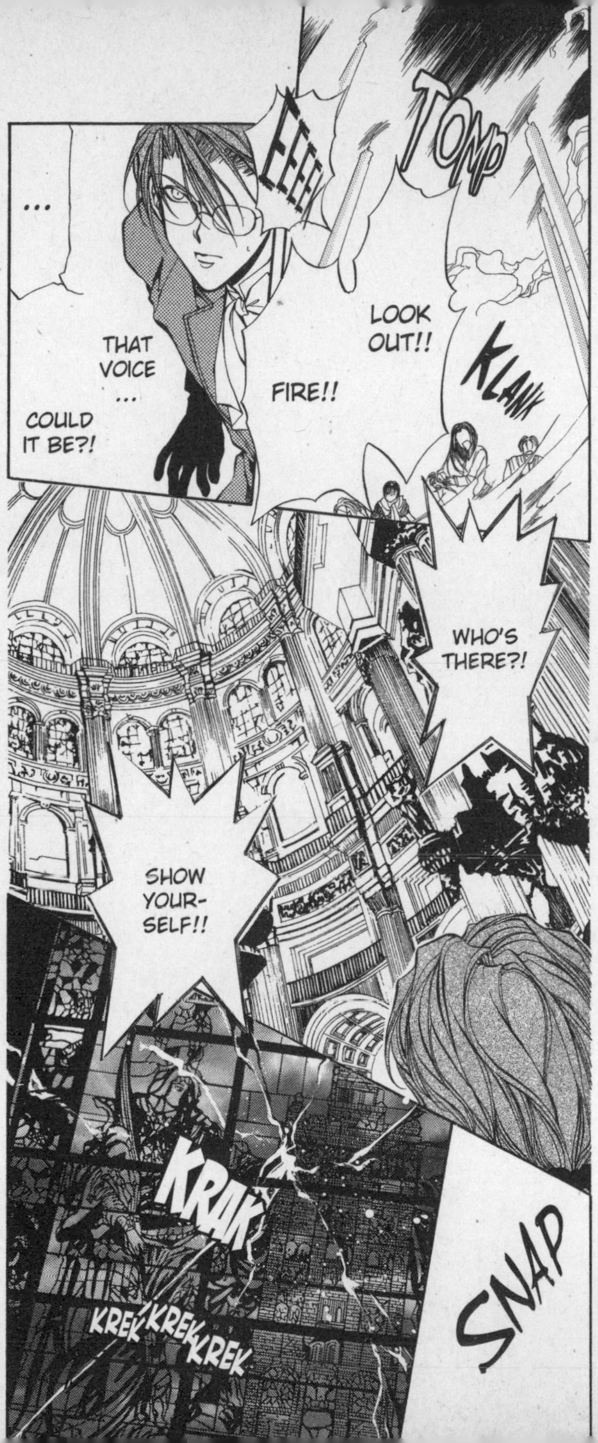
TONP
EEEE
KLANK
LOOK OUT!!
FIRE!!
...
THAT VOICE ...
COULD IT BE?!
WHO'S THERE?!
SHOW YOUR-SELF!!
SNAP
KRAK
KREK KREK KREK

I was able to cast the three supporting roles easily, but I had a much harder time deciding on the two leads, especially Tsuzuki. The gap between his serious side and his goofy side is huge, so it was hard to think of someone who could handle them both. Then my assistant lent me a CD, and that's where I found the voice of Tsuzuki, Kosuke Okano. Whoa! I thought: "I like his voice." So I contacted him, and he accepted right away. And right around the same time Shou Hayami (Muraki) accepted too. I was like "God, he really is Tsuzuki's doppelganger." We chose Fujiko Takimoto to be Hisoka after hearing her demo. I always thought that I wanted to use a woman for Hisoka, so I was glad to find someone who fit his character so well. All the other characters have male voices (very deep male voices) so her voice was a refreshing contrast. I'd like to do another project using this same cast someday.

BUT THEY TELL ME WE DON'T HAVE THE BUDGET.

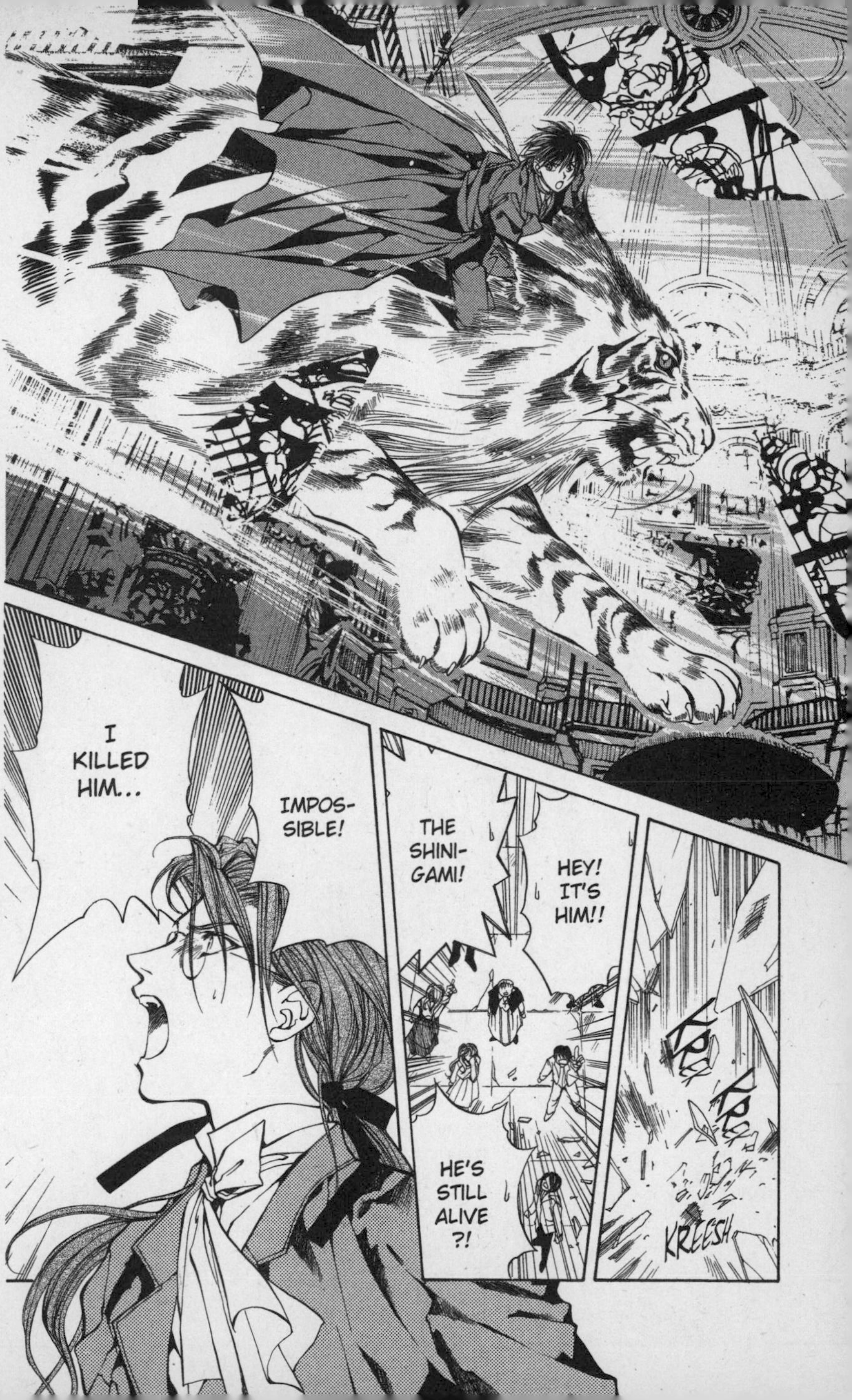
KRCK
KRCK
KREESH
HEY! IT'S HIM!!
THE SHINI-GAMI!
HE'S STILL ALIVE?!
IMPOS-SIBLE!
I KILLED HIM...

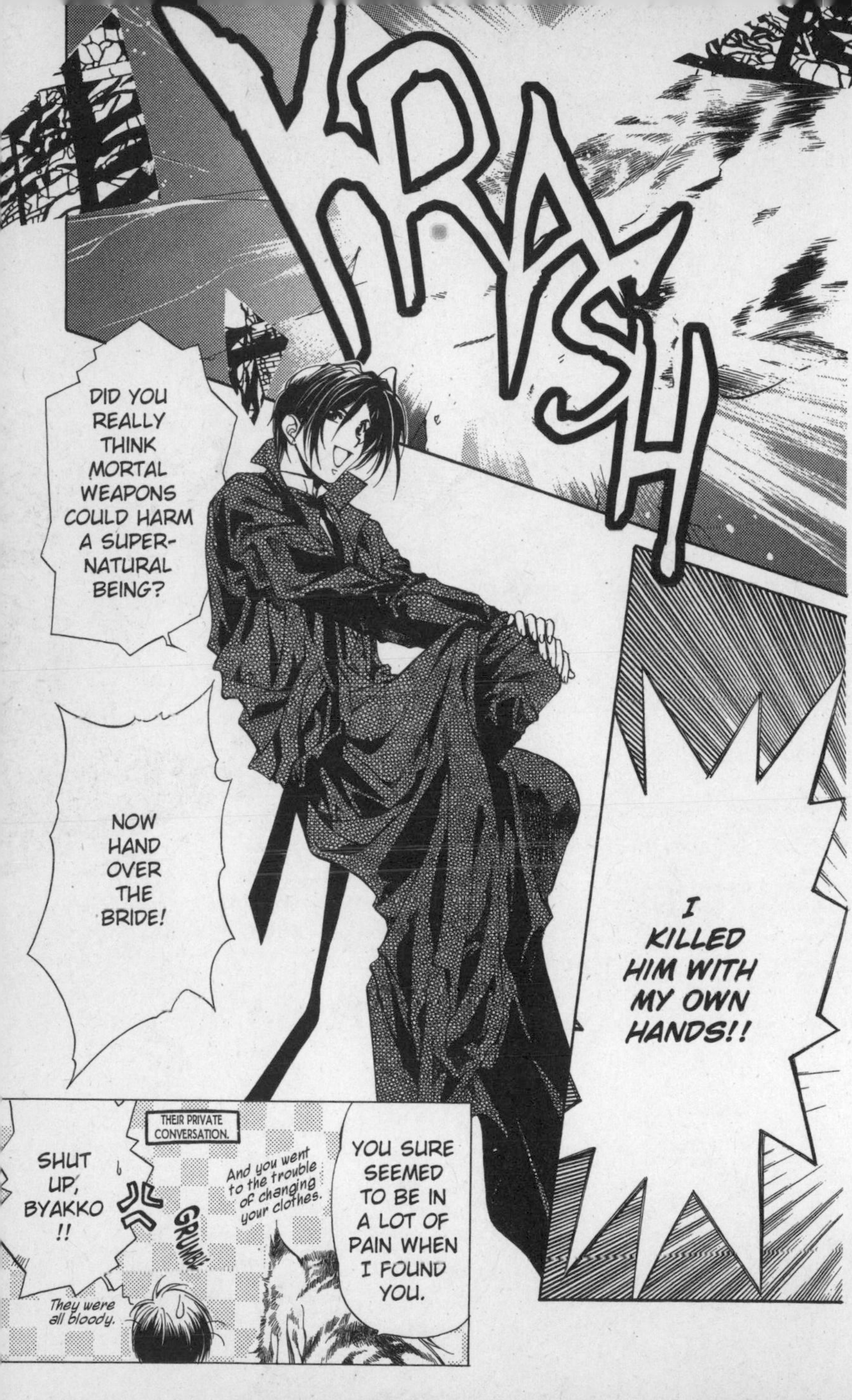
KRASH
I KILLED HIM WITH MY OWN HANDS!!
DID YOU REALLY THINK MORTAL WEAPONS COULD HARM A SUPER-NATURAL BEING?
NOW HAND OVER THE BRIDE!
YOU SURE SEEMED TO BE IN A LOT OF PAIN WHEN I FOUND YOU.
And you went to the trouble of changing your clothes.
THEIR PRIVATE CONVERSATION.
SHUT UP, BYAKKO!!
They were all bloody.

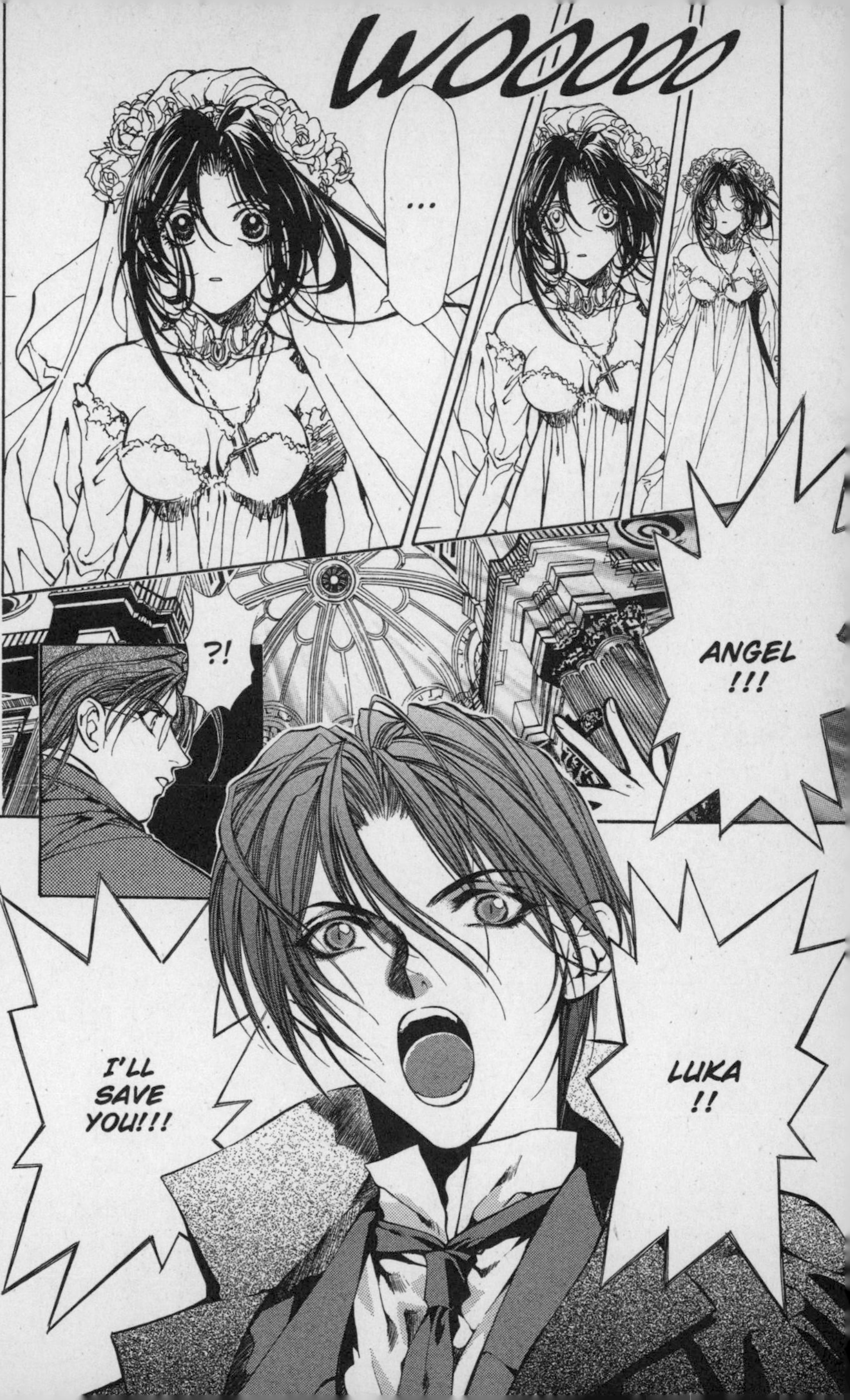
WOOOOO
...
ANGEL !!!
?!
LUKA !!
I'LL SAVE YOU!!!

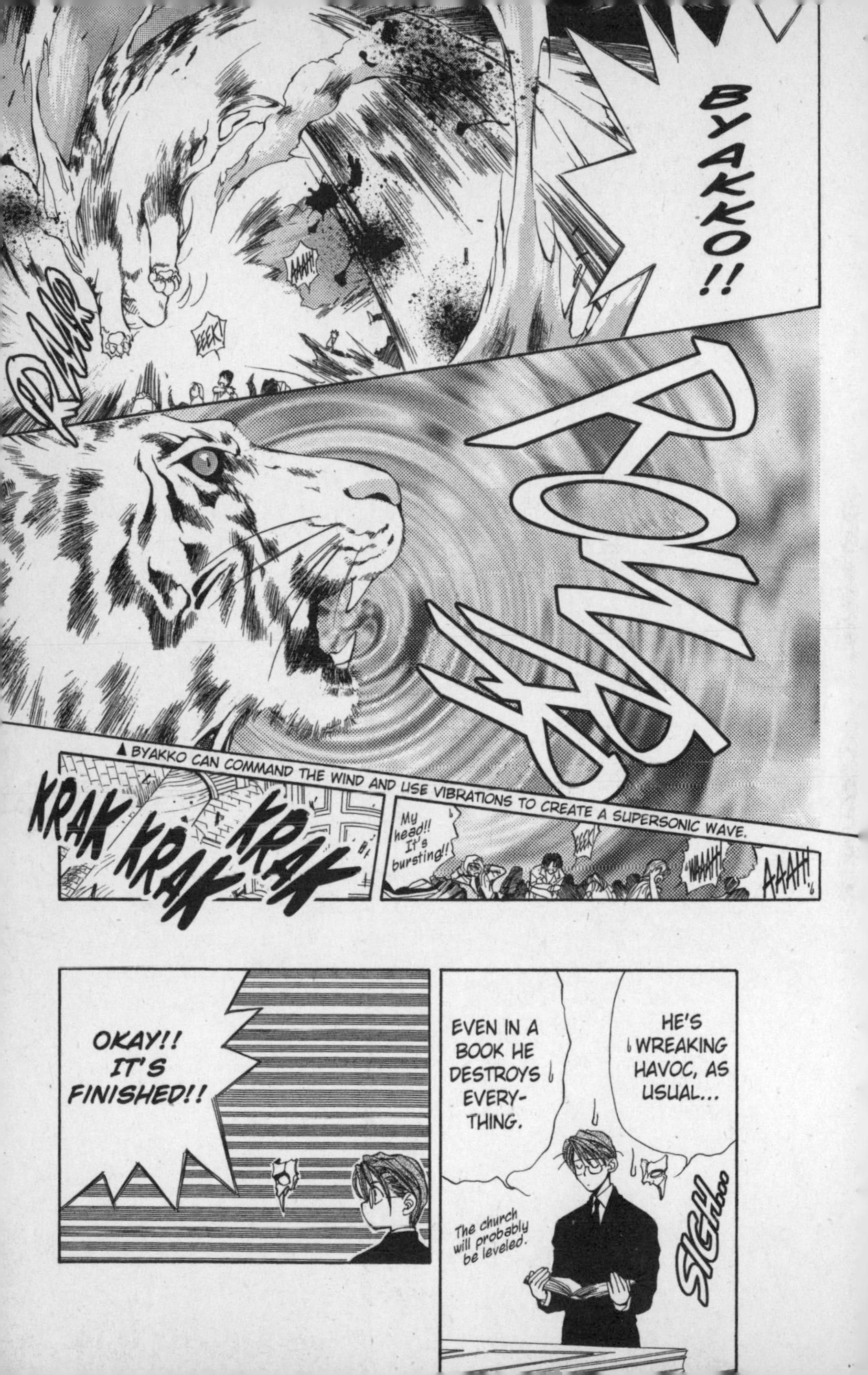
BYAKKO!!
AAAH!
EEEK!
▲ BYAKKO CAN COMMAND THE WIND AND USE VIBRATIONS TO CREATE A SUPERSONIC WAVE.
AAAH!
WAAAH!
EEEK!
My head!! It's bursting!!
KRAK KRAK KRAK
HE'S WREAKING HAVOC, AS USUAL...
EVEN IN A BOOK HE DESTROYS EVERY-THING.
The church will probably be leveled.
SIGH
OKAY!! IT'S FINISHED!!

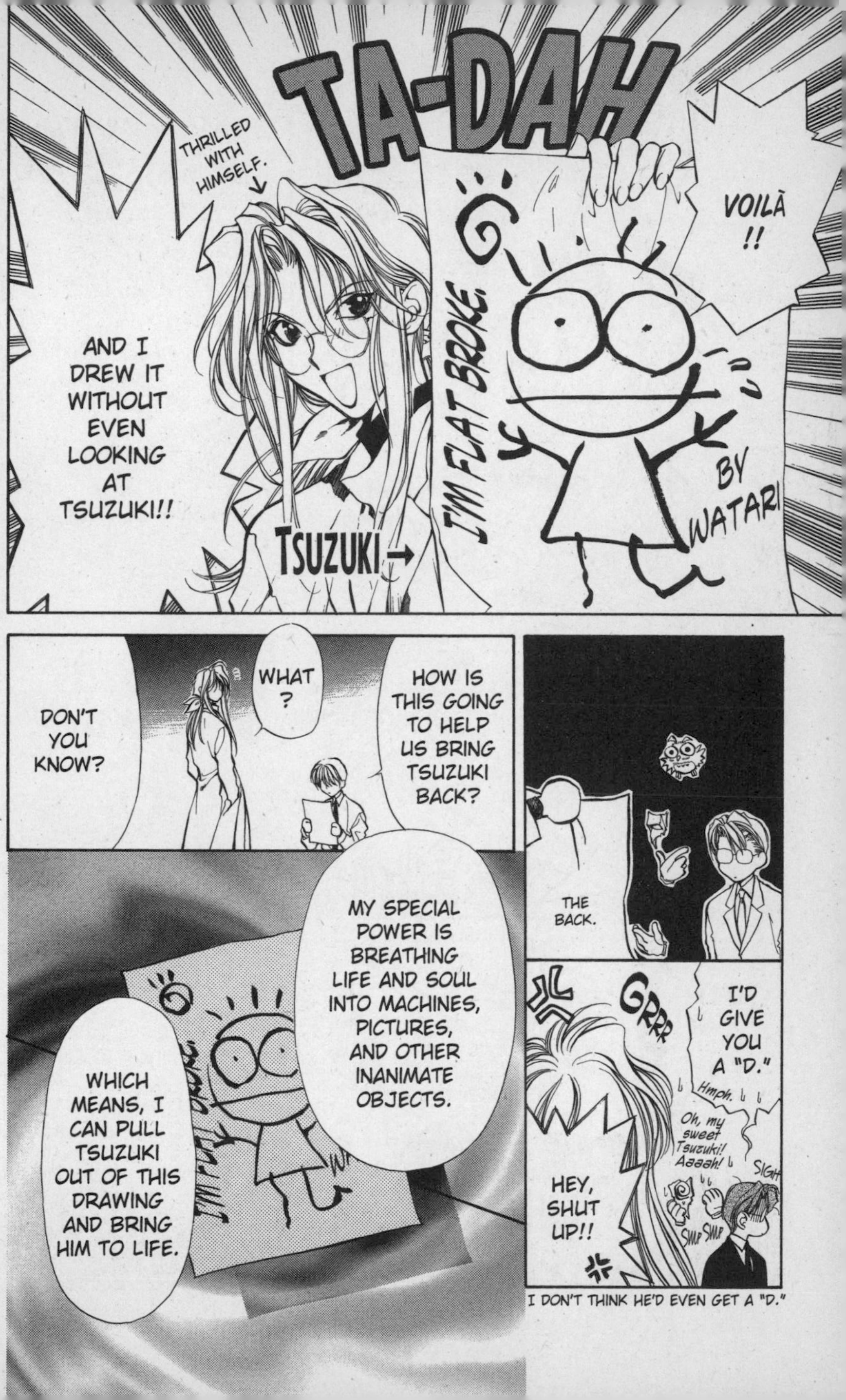
TA-DAH
VOILÀ !!
BY WATARI
I'M FLAT BROKE.
TSUZUKI →
THRILLED WITH HIMSELF.
AND I DREW IT WITHOUT EVEN LOOKING AT TSUZUKI!!
THE BACK.
I'D GIVE YOU A "D."
Hmph.
GRRR
Oh, my sweet Tsuzuki! Aaaah!
SIGH
SNAP SNAP
HEY, SHUT UP!!
I DON'T THINK HE'D EVEN GET A "D."
HOW IS THIS GOING TO HELP US BRING TSUZUKI BACK?
WHAT?
DON'T YOU KNOW?
MY SPECIAL POWER IS BREATHING LIFE AND SOUL INTO MACHINES, PICTURES, AND OTHER INANIMATE OBJECTS.
WHICH MEANS, I CAN PULL TSUZUKI OUT OF THIS DRAWING AND BRING HIM TO LIFE.

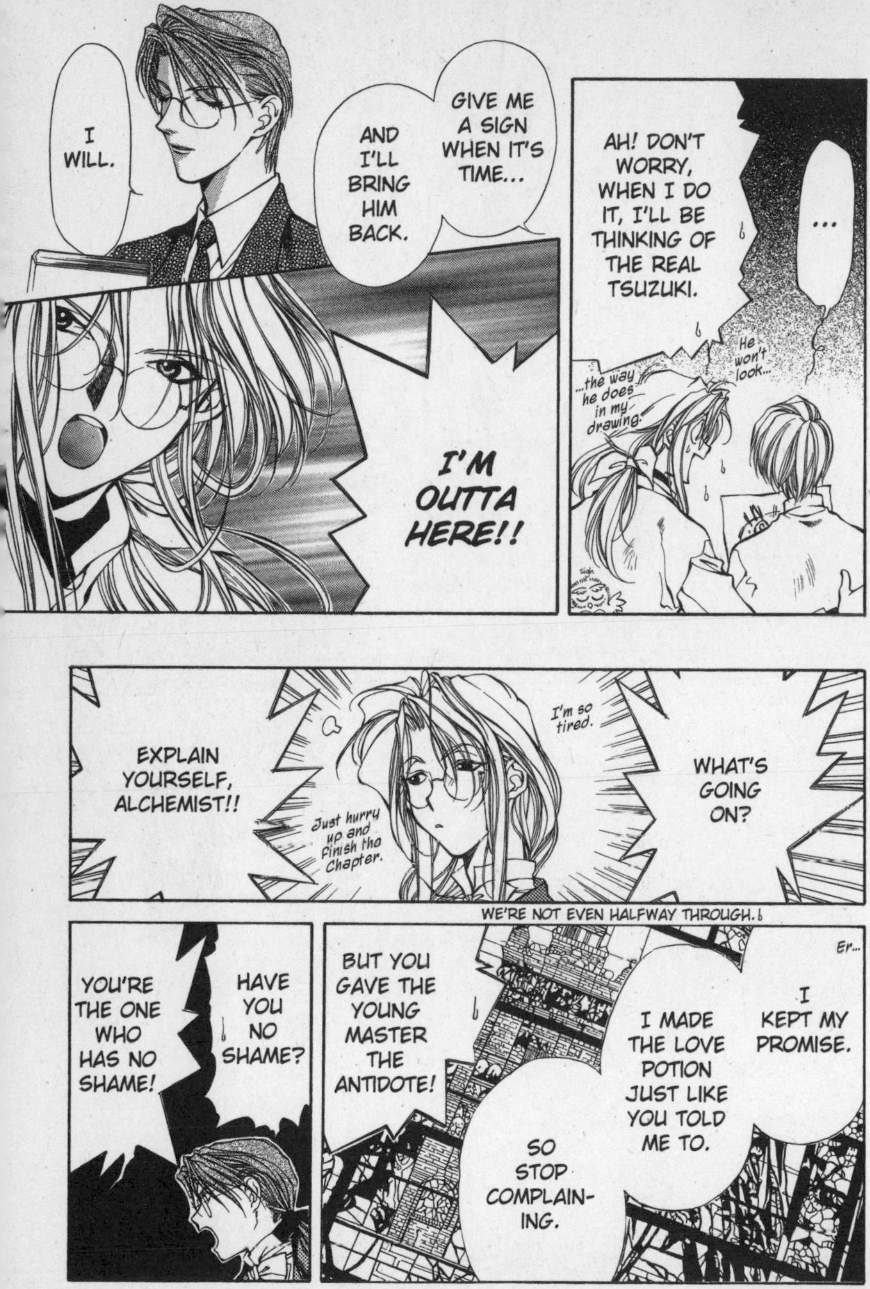
...
AH! DON'T WORRY, WHEN I DO IT, I'LL BE THINKING OF THE REAL TSUZUKI.
He won't look...
...the way he does in my drawing.
Sigh
GIVE ME A SIGN WHEN IT'S TIME...
AND I'LL BRING HIM BACK.
I WILL.
I'M OUTTA HERE!!
WHAT'S GOING ON?
I'm so tired.
EXPLAIN YOURSELF, ALCHEMIST!!
Just hurry up and finish the Chapter.
WE'RE NOT EVEN HALFWAY THROUGH.
Er...
I KEPT MY PROMISE.
I MADE THE LOVE POTION JUST LIKE YOU TOLD ME TO.
SO STOP COMPLAIN-ING.
BUT YOU GAVE THE YOUNG MASTER THE ANTIDOTE!
HAVE YOU NO SHAME?
YOU'RE THE ONE WHO HAS NO SHAME!

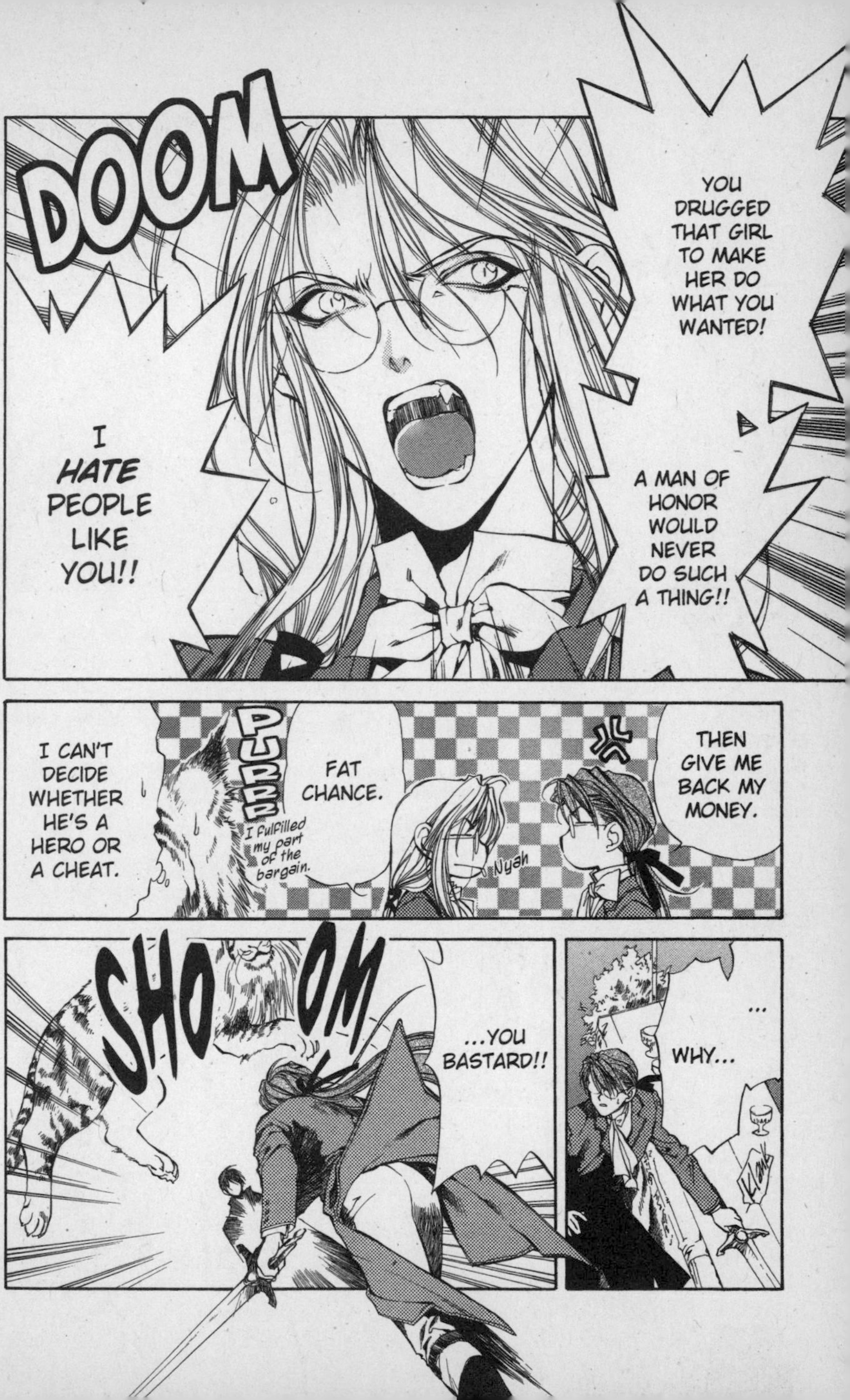
YOU DRUGGED THAT GIRL TO MAKE HER DO WHAT YOU WANTED!
DOOM
A MAN OF HONOR WOULD NEVER DO SUCH A THING!!
I *HATE* PEOPLE LIKE YOU!!
THEN GIVE ME BACK MY MONEY.
Nyah
FAT CHANCE.
PURRR
I fulfilled my part of the bargain.
I CAN'T DECIDE WHETHER HE'S A HERO OR A CHEAT.
...
WHY...
Klank
SHOOM
...YOU BASTARD!!

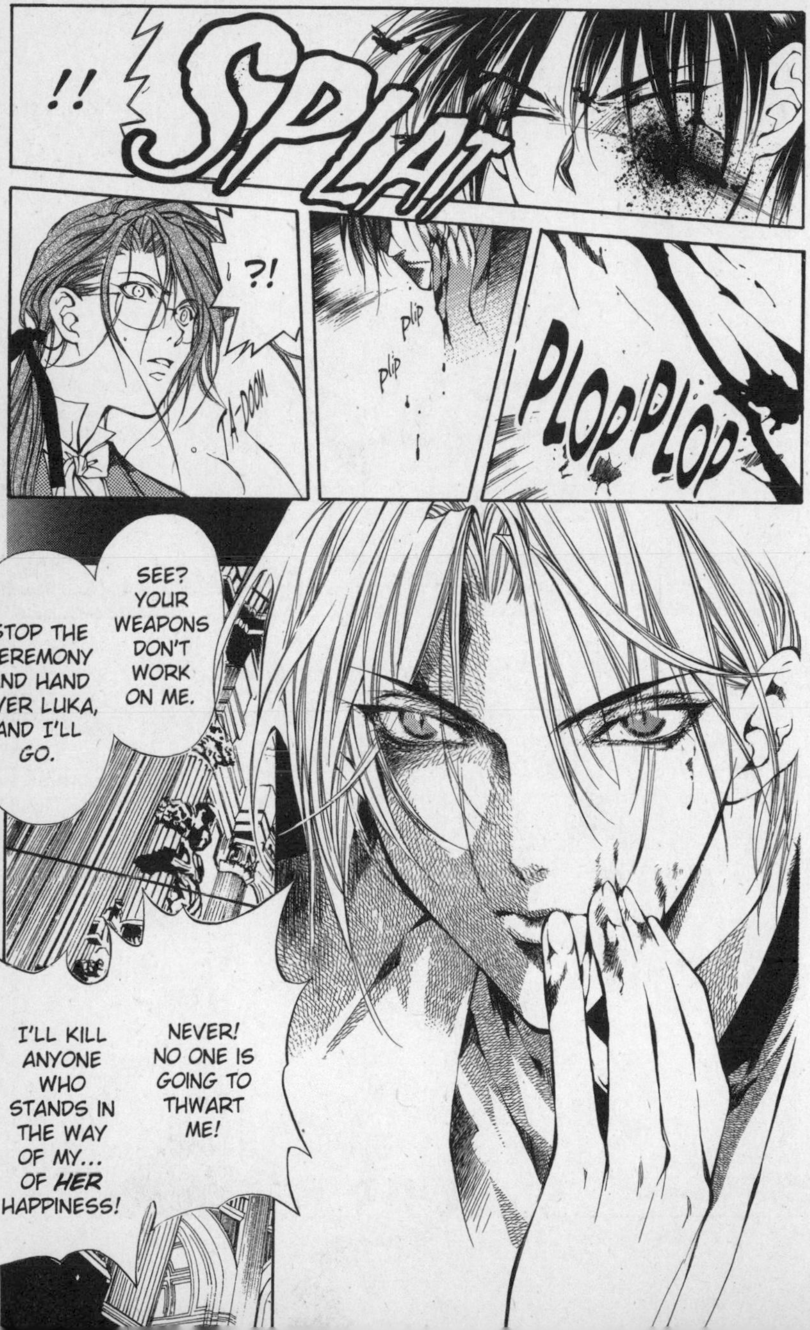

SPLAT
!!
PLOP PLOP
plip
plip
?!
TA-DOOM
SEE? YOUR WEAPONS DON'T WORK ON ME.
STOP THE CEREMONY AND HAND OVER LUKA, AND I'LL GO.
NEVER! NO ONE IS GOING TO THWART ME!
I'LL KILL ANYONE WHO STANDS IN THE WAY OF MY... OF *HER* HAPPINESS!

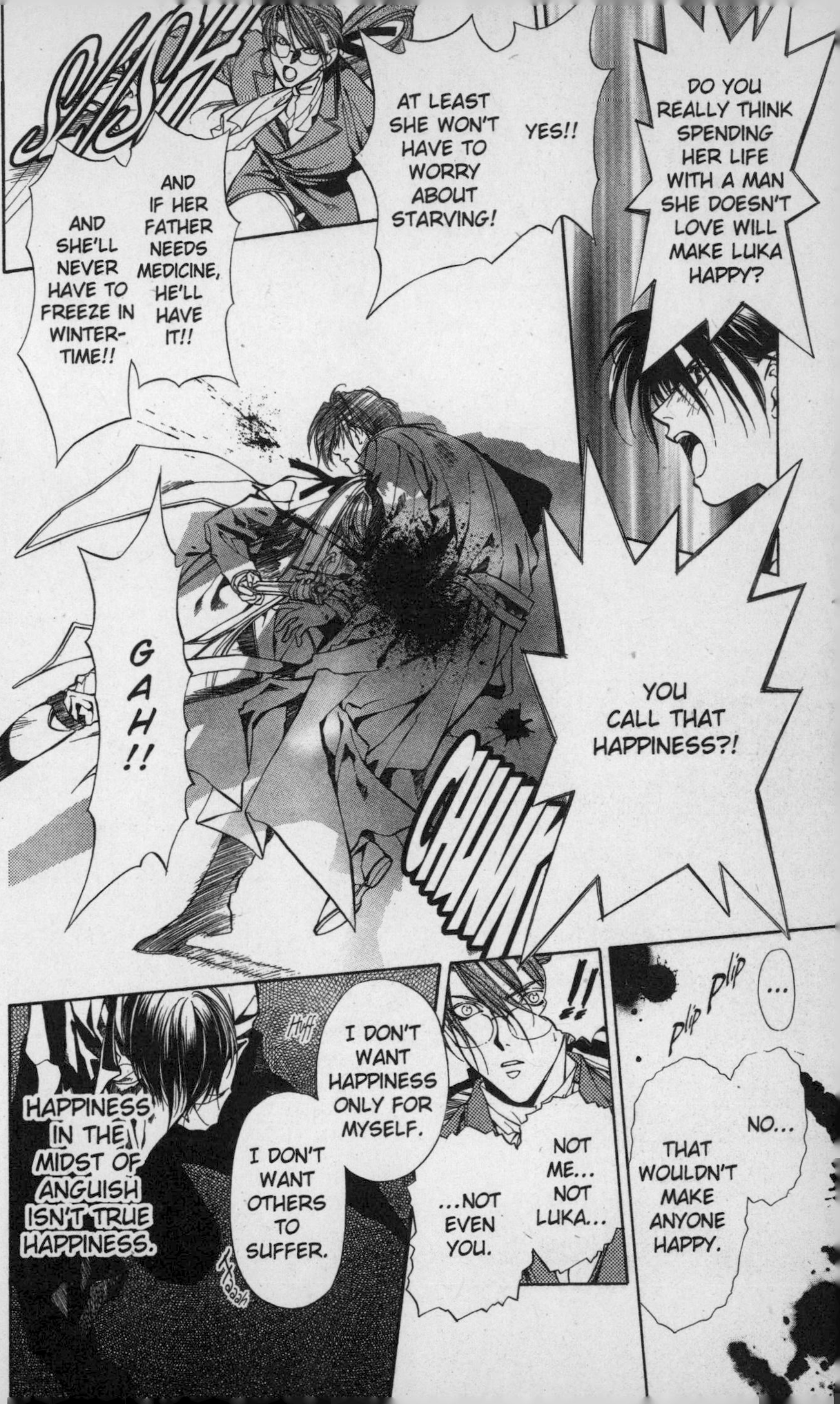
DO YOU REALLY THINK SPENDING HER LIFE WITH A MAN SHE DOESN'T LOVE WILL MAKE LUKA HAPPY?
YES!!
AT LEAST SHE WON'T HAVE TO WORRY ABOUT STARVING!
AND IF HER FATHER NEEDS MEDICINE, HE'LL HAVE IT!!
AND SHE'LL NEVER HAVE TO FREEZE IN WINTER-TIME!!
SLASH
YOU CALL THAT HAPPINESS?!
CHUNK
GAH!!
...
plip plip
NO...
THAT WOULDN'T MAKE ANYONE HAPPY.
!!
NOT ME... NOT LUKA...
...NOT EVEN YOU.
Huff
I DON'T WANT HAPPINESS ONLY FOR MYSELF.
I DON'T WANT OTHERS TO SUFFER.
Haaah
HAPPINESS IN THE MIDST OF ANGUISH ISN'T TRUE HAPPINESS.

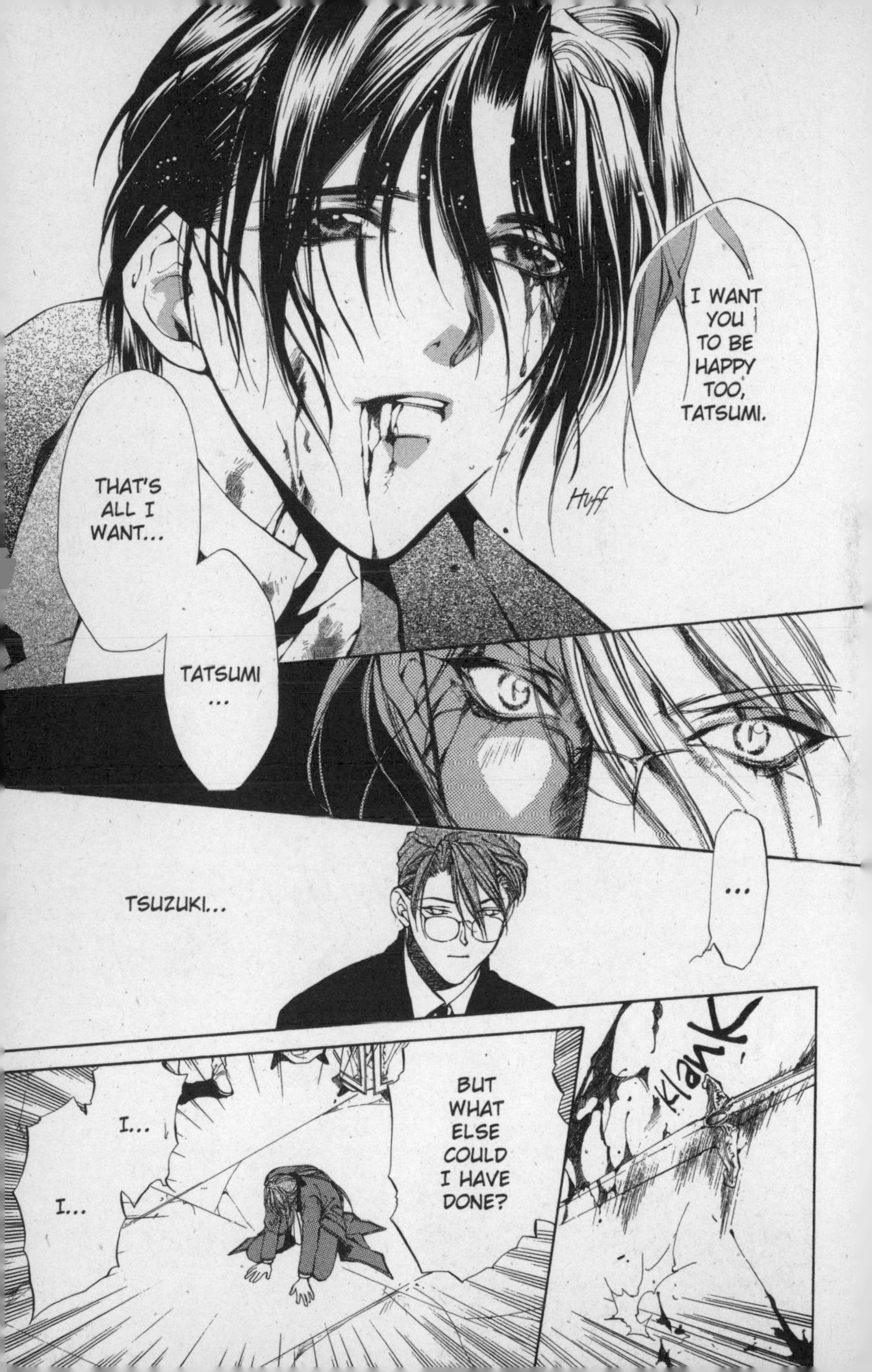
I WANT YOU TO BE HAPPY TOO, TATSUMI.
Huff
THAT'S ALL I WANT...
TATSUMI ...
...
TSUZUKI...
klank
BUT WHAT ELSE COULD I HAVE DONE?
I...
I...

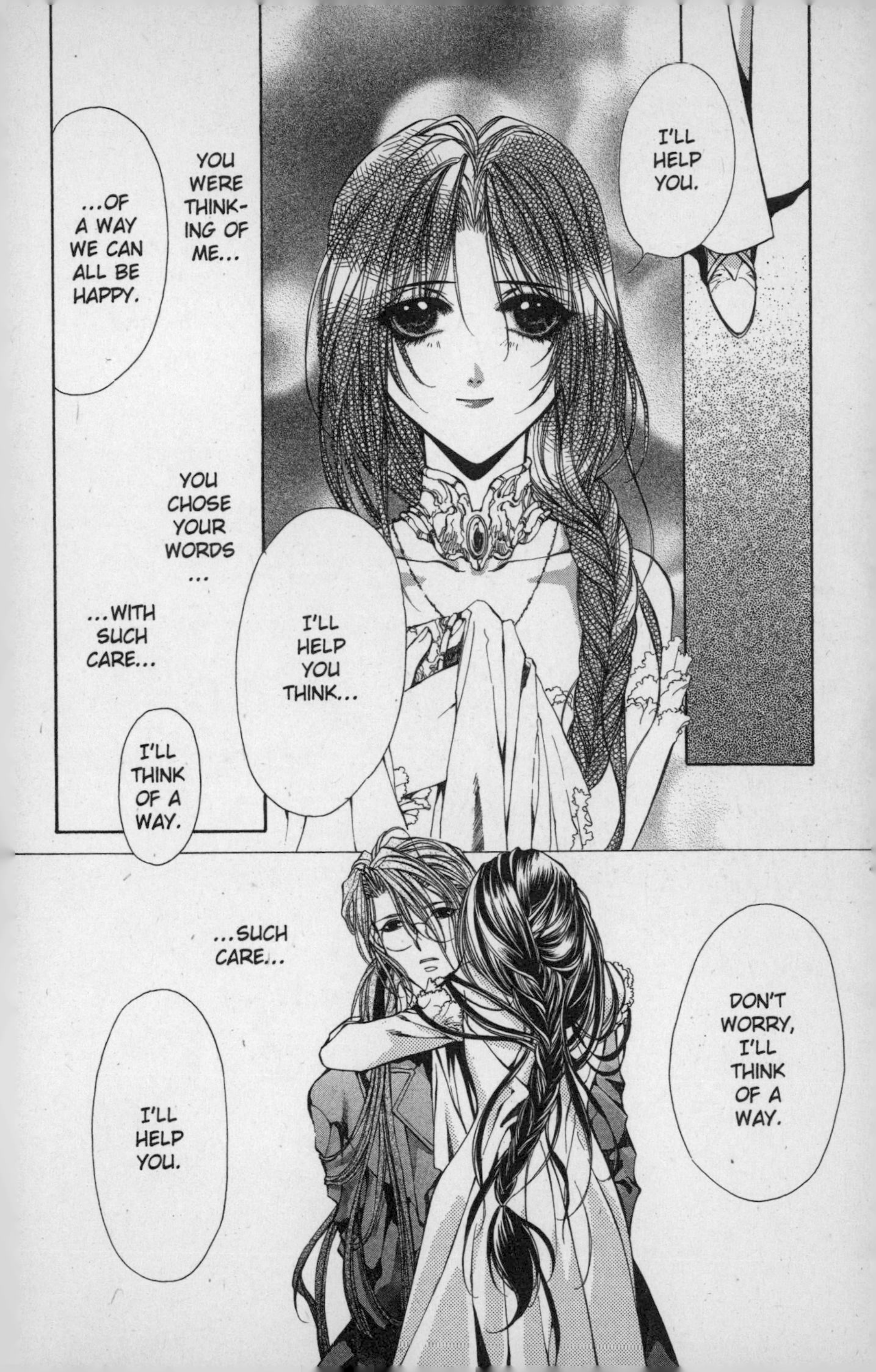
I'LL HELP YOU.
I'LL HELP YOU THINK...
YOU WERE THINKING OF ME...
...OF A WAY WE CAN ALL BE HAPPY.
YOU CHOSE YOUR WORDS ...
...WITH SUCH CARE...
I'LL THINK OF A WAY.
DON'T WORRY, I'LL THINK OF A WAY.
...SUCH CARE...
I'LL HELP YOU.

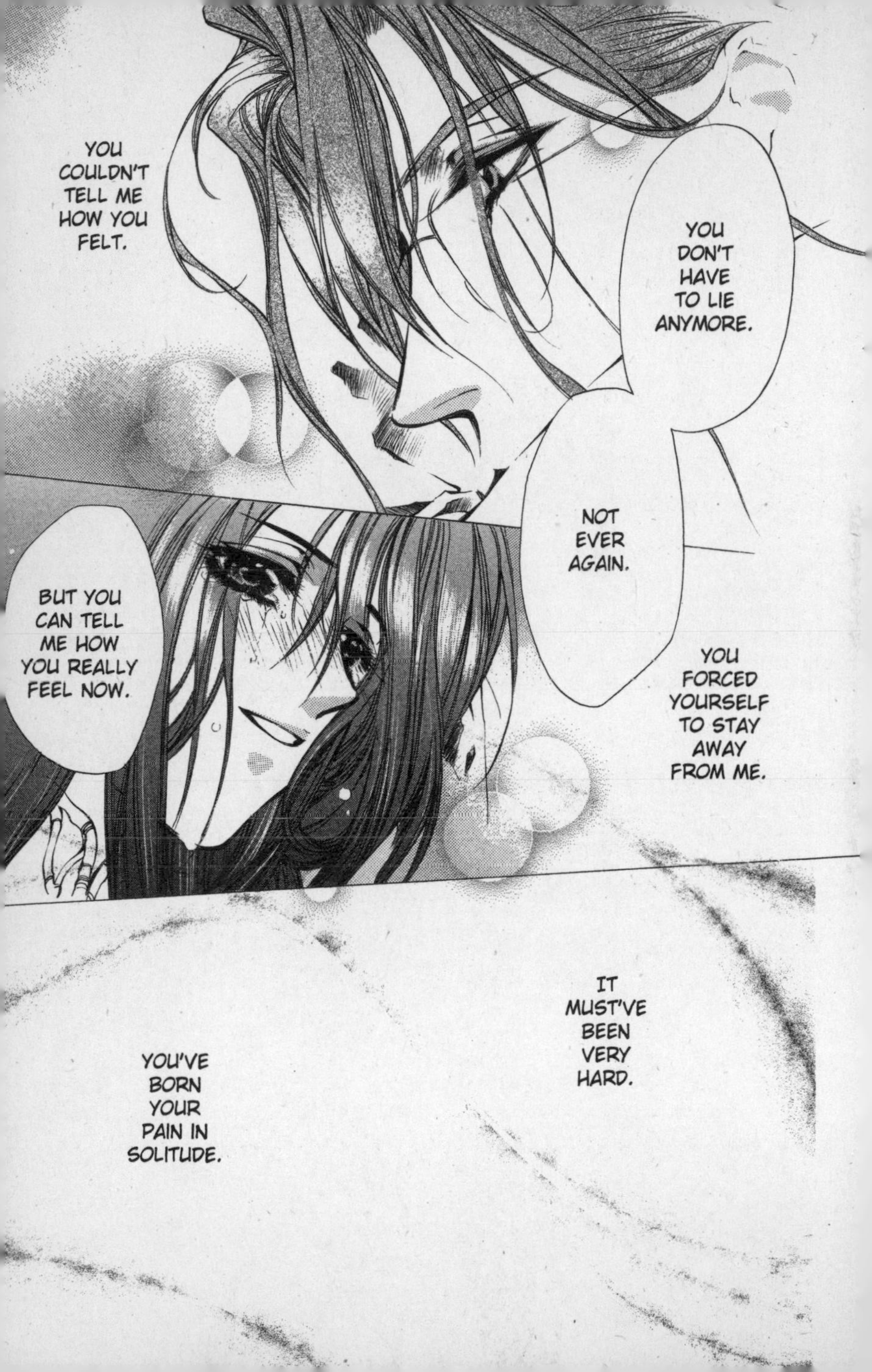
YOU DON'T HAVE TO LIE ANYMORE.
NOT EVER AGAIN.
YOU COULDN'T TELL ME HOW YOU FELT.
YOU FORCED YOURSELF TO STAY AWAY FROM ME.
BUT YOU CAN TELL ME HOW YOU REALLY FEEL NOW.
IT MUST'VE BEEN VERY HARD.
YOU'VE BORN YOUR PAIN IN SOLITUDE.

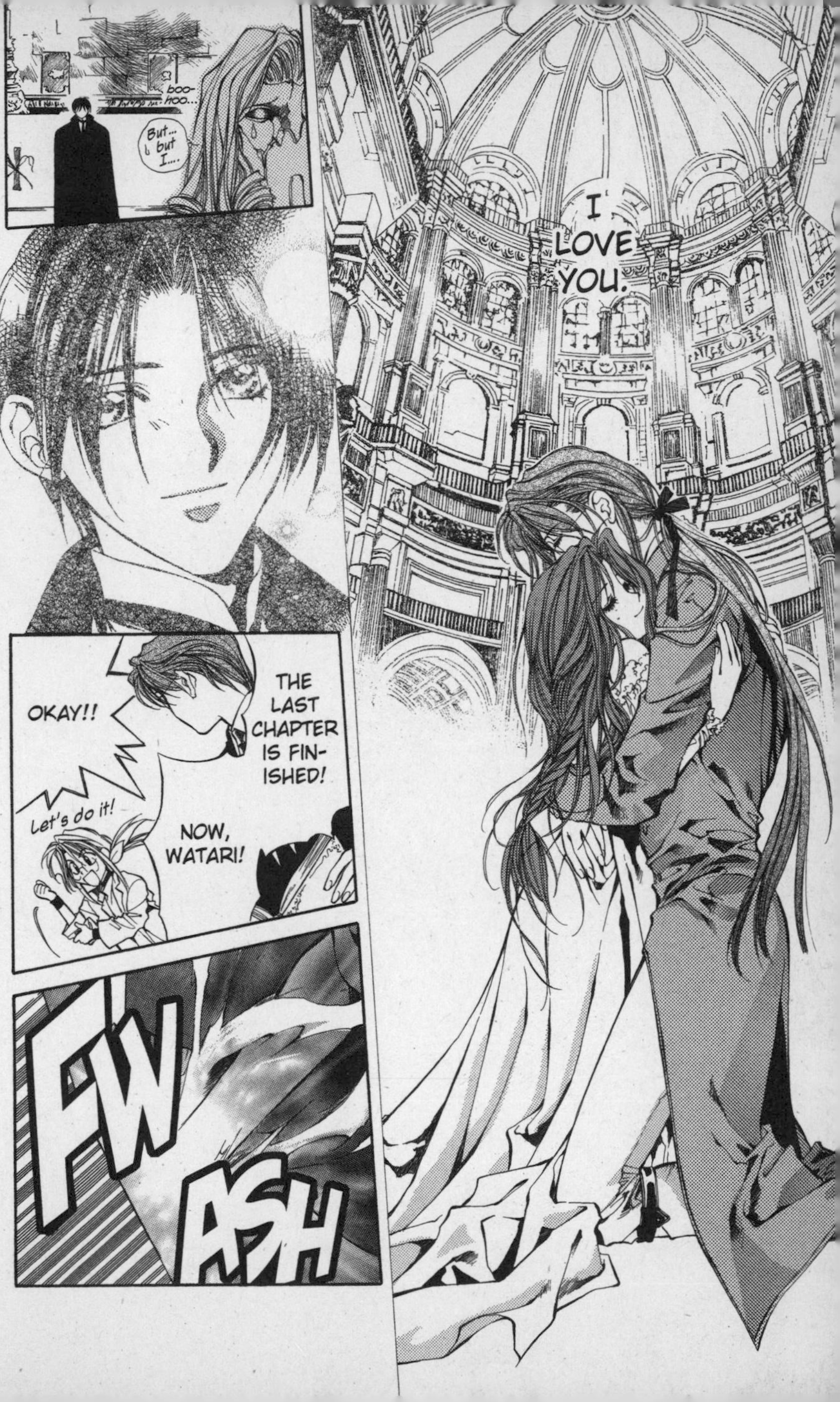
I LOVE YOU.
boo-hoo...
But... but I...
THE LAST CHAPTER IS FIN-ISHED!
OKAY!!
NOW, WATARI!
Let's do it!
FWASH

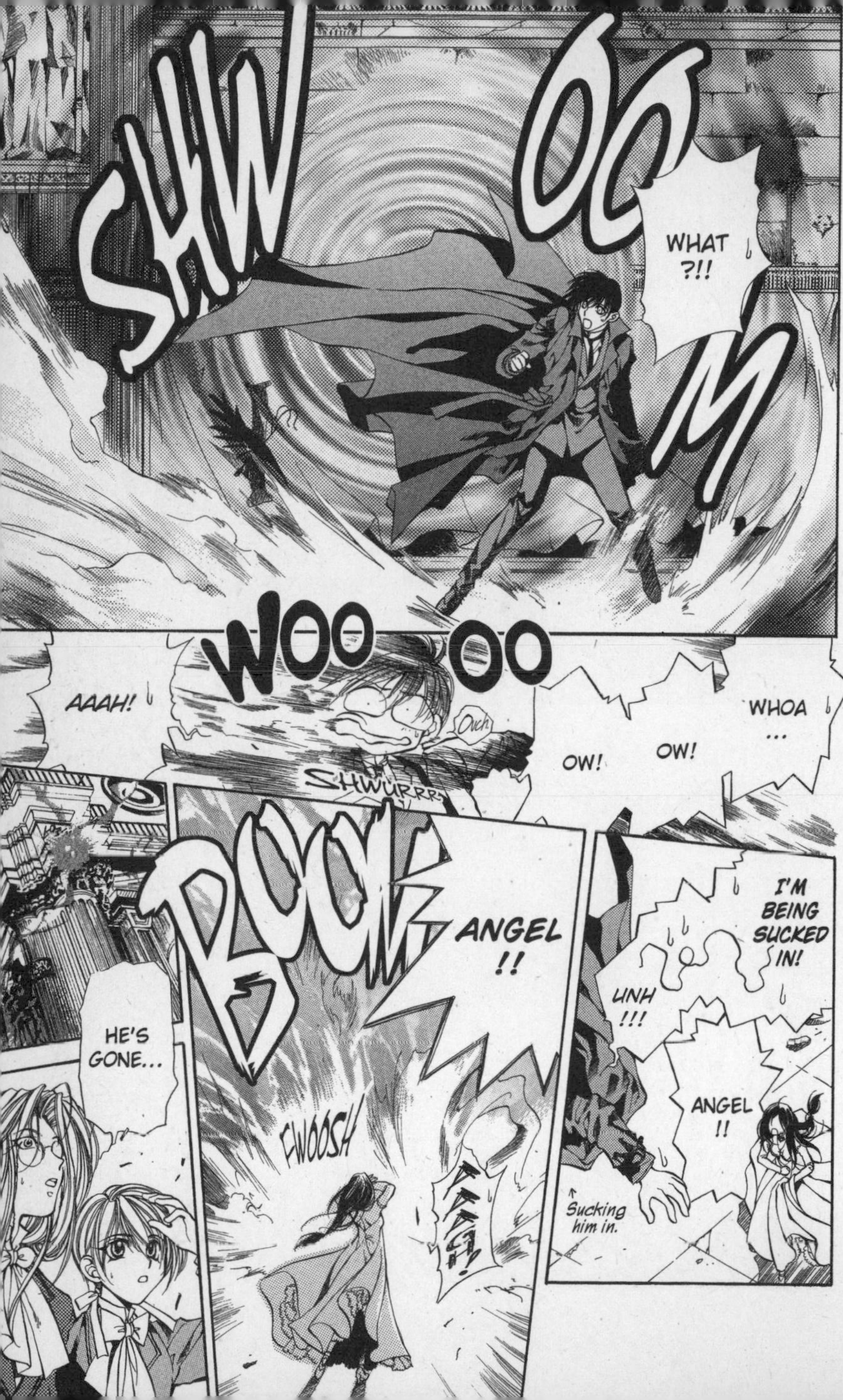
SHWOOOM
WHAT ?!!
WHOA ...
OW!
OW!
WOO OO
Ouch
AAAH!
SHWURRR
I'M BEING SUCKED IN!
UNH !!!
ANGEL !!
Sucking him in.
BOOM
ANGEL !!
FWOOSH
HE'S GONE...

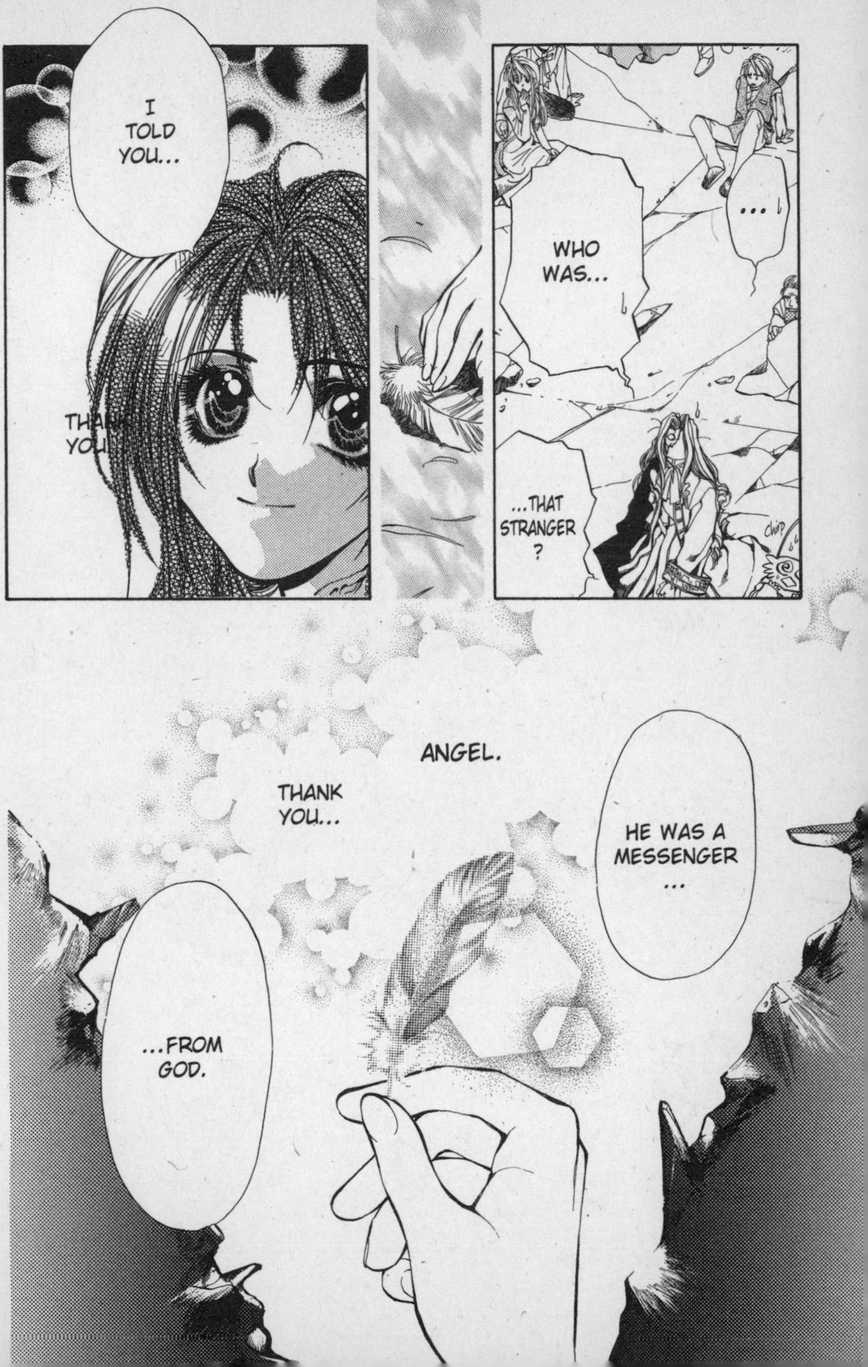
...!
WHO WAS...
...THAT STRANGER?
chirp
I TOLD YOU...
HE WAS A MESSENGER...
ANGEL.
THANK YOU...
...FROM GOD.

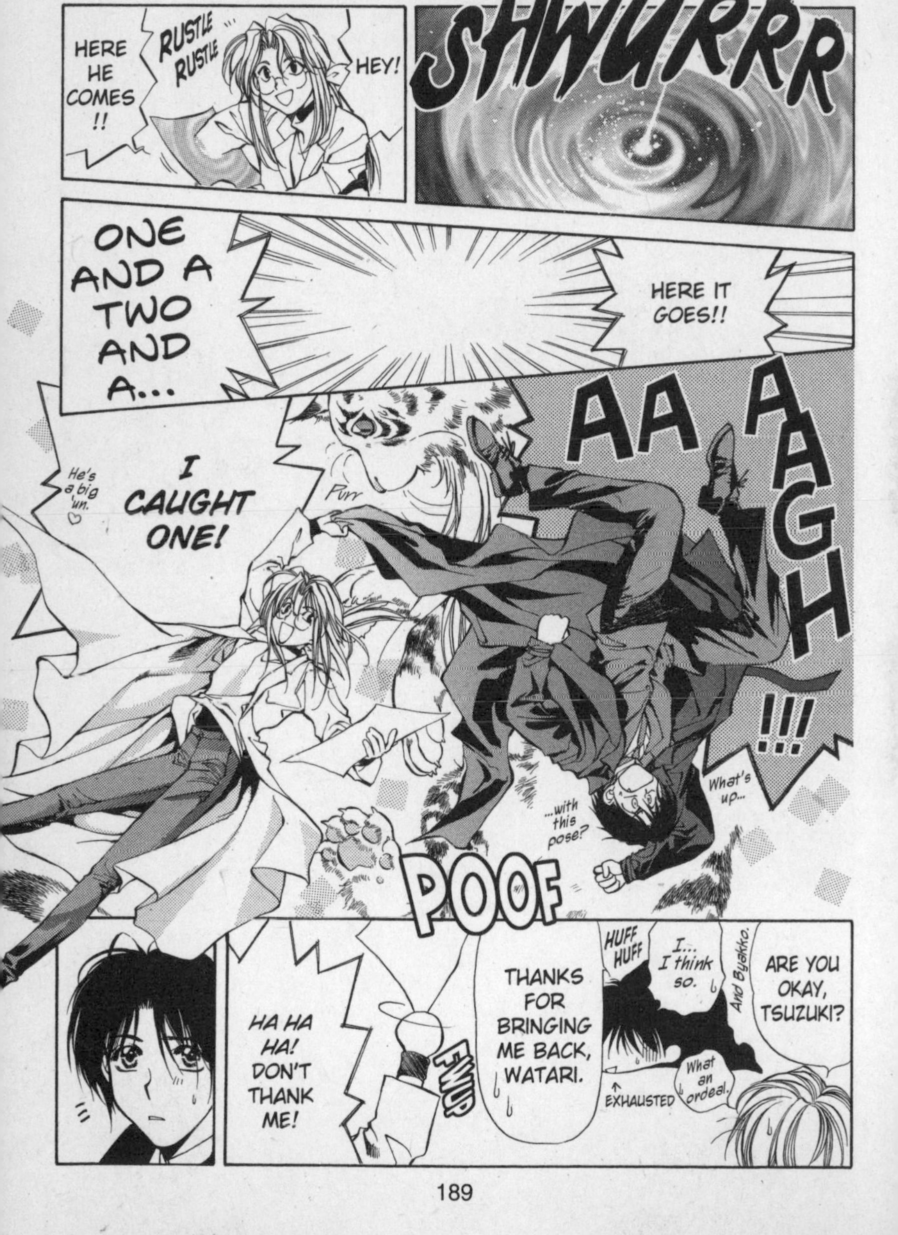
SHWURRR
HEY!
RUSTLE RUSTLE
HERE HE COMES!!
HERE IT GOES!!
ONE AND A TWO AND A...
AAAAGH!!!
What's up...
...with this pose?
POOF
Purr
I CAUGHT ONE!
He's a big 'un.
ARE YOU OKAY, TSUZUKI?
And Byakko.
I... I think so.
HUFF HUFF
What an ordeal.
EXHAUSTED
THANKS FOR BRINGING ME BACK, WATARI.
FWUP
HA HA HA! DON'T THANK ME!

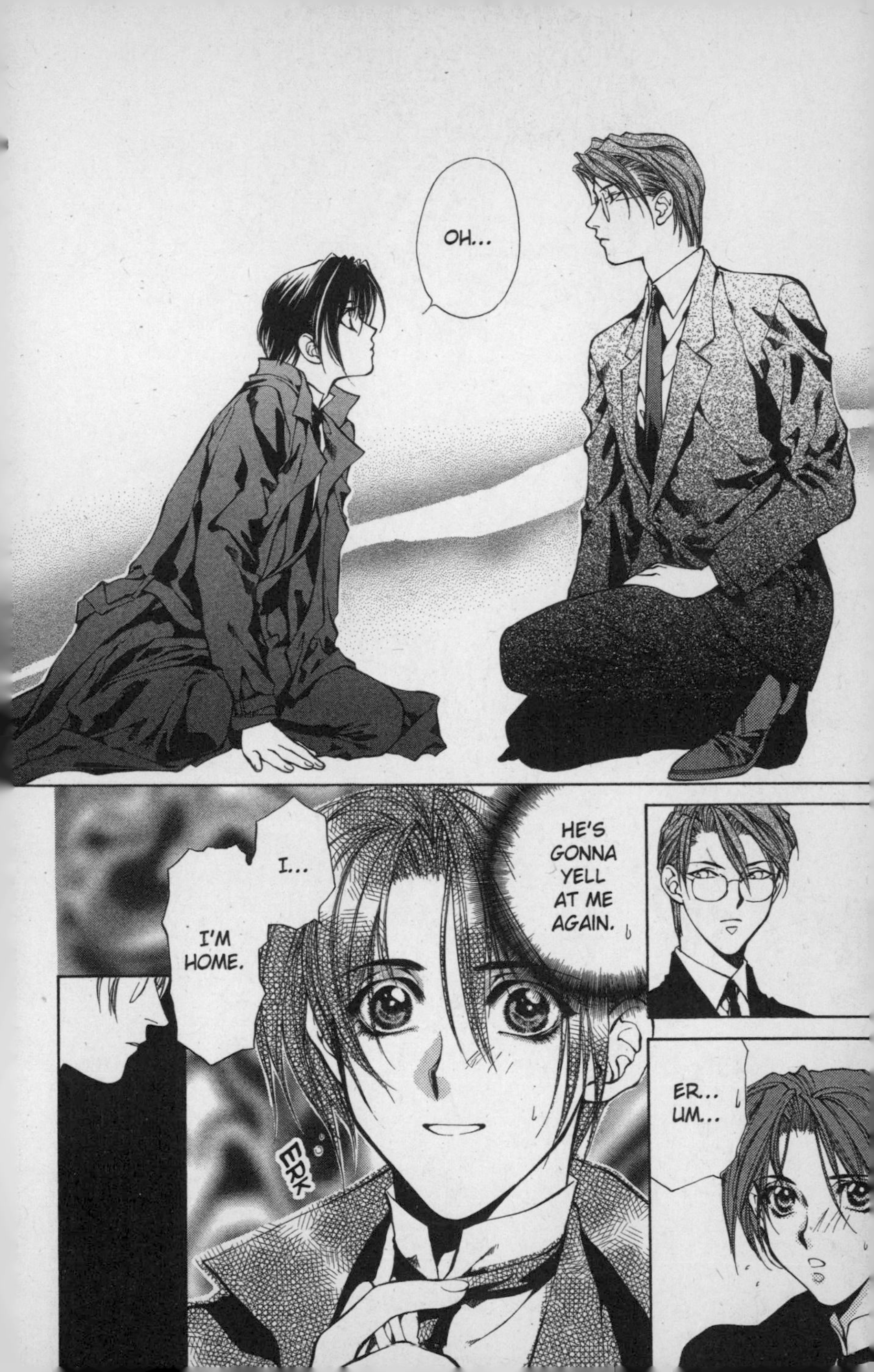
OH...
HE'S GONNA YELL AT ME AGAIN.
ER... UM...
I...
I'M HOME.
ERK

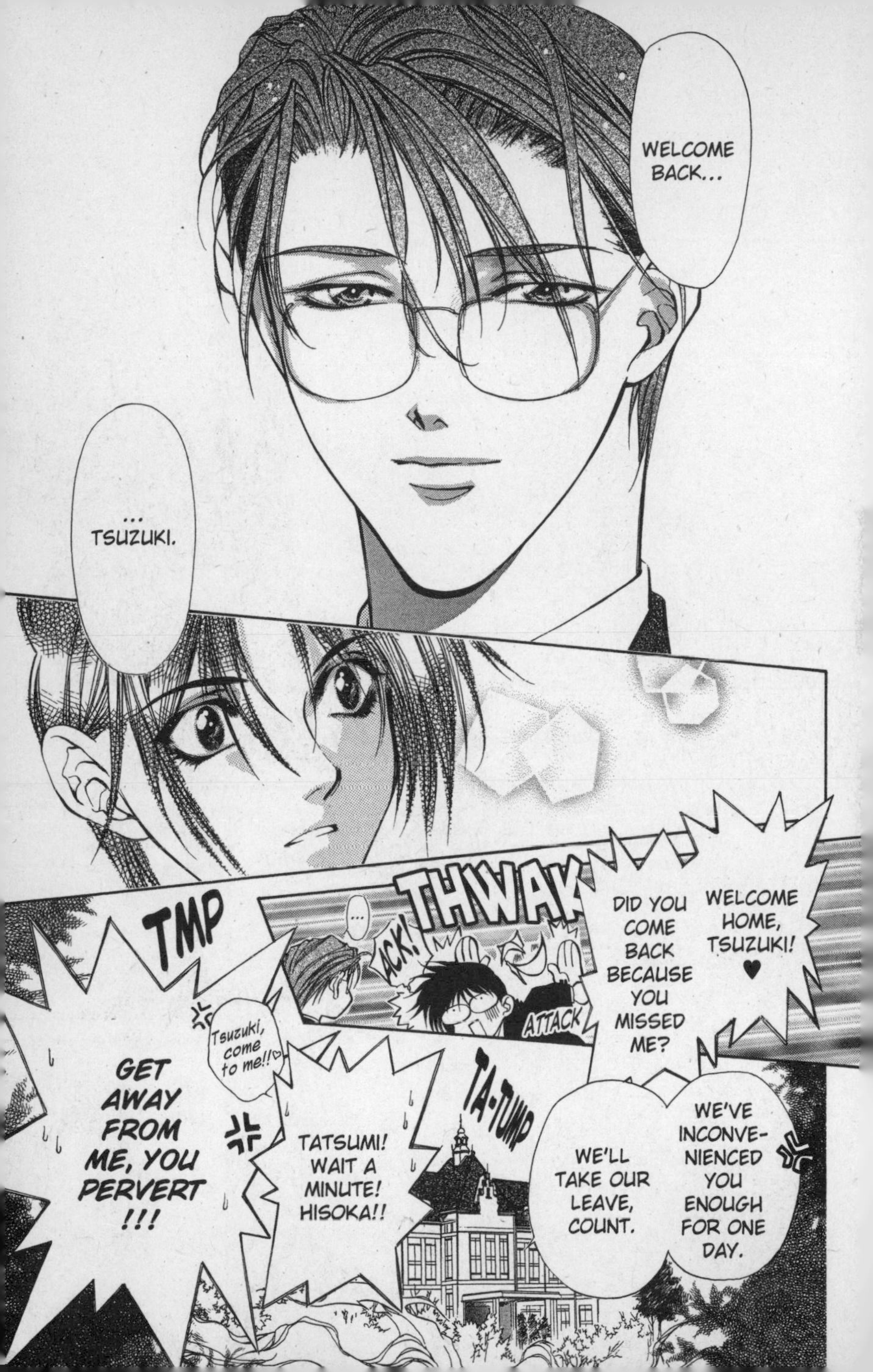
WELCOME BACK...
... TSUZUKI.
WELCOME HOME, TSUZUKI! ♥
DID YOU COME BACK BECAUSE YOU MISSED ME?
THWAK
...
ACK!
ATTACK
TMP
Tsuzuki, come to me!!♡
WE'VE INCONVENIENCED YOU ENOUGH FOR ONE DAY.
WE'LL TAKE OUR LEAVE, COUNT.
TA-TUMP
TATSUMI! WAIT A MINUTE! HISOKA!!
GET AWAY FROM ME, YOU PERVERT!!!

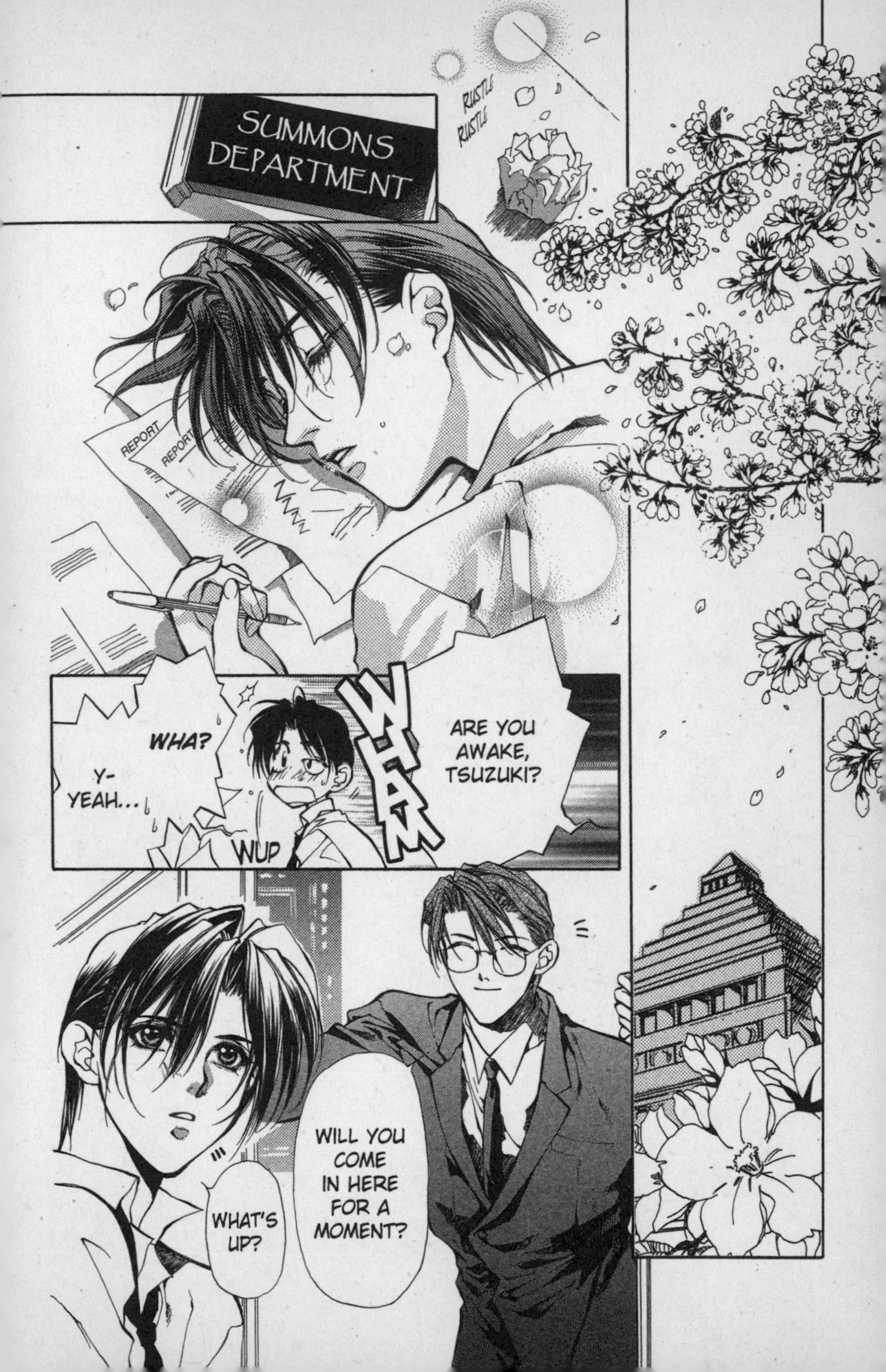
RUSTLE RUSTLE
SUMMONS DEPARTMENT
REPORT
REPORT
ARE YOU AWAKE, TSUZUKI?
WHAM
WHA?
Y- YEAH...
WUP
WILL YOU COME IN HERE FOR A MOMENT?
WHAT'S UP?

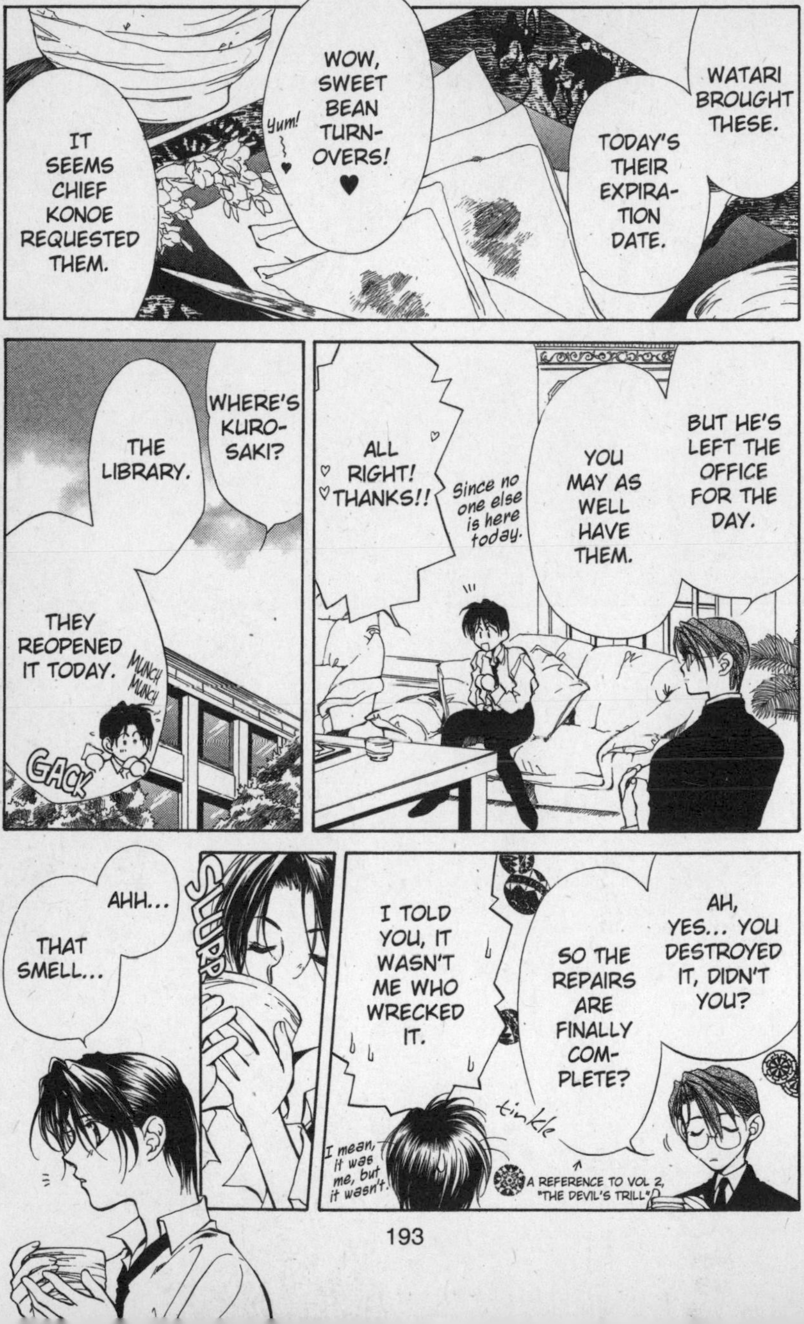
WATARI BROUGHT THESE.
TODAY'S THEIR EXPIRATION DATE.
WOW, SWEET BEAN TURNOVERS!
Yum!
IT SEEMS CHIEF KONOE REQUESTED THEM.
BUT HE'S LEFT THE OFFICE FOR THE DAY.
YOU MAY AS WELL HAVE THEM.
Since no one else is here today.
ALL RIGHT! THANKS!!
WHERE'S KUROSAKI?
THE LIBRARY.
THEY REOPENED IT TODAY.
MUNCH MUNCH
GACK
AH, YES... YOU DESTROYED IT, DIDN'T YOU?
SO THE REPAIRS ARE FINALLY COMPLETE?
tinkle
A REFERENCE TO VOL 2, "THE DEVIL'S TRILL"
I TOLD YOU, IT WASN'T ME WHO WRECKED IT.
I mean, it was me, but it wasn't.
SLURP
AHH...
THAT SMELL...

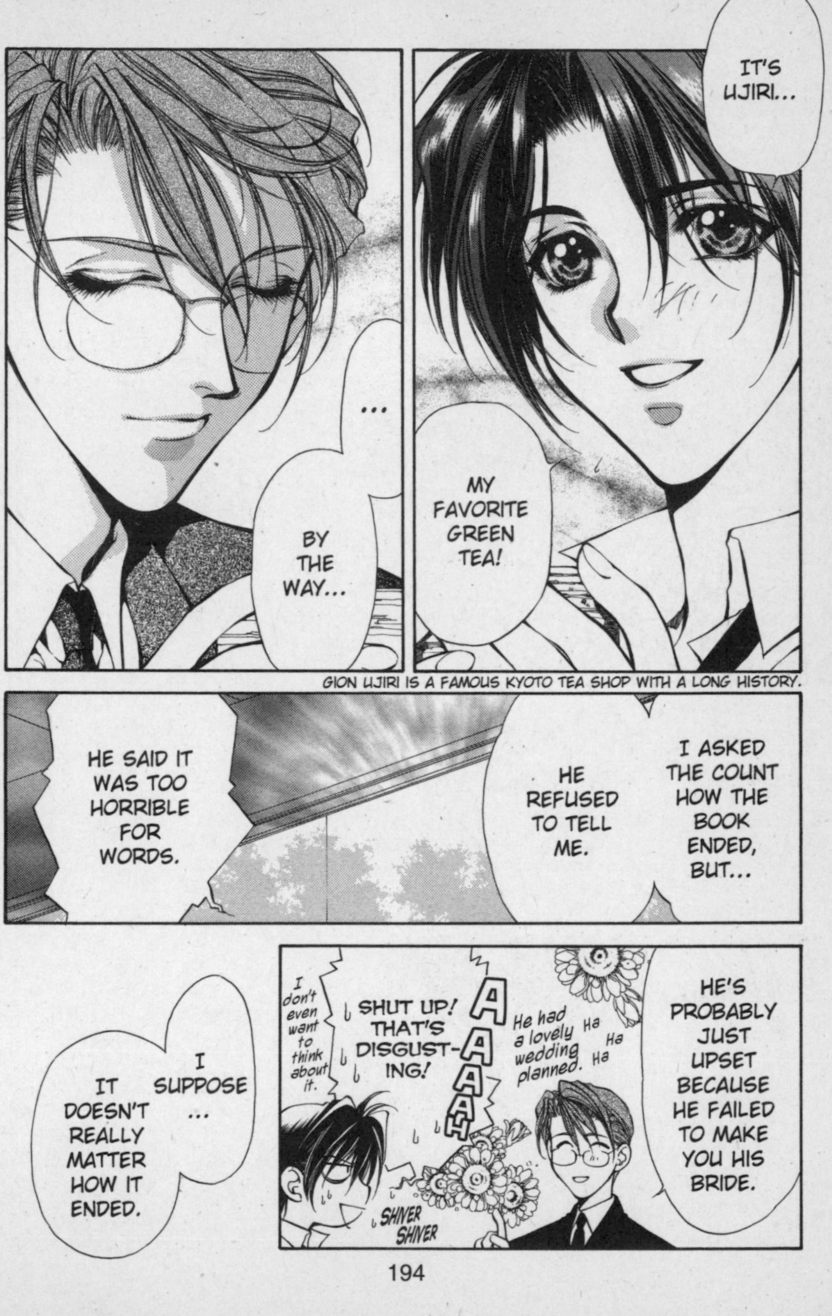
IT'S UJIRI...
MY FAVORITE GREEN TEA!
...
BY THE WAY...
GION UJIRI IS A FAMOUS KYOTO TEA SHOP WITH A LONG HISTORY.
I ASKED THE COUNT HOW THE BOOK ENDED, BUT...
HE REFUSED TO TELL ME.
HE SAID IT WAS TOO HORRIBLE FOR WORDS.
HE'S PROBABLY JUST UPSET BECAUSE HE FAILED TO MAKE YOU HIS BRIDE.
He had a lovely wedding planned.
Ha Ha Ha
AAAAAH
SHUT UP! THAT'S DISGUST-ING!
I don't even want to think about it.
SHIVER SHIVER
I SUPPOSE...
IT DOESN'T REALLY MATTER HOW IT ENDED.

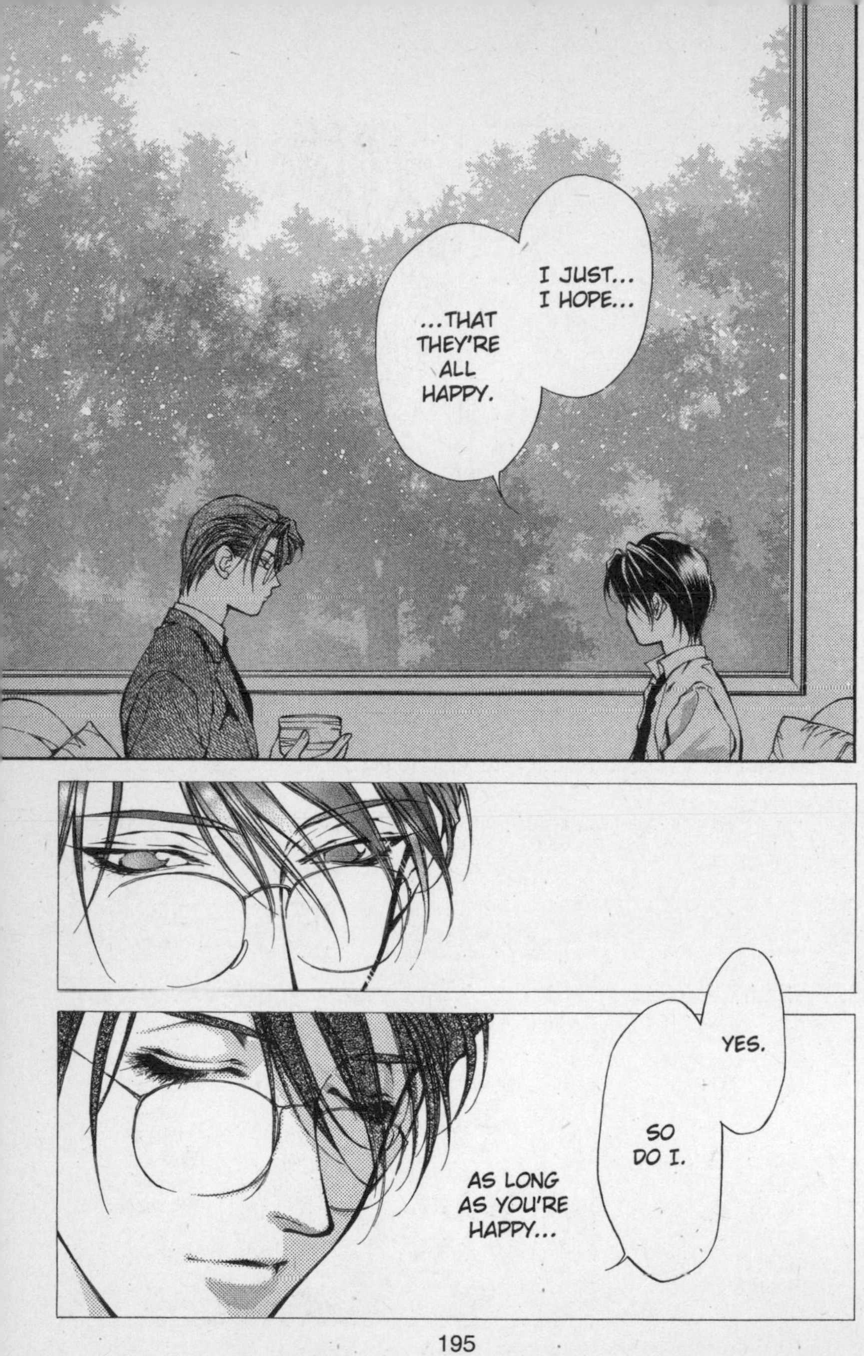
I JUST... I HOPE...
...THAT THEY'RE ALL HAPPY.
YES.
SO DO I.
AS LONG AS YOU'RE HAPPY...

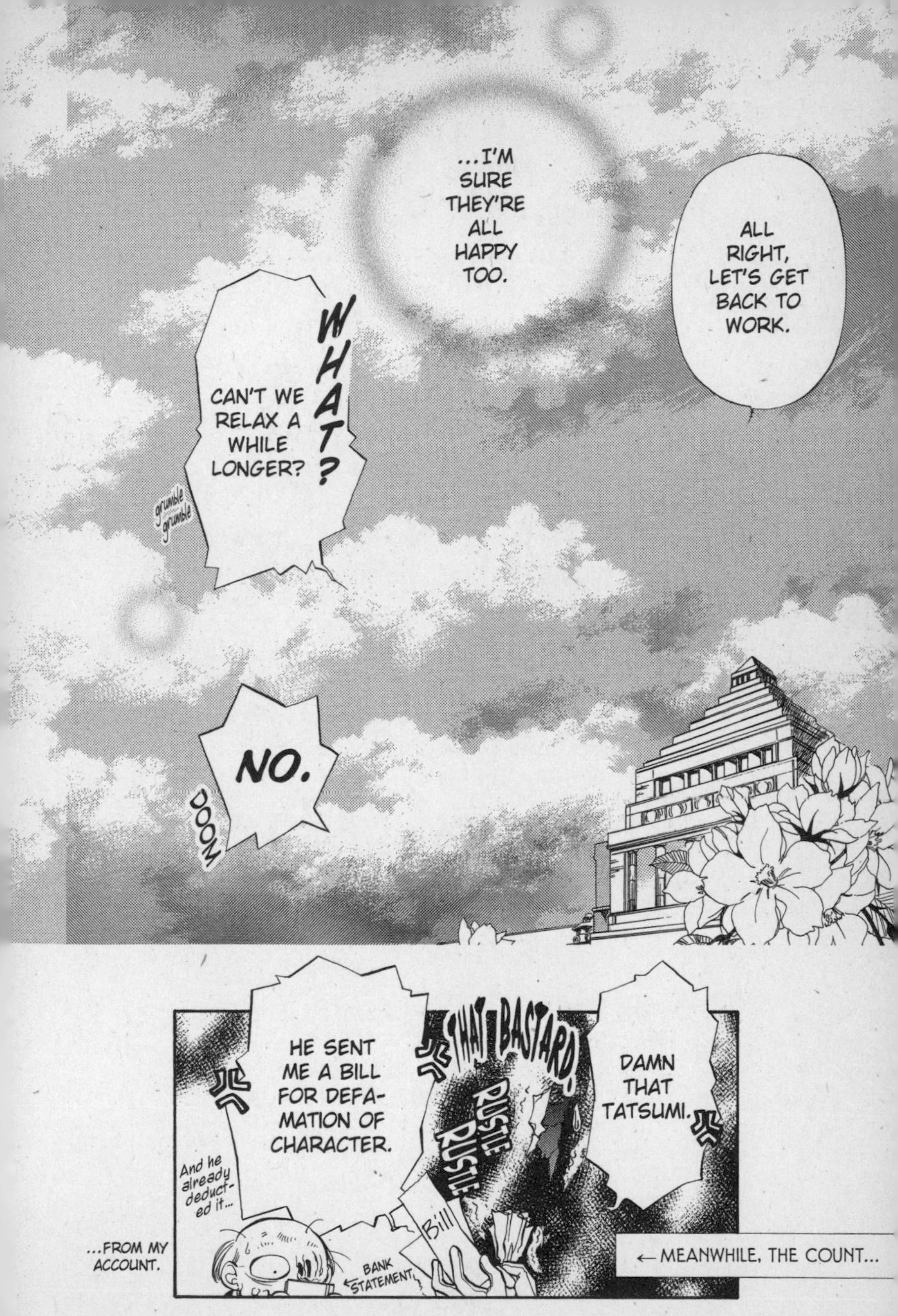
...I'M SURE THEY'RE ALL HAPPY TOO.
ALL RIGHT, LET'S GET BACK TO WORK.
WHAT?
CAN'T WE RELAX A WHILE LONGER?
grumble grumble
NO.
DOOM
← MEANWHILE, THE COUNT...
DAMN THAT TATSUMI.
THAT BASTARD.
RUSTLE RUSTLE
HE SENT ME A BILL FOR DEFA-MATION OF CHARACTER.
And he already deduct-ed it...
...FROM MY ACCOUNT.
Bill
BANK STATEMENT

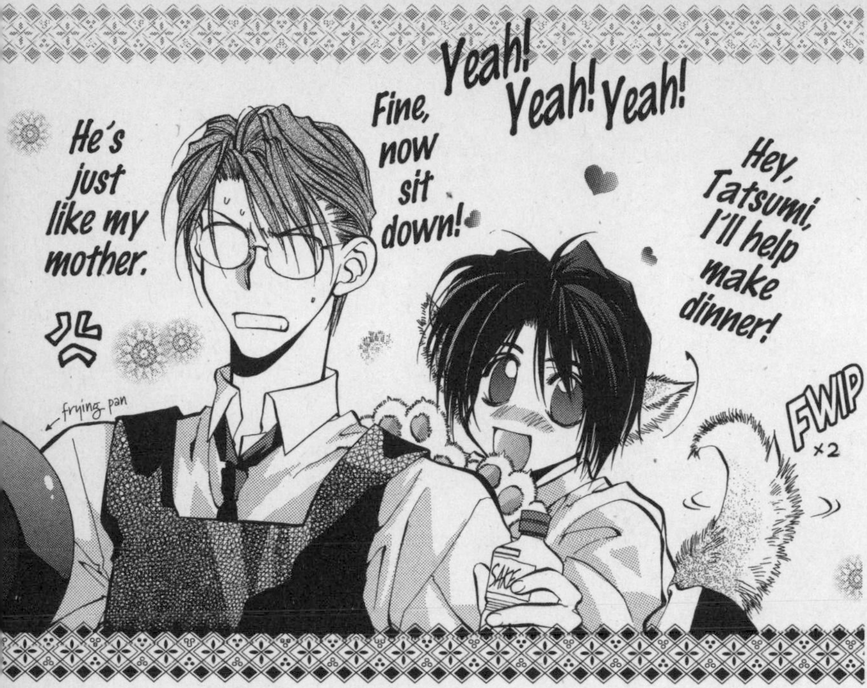
Yeah! Yeah! Yeah!
Hey, Tatsumi, I'll help make dinner!
Fine, now sit down!
He's just like my mother.
FWIP ×2
frying pan
SAKE

THIS IS HOW TATSUMI BECAME A MASTER CHEF.

AFTERWORD

IN THIS VOLUME, TATSUMI CEMENTED HIS PLACE AS A MAJOR CHARACTER. BUT I'M SURE HE'LL KEEP TRYING TO STRAIGHTEN OUT TSUZUKI. BY THE WAY, AT GION UJIRI THEY HAVE A TEA CALLED "TATSUMI OF KYOTO." IF YOU'RE EVER IN KYOTO, CHECK IT OUT! (HEE)

COMPLETE OUR SURVEY AND LET US KNOW WHAT YOU THINK!

☐ Please do NOT send me information about VIZ products, news and events, special offers, or other information.

☐ Please do NOT send me information from VIZ's trusted business partners.

Name: _____

Address: _____

City: _____ **State:** _____ **Zip:** _____

E-mail: _____

☐ Male ☐ Female **Date of Birth** (mm/dd/yyyy): ___ / ___ / _____ (Under 13? Parental consent required)

What race/ethnicity do you consider yourself? (please check one)

☐ Asian/Pacific Islander ☐ Black/African American ☐ Hispanic/Latino

☐ Native American/Alaskan Native ☐ White/Caucasian ☐ Other: _____

What VIZ product did you purchase? (check all that apply and indicate title purchased)

☐ DVD/VHS _____

☐ Graphic Novel _____

☐ Magazines _____

☐ Merchandise _____

Reason for purchase: (check all that apply)

☐ Special offer ☐ Favorite title ☐ Gift

☐ Recommendation ☐ Other _____

Where did you make your purchase? (please check one)

☐ Comic store ☐ Bookstore ☐ Mass/Grocery Store

☐ Newsstand ☐ Video/Video Game Store ☐ Other: _____

☐ Online (site: _____)

What other VIZ properties have you purchased/own? _____

_____

How many anime and/or manga titles have you purchased in the last year? How many were VIZ titles? **(please check one from each column)**

ANIME	MANGA	VIZ
☐ None	☐ None	☐ None
☐ 1-4	☐ 1-4	☐ 1-4
☐ 5-10	☐ 5-10	☐ 5-10
☐ 11+	☐ 11+	☐ 11+

I find the pricing of VIZ products to be: **(please check one)**

☐ Cheap ☐ Reasonable ☐ Expensive

What genre of manga and anime would you like to see from VIZ? **(please check two)**

☐ Adventure ☐ Comic Strip ☐ Science Fiction ☐ Fighting

☐ Horror ☐ Romance ☐ Fantasy ☐ Sports

What do you think of VIZ's new look?

☐ Love It ☐ It's OK ☐ Hate It ☐ Didn't Notice ☐ No Opinion

Which do you prefer? **(please check one)**

☐ Reading right-to-left

☐ Reading left-to-right

Which do you prefer? **(please check one)**

☐ Sound effects in English

☐ Sound effects in Japanese with English captions

☐ Sound effects in Japanese only with a glossary at the back

THANK YOU! Please send the completed form to:

VIZ Survey
42 Catharine St.
Poughkeepsie, NY 12601

rmation provided will be used for internal purposes only. We promise not to sell or otherwise your information.